MW00973483

GREEN EDITION

REA's *Annotated* LSAT

With REA's TestWare® on CD-ROM

Robert Webking, Ph.D.
Co-founder, Law School Preparation Institute
University of Texas at El Paso

Research & Education Association
Visit our website at
www.rea.com

Research & Education Association
61 Ethel Road West
Piscataway, New Jersey 08854
E-mail: info@rea.com

The Annotated LSAT
With TestWare® on CD-ROM

Published 2010

Printed in the United States of America

Library of Congress Control Number 2008940491

ISBN-13: 978-0-7386-0374-2
ISBN-10: 0-7386-0374-0

C10-0101

CONTENTS

Foreword

Finally, the book law school applicants have been waiting for! REA's *Annotated LSAT with CD-ROM* is the *only test prep* on the market with question-level analysis of an actual LSAT exam!

Our new test prep will familiarize you with everything you need to do well on the Law School Admission Test and get into the law school of your choice. From how to prepare for the actual exam, to detailed explanations of how the test's sections are scored, this is your opportunity to "practice for real" before you actually take the test.

This in-depth test prep by Dr. Robert Webking, author of REA's top-selling *LSAT Logic Games*, breaks down and fully explains the methodology and reasoning of each section of an actual LSAT exam, including Logical Reasoning, Analytical Reasoning, and Reading Comprehension. An instructive Writing Sample section is also included for further study and review.

It's a well-known fact that once test-takers become familiar with the style, structure, and overall concept of the LSAT, they will become calmer, more focused, and more relaxed on test day. Preparation helps test-takers answer questions with more confidence, which translates into higher test scores and greater career opportunities down the road.

This is not practice for its own sake but rather a focused workout.

This one-of-a-kind test prep gives you many opportunities to review the material and test what you've learned. It contains an annotated review and three full-length practice tests with detailed explanations for all practice test answers, a study guide, and powerful test-taking strategies.

REA's exclusive Test*ware*® CD-ROM features two of the book's three practice tests in a timed format with instant, automatic scoring and feedback. The CD allows you to stop a practice test at any time to review the material (or take a study break) and resume the test when you're ready.

Our test prep contains a wealth of information, so it's important to pace yourself as you study. Don't try to cram the whole book in overnight! Instead, spend a few hours each day reviewing small sections at a time. Working at a steady, structured pace will allow you to monitor your progress, practice what you've learned, and identify your strengths and weaknesses. By the time you take the actual LSAT, you'll be familiar with the test and confident in your knowledge and abilities.

We hope you find this test prep to be a great companion in your LSAT studies and the first step toward a successful law career. Good luck on the test!

Larry B. Kling
Chief Editor

How to Use This Book and TESTware®

It's all about well-focused practice.

Improvement on the Law School Admission Test takes a lot of practice. And it's not just about putting in time, but putting in time well spent. Use this book as a resource to help you do the intense, arduous, and well-focused practice that will improve your LSAT score.

The LSAT is unique among standardized tests. It covers many subjects, but does not test your knowledge of any of them. The heart of the test is the human faculty of reasoning, and the LSAT attempts to assess the development of that faculty in the test-taker. For someone trying to improve his or her score, there is no substitute for working with real LSAT tests. That is why this book centers on the analysis of an actual LSAT exam. (Content taken from the actual LSAT exam is set off in its official font.)

The goal of this book is for you to understand what the LSAT is asking you to do and then doing that well. (Basically, you should get better at the test by getting better at doing what the test tests.) Each major chapter (1 through 3) is devoted to understanding a particular section of the LSAT. This helps you learn what to focus your practice on, so you can use your study time to your best advantage.

You can improve your test score by analyzing what the exam is testing. This may seem hard at first, but the more you practice, the easier it will be to understand what the problems, tasks, and situations are asking you to do.

Take, for example, Chapter 1 on Logical Reasoning problems. Work through the analysis there to understand what that section is testing, how it does so, and consequently, what you want to be able to do in order to answer questions correctly. Then, practice developing that ability: work logical reasoning problems using those techniques and applying the understanding from the chapter. The key here is to take the theory and use it to analyze the problem so you can address it effectively.

Follow this method with each of the three major question types and keep doing the focused practice. Use this book as a resource for the kinds of questions found on the exam and refer back to it as often as necessary. It is likely that for most questions you encounter on the LSAT, we have analyzed a similar question you can use as a model.

Try to learn from everything you do when practicing. The more you recognize or understand particular problems or processes, the better and faster you will become at answering the problems. Don't settle for not understanding why a correct answer is correct. Use the analysis in these chapters to develop that understanding. After practicing for a couple of weeks, go back and reread the chapters. Your experience with LSAT questions may have helped you develop a background that will increase your analytical skills.

While there is no adequate substitute for practicing on real LSATs with LSAT questions, the practice tests included here will prepare you for the exam. These problems, tasks, and situations are built to boost your familiarity with the types of problems you will encounter on the LSAT. You may find it useful to refer to the sections of the test as you review the chapters. This will help you practice and develop your understanding of the particular test sections before taking actual LSAT exams.

Our interactive CD-ROM includes two timed practice tests with automatic, instant scoring. The CD enables you to access the practice questions by type—which can be useful for initial practice or for focusing on a type of question you find particularly difficult. Detailed explanations of all practice test answers are provided, so you can follow the process of working through the question to determine the right answer. Presenting the answers in this way will help you learn what to focus on as you practice.

And that's what it's all about: well-focused practice.

LSAT Preparation Schedule

	Day 1	Day 2	Day 3	Day 4	Day 5	Day 6
Week 1	Introduction Chapter 1	Chapter 1 Practice *Logical Reasoning*	Chapter 1 Practice *Logical Reasoning*	Chapter 2 Practice *Logical Reasoning*	Practice *Logical Reasoning*	Practice *Logical Reasoning*
Week 2	Chapter 2	Practice *Logical Reasoning* Chapter 2	Practice *Reading Comprehension*	Practice *Logical Reasoning* Practice *Reading Comprehension*	Practice *Logical Reasoning* Practice *Reading Comprehension*	Test 1 on CD-ROM
Week 3	Chapter 3	Practice *Logical Reasoning* Chapter 3	Practice *Analytical Reasoning*	Practice *Logical Reasoning* Practice *Analytical Reasoning*	Practice *Reading Comprehension* Practice *Analytical Reasoning*	Test 2 on CD-ROM
Week 4	Practice *Logical Reasoning* Chapter 4	Re-read Chapter 1 Practice *Logical Reasoning*	Practice *Logical Reasoning* Practice *Reading Comprehension*	Re-read Chapter 3 Practice *Analytical Reasoning*	Practice *Logical Reasoning* Practice *Reading Comprehension* Practice *Analytical Reasoning*	Test 3

About the Author

Robert Webking, Ph.D., is professor of political science at the University of Texas at El Paso, where he has taught since 1978. As co-founder of UTEP's Law School Preparation Institute, and through extensive activities with the Council on Legal Education Opportunity, he has worked to help students develop the sophisticated analytical skills that will serve them on the LSAT, in law school, and in their futures.

Acknowledgments

In addition to our author, we would like to thank Larry B. Kling, Vice President, Editorial, for his overall direction; Pam Weston, Vice President, Publishing, for setting the quality standards for production integrity and managing the publication to completion; John Paul Cording, Vice President, Technology, for coordinating the design and development of REA's TestWare® software; Michael Reynolds, Managing Editor, for editorial contributions and project management; Heena Patel, Technology Project Manager, for software testing; Rachel DiMatteo, Graphic Designer, for designing this book; Christine Saul, Senior Graphic Artist, for designing our cover; Jeff LoBalbo, Senior Graphic Designer, for coordinating prepress electronic file mapping, and ATLIS Graphics for typesetting this edition.

A special thank-you to Maria M. DeFilippis, Esq., for her technical review of the manuscript.

We would also like to thank the following contributors: Robert K. Burdette, Ph.D., J.D.; Anita Price Davis, Ed.D.; Christopher Dreisbach, Ph.D.; Theodora Glitsky, M.A.; Timothy M. Hagle, J.D., Ph.D.; H. Hamner Hill, Ph.D.; Clayton Holland, J.D.; Connie Mauney, Ph.D.; John E. Parks-Clifford, Ph.D.; Wesley G. Phelan, Ph.D.; John G. Robinson, Ph.D.; Garrett Ward Sheldon, Ph.D.; and Paul C.L. Tang, Ph.D.

About REA

Founded in 1959, Research & Education Association (REA) is dedicated to publishing the finest and most effective educational materials—including software, study guides, and test preps—for students in middle school, high school, college, graduate school, and beyond.

Today, REA's wide-ranging catalog is a leading resource for teachers, students, and professionals.

We invite you to visit us at *www.rea.com* to find out how "REA is making the world smarter."

INTRODUCTION

Every year more than 80,000 people apply to law school. They are, or will soon be, college graduates, which makes them quite accomplished compared to most people in the country. Most of these graduates have excellent academic records: they are A or B students, which makes them quite successful compared to other college graduates. And they want to do the work to become lawyers, which separates them from other accomplished college graduates. Yet about a third of them will not be admitted to law school, and many of the other two-thirds will not get into all the schools they apply to or hope to get into. What separates these accomplished students who get in from the often equally accomplished students who do not? The most important thing is a test designed to draw distinctions between the outstanding and the merely competent people. It is the **Law School Admission Test**.

Take a look at this; it's a real question from a real LSAT:

23. An air traveler in Beijing cannot fly to Lhasa without first flying to Chengdu. Unfortunately, an air traveler in Beijing must fly to Xian before flying to Chengdu. Any air traveler who flies from Beijing to Lhasa, therefore, cannot avoid flying to Xian.

    The pattern of reasoning exhibited by the argument above is most similar to that exhibited by which one of the following?

    (A) A doctor cannot prescribe porozine for a patient without first prescribing anthroxine for that patient. Unfortunately, anthroxine makes most patients who take it feel either extremely drowsy or else extremely nervous. It is likely, therefore, that a patient who has taken porozine has felt extremely nervous.

    (B) An ice-sculpture artist cannot reach the yellow level of achievement without first achieving the green level. The green level is impossible to achieve unless the white level has already been achieved. Therefore, an ice-sculpture artist who has reached the yellow level must have previously achieved the white level.

    (C) One cannot properly identify a mushroom without first examining its spores. A powerful microscope can be used to examine the spores of a mushroom. A powerful microscope, therefore, is necessary for anyone wishing to identify mushrooms properly.

(D) It is impossible to be fluent in a language without knowing its grammatical rules. A person who knows the grammatical rules of a language has learned them by means of exhaustive and difficult study or else by growing up in an environment in which the language is spoken. There are two major ways, therefore, for a person to become fluent in a language.

(E) In the City Ballet Company any dancer who has danced in *Giselle* has also danced in *Sleeping Beauty*, and some dancers who have danced in *Sleeping Beauty* have also danced in *Swan Lake*. Therefore, some dancers in the City Ballet Company who have danced in *Giselle* have also danced in *Swan Lake*.

If you have not yet taken an LSAT, you have probably not seen a question like this on any standardized test you have taken. Those other tests may have been about academic subjects, like history or chemistry; or they may have been about language skills, vocabulary, or analogies; or they may have been about mathematical concepts, solving a problem or interpreting a graph.

But this may be the first test where you have bumped into a question about Chinese air travel and an answer that is about medical prescriptions, or ice sculptures, or mushrooms, or language learning, or ballet.

And that difference captures the essence of the LSAT. It is a test unlike any other because it is directly testing something that the others are not. It is about air travel, prescriptions, ice sculptures, mushrooms, language learning, ballet, and just about everything else, while also being about none of those things. It concerns all subject matter but it's about no subject matter. The test does not cover material that you think about or learn about; it covers thinking and learning. It is about the human faculty of reasoning, and it tests how well that faculty is developed in the person taking the test.

As LSAT questions go, this example seems unusual, long, and apparently complex. But when examined more carefully, it is not unusual, but, in fact, prototypical. And while it is longer than most, the question is actually less complex than it appears on the surface and less complicated than many other questions. Though challenging, for an LSAT question it is actually fairly easy!

While the particular form of this question appears on fewer than 5% of the LSAT questions, they are all like this in substance. As a matter of fact, this question is very representative of what the LSAT is and what it's about. This is so because the question is not about Chinese air travel, but about reasoning regarding Chinese air travel. And sound reasoning about Chinese air travel is the same as sound reasoning about anything else. And if someone makes a mistake in thinking about Chinese air travel, that mistake is no different than one someone might make thinking about prescriptions or mushrooms or language learning.

The LSAT is about reasoning. Its questions ask you to demonstrate that you understand what reasoning is and how good reasoning works. Almost all of them do that in some way or other, and this particular question does it directly by asking you to understand how the reasoning in the main passage works and then to find another passage, one of the five answer choices, where the reasoning works exactly the same way. Answering the question is as simple as that: determine how the main passage goes about moving from its premises to its conclusion, which is like this:

$$B \rightarrow (L \rightarrow C)$$
$$(C \rightarrow X)$$
$$B \rightarrow (L \rightarrow X)$$

And then find the one answer among the five choices that does exactly the same thing—which turns out to be the one about ice sculptures because its reasoning is like this:

$$I \rightarrow (Y \rightarrow G)$$
$$(G \rightarrow W)$$
$$I \rightarrow (Y \rightarrow W)$$

That is what the LSAT is about, and that is what makes it different from other tests. That and this other thing: the LSAT tests reasoning at a very high and sophisticated level.

This book aims to help you do better on that test by

- understanding how the LSAT tests reasoning;
- understanding how to approach the reasoning skills it tests, and
- helping you to do well-focused practice to improve your reasoning and to show that improvement on the test.

HOW THE TEST TESTS REASONING

The LSAT includes six sections. For each section exactly thirty-five minutes are allotted. Five of the sections are made up of multiple-choice questions, and the sixth, the last one in the test, is a writing sample. The writing sample may be used by law schools in making admissions decisions, but it is not used in calculating the LSAT score. That score is based upon the number of right answers to the multiple-choice questions in four of the five multiple-choice sections (the fifth is an experimental section being assessed for future test takers).

These multiple-choice sections are of three types:

- Logical reasoning
- Analytical reasoning
- Reading comprehension

Each section tests a part of the reasoning process, and together they judge abilities to understand the things that we know and to use good reasoning skills to learn what else we know, and don't know, as a result.

In this book we use real questions from an actual LSAT test to help you understand the differences between the three kinds of multiple-choice questions; what each of the three assesses; and how each section tests what it tests.

HOW TO APPROACH THE TEST

Of course the best way, the most important way, the most interesting and satisfying way, and, in the long run, the most helpful way to improve on a test of your reasoning skills is to improve your reasoning skills. Preparing for the LSAT, because it is such a rigorous and demanding test, is an excellent way to improve those very skills. Improving significantly on the LSAT requires that you do it.

In this book, you work with actual LSAT problems of all three types to help you understand what they test and how they do it. Using the understanding that you can get from working in depth with actual LSAT questions, you can learn better how to approach them, and what to do—what skills to use and develop—to reason better. With better reasoning, you can work with the test more effectively to improve your skills and your score.

For example, working actively with questions like this one from a reading comprehension section can develop the ability to read carefully, attentively, and precisely:

5. The primary function of the last paragraph of the passage is to

(A) offer a synthesis of the opposing positions outlined in the first two paragraphs
(B) expose the inadequacies of both positions outlined in the first two paragraphs

(C) summarize the argument made in the first two paragraphs
(D) correct a weakness in the political economists' position as outlined in the second paragraph
(E) suggest policy implications of the argument made in the first two paragraphs

Doing the analysis that a question like this next one from an analytical reasoning section requires, and doing that analysis consciously, builds the crucial skill of understanding what conditional statements mean and do not mean:

8. If jays are not in the forest, then which one of the following must be false?

(A) Martins are in the forest.
(B) Harriers are in the forest.
(C) Neither martins nor harriers are in the forest.
(D) Neither martins nor shrikes are in the forest.
(E) Harriers and shrikes are the only birds in the forest.

And working with the following question from the test, and others like it, makes for realization of the important notion that, in a good argument, the conclusion cannot introduce something that has not first been used in one of the premises:

10. Art historian: Great works of art have often elicited outrage when first presented; in Europe, Stravinsky's *Rite of Spring* prompted a riot, and Manet's *Déjeuner sur l'herbe* elicited outrage and derision. So, since it is clear that art is often shocking, we should not hesitate to use public funds to support works of art that many people find shocking.

Which one of the following is an assumption that the art historian's argument requires in order for its conclusion to be properly drawn?

(A) Most art is shocking.
(B) Stravinsky and Manet received public funding for their art.
(C) Art used to be more shocking than it currently is.
(D) Public funds should support art.
(E) Anything that shocks is art.

Working with this next question, also from a logical reasoning section, develops understanding of the difference between ratios and absolute numbers and of the importance of not confusing the two:

12. A nationwide poll of students, parents, and teachers showed that over 90 percent believe that an appropriate percentage of their school's budget is being spent on student counseling programs. It seems, then, that any significant increase in a school's budget should be spent on something other than student counseling programs.

Which one of the following describes a flaw in the reasoning of the argument above?

(A) The argument confuses a mere coincidence with a causal relationship.
(B) The argument confuses the percentage of the budget spent on a program with the overall amount spent on that program.
(C) The argument fails to justify its presumption that what is true of a part of the budget is also true of the total budget.
(D) The argument fails to consider the possibility that money could be saved by training students as peer counselors.
(E) The argument fails to consider that if more money is spent on a program, then more money cannot also be used for other purposes.

By allowing you to learn from these and other actual questions from the LSAT exam, this book helps to build understanding of what is tested on the LSAT, how it is tested, and what to learn to do better on it. In doing so, the book attempts to sharpen the human ability to develop, critique, and execute rational arguments to a high level.

WORKING TO IMPROVE ON THE TEST

Improvement on the LSAT is difficult, but it can and does come with a lot of practice. But practice doesn't mean simply putting in time. Time and effort are required, but they are not enough. The time and energy have to be used well. Learning to play the violin takes more than just spending a lot of time holding one. Becoming a competitive high jumper requires more than hours and hours of time spent hopping around. In each case the time must be well spent doing things that will develop the precise skills in view. So it is with reasoning and the LSAT. A lot of time is needed, to be sure, but that time has to be ***well focused***: it has to be spent practicing the right things, or the things that will improve performance on the test by improving the abilities that are tested on the test. Indeed, time spent on the wrong things or in the wrong way might actually be counterproductive!

In working with the questions from the various sections on the LSAT throughout this book, you learn what to spend your practice time practicing. You learn what to focus your efforts doing. You can acquire the understanding and the tools you need to do well-focused practice.

From time to time you will encounter a focus box. These are meant to draw your attention to and to emphasize things to be especially aware of as you work with developing your critical thinking on LSAT problems, tasks, and situations.

Focus on

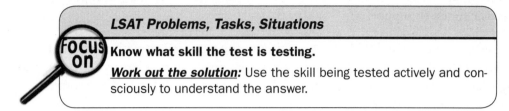

LSAT Problems, Tasks, Situations

Know what skill the test is testing.

Work out the solution: Use the skill being tested actively and consciously to understand the answer.

As an example of using understanding and skill to practice, return to this logical reasoning problem from the test, and let's work it through:

10. Art historian: Great works of art have often elicited outrage when first presented; in Europe, Stravinsky's *Rite of Spring* prompted a riot, and Manet's *Déjeuner sur l'herbe* elicited outrage and derision. So, since it is clear that art is often shocking, we should not hesitate to use public funds to support works of art that many people find shocking.

Which one of the following is an assumption that the art historian's argument requires in order for its conclusion to be properly drawn?

(A) Most art is shocking.
(B) Stravinsky and Manet received public funding for their art.
(C) Art used to be more shocking than it currently is.
(D) Public funds should support art.
(E) Anything that shocks is art.

The question (the part in the middle of the problem) asks for the identification of an assumption that the argument "requires" for the conclusion to be properly drawn. An assumption is a premise, or a piece of information which is not stated in the passage that helps to lead to the conclusion. To find it, begin by identifying the conclusion, which is stated in the passage, and in the final sentence. The conclusion is that we should not hesitate to use public funds to support artwork that many people find shocking.

The conclusion is new. It is what the passage is there to demonstrate to the reader. So consider why, according to the passage, it is the case that we should not hesitate to use public funds to support artwork that people find shocking. The passage explains, with the use of examples, that great works of art often seem outrageous or shocking when they are first presented. And it uses that information to back up the claim that art is often shocking. So that is one thing: art can be shocking. But the conclusion is not just about art, but links art to "public funds." Well, "public funds" is a term and a thing that has not appeared heretofore. It is new in the conclusion. But that cannot be: conclusions are based on premises. There cannot be a "properly drawn" conclusion that is about something that is not in the premises leading to that conclusion. So since the question tells us that the conclusion is to be taken as "properly drawn," we have to come up with the premise that includes "public funds." That unstated premise, that assumption, must be about using public funds to support art.

So now we have worked with the reasoning in the passage and with what the LSAT question told us about that reasoning to determine what the correct answer has to do. It must provide the missing premise that says that public funds should support art. Having determined that, we can find the correct answer fairly easily in choice (D).

Now, what did we just do? We solved an LSAT problem, and that is always satisfying. But we can learn from solving that LSAT problem if we focus on what we did, or what we realized in solving it.

Focus on

Assumption Problems

Anything in a properly drawn conclusion must be in a premise first.

Look For: Is there something mentioned explicitly for the first time in the conclusion?

A NOTE ON TACTICS

Notice the approach to the art history problem. Before we even considered the answer choices, we analyzed the passage. Knowing that the question had asked for the identification of a required assumption, we analyzed the passage to find the conclusion. Then we located the explicit premises, and comparing those to the conclusion we realized that there was something introduced in the conclusion that was not an explicit premise. That led to the realization that the missing assumption needed to connect that item in the conclusion to the ones that were mentioned in the explicit premises. We made that connection. Then we went and found the right answer.

The point is this: the time with the answer choices was fairly limited, and we utterly ignored them until we knew what the right answer had to do. The most dependable and efficient way to get the correct answer to an LSAT question is to determine as much as you can about what that right answer will be or will have to accomplish before going to the answer choices. In some cases, this will enable you to spend very little time with the answer choices because you will know exactly what the right answer is. In other cases it will keep you from being led astray by answer choices that might seem likely unless you know what the right answer has to do.

Going to the answer choices without knowing what the right answer has to do is unlikely to be helpful: 80% of them are wrong, just wrong; only one and exactly one—20%—is right. One out of five. The odds are four to one against you! You improve those odds by being in charge of the answer choices by knowing what the right answer has to do. No window shopping; no browsing;

you go there to buy exactly one thing. Insist on it. You can eliminate incorrect answers effectively only when you know what the right answer has to do. You may not know exactly what the right answer will be, but you can know what it has to do. Without taking the time and making the well-focused effort to acquire that knowledge, you have no reliable basis for eliminating any of the answer choices.

Take this example from our test:

9. At some point in any discussion of societal justice, the only possible doctrinal defense seems to be "That is the way we do things here." Different communities that each recognize the dignity and equality of all citizens will, for example, nevertheless settle on somewhat different provisions for the elderly. So we can see that general principles of justice are never sufficient to determine the details of social policies fixed within a particular state.

Which one of the following statements, if true, most strengthens the argument concerning the general principles of justice?

(A) Although two socialist states each adhered to the same electoral principles, one had a different type of machine for counting ballots in public elections than the other did.

(B) Two democratic industrial states, both subscribing to capitalistic economic principles, differed markedly in the respective proportions of land they devoted to forestry.

(C) Although each adhered to its own principles, a democracy and a monarchy each had the same distribution of wealth in its population.

(D) Two states founded on and adhering to similar principles of justice had different requirements that had to be met in order to be eligible for government-subsidized day care.

(E) Two societies based on different principles of justice, each adhering to its own principles, had the same unemployment benefits.

Suppose you read the passage and discover it has to do with the principles of justice in a society and the details of social policies. Based on that, you go to the answer choices to see what might seem a likely candidate to strengthen the passage about principles of justice. Well, all of them talk about "principles," so we can't eliminate any on that basis. The passage talks about "provisions for the elderly," so if we can eliminate all of the answer choices that don't deal with that, we can eliminate them all! That didn't work. So let's get a little more precise: the passage is not about elections, so eliminate choice (A). And it's not about forestry, so let's eliminate choice (B). It mentions neither democracy nor monarchy, so we'll eliminate (C). There's nothing in it about government subsidized day care, so (D) can be eliminated. But there's also nothing about unemployment benefits, so we'll eliminate (E) as well. That still didn't work.

OK, now let's start over, but this time spend some more time analyzing what the passage does and what the question asks for. It asks for something to strengthen the conclusion. This might be something new, a premise about some specific thing that is not mentioned already in the passage. But in order to determine whether some new information will strengthen the argument, let's take the time to be precise on what that argument is. The conclusion to the passage's argument is in the final sentence, and it is that general principles of justice will not determine the particular social policies within a particular state. The evidence that leads to this conclusion is that even in states with the same general principles, particular social policies differ. And to make the point, the passage offers the example of policies regarding provisions for the elderly. On analysis, then, we realize that a general principle is drawn largely on the basis of a single example. Additional examples would surely strengthen it. But be clear on what they need to be examples of: a case with two states that believe in the same idea of justice yet have particular social policies on some matter that differ would provide additional information to back up the conclusion.

Now, with that understanding of what the right answer will need to do—it will need to provide evidence that makes it more likely that the general principles of justice did not determine particular social policies because even states with the same general principles will have different particular policies—go back to the answer choices and ask of each answer choice whether it makes this situation more likely.

Now we find only one, and exactly one, answer choice that provides what we are looking for: two states with the same principles of justice yet different particular policies (in this case, on day care). Choice (D) does what needs to be done. The others can be eliminated simply because they do not do what needs to be done. To eliminate them, we learned what needed to be done. It's not so much that process of elimination leads you to the answer, but that knowing the answer leads you to eliminate the choices that do not articulate it.

STRATEGY FOR A HIGHER SCORE

You are more likely to answer an LSAT question correctly by doing the work and analyzing the problem before going to the answer choices to identify the correct one. But the questions are still difficult—very difficult. Remember that the LSAT is an examination designed to draw distinctions among highly intelligent and academically accomplished people. Almost everybody who takes the test is a successful student with very high expectations. Yet almost everybody who takes the test gets fewer than 75% of the answers correct!

The exact number of correct answers it takes to get a particular scaled score varies a little from exam to exam, but see the conversion chart for how it works out on the test we use in this book.

Remember that the goal, when it comes to being admitted into law school, is a higher rather than a lower LSAT score. It is not a perfect LSAT score, or even what is usually considered an "A" or "B" in university courses (something like 80% or higher correct). Most people just will not get that many answers correct. The average scaled score is about 151, which on this test meant

Conversion Chart
For Converting Raw Score to the 120-180 LSAT
Scaled Score
LSAT Form 0LSS46

Reported Score	Raw Score Lowest	Raw Score Highest
180	98	101
179	97	97
178	96	96
177	95	95
176	94	94
175	93	93
174	92	92
173	91	91
172	90	90
171	89	89
170	87	88
169	86	86
168	85	85
167	83	84
166	81	82
165	80	80
164	78	79
163	77	77
162	75	76
161	73	74
160	72	72
159	70	71
158	68	69
157	66	67
156	65	65
155	63	64
154	61	62
153	59	60
152	58	58
151	56	57
150	54	55
149	53	53
148	51	52
147	49	50
146	48	48
145	46	47
144	45	45
143	43	44
142	42	42
141	40	41
140	39	39
139	37	38
138	36	36
137	34	35
136	33	33
135	32	32
134	31	31
133	29	30
132	28	28
131	27	27
130	26	26
129	25	25
128	24	24
127	23	23
126	22	22
125	21	21
124	20	20
123	19	19
122	18	18
121	17	17
120	0	16

answering 56 of the 101 questions correctly. The test usually has 101 scored multiple choice questions, thought the number can sometimes be 100. They are divided among the four scored sections, each of which will include somewhere between 22 and 28 questions, with the exact number varrying by test. A scaled score of 158 is better than the scores of three-fourths of the people who take the test (and these are, we recall, generally excellent students!). Yet it means answering fewer than 70% of the questions correctly! And many people earn fine LSAT scores and get into law school and do well there and then live happy and productive lives with fewer—a lot fewer—correct answers than that. Your goal as test taker is simply to get as many correct answers as possible.

So work to earn a higher score. Getting a higher score does not mean spending time working every one of the questions on the test. It does mean using the time you spend well, so that you answer correctly the questions you do give attention to. Remember that the goal is more correct answers. That may well mean—and for most test takers it does mean—that you will not be able to devote time to every one of the 101 questions on the test. That is all right. That is acceptable. That really doesn't matter very much. The goal is more right answers, not "getting to" every question. You earn exactly no points for doing that. The most effective means to get a better score is to get right answers to the questions that you actually spend your time on.

Getting wrong answers quickly does not do you much good. Spending time on half of the questions on the exam, only half, but getting the bulk of those correct because you have done the analysis and learned the right answer, will earn a significantly higher LSAT score than sacrificing accuracy for speed and spending time on all of the questions on the test. In general, then, it makes no sense to sacrifice accuracy for speed. Speedy errors are errors. Slower right answers are right answers. The more right answers you have, the higher your score will be. Get right answers.

Especially when practicing, it makes no sense to practice getting wrong answers quickly. Use your practice time effectively to focus on understanding the problems, how the logical analysis works, and what makes the correct answers correct. Learn how to improve your reasoning skills to make yourself more able to do the analysis to know what the one right answer to each question will have to do. Only when you are able to get right answers dependably, only when you get them right and know that you have them right, does it make sense to begin thinking about getting right answers quickly. Enhancing your ability to do things accurately can lead to more right answers more quickly. But *speed alone* will not improve accuracy or analytical ability.

So let's learn how to do the analysis well to earn those right answers.

1

LOGICAL REASONING

Logical reasoning is a skill of human beings. It is using logic to take the things we know and to determine what else we know because of them. Reasoning logically is arguing, and arguing is what lawyers do. We might even say that being a lawyer means arguing. Being a good lawyer means arguing well.

The logical reasoning sections are the most important on the LSAT. First, the two logical reasoning sections make up half of the multiple-choice questions on the test. Second, the logical reasoning problems bring together what the test as a whole is about: your ability to reason well. Working with them involves using the skills that are tested on the reading comprehension section and the skills that are tested on the analytical reasoning section. Those skills are combined and developed at another level to come together in a sophisticated reasoning process.

The logical reasoning section presents a number of problems that test your ability to understand, analyze, critique, and create arguments. Overall, this section is about arguments.

WHAT IS AN ARGUMENT?

Argument does not necessarily mean a dispute or disagreement. An argument need not be contentious or combative. An argument is a claim that something is true for certain reasons. It brings together some things that we know and then, through the use of reasoning, takes us to the realization that we know other things because of those things that we know.

An argument is a set of statements where one of the statements follows from the other ones. We know, for example, that autumn includes every day in the month of October and every day in the month of November, and when we know that today is a day in November, we know also from those two things together that today is a day in autumn.

An argument shows that a particular statement which follows from the others is a fact because the others are statements of fact. Not every group of statements allows us to realize that another statement is correct. The statement that "today is a day in November," added to the statement that "every day in November is in autumn," does allow us to know that the additional statement "today is a day in autumn" is correct. But the statement that "today is a day in November," grouped with the statement that "squash soup is full of nutrients," does not allow us to say that some other statement is the case.

So, an argument is made up of statements, but not all collections of statements are arguments. It is important to know which ones are arguments and which ones are not—and then which ones are *good* arguments and which ones are not.

Parts of an Argument

Again, an argument moves from some things that you know to let you realize something that you did not know. The something that you realize, or learn, is the **CONCLUSION**. The things that you start with, the things that you know, are called **PREMISES**.

Every argument contains a conclusion. After all, that is what an argument is for—drawing a conclusion. An argument draws a conclusion from at least one premise, and in the LSAT from more than one premise. Working with any argument requires identifying the premises and separating them from one another and from the conclusion.

So, an argument is a group of statements, some of which are premises and one of which is a conclusion. The order of the statements in the passage alone does not indicate which of them is the conclusion. The conclusion could come anywhere among the statements. Often it is its own sentence, but it might be combined in a sentence with one or more premises. In fact, the conclusion might not even be explicitly stated, but in that case it will be clearly understood or will clearly follow from what is stated in the premises.

Similarly, the premises may or may not be stated explicitly, and when they are stated they can come in any order in a passage. In order to understand the argument, then, you need to be able to sort out these things:

- Which of the statements in a passage form an argument?
- Which of the statements in the argument is the conclusion?
- Which of the statements in the argument are the premises?

As an example, look at this passage:

> Gregory Peck played Atticus Finch in the film version of Harper Lee's novel *To Kill a Mockingbird*. Of course, Atticus Finch is a fictional character. Yet many lawyers name Atticus Finch as the role model who inspired them to follow their profession. It goes to show you that literature can have a real and important effect on many people's lives.

Some of the statements here make up an argument, one whose purpose is to advance the conclusion highlighted at the end of the passage:

> Gregory Peck played Atticus Finch in the film version of Harper Lee's novel *To Kill a Mockingbird*. Of course, Atticus Finch is a fictional character. Yet many lawyers name Atticus Finch as the role model

> who inspired them to follow their profession. It goes to show you that literature can have a real and important effect on many people's lives.

And the conclusion is based on premises:

> Gregory Peck played Atticus Finch in the film version of Harper Lee's novel *To Kill a Mockingbird*. Of course, Atticus Finch is a fictional character. Yet many lawyers name Atticus Finch as the role model who inspired them to follow their profession. It goes to show you that literature can have a real and important effect on many people's lives.

Note the argument is introduced by a statement that is not a part of it, but nonetheless offers interesting information:

> Gregory Peck played Atticus Finch in the film version of Harper Lee's novel *To Kill a Mockingbird*. Of course, Atticus Finch is a fictional character. Yet many lawyers name Atticus Finch as the role model who inspired them to follow their profession. It goes to show you that literature can have a real and important effect on many people's lives.

In order to do the LSAT Logical Reasoning sections well, you need to start with the ability to identify the role in the argument played by the statements in a passage.

Sorting Out the Argument

The best place to start in figuring out the argument in a passage is with the conclusion: *what is it that the statements want you to learn or to realize that you did not know?* Since you cannot say that the conclusion will be the first among a set of statements, or the last, or the third of five, or something of the kind, then how can you tell which statement is the conclusion? You know the conclusion by its logical relationship to the other statements. The parts of an argument that are not the conclusion will be presented as things that are given, or things brought up exactly because they help you to see something else. That something else is the conclusion.

Often conclusions are introduced by particular words called "conclusion indicators." A sentence that uses one of these words is likely to be a conclusion. The most commonly used of these words are "therefore," "thus," "hence," and "so." When these words are used, what follows is likely to be a conclusion, as we see in the following example:

> All third graders at Wonderland Elementary School have read *Ivanhoe*. Therefore, Billy has read *Ivanhoe,* since Billy is a third grader at Wonderland Elementary School.

In this passage the second of the statements is the conclusion, and that is clearly indicated by the use of the word "therefore."

However, many times conclusion statements do not include one of the conclusion indicators. Still, in those cases those indicators are suggested, or implied by the logical structure. What if the passage about Billy had read as follows:

> Billy has read *Ivanhoe* since Billy is a third grader at Wonderland Elementary School, and all third graders at Wonderland Elementary School have read *Ivanhoe*.

The two Billy passages mean the same thing, and the conclusion is the same in both even though in the second case it is not introduced by one of the words that signals a conclusion. To test this, try adding a conclusion indicator at the beginning of a statement that you think might be a conclusion. If the conclusion indicator makes sense there, then, indeed, there is a conclusion. It will not make sense, or sound right, to introduce a premise with one of these conclusion indicators. So adding "and so" to the beginning of the first statement in the second Billy passage makes that statement say "**and so** Billy has read *Ivanhoe,*" something that sounds right and makes sense because it clarifies that this is exactly the point that the passage is designed to make. But to say "**and so** Billy is a third grader at Wonderland Elementary" does not similarly make sense because the fact that Billy is a third grader is something taken as given. It is something we already knew.

So whether they are stated explicitly or not, conclusion indicators are things that point the way to the argument's new knowledge as opposed to the things that are known at the start of the argument.

Those things that you know already are the premises. And once you have determined what the conclusion is you can ask what the premises are. Just as certain words or thoughts indicate the presence of a conclusion, so there are particular words or thoughts that indicate reasons that lead to conclusions, or premises. In fact, some of those are plain in the *Ivanhoe* example. Premise indicators include words or thoughts like "because," or "since." There are many more, but they all carry this meaning: "**because** we know this," or "**since** we know this," we know this other thing.

> Since we know that third graders at Wonderland elementary have read *Ivanhoe,* we know that Billy has read *Ivanhoe,* because Billy is a third grader at Wonderland Elementary.

Here both premises have been introduced with premise indicators, and even if those words weren't actually used in the statements, it makes sense to include them. It would *not* make sense to introduce the statement "Billy has read *Ivanhoe*," with one of those words, and it would not make sense to do so exactly because that statement is not a premise, but the conclusion.

Look at this distinction between premises and conclusion in an actual LSAT passage:

7. Unlike newspapers in the old days, today's newspapers and televised news programs are full of stories about murders and assaults in our city. One can only conclude from this change that violent crime is now out of control, and, to be safe from personal attack, one should not leave one's home except for absolute necessities.

   Which one of the following, if true, would cast the most serious doubt on the conclusion?

   (A) Newspapers and televised news programs have more comprehensive coverage of violent crime than newspapers did in the old days.
   (B) National data show that violent crime is out of control everywhere, not just in the author's city.
   (C) Police records show that people experience more violent crimes in their own neighborhoods than they do outside their neighborhoods.
   (D) Murder comprised a larger proportion of violent crimes in the old days than it does today.
   (E) News magazines play a more important role today in informing the public about crime than they did in the old days.

For now, focus on these two statements:

(s1) Newspapers and televised news programs are full of stories about murders and assaults in our city.

(s2) Violent crime is now out of control.

Of course, the language in the passage ("one can only conclude") shows plainly which is a conclusion, but to see how these words and thoughts work, confirm what is the conclusion by using the premise indicators and conclusion indicators. The phrase "and so..." makes sense and it fits before statement s2, but certainly not before s1. The first statement is presented as something that we know and not something that we learn from argument. But a premise indicator like "because" does make sense as an introduction to s1 and not at all as an introduction to s2.

The first thing that is tested in a logical reasoning section is your ability to sort out the parts of an argument: the premises and the conclusion. *Can you tell which is which?*

What Makes an Argument into a Good Argument?

So we know that not all collections of statements are arguments. We also know that a passage that includes an argument may also include statements that are not part of the argument. Finally, we know that in the statements that make up an argument, one is a conclusion and the others are premises.

Now consider that some arguments are good, like this:

All dogs are mammals. Sally is a dog. So Sally is a mammal.

And some are not, like this:

Some dogs can do arithmetic. Nick can do arithmetic. So Nick is a dog.

What makes any argument into an argument is a ***claim*** that a conclusion follows from certain premises. In a good—or **sound**—argument the conclusion actually does follow from the premises. A good argument establishes its conclusion as true. Indeed, that is what it is for: we learn that something is the case because of the other things that we know are the case.

So what makes an argument into a good argument? Two things. When both of them are present the argument is a good argument and its conclusion is dependable. The two things are:

(1) **true premises**, and
(2) **valid reasoning**.

True premises

As mentioned earlier, an argument is a claim that, because we know certain things, we in fact also know something else because of knowing them. Because we know thing One and thing Two, we also know thing Three. Well, we can really be certain that we actually do know thing Three only when we are really certain that we do know things One and Two, or that the information contained in the premises is really true.

I have Shakespeare class today because my Shakespeare class meets every Monday Wednesday, and Friday, and today is Wednesday.

The student doing this reasoning can dependably conclude that she has Shakespeare class because she is certain about the other information. The conclusion follows from the truth of the premises.

But suppose she's a bit disoriented and thinks that it's Wednesday when in fact today is Tuesday. Now one of the premises—that today is Wednesday—is not true. And although the conclusion might seem to follow, it does not follow. And it does not follow because one of the premises is false.

Valid reasoning

But true premises alone do not guarantee a true conclusion. For one thing, of course, the premises have to be related to one another through the subject matter. They have to have something to do with the same thing or things so that it makes sense to reach a conclusion about one of those things. Information about apples together with information about bananas cannot give you information about oranges. But information about apples, combined with information about heat, might lead to knowledge about applesauce. And there's more: it's not enough for the premises to be about the same thing, for true premises have to relate to one another appropriately in order for them to show that something more than sharing a common subject is true. Not all premises, even if they are true and about the same things, lead to conclusions.

Consider this:

I do not have Shakespeare class today because my Shakespeare class meets on Monday, Wednesday, and Friday, and today is not Wednesday.

If today is, say, Friday, then both of the premises in this argument are true. Yet the conclusion (that I do not have Shakespeare class today) is *not* true. That I do not have class today did not dependably follow from these premises even though we do know the things in the premises and they are correct.

In this case (for reasons discussed later on) the reasoning is **not valid** and so the conclusion does not follow.

And so...

Not all true premises lead to a true conclusion, just as not all good reasoning leads to a true conclusion. But both things **together**, true premises and good reasoning, **always** lead to a true conclusion, as they did with the Sally argument:

All dogs are mammals. Sally is a dog. So Sally is a mammal.

Now back to the example from the LSAT:

7. Unlike newspapers in the old days, today's newspapers and televised news programs are full of stories about murders and assaults in our city. One can only conclude from this change that violent crime is now out of control, and, to be safe from personal attack, one should not leave one's home except for absolute necessities.

   Which one of the following, if true, would cast the most serious doubt on the conclusion?

(A) Newspapers and televised news programs have more comprehensive coverage of violent crime than newspapers did in the old days.
(B) National data show that violent crime is out of control everywhere, not just in the author's city.
(C) Police records show that people experience more violent crimes in their own neighborhoods than they do outside their neighborhoods.
(D) Murder comprised a larger proportion of violent crimes in the old days than it does today.
(E) News magazines play a more important role today in informing the public about crime than they did in the old days.

In the part of the question that we worked with earlier, the conclusion that violent crime is out of control is made based on the premise that more such crime is reported in the newspapers than there used to be. But suppose the speaker were wrong, and that however much it might seem that the paper is reporting more violent crime than it used to, in fact the paper is not reporting more such crime. In this case the conclusion would not follow, because the premise would be false (or the "thing that we know" turns out to be something that in fact we do not know, because it is not the case). The premise would be false and the conclusion would not be dependable for that reason. Note that this does not mean that the opposite of the conclusion is the case, but simply that the argument does not compel any conclusion. We could say neither that the conclusion is true nor that the conclusion is false, but only that the argument does not lead to the conclusion claimed.

Or suppose that in fact the paper does report more crime than it used to do, and the statement that it does is combined with another statement that says:

if there were more crime surely the newspaper would report it.

In that case even if both premises were true, the conclusion (that there is more crime) would not follow (the paper might still report more crime even if the crime rate were actually down). In this example the true premises would not be related in such a way as to lead, dependably, to the conclusion claimed. The argument would not be logically valid, and we could not know from the argument alone whether the conclusion was true.

So either a false premise or reasoning that is not valid would prevent the argument from being a good one, from successfully showing that its conclusion is true.

The logical reasoning section tests your understanding that a good argument has true premises and valid reasoning. It challenges you to prove that you can assess the truth of a statement and show the impact of that truth or falsity on the conclusion. And it tests your understanding of when true premises dependably lead to conclusions and when they do not. It asks: Do you know what makes reasoning valid and invalid?

Extended Arguments

An argument, strictly speaking, has exactly one conclusion. But a passage, a discussion, a paragraph is likely to be much more complex than that. Most discourse will include arguments with conclusions, and then those conclusions themselves will become parts of larger arguments. In this case the passage becomes a group of arguments, and you can analyze it best by separating out the arguments and then trying to understand how they relate to one another.

7. Unlike newspapers in the old days, today's newspapers and televised news programs are full of stories about murders and assaults in our city. One can only conclude from this change that violent crime is now out of control, and, to be safe from personal attack, one should not leave one's home except for absolute necessities.

Which one of the following, if true, would cast the most serious doubt on the conclusion?

(A) Newspapers and televised news programs have more comprehensive coverage of violent crime than newspapers did in the old days.
(B) National data show that violent crime is out of control everywhere, not just in the author's city.
(C) Police records show that people experience more violent crimes in their own neighborhoods than they do outside their neighborhoods.
(D) Murder comprised a larger proportion of violent crimes in the old days than it does today.
(E) News magazines play a more important role today in informing the public about crime than they did in the old days.

Consider the LSAT problem again. The main point or main conclusion that the passage wishes to draw is that "one should not leave one's home except for absolute necessities." And the argument is that one should not go out ***because*** violent crime is out of control.

Notice that we introduced the phrase "violent crime is out of control" with a premise indicator: "because." Yet earlier when analyzing the relationship between that phrase and the sentence that precedes it about the number of crime stories in the newspaper, we noted that a conclusion indicator, "therefore," introduced the information that violent crime is out of control, and, indeed, the passage says the statement is a conclusion.

So which is it? It makes sense introduced by "and so..," and thus seems to be a conclusion.

But it also makes sense introduced by "because," which seems to make it into a premise.

Which is it? It is both a conclusion and a premise. We don't have to choose! The passage includes one argument that produces the conclusion that crime is out of control. It then uses that conclusion as a premise in another argument—another argument that is more important to the passage as a whole—that establishes the bigger conclusion that one should not leave home.

> Unlike newspapers in the old days, today's newspapers and televised news programs are full of stories about murders and assaults in our city. One can only conclude from this change that violent crime is now out of control, and, to be safe from personal attack, one should not leave one's home except for absolute necessities.

In fact most discourse involves multiple arguments. One argument reaches a conclusion, and that same conclusion then serves as a premise in a larger, more extended argument.

For example, look at an expanded version of the Shakespeare passage:

I have Shakespeare class on Monday, Wednesday, and Friday. Today is Wednesday. I know it is Wednesday because yesterday I went to the movies, and I go to the movies only on Tuesdays, and, of course, Wednesday is the day after Tuesday. So I have Shakespeare class today.

The main conclusion of the passage's main argument remains the same: that I have Shakespeare class today. But now the evidence for that conclusion—the claim that the premises are true—is backed up by evidence for the truth of the premise establishing what day it is. That evidence appears as an argument itself proving the conclusion that today is Wednesday. And the argument that it is Wednesday works like any other: it moves from things that we know (I know that I go to the movies only on Tuesday, and I know that I went to the movies yesterday, and I know that the day before Wednesday is Tuesday) to reveal something we did not know. So the argument with the conclusion that today is Wednesday is an argument within an argument. It reaches a conclusion that is a real conclusion to one argument and then a real premise, a key thing that we know, for another argument that is more important. The statement "Today is Wednesday" is both a conclusion and a premise in the complete passage.

Why is the one argument in a passage more important than the other? The primary objective of the passage is to make an overall main point or conclusion. In the Shakespeare passage the main idea being developed is not that it is Wednesday, but that there is Shakespeare class today. One way to determine that is to use the conclusion test: "*and so...*" placed after the statement that it is Wednesday, which leads to the statement that there is Shakespeare class. But "and so..." placed after the statement that there is Shakespeare class leads nowhere else in the passage. There is no more important conclusion in the passage.

Another way to figure it out is this: what does the author most want the reader to gain from the passage? In the Shakespeare passage does the author care more that the reader walk away convinced it is Wednesday or that the reader walk away convinced that there is Shakespeare class?

Clearly the second. The author may not care whether the reader remembers why, but does care that the reader remembers to go to class. Similarly with this LSAT passage,

> 7. Unlike newspapers in the old days, today's newspapers and televised news programs are full of stories about murders and assaults in our city. One can only conclude from this change that violent crime is now out of control, and, to be safe from personal attack, one should not leave one's home except for absolute necessities.

Two conclusions here are (1) violent crime is out of control and (2) one should not leave one's home except for absolute necessities. Is the nervous author of the passage more concerned that the reader realize that crime is out of control or that the reader take heed of the counsel to stay home unless absolutely necessary to venture out? The point is to keep the reader home so as to keep the reader safe. It might be better for the reader to remember why he or she ought to stay home, but it is more important that the reader remember to stay home than it is that the reader recognize that violent crime is out of control.

So a passage may be made up of several arguments, and those arguments will be related together to make a main point, or a main overall argument. Each argument has exactly one conclusion. And remembering that can help you to sort out the overall argument that a passage presents.

A logical reasoning section tests your ability to sort out the arguments within an argument. Can you tell which role each plays? Do you understand which arguments are included so that their conclusions can be used as premises in larger, more important, arguments?

THE LOGICAL REASONING PROBLEM

So the logical reasoning section is about arguments, and it measures whether the test taker

- knows what an argument is.
- can sort out the parts of an argument: its premises and conclusion.
- can distinguish between the main conclusion and subsidiary conclusions in extended arguments.
- understands that a good argument requires both true premises and logical reasoning.
- can assess whether a given argument presents premises that are true.
- can assess whether a given argument exhibits logical reasoning.

The logical reasoning section of the LSAT tests these things by presenting about fifty individual passages and asking you to analyze the passages in different specific ways. Each analysis of the passage, however, has this in common: it is testing whether you understand what an argument is and can see how this particular argument in this passage is made.

To begin to understand the different ways the problems do that, look again at the example problem we have been considering:

7. Unlike newspapers in the old days, today's newspapers and televised news programs are full of stories about murders and assaults in our city. One can only conclude from this change that violent crime is now out of control, and, to be safe from personal attack, one should not leave one's home except for absolute necessities.

Which one of the following, if true, would cast the most serious doubt on the conclusion?

(A) Newspapers and televised news programs have more comprehensive coverage of violent crime than newspapers did in the old days.
(B) National data show that violent crime is out of control everywhere, not just in the author's city.
(C) Police records show that people experience more violent crimes in their own neighborhoods than they do outside their neighborhoods.
(D) Murder comprised a larger proportion of violent crimes in the old days than it does today.
(E) News magazines play a more important role today in informing the public about crime than they did in the old days.

Each logical reasoning problem on the LSAT includes three parts. The problem begins with the **passage** that is usually six to ten lines long and presents an argument. In this example that passage is about the reporting of violent crime and the conclusion that follows from the observations about it. Next the problem includes a short **question**. In this example the question asks for something that would cast serious doubt on the conclusion in the passage. Last, there is a set of five **answer choices**, exactly one of which is correct.

There are always many things that could be said about any passage or any argument that might be presented for your consideration. It is the short question that follows the passage that tells you which particular thing you need to identify about the passage in the current problem. Broadly, every question asks, "*Do you understand this argument?*" But specifically each question is more in this form: "*If you understand this argument well, then you will understand this particular thing about it. So show that you do understand this particular thing.*"

There are about ten "particular things" that the short questions ask about. By knowing what those ten things are and how they go about testing your understanding of the argument in the passage more broadly, you can learn to understand the arguments in the passages and to deal with the particular questions about them effectively.

Those ten types of questions in logical reasoning problems can, in turn, be understood as falling into four basic clusters:

(I) What Follows? Cluster
- (1) Conclusion
- (2) Inference
- (3) Most Strongly Supported

(II) Missing Information Cluster
- (4) Assumption
- (5) Principle
- (6) Discrepancy

(III) True Premises? Cluster
- (7) Weaken
- (8) Strengthen

(IV) Reasoning Form Cluster
- (9) Structure
- (10) Reasoning Flaw

We will take each of these in order.

WHAT FOLLOWS? CLUSTER

An argument is made up of premises and a conclusion. It moves from things that we know—the premises—to things that we learn because we know the things that we know. True premises that are logically related in appropriate ways lead inescapably to, or compel, conclusions. There are things that follow from true premises that relate to one another logically. This is why we engage in argument: to make it clear that some things follow from other things that we know when those other things are considered together. One cluster of LSAT logical reasoning problems tests the ability to tell the difference between premises and conclusions in this process, and to determine what follows from a set of true, logically related premises. This cluster includes three specific sorts of logical reasoning problems: **conclusion problems**, **inference problems**, and **most strongly supported problems**. In these sorts of problems the argument is always a good one, meaning it features premises that can be taken to be true and a conclusion that in fact does follow from those premises. The questions ask you to demonstrate your knowledge of what the conclusion is and what the premises are in that good argument.

(1) Conclusion Problems

Every argument has a conclusion. Knowing the conclusion is essential to understanding any argument. So *every* logical reasoning problem requires you to identify the conclusions in the argument. But there are a few questions—usually about 3—on any LSAT exam that ask directly what the conclusion to the passage is.

Conclusion problems present a passage that features a good argument. The task is to identify the conclusion, or the new knowledge, advanced in that argument. The classic form of an argument is this:

Premise: if it is January then it is winter.

Premise: it is January.

Conclusion: Therefore it is winter.

The model form of an argument consists of two premises followed by a conclusion. In the model the conclusion is the last thing stated, and it is introduced by a "conclusion indicator" (words like "therefore," "hence," "thus," "and so," and the like). The conclusion is something that must be true if the premises are true, and in a good argument the premises are taken to be true.

The following always applies to the passages in conclusion questions: The argument is good, and the premises are taken to be true and to compel the conclusion. What complicates the matter in LSAT logical reasoning section conclusion problems is that the argument is not presented in model format. Instead of premise, premise, conclusion—or because, because, therefore—the conclusion is not written last in order of the statements in the passage, and it is unlikely to be introduced by a word that clearly indicates that it is the conclusion. So the task is to understand what the passage means, and to sort out the premises and the conclusion. You prove that you understand what point the argument is making by identifying which among the statements included in the passage is the conclusion. And you accomplish that by analyzing the content of the argument, since the form of the passage (the order of the statements and the use of conclusion and premise indicator words) does not make the task simple.

Take an example:

War and Peace is a very long book. Yet I know that Oscar has read it. With my own eyes I saw Oscar purchase *War and Peace* at the bookstore using his own money. Oscar told me once that he always reads any book that he pays for. And there is no reason he would lie about a thing like that.

Suppose the task is to identify the conclusion in the passage. Start by looking for conclusion indicators: "therefore," "hence," "and so," "thus," or something with the same meaning. But there is no such conclusion indicator anywhere in the passage, and so that simple signal does not show the solution. OK, so try looking to the last statement in the group. But here that last statement, "there is no reason he would lie about a thing like that," is surely not what the passage is meant to present as new knowledge. It is not what the argument is there to show. So you have to use other means to find the conclusion.

Remember that the conclusion is the new knowledge, or the thing that the premises, the things we already know, are brought together to show to be true. Even though a conclusion indicator is not used in the passage, it will always make sense to inset such an indicator at the beginning of an argument's conclusion, and it will not make similar sense to use a conclusion indicator at the beginning of a premise.

So try that out first by sorting out the statements in the passage:

(s1) *War and Peace* is a long book.

(s2) Oscar has read *War and Peace*.

(s3) Oscar bought *War and Peace*.

(s4) I saw Oscar purchase *War and Peace*.

(s5) Oscar reads a book that he buys.

(s6) Oscar would not lie about a thing like that.

Now, considering the passage as a whole and keeping everything within that context, place a conclusion indicator at the beginning of each of the statements and see whether it makes sense. For example, it does not make sense to say in the last statement "and so Oscar would not lie about a thing like that." This is not something that is established in the argument, but something that we know that helps make the argument work. It makes much more sense to use a premise indicator at the beginning of that statement: "because Oscar would not lie about a thing like that," leads to the rest of the passage—because Oscar wouldn't lie about a thing like that, it is the case that we know that he reads what he buys, and he has bought *War and Peace,* and so...

It is becoming apparent where this is going. Try the conclusion indicator before the first statement: "and so War and Peace is a long book." Again the conclusion indicator does not fit because the passage is not trying to establish that *War and Peace* is a long book, but rather takes that as a given, as a premise, as a thing that we know. The same is true of the third and fourth statements.

But with the statement "Oscar has read *War and Peace,*" the conclusion indicator makes perfect sense. "And so Oscar has read *War and Peace*." That is what the argument is trying to establish and so that is the conclusion of the argument. It is the conclusion even though it is not a final statement in the list, and even though in the passage itself the conclusion is not announced with the word or words that serve as a conclusion indicator.

What did we just do? We found the conclusion for a passage by looking at the content of the passage. We used the understanding that an argument is made up of premises, things that we know, or take as given, or things established by evidence rather than by argument, and the conclusion that is derived from those things that we already know. We applied that knowledge to a set of statements in a passage that *we knew made up a good argument* and decided which among those statements was the conclusion. That is ***analysis***, and exactly the kind of analysis that an LSAT logical reasoning section conclusion problem asks you to do.

Now let's apply this to an actual LSAT question in our sample test [All LSAT sample questions in this book are taken from the Official LSAT which was administered in December 2000. For convenience' sake, let's name this test "Proto," and then we can simply refer to it by name in the rest of the book.]:

A recent national study of the trash discarded in several representative areas confirmed that plastics constitute a smaller proportion of all trash than paper products do, whether the trash is measured by weight or by volume. The damage that a given weight or volume of trash does to the environment is roughly the same whether the trash consists of plastics or paper products. Contrary to popular opinion, therefore, the current use of plastics actually does less harm to the environment nationwide than that of paper products.

5. The main conclusion of the argument is that

(A) plastics constitute a smaller proportion of the nation's total trash than do paper products
(B) the ratio of weight to volume is the same for plastic trash as it is for paper trash
(C) popular opinion regards the use of paper products as less harmful to the environment than the use of products made from plastic
(D) contrary to popular opinion, a shift away from the use of paper products to the use of plastics would benefit the environment nationwide
(E) at this time more harm is being done to the environment nationwide by the use of paper than by the use of plastics

This is our first LSAT problem, so let's go through it to establish the recommended steps to follow with any logical reasoning problem:

Step 1. Always begin looking at the question that the problem presents. Here the question wants us to identify the main conclusion.

Step 2. Now read the passage, being alert to its precise meaning and with an eye to the conclusion that the passage is presented to establish. We want to know what the author most wants us to walk away with or to remember.

Step 3. Now analyze the passage by sorting out the various statements that make it up:

(s1) Plastics constitute a smaller proportion of all trash than do paper products.

(s2) The damage that a given volume or weight of trash does is about the same for both paper trash and plastic trash.

(s3) The current use of plastics does less harm to the environment than the use of paper.

(s4) The use of plastics does less harm is contrary to public opinion.

Step 4. Now do the work and find the conclusion. Do this before even looking at the answer choices.

We know there is an argument and we know that at least some of the statements are parts of that argument. And we know that one of those statements that are part of the argument is the conclusion and that some of the others are premises. When working with an LSAT question it may not be necessary to test every statement initially, or it may seem clear that some are premises and that some are not actual parts of the argument. In this case, in order to demonstrate the approach, test each one of the statements for whether it is the conclusion:

Try adding the conclusion indicator "and so..." at the beginning of each statement to see whether it seems to make sense in the context of the passage:

(s1) "*And so* plastics constitute a smaller proportion of all trash than do paper products." Does that make sense? Probably not. Indeed, that statement is introduced by a clause that suggests it is one of the things that we know to begin with, due to "a recent study." This is something we know by evidence, not by argument. It is a premise—something that is brought into the passage to make something else clear.

(s2) "*and so* the damage that a given volume or weight of trash does is the same for both paper and plastic." Does that make sense in terms of the passage? Is that a fact that is deduced from other things, or one of those other things that is used to deduce some new fact? Again, it seems that "because" makes much more sense at the beginning of this statement than "and so..." does, making the statement a premise rather than the conclusion.

(s3) "*and so* the current use of plastics does less harm to the environment than the use of paper." This seems to make sense. This statement is not something that is taken to be common knowledge or supported by evidence, but something that we learn because we know the material in s1 and s2. So even though the conclusion indicator is not expressed at the beginning of s3, in terms of the passage it belongs there, which indicates the conclusion!

(s4) what about this statement? Neither "and so..." nor "because" seems to fit in a way that makes sense at the beginning of this statement. In fact, this is a statement that is not part of the argument but an extra part of the passage, extra information that might give some perspective or some side thing about the argument itself.

So our test for conclusion and premise indicators shows us that the argument works like this: because s1 and because s2, therefore s3. Thus, s3 is the conclusion.

Step 5. Now that you have done the work and found the conclusion, you are ready to find the one correct answer among the five choices that the problem offers you. It is not helpful to go to the answer choices before you have analyzed the passage. They will not make that analysis easier, but will distract from it. Remember, 80% of the answer choices are just plain wrong. Unless you have some advantage when you go to them, the odds are not with you. Create that advantage by analyzing the passage and determining what the right answer will be, or what the right answer will have to do, before you go to the answer choices.

In this case you have determined what the right answer is. You can usually do that with a conclusion problem. Here the main conclusion is that the current use of plastics does less harm nationwide than the use of paper. Armed with that information, you go to the answer choices determined to be in charge of them. There is information in them that you want to find. Maintain your determination to find it. Do not invite each answer choice to be your answer, but rather interrogate each answer choice to determine whether it does what you need done. As long as you know what you need—as long as you have done the work and done the analysis—you will be able to find the one correct answer choice. There is only one. There is exactly one. The LSAT will never make you choose between two correct answers.

Here, you know what the correct answer has to say. Review the answer choices to ask each one whether it says what you need.

Choice (A) restates one of the premises in the argument, but it is not the conclusion.
Choice (B) restates another premise in the argument, but it is not the conclusion.
Choice (C) restates a statement made in the passage that is actually neither a premise nor the conclusion to the argument.
Choice (D) goes further than the passage does in addressing things that might help the environment nationwide.
Choice (E) is exactly what you are looking for. It correctly states the main conclusion to the passage. Three of the other answer choices mention things in the passage, but your analysis makes it clear which is the conclusion. And the ability to do that analysis is what the test is testing.

> Focus on
>
> ***Conclusion Problems***
>
> **Find the statement in the passage that is the main conclusion the author wants the reader to see.**
>
> ***Interrogate the choices:*** "Does this mean [main conclusion]?"

(2) Inference Problems

A second type of problem in the What Follows? Cluster is the **inference problem**. Three to five of the logical reasoning problems on any LSAT ask for the identification of an inference. On the LSAT, "inference" has a precise meaning: an inference is something that follows from a set of premises or statements. It is an *inescapable* result or consequence of those statements.

An "inference" problem differs from a "conclusion" problem in this way: a "conclusion" question asks for the main conclusion of the passage, or what the passage is there to establish. The conclusion problem wants to know what the author of the passage wants the reader of the passage to walk away having learned.

The category of "inference" is a broader one. An inference is anything that must be true, or anything that follows from, the statements that are included in a passage. Like the "main conclusion," an inference is something that is compelled by the premise statements, something that is inescapably true. But while all main conclusions are inferences, it is not the case that all inferences are main conclusions. So the distinction between the two is important in the world of the LSAT.

An important practical difference between an "inference" problem and a "conclusion" problem on the LSAT is this: with a conclusion problem the main conclusion will be among the statements in the passage, though almost never at the end and not introduced by a conclusion indicator. With an inference problem the inference will *not* be among the statements in the passage. It will be *implicit,* meaning that it is not explicitly said, not there in black and white, but that it is nonetheless compelled by what is said. So the inference is there in that it necessarily follows from what is said, even though it is not stated out loud or explicitly among the statements in the passage.

It is important to distinguish between an inference and an implication. An "implication" is often taken to be a suggestion or something that is likely to be the case or is perhaps the case

and that we have determined to be so from some sort of evidence or sign.
example:

> George ignored what Martha had to say, implying that he did not trust her judgment.

In this statement there is a suggestion that George does not trust Martha, but there is no claim that the evidence compels that judgment. It would be consistent with the statement to say that there are other reasons why George might have ignored what Martha had to say. So the "implication" is not something that has to be true, but something that seems likely under a set of circumstances.

An inference, by distinction, *has to be true.* On the LSAT in a legal reasoning section when a problem asks for an inference it is asking for something that is inescapably true if the statements in the passage are true. So here:

> When George ignores what someone else has to say it is because he does not trust that other person. And George ignored what Martha had to say.

It is inescapably true: it is compelled—not just suggested or even likely, but compelled—that George does not trust Martha.

LSAT inference questions are like that. They ask for something that must be true if the statements in the passage are true. What must be true can be something major, or something minor. Often it has the characteristic of a "side effect." That is, a legal reasoning problem that asks for an inference is not asking for the main conclusion, but for something else that must be true because the statements in the passage are true.

Working with Inference Problems

The question stem of an inference problem will ask either for an inference or for something that "must be true" if the statements in the passage are true. In either case, in working with the problem, recognize and take advantage of this "must be true" feature. Since an inference question does not ask for the main conclusion or for a missing premise needed to establish the conclusion, it is the type of problem whose correct answer is difficult to identify ahead of time (though there are exceptions to this). Test for an inference by interrogating the answer choices with this simple question: "The statements in the passage are true, can this one [in choice _] be false?" If the answer to that question is "no," then that is an inference. Use the question rigorously, insistently, to answer the inference questions correctly. There will be exactly one inference among the five answer choices.

Consider this typical example from Proto:

8. Most people invest in the stock market without doing any research of their own. Some of these people rely solely on their broker's advice, whereas some others make decisions based merely on hunches. Other people do some research of their own, but just as often rely only

on their broker or on hunches. Only a few always do their own research before investing. Nonetheless, a majority of investors in the stock market make a profit.

If the statements in the passage are true, which one of the following must also be true?

(A) Some people who make a profit on their investments in the stock market do so without doing any research of their own.
(B) Most people who invest in the stock market either rely solely on their broker or make decisions based merely on hunches.
(C) Some people who do investment research on their own, while just as often relying on their broker or on hunches, make a profit in the stock market.
(D) Most people who invest in the stock market without doing any research of their own make a profit.
(E) Most people who rely solely on their broker rather than on hunches make a profit in the stock market.

Begin working a logical reasoning problem by looking at the short question. Here it asks for something that "must be true" if the statements in the passage are true. That is the very definition of an inference. The question stem does not care about the role played by that thing that must be true—it might be a main conclusion or something more minor—but it will be something that cannot be false consistent with the passage.

So to approach this question correctly, read the passage for precision on what it says to be able to determine what else is true. Sorting it out patiently, find these statements:

(s1) Most of those who invest in the stock market do not do any research of their own.

(s2) Some non-researching investors rely only on brokers.

(s3) Some non-researching investors rely merely on their own hunches.

(s4) Some of those who invest in the stock market do some research of their own.

(s5) These researchers, just as often, rely on hunches or brokers.

(s6) A few investors always do their own research.

(s7) A majority of investors make a profit.

Next, analyze the statements. Inference problems are the category where it is most difficult to analyze the passage for the answer to the question that is being asked. That is because with a set of statements there might be many things that must be true based upon them (whereas there is only *one* main conclusion). Still, it makes sense to analyze the problem for some of the inferences that might plainly be made, or at least to focus on statements that could easily be involved in inferences. For example, if one statement says that everything in a category has some characteristic, and another statement says that something is in that category, then an inference follows that that something has that characteristic. Like this:

> Francis decided that it was best for them to take Judy's car to get to court that morning. The alarm clock did not ring when it was supposed to, and so the two of them had awakened late. Still, they had to get to court on time and so Judy's Porsche—of course all Porsches are fast—seemed a better choice than Francis's Edsel hybrid.

One might take this passage to imply several things:

Francis and Judy take the same car to court.

Francis's car is not fast.

While driving to court Francis and Judy might exceed the speed limit.

Traffic on the route to court is light enough to allow Francis and Judy to drive more or less quickly.

Francis and Judy habitually use an alarm to awaken them.

Each of these things, and several others, seems possible, perhaps even likely to be true. But none of them has to be true. None of them is an inference that is compelled by the statements. But now consider the statements that are also part of the passage:

All Porsches are fast.

Judy's car is a Porsche.

The inference from those two statements is inescapable that **Judy's car is fast**.

Of course the statements in the passage might make other things that must be true as well, and that you have discovered one of them does not preclude others. With an inference question analyze the passage to be as clear as possible about the meaning of each statement. Pay particular attention to inconclusive and exclusive terms like **all, none, some, few, majority**, and the like, because statements using such terminology frequently lead to inferences when the statements are considered together. Then, having been precise about what the statements say and do not say, move to testing each of the five answer choices to determine whether it must be true.

Again, with an inference question the standard is ironclad and the inference *must be true*. Not "sort of," or "almost certainly," but "certainly." One way to test this is to interrogate each answer choice and ask of it: "can this be false and the statements in the passage still be true?" Note, do not ask "is this likely to be false," but exactly "is it *possible* for this to be false, however likely or unlikely that might be." If it is possible for the statement to be false, then the statement is not something that must be true, and it is not an inference to be drawn from the passage. The one correct answer will be something that must be true and cannot be false.

So back to the question from the LSAT, having clarified precisely what the statements say. Again, inference problems are different from most others in that it is not dependably possible to work out what the single correct answer will be or will involve. But it may be that the statements in a particular passage do relate to one another so as to compel an inference or two that it may be worthwhile to draw before going to the answer choices. This is especially likely to be the case if the passage involves categories and things that are partially or wholly included in and excluded from categories.

So consider the statements in the passage in this problem. Begin with the s1 and s7. Most do no research and a majority make a profit. Those two groups, each more than 50%, must overlap somewhat. So one inference, one thing that must be true, is that some who do no research do make a profit. Take caution not to go further than what must be true: the statements compel the inference that some make a profit who do no research, but they do not say how many.

It does not seem that there is anything else we know *for certain* from the collection of statements. Do we know, for example, whether any of the few who do research actually make a profit? Our common sense might tell us an answer here, but the passage demands no inference. It might be true that the minority which does not make a profit also wholly includes the minority which does their own research. We cannot say with certainty either way from the passage and therefore, unless an answer choice adds information, there is no inference possible on this point. In general, statements about "some" are unlikely to compel an inference.

Having worked the passage to find any inferences that it plainly compels, approach the answer choices with the determination to interrogate them carefully to determine whether it is at all possible for each that it be false, consistent with the statements in the passage. Any answer choice that might be false we reject.

Choice (A). Can it be false that some make a profit do so without doing any research? No, it cannot. It must be true from s1 and s7. This is the very inference that we made and that we were on the lookout for in the answer choices. Since more than half do no research and more than half make a profit, some must be included in both of those groups. Remember, with inferences the standard is very high and very rigorous. But this simply cannot be false.

Choice (B). This choice deals with the first two sentences in the passage. The "most" investors who do no research of their own include "some" who rely only on brokers' advice and "some" who rely only on hunches. But does the passage indicate that the "most" includes only and exactly these two groups? It does not. It could be false, therefore, that most are in one or the other of these categories, since neither "some" is exclusive. (So there might be some who rely on hunches and some on brokers, some who rely on neither, and so on.)

Choice (C). Must it be true that some who do research on their own make a profit? There is nothing that compels the majority that makes a profit to include any of the "some" who do some research. Recall that "some" is quite indeterminate in that it means "at least one." So it could mean exactly one, or it could mean all, or any number in between. And it could be false that the some who do their own research are among the majority who make a profit.

Choice (D). Must it be true that *most* who do no research make a profit? To be sure, we know that most do no research and that most make a profit, but in each case that "most" or "majority" means for certain no more than 50% plus one. The two majorities must overlap, but they need not overlap extensively. It could be simply the "plus one" that overlaps. So could it be true that most who do no research make a profit? Yes, it could be consistent with the statements in the passage. But could it be false that most who do no research make a profit? Yes, it could also be false consistent with the statements. It cannot be false that some who do no research make a profit, but nothing is compelled as to whether the majorities in the two groups are the same.

Choice (E). Does it have to be true that most who rely solely on the broker rather than on hunches make a profit? This choice tries to appeal to common sense, perhaps, but the inference question is not about common sense. Do the statements compel the conclusion that most of the "some" who rely on brokers make a profit? They do not. It is consistent with the passage for all of the profit makers from the group of those who do no research to be among those who rely on hunches. So this could be false and is not the answer to the question.

With this inference problem it was quite possible to make the inference before going to the answer choices. That very inference is in choice (A), which, indeed, has to be true. Examination of the others showed that none of the others had to be true, though each of the others might have been true. Rigorous interrogation of the answer choices and rigorous interpretation of the passage is required in all questions, but especially in inference questions since the standard is so exact and so severe. That something could be true is not enough to make it an inference. An inference is something that "must" be true. It cannot be false. Not even a little.

Inference Problems

Something else that MUST BE TRUE because the statements in the passage are true.

Interrogate the choices: "Can this be false while the statements in the passage are true?" (If so, it is not an inference.)

(3) Most Strongly Supported Problems

It is helpful to distinguish a third type of problem in the What Follows? Cluster. These are called **most strongly supported problems**, and there are three or four of them on every LSAT. Like conclusion problems and inference problems, these questions feature passages with true premises and valid reasoning. The question will ask for something that is "most strongly supported" by those premises. So like inference problems and conclusion problems, these ask you to identify something that follows from the statements in the passage.

Most strongly supported problems might be about something big and important or something more like a side effect. They are more likely to be about broader themes than inference problems, often asking about something quite important in reaching the passage's main conclusion. But they almost never ask for the main conclusion of the argument. Unlike conclusion problems, but like other inference problems, the most strongly supported problems ask for something that is implicit rather than explicit. That is, they ask you to identify something that follows from the statements in the passage, but is not itself included among those statements. Finally, the other difference between most strongly supported problems and problems that ask for an "inference" either using that word or asking for something that "must be true" is that, in the case of the most strongly supported problem, the standard of proof will be a little bit less certain. But only a little bit. With the most strongly supported problem it might be conceivable, but only barely, that what is most strongly supported is not in fact proven absolutely to be true by the statements in the passage. But the correct answer will be very very strongly supported. Someone who understands the statements in the passage will have no reasonable doubt that the correct answer follows from them.

As a practical matter, it is most helpful to treat most strongly supported problems like inferences, and look for something that (at least almost certainly) must be true based upon the statements in the passage, and to realize that the one correct answer will be very strongly supported by the statements in the passage. The four incorrect answer choices will not be supported by the statements in the passage to any significant degree at all. Perhaps the incorrect ones could be true, but the correct one will be the only one that has to be, or almost has to be, true.

Interrogate the answer choices using a "reasonable doubt" test. Ask each answer choice: Given the information in the passage, must this be true beyond a reasonable doubt? Exactly one of the answer choices will demand an answer of "yes." For that answer choice it will be highly unlikely that it could be false. For the other four answer choices it will be quite possible, perhaps even likely or certain, that the answer will be false.

Be alert here! The problem is not asking you for something that "could be true," but for something that almost certainly *must* be true. Something that *could be true* is merely something that is not contradicted by the information in the passage. Something that *must be true,* or almost certainly must be true, is a conclusion that follows from the statements in the passage. Remember, the LSAT will not give multiple correct answers to choose between. So that with these questions there is no need to choose among strongly supported alternatives and judge which one is the "most" strongly supported. There will be one, and only one, that clearly follows from the statements in the passage.

Start with this one from Proto:

7. Consultant: Most workers do not have every item they produce judged for quality, but each piece a freelance writer authors is evaluated. That is why freelance writers produce such high-quality work.

The consultant's statements, if true, most strongly support which one of the following?

(A) A piece authored by a freelance writer is generally evaluated more strictly than the majority of items most workers produce.

(B) By having every piece of their work evaluated, some workers are caused to produce high-quality work.
(C) No other workers produce higher quality work than do freelance writers.
(D) Only freelance writers have every item they produce evaluated for quality.
(E) Some workers produce high-quality work in spite of the fact that not every item they produce is judged for quality.

Begin as with any logical reasoning problem by looking at the question. Here the problem asks you to identify something that is "most strongly supported" by the statements in the passage from the consultant. As with all most strongly supported problems, the statements in the passage are taken to be true and the argument is good. The task is to identify something else that is not stated that is also true.

First, read the statements and analyze them for anything else that seems to follow that is not explicitly stated:

(s1) Most workers do not have everything they produce judged for quality.

(s2) Each thing a freelance writer produces is judged for quality.

(s3) That is the reason freelance writers produce such high-quality work.

Using the "and so..." test we can realize that s3 is the main conclusion to the passage, or what the passage is trying to establish. Now we ask: are there other things that are likely to be true based upon the statements? One such thing is that most workers are not freelance writers, since those two categories seem to be treated as exclusive of one another. And that might be the answer to the question, though we will be alert for its being something else as well.

If nothing else clearly follows from the statements as given, go to the answer choices to test them. Interrogate each answer choice and ask if it is true: "Based on the statements in the passage, is this true?" Remember, the one correct answer will almost certainly be true, and the four incorrect answers will be things that might or might not be true, but that could easily be false and still have the statements in the passage be true.

Choice (A) speaks of items being evaluated "more strictly" for freelance writers than for other workers. None of the statements speaks of the strictness with which items are evaluated, so this is something that may or may not be true, consistent with the statements.

Choice (B) speaks of workers who have every piece evaluated, something that seems to apply in s2 to freelance writers but in s1 not to most workers. It connects that evaluation to producing high-quality work, a connection which is maintained in the conclusion to the passage. Given the truth of that conclusion based upon the evidence in s1 and s2, it seems that it must be true that those who have every item evaluated are more likely to produce high-quality work. This is true beyond a reasonable doubt. Indeed, it is difficult to see how it could be false and still have s3 (introduced by "that is why") follow from s1 and s2. Confirm that this is the one correct answer by asking if any of the remaining three is true beyond a reasonable doubt.

Choice (C) speaks of other workers not mentioned in the statements. The truth of the statements in the passage does not demand anything one way or the other as to whether there are other workers whose work is higher quality than freelance writers.

Choice (D) is more restrictive than the statements in the passage by including the word "only." The statements in the passage do not require or prevent others from having their work evaluated. So the statement could be either true or false and have no effect on the passage.

Choice (E) asserts that there are some workers who produce high-quality work without their work being evaluated. Do the statements in the passage care about that? They do not. Again, this is a statement that might or might not be true and have no effect on the truth of the statements in the passage.

So the answer is in choice (B). The statement there must be true, and that is the case with none of the other four. Notice that it is not that the wrong answers must be false, but that they could be either true or false, consistent with the statements in the passage. So long as you do not ask "could it be choice (x)?" bur rather "is choice (x) something that the passage makes true?" there is no doubt what the one correct answer is.

This problem is like a straightforward inference problem: the "could this be false?" test would probably lead equally well to the one correct answer. It would take an awful lot of creativity to find a way to make choice (B) false and still have the statements in the passage be true.

But consider another most strongly supported problem from test Proto:

13. Editorialist: Some people argue that ramps and other accommodations for people using wheelchairs are unnecesssary in certain business areas because those areas are not frequented by wheelchair users. What happens, however, is that once ramps and other accommodations are installed in these business areas, people who use wheelchairs come there to shop and work.

Which one of the following is most strongly supported by the editorialist's statements?

(A) Owners of business areas not frequented by wheelchair users generally are reluctant to make modifications.
(B) Businesses that install proper accommodations for wheelchair users have greater profits than those that do not.
(C) Many businesses fail to make a profit because they do not accommodate wheelchair users.
(D) Most businesses are not modified to accommodate wheelchair users.
(E) Some business areas are not frequented by wheelchair users because the areas lack proper accommodations.

The question stem clearly establishes this as a most strongly supported problem. The argument is taken to be a good one and the statements are true. So read them for what they say:

(s1) Some argue ramps are unnecessary in certain places since those places are not places wheelchair users go.

(s2) When ramps are put in those places people in wheelchairs do come there.

The passage does not draw a main conclusion, but stops with the listing of these two statements. The question is what they strongly support. That might be something in the nature of a main conclusion, although it seems that such a conclusion would need to reach the question of "necessity" mentioned in s1, and perhaps there is not enough data here to do that. Yet the statements do have to do with the same thing—installing ramps in certain business areas—and the question tells us that together they support some other statement, or that they make some other statement true beyond a reasonable doubt. So ask the answer choices "Do the statements in the passage make this have to be true?" (Don't focus on the reasonable doubt, but on the "*strongly*" in "most strongly supported.")

Choice (A) speculates that the owners of businesses are reluctant to modify their businesses by adding the ramps. Is this something that needs to follow for the s1 and s2 to be true? Probably not. It could be true or false consistent with the statements.

Choice (B) discusses profits. Again, it might or might not be the case that businesses with accommodations make higher profits. To know that would require knowledge beyond what the statements provide. It is something that might or might not be the case without affecting s1 or s2.

Choice (C) again discusses profits. Since neither s1 nor s2 mentions profits, something about profits could be true or not and not affect the truth of the statements or be affected by them.

Choice (D) speaks of a category of "most businesses," a category that is not mentioned or required or affected by either s1 or s2. Both can be true and not support this.

Choice (E) addresses businesses frequented by those in wheelchairs and accommodations, things addressed in s1 and s2. It makes the links between the two statements and seems likely to be true in light of the truth of both of those statements. It is, indeed, strongly supported by the passage. Note that it does not go beyond observing that wheelchair users use the place with accommodations when they did not use the place without accommodations. It does not speculate as to why. It does not go too far, but does state something that seems true beyond a reasonable doubt. None of the others comes close to doing this. This is the one correct answer, and it is a kind of subsidiary conclusion that might be used to address other questions such as necessity and profitability that are suggested by the passage in the choices. It differs from a conclusion problem at least in that the answer is not among the explicit statements in the passage. It differs from an inference problem in that the answer could conceivably be false and still have the premises be true, though it would be quite unlikely to be so.

Focus on

Most Strongly Supported Problems

Something else that is not stated that is ALMOST CERTAINLY TRUE because the statements in the passage are true.

Interrogate the choices: "Does this have to be true when the statements in the passage are true?"

MISSING INFORMATION CLUSTER

Another cluster of LSAT logical reasoning problems tests the ability to identify premises and conclusions in an argument and to determine when a needed premise is missing or not included among the statements in a passage. This cluster includes **Assumption** problems, **Principle** problems, and **Discrepancy** problems. As is the case with the What Follows? Cluster, in the problems in the Missing Information Cluster the argument is always a good one, meaning it features premises that can be taken to be true and a conclusion that in fact does follow from those premises. The questions ask you to demonstrate your knowledge of what the conclusion is and what the missing or unstated premise must be in that good argument.

(4) Assumption Problems

A large and important category of logical reasoning problems asks you to identify an assumption that is part of the argument. Usually six to nine logical reasoning problems on an LSAT ask directly about assumptions. So to do well on the LSAT you want to be able to identify assumptions well. And it is even more important than those numbers suggest, since there are several other sorts of problems in the logical reasoning section whose solutions require you to identify missing assumptions. In fact, identifying assumptions is a task that is at the core of analytical thinking.

Assumptions are familiar to us in ordinary language and discussion. An assumption is a thing that we take for granted. It is something that is known and needs to be the case for an argument to work, but something that does not need to be proven itself or usually even stated out loud. That last part is the key: an assumption is something that is not stated explicitly, but nonetheless it is needed by the argument for the premises to compel the conclusion.

Because it is needed for the conclusion to follow from the premises that are stated, an assumption is something that *must be true*. It is a premise that has to be there for the conclusion to follow from the other premises. It differs from most other premises only in that it is not explicitly stated.

On the LSAT, when a problem asks you to identify an assumption it is equipping you with some powerful information: it is telling you that the argument is a good one that does compel its conclusion. But one of the premises that has to be there for the argument to compel its conclusion is not included among the explicit statements. There is a gap, something missing among those statements. Your job is simply to fix it! Identify the gap and fill it. Take an example.

Suppose you are told to identify an assumption that is part of this argument:

Professor Acosta's course requires a paper because all political philosophy courses require a paper.

Here the first statement is the conclusion, and since it is an assumption problem you know for certain that the conclusion is compelled by the premises. But the only explicit premise connects political philosophy courses and courses that require a paper. There is no explicit premise that says anything about Acosta's course. But the conclusion is about Acosta's course. To compel a conclusion about that, some premise that is part of the argument has to introduce it. An argument cannot draw a conclusion about something that is not mentioned in the premises! So knowing that the conclusion is a good one, and that it follows from the premises, what else do the premises have to say? They have to say that

Acosta's course is a political philosophy course.

That must be true for the other premise to compel the conclusion.

So this is what enables you to answer assumption problems effectively:

In a logical reasoning problem that asks for an assumption, the conclusion is good and does follow from the premises. The assumption is an unstated premise that must be true for that conclusion to follow. Not only does this tell you what an assumption certainly is—missing information essential for the conclusion to follow—but also that it is strictly limited to information that must be true for that conclusion to follow.

So in the Acosta example: perhaps it is true that Acosta's course is an upper division one, or that it is a required course, or that it is a boring course, or that it is a course that is poorly classified as a political philosophy course, or that it is an especially popular course, or that the paper it requires is exceptionally demanding. There might be all sorts of things about Acosta's political philosophy course, but the conclusion that the course requires a paper does not require that any of that other information be the case. None of that can be said to be assumed. These are things that *could* be true, but not one of them *must* be true, and so not one of them is assumed in the passage.

So an assumption is something that fills a gap in the explicit statements to make the premises compel the conclusion, but it fills that gap with the minimum that is required to do so, not with what may be true or could be true, but with what must be true since you know that the conclusion follows. One of the great dangers with assumption problems is a temptation to choose an answer choice that is correct but that goes too far, meaning it says that something *must* be true that merely *could* be true.

Take this example from Proto:

10. Art historian: Great works of art have often elicited outrage when first presented; in Europe, Stravinsky's *Rite of Spring* prompted a riot, and Manet's *Déjeuner sur l'herbe* elicited outrage and derision. So, since it is clear that art is often shocking, we should not hesitate to use public funds to support works of art that many people find shocking.

Which one of the following is an assumption that the art historian's argument requires in order for its conclusion to be properly drawn?

(A) Most art is shocking.
(B) Stravinsky and Manet received public funding for their art.
(C) Art used to be more shocking than it currently is.
(D) Public funds should support art.
(E) Anything that shocks is art.

As always, approach the problem by reading the question first. Here it says that your task is to identify an assumption that is required for the conclusion to be properly drawn. So you know these things:

- The conclusion does follow from the premises.
- One of those premises, a missing assumption, is not explicitly stated, but has to be true because the conclusion does follow.
- Your task is to state that unstated premise.

So analyze the argument as presented, and begin that analysis, again as always, by identifying the conclusion. In this case the conclusion indicator "so" that introduces the final sentence points the way to the main conclusion of the passage, which is that we should not hesitate to use public funds on art that some people find shocking.

That conclusion is a good one: it does follow from the premises. But look at it closely: one of the major terms in the conclusion is something that is not mentioned at all in the premises that are explicitly stated. The conclusion has to do with using public funds, but "public funds" does not appear in any of the statements in the passage. The conclusion cannot be about something that is not in the premises, so an unstated premise has to link the artworks to those public funds. And the link has to be one that says that public funds need to be used to support art. Then the explicit argument will go like this:

(p1) If public funds should be used to support art and some art is shocking, then public funds should be used to support some shocking things.

(p2) And public funds should be used to support art.

(C) So public funds should be used to support some shocking things.

The premise that public funds should be used to support art provides the necessary link between what is stated in the explicit premises and the conclusion that does follow from them. So it has to be the case. It may not be the only assumption that the argument requires, but it is certainly an assumption that the argument requires. So the next step is to interrogate the answer choices and ask each of them whether it in fact makes that connection between "using public funds" and "supporting art." Put that way, the question becomes easy (as these questions often appear to be after the difficult analysis is done!). And the one correct answer is choice (D).

Notice how important it is to be very clear on what the problem is asking for and then, based on your analysis, to know exactly what the right answer has to do. Each of the four wrong choices is something that could be true, consistent with the passage. But none of those four comes close to filling the gap that needs to be filled to make the explicitly stated premises compel the conclusion. Remember: ***do not ask*** "could it be this?" of the answer choices. The right answer is not something that merely "could be," but something that "must be." If you look for a "could be" there is an 80% probability that you will select a wrong answer! Instead, know what the right answer has to do and ask "does this make the connection between art and public funding?" That connection must be made.

But sometimes it isn't quite that clear. There are assumption problems where the missing link or the gap is not so plain. And there are others where there is a clear gap but the question asks about a different assumption that is required for the conclusion to follow. In those cases you may not be able to be as exact as you can be about the public funding example in interrogating the answer choices. But still you can—and should—insist on finding something that does what an assumption has to do. Remember an assumption is an unstated premise that *must be true* for the conclusion to follow, and in an assumption problem the conclusion *does* follow. So take advantage of that and use this assumption test to interrogate the answer choices: "Does this have to be true for [the conclusion] to follow?"

Apply that consideration to the public funding question: take choice (A). It could be true that most art is shocking, but you don't care about that. Ask "Does it have to be true that most art is shocking for it to follow that public funds should be used to support some shocking art?" The answer is no. All that needs to be true is some shocking art and the premises give us that. So choice (A) is not a missing assumption. Ask the same question of the other answer choices and you get the same return, except with choice (D), where the answer is yes, that has to be true. If it is not true that public funds should be used to support art, then the other premises do not compel the conclusion that public funds should be used to support shocking things.

Try this out with another problem from Proto:

19. Historian: The spread of literacy informs more people of injustices and, in the right circumstances, leads to increased capacity to distinguish true reformers from mere opportunists. However, widespread literacy invariably emerges before any comprehensive system of general education; thus, in the interim, the populace is vulnerable to clever demagogues calling for change. Consequently, some relatively benign regimes may ironically be toppled by their own "enlightened" move to increase literacy.

Which one of the following is an assumption on which the historian's argument depends?

(A) A demagogue can never enlist the public support necessary to topple an existing regime unless a comprehensive system of general education is in place.

(B) Without literacy there can be no general awareness of the injustice in a society.
(C) Any comprehensive system of general education will tend to preserve the authority of benign regimes.
(D) A lack of general education affects the ability to differentiate between legitimate and illegitimate calls for reform.
(E) Any benign regime that fails to provide comprehensive general education will be toppled by a clever demagogue.

Start with the question that the problem poses, and, again you see that you are asked to identify an assumption, one on which the argument "depends." That reinforces the thought that the assumption is something that must be true for the conclusion to follow.

So now read the passage and isolate the conclusion, which is contained in the final sentence and introduced by the conclusion indicator "consequently." What the argument says it establishes is that some regimes may be toppled by their efforts to increase literacy. So now consider the rest of the statements, looking for the premises that lead to that conclusion.

(s1) If literacy spreads and circumstances are right, then there is increased capacity to distinguish true reformers from opportunists.

(s2) Widespread literacy emerges before comprehensive general education.

(s3) In between the emergence of literacy and the education, the populace is vulnerable to clever demagogues.

(s4) Consequently some benign regimes may be toppled by increasing literacy.

Begin analysis looking for an assumption as we did with the previous problem. Ask whether one of the major terms in the conclusion is something that appears for the first time there. Indeed, in this case, "toppling regimes" comes up for the first time in the conclusion, so there is a missing link connecting information about literacy and demagogues to toppling regimes. But after interrogating the five answer choices, you discover that none of the five is about such a link. What does that mean? It does not mean that the link is not necessary, or that such an assumption is not lacking, but that there is some other assumption that is also lacking that the problem wants you to identify.

So review the statements in the passage and formulate the question to use in order to interrogate the answer choices. Ask of each choice: "(given the information in the passage) Does this have to be true for some regimes to be toppled by increasing literacy?"

Anything that does not have to be true will not be the missing assumption. But if the missing assumption is not true, then the conclusion will not follow. So now, appropriately armed, interrogate the answer choices:

Choice (A) does not have to be true, and indeed the passage seems to suggest that the opposite of it is the case and that demagogues are likely to get public support without a system of general education.

Choice (B) could be something that is true, but it does not have to be the case that there could be "no" awareness of injustice without literacy for it to be the case that literacy increases awareness of injustices. So this isn't it.

Choice (C) says that general education tends to preserve authority. Does that have to be true for increasing literacy to endanger benign regimes? It does not. The conclusion is not about not preserving authority in regimes, but endangering them. There may be a relationship between those things, but it is not needed for this conclusion to follow.

Choice (D) claims a lack of general education affects the ability to tell the difference between legitimate and illegitimate calls for reform. Does this have to be the case? The argument is precisely that because uneducated people are vulnerable to demagogues making illegitimate claims, then this has to be the case. Notice that the statement in choice (D) in no way goes too far, since it does not say how the ability to differentiate is affected by education and does not insist that it is affected to a particular degree, but does suggest that it must be true that it is affected. Indeed that must be true, for if it were not true, s3 would not be true, and the conclusion would not follow. So here is the missing assumption!

You confirm this by checking choice (E), which includes information that could be true, but certainly would not have to be true for the conclusion of affecting "some" benign regimes to follow from the information in the statements.

Both examples from test Proto take us to things that MUST BE TRUE for the conclusion to follow. Asking for what "could be" would take you to incorrect answers. Be very clear on exactly what the right answer will *do*, even if, as in this case, you cannot say ahead of time exactly what it will *be*. The assumption is a necessary part—not optional—of a good argument. Sometimes it is easy to see the necessary part the problem asks you to identify, and other times it is not apparent. But maintain the clarity that you are looking for something that must be true because the argument is good, and insist on that in interrogating the answer choices. As long as you have the conclusion identified correctly, you will not allow yourself to be misled.

Focus on

Assumption Problems

Identify a gap between things in the conclusion and things mentioned in the explicit premises.

<u>Interrogate the choices</u>: "Does [answer choice] have to be true for [conclusion] to follow from the explicit premises?"

A Variation: The "If Assumed" Problem

Again, a missing assumption is a premise that must be true for the conclusion to follow. And an LSAT assumption problem will leave no doubt about that, since the question will ask for an assumption on which the conclusion "depends" or "relies." The question itself will make it clear that the assumption must be true since the conclusion is to be taken as true. The assumption will be the minimum that has to be true for the explicit premises to make the conclusion follow.

But there are a few LSAT problems, usually between one and three on any LSAT, that pose the question differently and require a somewhat different standard of proof. These are the **"if assumed" problems**, and they ask you to identify not an assumption that must be true, but something that if it were assumed would allow the conclusion to be drawn. This is the difference between an essential assumption and something that serves adequately to fill in a gap in the argument. A missing assumption, both by definition and in ordinary usage or common sense, has to be true. The "if assumed" statement could include details that do not have to be true, but that will nonetheless serve to fill in a gap in the argument. Consider this:

All dogs bark, so Sally barks.

There is something introduced in the conclusion here that is not mentioned in the explicit premise: Sally. We are assuming that

Sally is a dog.

That assumption MUST BE TRUE for the conclusion to follow from the information that all dogs bark.

Suppose we were supplied with this premise:

Sally is a golden retriever.

That premise does not have to be true for the conclusion to follow (Sally might be a beagle, an Irish wolfhound, a dachshund, or a mutt, and still be a dog), but it is surely the case that if it is true that Sally is a golden retriever then the conclusion that Sally barks does indeed follow. So the statement that Sally is a dog must be true and it is an assumption made by the argument. The alternative statement that Sally is a golden retriever includes within it required information that Sally is a dog, and so fills in the gap that needs to be filled in for the conclusion to be compelled by the premises. So, indeed, *if* we assume that Sally is a golden retriever, the conclusion follows.

So the "if assumed" problem requires a different standard of proof than the pure assumption problem. The detail in the "if assumed" answer may not have to be true for the conclusion to follow, but it is ***enough*** to make the conclusion follow. With an assumption question an answer choice that offers information beyond the bare minimum required is incorrect. But with an "if assumed" problem that is not the case.

Still, as a practical matter, it is best to treat an "if assumed" problem like an assumption problem, to look for a gap between the explicit premises in the conclusion, and to look for an answer choice that fills that gap. On an "if assumed" problem (like on any other), the LSAT will not require you to choose between two that do that job.

Take this example from test Proto:

21. Some government economists view their home countries as immune to outside influence. But economies are always open systems; international trade significantly affects prices and wages. Just as physicists learned the shortcomings of a mechanics based on idealizations such as the postulation of perfectly frictionless bodies, government economists must look beyond national borders if their nations' economies are to prosper.

    The argument's conclusion follows logically if which one of the following is assumed?

    (A) A national economy cannot prosper unless every significant influence on it has been examined by that nation's government economists.
    (B) Economics is weakly analogous to the physical sciences.
    (C) Economic theories relying on idealizations are generally less accurate than economic theories that do not rely on idealizations.
    (D) International trade is the primary significant variable influencing prices and wages.
    (E) Some government economists have been ignoring the effects of international trade on prices and wages.

The question asks you to find something that, if assumed, makes the conclusion follow. So it tells you that the argument is a good one, but that there is some piece missing in the explicitly stated premises. So find the gap.

The conclusion is contained in the final statement: government economists must look beyond national borders if their economies are to prosper. The premises establish the point that international factors affect a domestic economy. But pay careful attention to the conclusion—to its exact language—and be alert to the fact that it includes something that is not mentioned in that explicit premise: prosperity. The conclusion is about prosperity, but no explicitly stated premise is about prosperity. There is a gap that needs to be filled: a premise must be there to connect prosperity to studying international influences on an economy.

Looking to fill that gap, interrogate the answer choices to ask each whether it fills that gap, or: "Does this have to be true for it to be true that 'for the economy to prosper the economists must look beyond their borders'?"

Here the interrogation question for an assumption takes you to choice (A). Indeed, it is the only one that addresses the prosperity that needs to be a part of the missing premise. But now notice that choice (A) speaks of examining "every" significant influence on an economy. It probably does not have to be true that *every* influence needs to be examined for the conclusion to follow, and so, strictly speaking, the statement in choice (A) is not a required assumption. But is it the case that if the statement in choice (A) is taken to be true then the conclusion follows? Yes it is. And here is the subtle difference between a required assumption problem and an "if assumed" problem. Again, however, as a practical matter the difference is unlikely to affect decision-making when you are looking for the correct answer to an "if assumed" problem. Only one of the five choices will provide information that fills in the missing link in the argument.

The place to be cautious on this is with the more common pure assumption problem, where an answer choice might go further than is required (like the Sally is a golden retriever statement does). The pure assumption question is more rigorous in that the assumption *must* be true for the conclusion to follow. With the "if assumed problem," on the other hand, the correct answer is enough—though it might be more than necessary—to make the conclusion follow.

(5) Principle Problems

There are some LSAT logical reasoning problems, usually three to five on a test, that ask you to identify a principle that underlies the reasoning in the passage. These **principle problems** fall into the Missing Information Cluster and are quite similar to assumption problems, and especially to "if assumed" problems. Like assumption problems, principle problems present you with a passage that includes a good argument, one where the premises compel the conclusion. But also, as with the assumption problem, there is some missing information in those explicitly stated premises.

You know the argument is good, and you need to identify a premise that is not said out loud and helps to enable it to be good. With an assumption problem this means to fill in a gap or to supply the missing information between the things mentioned in the premises and the things the conclusion is about. In the case of a principle problem there is something missing that makes a particular choice that the argument describes, or takes for granted, make sense. Take this example:

> Terry chose the green sweater instead of the yellow one because the green one seemed heavier, and so warmer.

Here the conclusion is that Terry chose the green sweater. The premise is that the green sweater appeared warmer. But if you think about it, while that premise is true and the conclusion is true (again, in a principle problem, as in an assumption problem, we accept that we are presented with true premises and a good conclusion), it is not really enough to compel the conclusion. In fact, the passage depicts a choice that Terry made, and that was to take the warm green sweater over the less warm yellow sweater, and because of the warmth factor. So it seems that warmth was more important to Terry than color. The choice, then, was based on a "principle" that would make Terry judge that in choosing a sweater warmth is the more important thing. Many different principles could lead Terry to his choice: warmth is the most important thing; or color is the least important thing; or function is more important than style; or something like that. The principle is not something that has to be true, but something that, if believed, would lead to the choice depicted in the passage.

This is the pattern that ordinary principle questions follow: the passage offers evidence in the premises to compel a conclusion, but on examination—usually it takes very careful and conscious examination—you realize that the premises compel the conclusion only with a careful choice that some characteristic or outcome is to be preferred to another. That is the principle that says that something is more valuable than something else, and the problem is testing your ability to analyze the passage to see that there is a choice being made, and that there is some principle at work in the choice, and then to identify it.

Here's one from test Proto:

21. Attacks on an opponent's character should be avoided in political debates. Such attacks do not confront the opponent's argument; instead they attempt to cast doubt on the opponent's moral right to be in the debate at all.

Which one of the following principles, if valid, most helps to justify the reasoning above?

(A) Attacks on an opponent's character result from an inability to confront the opponent's argument properly.
(B) Attacks on an opponent's character should not impress those watching a political debate.
(C) Debating techniques that do not confront every argument should be avoided.
(D) Attacking the character of one's opponent does nothing to preserve one's moral right to enter into further political debates.
(E) Questions of character should be raised in political debate if they are relevant to the opponent's argument.

The question asks in a straightforward way for a principle to justify the reasoning. So go to the passage and look for the reasoning. The conclusion is in the first sentence that says that attacks on character should be avoided. The premise says that attacks on character do not confront argument but instead cast doubt on the opponent's moral right to be in the debate.

Like most principle questions, the argument here presents the conclusion as following "of course," or quite naturally and easily from the premise. But if you examine it closely you'll find a subtle choice: so what if the attacks on character do not confront the opponent's arguments? For that argument to have force, you have to judge that it is more important to confront arguments than to consider this "moral right." That is the subtle choice involved in reaching the conclusion here. It is the "value judgment" or principle that lies behind the choice. Typically, with a principle question the challenge lies in identifying the choice. Once you have done so you can articulate it and then interrogate the answer choices to find the one that accurately represents the judgment employed.

With a principle problem, interrogate the answer choices this way: "If I believed this, would I make that choice?" Specifically, for this problem, ask: "If I believed this would I believe that it's more important to address arguments than character?" Notice that the principle will not be something that must be true, but a belief that, if held, would lead to making the choice found in the passage. Here that belief is found in answer choice (C). Note that the other choices have to do with attacking character, but none comes close to representing the kind of opinion that you are looking for that says that argument is more important than character. So clarity on what the principle question is asking for and then a rigorous interrogation of the answer choices to find the appropriate principle will lead to success here.

Focus on

Principle Problems

Finding the subtle choice being made in the passage.

Interrogate the choices: "If I believed [this choice] would I make [the choice that is made in the passage]?"

Sometimes principle questions go at it the other way around, and instead of asking you to identify the principle that is applied in the passage, they will enunciate the principle and ask you to apply it yourself. The idea remains the same: take a belief and use that belief in making a choice.

(6) Discrepancy Problems

Another type of logical reasoning problem in the Missing Information Cluster is the "discrepancy" or "paradox" question. Like assumption questions and principle problems, **discrepancy problems** instruct you to take it as fact that the argument has true premises, valid reasoning, and compels the conclusion. In these other problems there is something missing in this good argument: something that is needed to fill a gap in the argument in the case of an assumption problem or something that explains a subtle choice in the case of a principle problem. With the discrepancy problems, though, the missing piece is something that explains how it could be that two things that seem contradictory are nonetheless true at the same time.

There are two or three of these problems on any LSAT. They are different from the others in what they ask you to do, and they are very straightforward in that task. They present a paradox: there are two things that are the case that it does not seem should be true at the same time. But the passage tells you that they are true. Believe it. Then accept the mission of finding some additional premise, something else that is also the case, that helps it make sense that the discrepant things, or apparently contradictory things, are true at the same time.

Here is one of the three discrepancy questions from test Proto:

14. After the United Nations Security Council authorized military intervention by a coalition of armed forces intended to halt civil strife in a certain country, the parliament of one UN member nation passed a resolution

condemning its own prime minister for promising to commit military personnel to the action. A parliamentary leader insisted that the overwhelming vote for the resolution did not imply the parliament's opposition to the anticipated intervention; on the contrary, most members of parliament supported the UN plan.

Which one of the following, if true, most helps to resolve the apparent discrepancy presented above?

(A) The UN Security Council cannot legally commit the military of a member nation to armed intervention in other countries.
(B) In the parliamentary leader's nation, it is the constitutional prerogative of the parliament, not of the prime minister, to initiate foreign military action.
(C) The parliament would be responsible for providing the funding necessary in order to contribute military personnel to the UN intervention.
(D) The public would not support the military action unless it was known that the parliament supported the action.
(E) Members of the parliament traditionally are more closely attuned to public sentiment, especially with regard to military action, than are prime ministers.

As always, begin working any logical reasoning problem by reading the question. The question here clearly identifies this as a discrepancy problem. Indeed, most such problems will use either the word "discrepancy" (which means "inconsistency") or the word "paradox" in the question itself. And when the question does not use one of those two words, it will make it clear that the task is to reconcile things that you would not expect to be true at the same time.

So read the passage determined to find the things that seem to be inconsistent with one another. Often these passages are not actual arguments with conclusions, but descriptions of situations where two things are said to be the case that it does not appear should be the case at the same time. This is the crucial step here. It is almost instinctive to do so, but do not yet try to make the discrepant things compatible. Instead, begin by being clear on the apparent paradox. Identify plainly the two things that it does not seem should be true at the same time. Give them both credit. Embrace them both. Make the case for each.

In this passage there is a seeming inconsistency between these two things, which we will label P and Q:

(thing P) The parliament of a nation passed a resolution condemning its prime minister for promising to commit military personnel to a UN intervention in another country.

(thing Q) Most members of the parliament support the UN plan.

Do not attempt to dodge or fudge either thing P or thing Q. Both are the case. Do not ignore, or slight, or downplay either one of them. Instead, embrace them: clarify the problem that needs to be explained. The correct answer will offer some additional information that shows how thing Q is true at the same time that thing P is true.

Once you have made yourself very clear about what those two things are, you are ready to interrogate the answer choices. "Does this help to explain how thing Q and thing P *are* true at the same time?" In this case that becomes:

"Does this explain why the members of the parliament support the plan on the one hand and why they passed a resolution condemning the prime minister for committing to it on the other?"

Armed with an interrogation question that gives equal dignity to both sides of the apparent discrepancy, you will find the one correct answer that addresses both sides. Here the only answer choice that does that is choice (B), which is clearly the one correct answer.

Choice (A) is about the UN Security Council, which is not the issue in the discrepancy.
Choice (C) is about funding, something that does not affect the truth of either of the things in question here. It is beside the point
Choice (D) is about public support, which, again, is not the issue at hand.
Choice (E) is also about public sentiment, which is not at issue in making either of the things be the case.

So once you have identified clearly what the seeming inconsistency or paradox is in a discrepancy problem you should be able to identify the exactly one correct answer that offers additional information—in this case information about the constitutional prerogatives of the parliament—that makes the two things make sense simultaneously. The difficulty with these is rarely in finding the correct answer once you know what to look for.

> **FOCUS on**
>
> ***Discrepancy Problems***
>
> **Identify and embrace the two things that are true but seem contradictory.**
>
> ***Interrogate the choices:*** "Does this help explain how [thing P] and [thing Q] are true at the same time?"

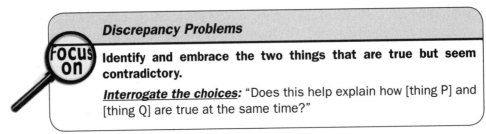

Many people seem to find discrepancy questions especially difficult. But they need not be so, and indeed are not especially difficult, when you take this step to clarify and then embrace the discrepancy. Don't try to avoid it. Make it as sharp as it can be, and then explain it.

TRUE PREMISES? CLUSTER

An argument takes things that we know, the premises, and considers them in relation to one another to lead us to realize something that we did not know, the conclusion. A good argument is one where the conclusion is compelled, or must be true. A good argument is characterized by two things: true premises and valid reasoning. One cluster of LSAT logical reasoning problems tests your understanding of what a good argument is with problems that address the question of the truth of the premises and, accordingly, affect an argument's ability to draw a conclusion. These problems make up what can be called the True Premises? Cluster of LSAT problems.

There are two basic forms of these problems: **weaken problems** and **strengthen problems**. Most LSAT exams will have between eight and eleven problems in this cluster. This is significant, then, for that means that these problems are about ten percent of the whole LSAT.

The issue of the truth of the premises is a crucially important one. Much of what goes on in classic courtroom testimony is an effort to establish or to challenge the truth of premises that, added together, might compel a conclusion. Suppose, for example, that Lucia is charged with robbing a bank in Seattle. The following reasoning might become critical in determining Lucia's guilt:

> If Lucia was not in Seattle on the day of the bank robbery, then Lucia could not rob the bank.
>
> And Lucia was in Dallas (and so not in Seattle) on the day of the bank robbery.
>
> And so Lucia did not rob the bank.

The logic, the reasoning in this syllogism, is valid, so that if the premises are true the conclusion is inescapably true. The question in a trial, then, would become, simply: "are the premises true?"

The defense would present testimony to establish the truth of the minor premise, which would constitute a classic alibi for Lucia. The defense would seek to strengthen the conclusion—that Lucia did not rob the bank—by offering evidence about the truth of the minor premise.

The prosecution, on the contrary, would try to weaken the argument, to make its conclusion less likely to be true, by challenging the truth of either or both of the premises. With regard to the minor premise—that Lucia was in Dallas—the prosecution might seek to question the reliability of the defense evidence that this was the case. The prosecution might also add additional evidence that it was not the case. Perhaps, for example, the eyewitness who claimed to see Lucia in Dallas was in fact seeing someone who just looked an awful lot like Lucia.

Or the prosecution might weaken the argument by attacking the major premise. Perhaps Lucia could be in both cities during the same day, given the speed of travel. Or perhaps Lucia could rob a bank in Seattle electronically from a terminal in Dallas. Evidence such as this, then, might be presented to challenge the truth of that first premise.

(7) Weaken Problems

To see how this works with **weaken problems** on the LSAT, begin with an LSAT problem that you have already seen, the passage that urges you to stay home because violent crime is out of control:

7. Unlike newspapers in the old days, today's newspapers and televised news programs are full of stories about murders and assaults in our city. One can only conclude from this change that violent crime is now out of control, and, to be safe from personal attack, one should not leave one's home except for absolute necessities.

   Which one of the following, if true, would cast the most serious doubt on the conclusion?

   (A) Newspapers and televised news programs have more comprehensive coverage of violent crime than newspapers did in the old days.
   (B) National data show that violent crime is out of control everywhere, not just in the author's city.
   (C) Police records show that people experience more violent crimes in their own neighborhoods than they do outside their neighborhoods.
   (D) Murder comprised a larger proportion of violent crimes in the old days than it does today.
   (E) News magazines play a more important role today in informing the public about crime than they did in the old days.

Perhaps you have already taken the time to figure out the answer to this problem, but now do it systematically and appreciate the process.

The question asks for something to "cast the most serious doubt on the conclusion." That means that it wants to weaken the argument, or to provide some additional information that makes the conclusion less likely to be true. That information will not be about the reasoning, since the reasoning is either good or not, but not more or less doubtful (there are no degrees of validity). What may cast doubt on the conclusion is something that makes a premise less likely to be true. When the reasoning is logical, the conclusion is as true as the premises are.

So begin the analysis of the passage by isolating the conclusion and then the premises. As always with strengthen and weaken questions, accurate identification of the conclusion is crucial. And here, as we know, the conclusion is that one should not leave one's home except for absolute necessities.

This conclusion follows from things that the passage claims that we know. It claims that there is an increase in the number of stories about violent crime. It also claims that if there is such an increase in stories, then there is an actual increase in crime. It then judges that the increase is so great as to make crime be out of control. This information, in turn, now becomes part of still another premise, the minor premise in the argument as a whole:

Major premise: If crime is out of control then one cannot be safe from personal attack outside the home.

The passage offers evidence to establish the truth of the minor premise: Crime is out of control.

Thus the conclusion: To avoid personal attack, do not leave home.

Having identified the premises in the argument, you can weaken it by challenging the truth of any premise. If it is less likely that the premises are true, then the conclusion is less likely to be compelled. Only true premises compel a conclusion. One way to address this in an LSAT problem is to formulate an interrogation question for the answer choices based on this understanding. Ask each of the answer choices: "Does this make it less likely that [the conclusion] is the case?" And then be specific: "Does this make it less likely that to avoid being the victim of violent crime one should not leave home?" Anything that makes one of the premises less likely to be true will make the conclusion less likely to be true. The question seems indefinite ("less likely" as opposed to "must be...") perhaps, but only one of the answer choices will do that. You find the one that does by understanding what the argument does. And, of course, it is testing just your ability to do that.

Here the correct answer challenges the minor premise. It disputes the truth of the thing that the passage claims to establish, that violent crime is out of control. And it does that, in turn, by attacking the evidence that is used to establish that violent crime is out of control. The major premise in the embedded argument establishing that point is that

If there are more newspaper stories about crime, there is more crime.

The correct answer here challenges the truth of that assumption, and by making it less likely to be true, therefore, weakens the conclusion.

So look at the answer choices, using the weaken interrogation question:

Does the information in choice (A) make it less likely that one should not leave home? It does, because it makes it less likely that there is actually more crime. It attacks the truth of the premise that crime is out of control.

Now look at choice (B). This does not make the conclusion less likely, but only suggests that the problem is more widespread.

Choice (C) also does not make it less likely that one should stay home to avoid being the victim of crime, because it means that crime is still there, indeed, right outside your door!

Choice (D) also does not address the evidence leading to the conclusion and so does not make it less likely.

And choice (E) offers some information about news media, but nothing about more or less crime, so nothing that addresses or weakens the argument.

Notice, then, that what is true of most logical reasoning problems is true of these weaken problems as well. When you take the time and have the patience to do the analysis that the test is designed to make you do, determining which one of the answer choices is the one correct one is a process of finding the one that accomplishes exactly what needs to be accomplished, given the nature of the question and the structure and content of the passage. Working it well leads to understanding the argument and to being able to answer the question correctly.

So the "stay at home to avoid being the victim of crime" argument was weakened by attacking the truth of one of the premises. Now go to another problem:

20. Recently discovered prehistoric rock paintings on small islands off the northern coast of Norway have archaeologists puzzled. The predominant theory about northern cave paintings was that they were largely a description of the current diets of the painters. This theory cannot be right, because the painters must have needed to eat the sea animals populating the waters north of Norway if they were to make the long journey to and from the islands, and there are no paintings that unambiguously depict such creatures.

Each of the following, if true, weakens the argument against the predominant theory about northern cave paintings EXCEPT:

(A) Once on these islands, the cave painters hunted and ate land animals.
(B) Parts of the cave paintings on the islands did not survive the centuries.
(C) The cave paintings that were discovered on the islands depicted many land animals.
(D) Those who did the cave paintings that were discovered on the islands had unusually advanced techniques of preserving meats.
(E) The cave paintings on the islands were done by the original inhabitants of the islands who ate the meat of land animals.

Here the question says that four out of the five answer choices will weaken "the argument against the predominant theory" about cave paintings in the passage. So you begin by being very clear on what that theory is:

The theory is that

The cave paintings were a description of the diets of the painters.

But the theory is not the conclusion to the argument. The conclusion to the argument is that the theory is wrong! And it is *that* conclusion you are challenged to make less likely. So now sort out the argument for that conclusion:

Major premise: If the paintings were of the diets of the painters, they would have included sea animals.
Minor premise: The paintings do not include sea animals.
And so it reaches the conclusion: The paintings were not of the diets of the painters.

This is the argument that four of the five choices weaken. So you will want to interrogate the answer choices with this question: "Does this make it less likely that the paintings were *not* of the diets of the painters?" But be careful! With four of the five choices, the answer will be "Yes it does make it less likely." The correct answer is the one choice that does not, or where the answer to the interrogation question is "No it does not make it less likely."

For the conclusion not to follow, since the logic in the syllogism is good, one or both of the premises has to be untrue, at least uncertain. The correct answer to a weaken question, again, does not have to make an argument clearly false, but only less likely to be true. You don't have to kill it; just wounding it severely is enough. And you do that by making a premise less likely to be true, which makes the conclusion also less likely to be true.

So interrogate the choices:

Choice (A) grants what the passage says, that the painters must have eaten sea animals at one time, but says that their diet now is of land animals. If that is the case (and the question tells you, take each of these choices as true) then it challenges the truth of the major premise, and so weakens the argument.

Choice (B) tells you that there are more paintings than you have seen. And if that is the case, it might be that some of the unseen paintings are of sea animals. If so, you cannot be sure that there are no sea animals among the paintings. So this choice challenges the truth of the minor premise and, therefore, makes the conclusion less likely to be true.

Choice (C) adds the information that the paintings depicted land animals, but does nothing to challenge the truth of either of the premises. If both premises are true, then the conclusion is true, and the argument is intact. This does not weaken the argument.

Choice (D) offers information to suggest that the major premise might not be true by providing evidence that the painters could have survived without eating sea animals.

Choice (E) challenges the truth of the major premise by saying that the painters were people who never traveled on the sea and who might have lived on diets made up of land animals and not sea animals.

Again, clarity on what you need to do enables you to see that choice (C) is the correct answer. Each of the other four attacks the truth of one of the premises leading to the conclusion, and, therefore, the truth of the argument as a whole. Be very careful with EXCEPT questions. Even though the "EXCEPT" will be emphasized, it is easy to lose track of it as you interrogate the answer choices. So you might read choice (D), for example, determine that "Yes, indeed, that weakens it," and then take that to be the answer! Focus carefully, and remind yourself, that what weakens the argument in this problem is NOT the answer.

The DANGER of EXCEPT

Be very careful with EXCEPT questions. Even though the "EXCEPT" will be emphasized, it is easy to lose track of it as you interrogate the answer choices. Focus carefully, and continually remind yourself, that what weakens the argument in this problem is NOT the answer.

Note that in both the "stay at home" question and the "cave paintings" question the same basic tactic is followed in weakening the argument. In both cases the argument is weakened by undermining the truth of one of the premises leading to the conclusion. The conclusion can be no more true than the premises are, and if the premises are less likely to be true the conclusion is less likely to be true. Most weaken questions will follow this pattern: they will undermine the truth of one of the premises. So when dealing with a weaken question be certain to sort out correctly the conclusion and the premises and be alert for new information in the answer choices that makes a premise less likely to be true. There will not be more than one answer choice that does this. When you successfully point out the one that does, you have shown as well your understanding of the structure of the argument, how it works, and what makes an argument into one that is not so good.

Focus on

Weaken Problems

Making a premise less likely to be true makes the conclusion less likely to be true.

Interrogate the choices: "Does this make it less likely that [conclusion]?"

(8) Strengthen Problems

Go back to Lucia's alleged bank robbery. You know that if you wanted to weaken the argument that she did not do it you could accomplish that by questioning the truth of either of the premises in the argument. But now you are on the other side, and you want to strengthen the argument that she did not do it. You want to make it *more* likely rather than *less* likely that she did not rob the bank. How could you do that? One way would be to provide additional evidence—new things that we know—to demonstrate that Lucia was out of town, or that, for some other reason, she was unable to commit the crime.

Where a **weaken problem** will typically try to make the conclusion less likely by undermining the truth of an existing premise, a **strengthen problem** will typically try to make the conclusion of an argument more likely by adding new information, additional premises that lead to the same conclusion.

In Lucia's case, you might offer credit card receipts proving that she was buying things in Dallas on that day, and you might even offer them spanning the course of the day to indicate that she was in Dallas during various times of the day. Such evidence would lead to an even stronger conclusion that she could not have been in Seattle.

Try this out with one of the five strengthen problems from LSAT Proto:

A recent national study of the trash discarded in several representative areas confirmed that plastics constitute a smaller proportion of all trash than paper products do, whether the trash is measured by weight or by volume. The damage that a given weight or volume of trash does to the environment is roughly the same whether the trash consists of plastics or paper products. Contrary to popular opinion, therefore, the current use of plastics actually does less harm to the environment nationwide than that of paper products.

6. Which one of the following, if true, most strengthens the argument?
   (A) A given weight of paper product may increase in volume after manufacture and before being discarded as trash.
   (B) According to popular opinion, volume is a more important consideration than weight in predicting the impact of a given quantity of trash on the environment.
   (C) The sum of damage caused to the environment by paper trash and by plastic trash is greater than that caused by any other sort of trash that was studied.
   (D) The production of any paper product is more harmful to the environment than is the production of an equal weight or volume of any plastic.
   (E) The proportion of plastic trash to paper trash varies from one part of the country to another.

As always, start your work with the problem by looking at the question, which asks you to strengthen the argument. Strengthening the argument means making its conclusion more likely to be true. And it wants you to do that by adding one of the statements presented in the five choices to the existing argument. So the question becomes which of these, if added to the argument as a true premise, makes the conclusion more likely to be true?

So analyze the passage for its conclusion (How can you make it more likely without knowing what it is?). That turns out to be contained in the final sentence, with the statement that "the current use of plastics actually does less harm to the environment" than the use of paper. The premises that lead to this conclusion are these:

The major premise establishes this relationship: If plastics constitute a smaller proportion of trash than paper does, then the damage that the plastic trash does to the environment is less than the damage that the paper trash does to the environment.

The minor premise is the fact that: There is less plastic trash by volume than paper trash.

And so the conclusion would be properly drawn that: Plastic trash does less harm to the environment than paper trash.

The premises are already presented as true and uncontroversial. So it seems unlikely that they need to be strengthened. But take a careful look at the conclusion, for it behaves as a conclusion in an assumption problem might behave. The premises are about plastic and paper trash, but the conclusion is more sweeping since it is about "the use of plastics and the use of paper," not just about their trash. The conclusion is broader than the premises!

But your job here is not to criticize the argument or to identify a missing assumption, but to strengthen it, which means to make its conclusion more likely to be true. So with that conclusion, broad as it is, firmly in mind, ask of the answer choices: "Does this make it more likely to be true that the use of plastics does less harm to the environment than the use of paper?"

And now interrogate the choices:

Choice (A) does not really help, since we already know about the difference in damage by weight, and this choice simply speaks to the weight of paper.

Choice (B) speaks about popular opinion, which is unlikely to have an effect on the actual harm that paper or plastics do to the environment.

Choice (C) is about the damage done by paper and plastics together, and so does nothing to make it more likely that plastic is less harmful than paper.

Choice (D) compares the environmental costs of the production of paper and the production of plastic and gives us the additional premise that the production of paper is more costly to the environment. If that is true, as the question tells us it is, then, indeed it is something else that we know that leads us to conclude that the use of plastic does less harm to the environment than the use of paper.

Choice (E) does not address that conclusion, since all it does is say that the proportion of plastic to paper varies from place to place.

So the correct answer here, Choice (D), is the only one that addresses the conclusion and offers an additional premise—something more that we know—that makes that conclusion more likely to be true. This is typically what a strengthen problem will do.

Look at that in another Proto problem:

1. Marmosets are the only primates other than humans known to display a preference for using one hand rather than the other. Significantly, more marmosets are left-handed than are right-handed. Since infant marmosets engage in much imitative behavior, researchers hypothesize that it is by imitation that infant marmosets learn which hand to use, so that offspring reared by left-handed parents generally share their parents' handedness.

   Which one of the following, if true, most supports the researchers' hypothesis?

   (A) A study conducted on adult marmosets revealed that many were right-handed.
   (B) Right-handed marmosets virtually all have at least one sibling who is left-handed.
   (C) According to the study, 33 percent of marmosets are ambidextrous, showing equal facility using either their left hand or their right hand.
   (D) Ninety percent of humans are right-handed, but those who are left-handed are likely to have at least one left-handed parent.
   (E) Marmosets raised in captivity with right-handed adult marmosets to whom they are not related are more likely to be right-handed than left-handed.

This question asks you to identify the one among the five choices that "most supports" the researchers' hypothesis. You can be sure at the outset that only one of the five will offer any real support. The LSAT will not make you choose between correct responses.

So read the passage and analyze it to find the hypothesis that you are charged to support or strengthen. That hypothesis is that marmosets learn which hand they use by imitation. And the argument goes like this:

Major premise: If marmosets learn handedness by imitation, then offspring would share their parents' handedness.

Minor premise: Offspring with left-handed parents are typically left-handed themselves.

Conclusion: Marmosets learn their handedness by imitation.

It is often the case with strengthen questions that the conclusion is presented as likely or possible or, as in this case, as a hypothesis. This is exactly the kind of qualified conclusion that additional information—additional knowledge or evidence—will help to confirm or make stronger. So now get that conclusion firmly in mind and formulate the interrogation question for the answer choices: "Does this make it more likely that marmosets learn their handedness by imitation?" Armed with that question, produced by careful analysis, you go to the answer choices.

Choice (A) offers information that there are many right-handed marmosets, which does not combine with anything else in the passage to confirm that marmosets learn their handedness by imitation.

Choice (B) continues with right-handed marmosets, adding that every right-handed marmoset has a left-handed sibling. This too is no help in making it more likely that they learn their handedness by imitation. If anything, this information might make that less likely.

Choice (C) says that about a third of marmosets are ambidextrous, something which, again, however interesting, simply does not do what you need done. Stay focused on what you need.

Choice (D) is about humans. It offers no premise to support a conclusion about marmosets.

Choice (E) does offer such a premise. Here is information—something that we know—that connects the dominant hand of the marmoset to imitation. It is new information, a new premise, that adds an additional reason to believe that the conclusion is true.

Again, this marmoset example shows that with strengthen questions the one correct answer is likely to be a new premise adding to the store of things that we know to make the conclusion more likely to be the case. Just as the correct answer to a weaken question does not have to make the conclusion impossible, so the right answer to a strengthen question does not have to make the conclusion one hundred percent ironclad, but only more likely. And clearly in this case, this additional information makes the hypothesis that they learn their handedness from imitation more likely to be the case.

Focus on

Strengthen Problems

Adding a relevant premise can make the conclusion more likely to be true.

Interrogate the choices: "Does this make it more likely that [conclusion]?"

So strengthen and weaken are very similar in that both affect the truth of the conclusion, but they typically do so in different ways. Weaken problems tend to attack existing premises. Strengthen questions tend to add new supporting premises.

A CAUTION FOR BOTH STRENGTHEN AND WEAKEN PROBLEMS:

Be sure that when you are interrogating the answer choices on a weaken or strengthen problem that you are looking for the one correct answer and *not* for incorrect answers. It is not the case that everything that does not weaken a conclusion strengthens it, so in a weaken problem look for the one that weakens a premise and not for others that strengthen the conclusion. And it is not the case that everything that does not strengthen a conclusion weakens it, so in a strengthen problem look for one that makes the conclusion more likely and not for others that make it less likely. Very often the incorrect answers will not do the opposite of what you are looking for (though sometimes they will), but instead will be neutral, or will neither weaken nor strengthen the conclusion.

REASONING FORM CLUSTER

An argument takes things that we know, the premises, and considers them in relation to one another to lead us to realize something that we did not know, the conclusion. A good argument—one where the conclusion is compelled, or must be true—is characterized by two things: true premises and valid reasoning. One cluster of LSAT questions, the Reasoning Form Cluster of problems, tests your understanding of that by asking you to analyze and evaluate the reasoning used in particular arguments and, accordingly, to decide whether in fact the argument logically compels its conclusion.

The Reasoning Form Cluster is quite important. It includes about fifteen questions, divided into two basic types: **structure problems**, which require you to describe the reasoning followed in a passage, and **reasoning flaw problems**, which require you to identify a reasoning error in an argument.

(9) Structure Problems

The LSAT is about the ability to understand and analyze arguments, and no type of question tests that more directly than the **structure problems** in the logical reasoning section. There are seven or eight of these on any LSAT. These problems ask for a description of how the argument goes from its premises to its conclusion. In other words, it asks quite simply: how does this argument work? Normally with structure problems the argument *does* work, or there is no flaw or reasoning error, so that the task is to describe accurately what goes on in relating the premises to one another to compel the conclusion.

One way the structure problems do this is to ask about the role of a particular part of the passage. That part might be a premise, a conclusion, or a subsidiary conclusion to the argument, or it might even be something extraneous to the argument itself. Take this example from test Proto:

14. Many people think that the only way to remedy the problem of crime is by increasing the number of police officers, but recent statistics show that many major cities had similar ratios of police officers to citizens, yet diverged widely in their crime rates.

The statistics cited function in the argument to

(A) establish that the number of police officers does not need to be increased
(B) illustrate the need for increasing the number of police officers in major cities
(C) prove that there are factors other than the number of police officers that are more important in reducing the crime rate
(D) demonstrate that there is no relation between the number of police officers and the crime rate
(E) suggest that the number of police officers is not the only influence on the crime rate

The question here makes it plain that the task is to understand how the argument works, how its pieces relate to one another, and to show that understanding by describing the place of a particular piece. So, as always, analyze the argument for its conclusion, and then for the premises leading to that conclusion.

When you look for the conclusion you bump into a problem, for the conclusion does not seem to be stated explicitly. But, of course, that does not mean there is no conclusion, as you can determine by using the good old "and so..." test. Here are the statements:

(s1) Many people think that the only way to remedy crime is more police.

(s2) Statistics show that many major cities have similar numbers of police officers but different amounts of crime.

Add "and so..." at the end of s2 and you are taken to the unstated conclusion that the ratio of police to citizens is not the only thing that accounts for crime rate. That is the argument's conclusion. So now its structure becomes something like this:

Major premise: If cities with different ratios of police to citizens have different amounts of crime, then the numbers of police officers is not the only thing that affects the amount of crime.

Minor premise: And it is the case that cities with the same ratio of police to citizens have different amounts of crime.

Conclusion: Numbers of police are not the only thing that affect crime rate.

Now that you understand the argument and how it works (which, again, is what any LSAT logical reasoning problem is about), you can address the particular question, which is to identify the role of the statistics. What the statistics are there to do is simply to establish the truth of the minor premise. They offer evidence that enables the conclusion to be drawn. Describe that role, and then, armed with that information, fiercely interrogate the answer choices to find the one that accurately describes that role.

The correct answer is plainly choice (E). But be conscious of exactly what you needed to do to know that. First you had to identify the statistics as being part of a premise and not the conclusion. Then you needed to identify the conclusion accurately, which means that you had to analyze the argument thoroughly and carefully for exactly what is compelled by the premises.

Each of the wrong answer choices requires the premises to demonstrate something that they do not do. There is no claim to show either that the number of officers needs to be increased or that it does not (choice (A) and choice (B)). Nor is there an assertion that the number of police officers is unimportant for crime (choice (D)). There is not even any claim that the other factors influencing the crime rate are more or less important than the number of police (choice (C)). But the conclusion is compelled that the ratio of police officers to citizens is not the only factor responsible for crime rate. So, again, to find the one correct answer you take the time and use the patience to sort out exactly what the argument says and to draw the accurate conclusion.

Look at another problem that focuses on the structure of an argument:

Some people claim that the reason herbs are not prescribed as drugs by licensed physicians is that the medical effectiveness of herbs is seriously in doubt. No drug can be offered for sale, however, unless it has regulatory-agency approval for medicinal use in specific illnesses or conditions. It costs about $200 million to get regulatory-agency approval for a drug, and only the holder of a patent can expect to recover such large expenses. Although methods of extracting particular substances from herbs can be patented, herbs themselves and their medicinal uses cannot be. Therefore, under the current system licensed physicians cannot recommend the medicinal use of herbs.

12. Which one of the following most accurately describes the argumentative technique used in the argument?

(A) questioning a claim about why something is the case by supplying an alternative explanation
(B) attacking the validity of the data on which a competing claim is based
(C) revealing an inconsistency in the reasoning used to develop an opposing position
(D) identifying all plausible explanations for why something is the case and arguing that all but one of them can be eliminated
(E) testing a theory by determining the degree to which a specific situation conforms to the predictions of that theory

Here the question asks about the technique that is used in the argument. In other words, the challenge is to identify how the premises are related to lead to the conclusion. As always, you begin by understanding what the conclusion to the argument is and how the premises relate.

In this case the conclusion is indicated pretty clearly in the final sentence with the classic conclusion indicator "therefore." So what we learn from the argument is that physicians cannot recommend medicinal use of herbs. From what premises do we derive that knowledge? Isolate and analyze the statements to decide which ones are actual parts of the argument:

(s1) Some think that doctors do not prescribe herbs because of doubtful effectiveness.

(s2) For a drug to be offered for sale, it must be approved by the regulatory agency for medicinal use.

(s3) It is costly to get regulatory approval, so that only patent holders can recover the expenses.

(s4) Herbs cannot be patented.

There seems to be quite a lot going on here. The things that we know are in s2, s3, and s4. But none of these mentions one of the key terms in the conclusion, which is "physicians recommending."

Statements s3 and s4 are premises that lead to a conclusion, a subsidiary conclusion which can become another premise:

(s5) Herbs cannot get regulatory approval.

Now an assumption relating regulatory approval and physicians recommending clarifies the argument:

Major premise (assumption): If something does not have regulatory approval, then physicians cannot recommend it for medicinal use.
Minor premise (from subsidiary conclusion): Herbs cannot get regulatory approval.
Conclusion: Physicians cannot recommend herbs for medicinal use.

So understanding the structure of the passage turned out to be quite challenging. It took your understanding of extended arguments and assumptions to see how the statements of fact made in the passage could compel the conclusion in the passage. Now return to statement s1. That introduces the rest. It turns out that the actual argument in the rest of the passage is presented to demonstrate that the "some people" who make this charge about the medicinal effectiveness of herbs are incorrect. And there is even a more important conclusion in the passage. The passage proves that these people are incorrect by accounting for physicians not recommending this medicinal use of herbs for another reason.

It took a lot of work, but now you understand what is going on in the passage. The goal is to explain that the "some people" that the passage begins with are incorrect and to show why. With that understanding you are ready to interrogate the answer choices asking each of them whether it articulates this fact about the argument well. It is a good idea simply to restate how the argument works: it states a belief and then provides an argument (a complex one involving a subsidiary conclusion and an assumption) to show that belief is incorrect.

As usual, the real work is involved in analyzing the passage itself. With that analysis, insisting on the correct answer enables you to appreciate that Choice (A) is correct. Not surprisingly, others are not close: they speak of attacking the validity of data in (choice (B)), of revealing an inconsistency (choice (C)), of identifying all plausible explanations (choice (D)), and testing whether a given situation conforms to predictions (choice (E)). While each of these things is a technique that some argument or other might use, none of them is even close to what goes on in this argument, as you readily realize, having understood how the argument works.

FOCUS on

Structure Problems

The argument is good. How are the premises related to compel the conclusion?

Interrogate the choices: "Does this state accurately that [describe how the premises lead to conclusion in the specific case]?"

Again, like all logical reasoning problems, these structure problems test your understanding of what an argument is and how it works. You will need to use that ability, sometimes to the fullest, to demonstrate that understanding.

A Variation: Parallel Structure

Every LSAT includes either one or two reasoning structure problems that ask you to analyze the logical structure of the main passage and then find another in one of the five choices that follows exactly the same pattern. These problems are typically quite lengthy, and can be time consuming in that they require careful analysis of six passages rather than just one. They are especially helpful, however, in practicing for the LSAT since they offer valuable exercises in analyzing arguments for the relationship between the premises and conclusion.

On test Proto this is the parallel reasoning structure problem:

22. If relativity theory is correct, no object can travel forward in time at a speed greater than the speed of light. Yet quantum mechanics predicts that the tachyon, a hypothetical subatomic particle, travels faster than light. Thus, if relativity theory is correct, either quantum mechanics' prediction about tachyons is erroneous or tachyons travel backward in time.

The pattern of reasoning in which one of the following arguments is most similar to that in the argument above?

(A) According to a magazine article, the view that present-day English is a descendant of the ancient Proto-Indo-European language is incorrect. Rather, English more likely descended from a Finno-Ugric language, judging from the similarities between English and other languages of Finno-Ugric descent.

(B) If the defendant committed the crime, then either the defendant had a motive or the defendant is irrational, for only irrational persons act with no motive. If the psychologist is correct, then the defendant is not rational; on the other hand, according to the evidence, the defendant had a strong motive. Thus, since there is no reason to disbelieve the evidence, the defendant is guilty.

(C) The human brain can survive without oxygen only for a few minutes, according to modern medicine. Surprisingly, a reliable witness reported that a shaman has survived for an entire week buried five feet underground. Thus, if modern medicine is not wrong, either the witness is mistaken or the shaman's brain did not suffer any lack of oxygen.

(D) Alexander the Great was buried either in Alexandria or in Siwa, Egypt. However, the burial place is more likely to be Siwa. A limestone table engraved by Ptolemy, Alexander's lieutenant, was found in Siwa, attesting to Alexander's burial place.

(E) If the big bang theory is correct, the universe is currently expanding: the galaxies are moving away from each other and from the center of an original explosion. The same theory also predicts that, eventually, the gravitational forces among galaxies will counterbalance the galaxies' kinetic energy. It follows that, at some point, the universe will stop expanding.

The question is quite clear on what you need: you want to find the one among the five choices that follows the same pattern of reasoning as the main passage. So begin by analyzing that passage for its conclusion, and then its premises, and then the relationship between the two.

On these parallel structure problems the specific content of either the main passage or the answer choices is not relevant. They will almost certainly differ. What matters is the logical structure, and so in analyzing the main passage it is a good idea to get away from the specific content. In this passage the argument goes like this:

(p1) If relativity correct then nothing travels forward at speed greater than light.

(p2) Quantum physics predicts that a tachyon travels at a speed greater than light.

(Conclusion) So if relativity is correct then either quantum physics is wrong or the tachyon does not travel forward.

Since the content does not matter, it can be helpful to simplify it so as to see the structure, like this:

(p1) If R then not both S and F

(p2) Q predicts T = S

(Conclusion) If R then (Q's prediction wrong) or (T is not F)

One of the five choices will follow exactly this pattern. There will be exactly five players playing the roles of R, S, F, Q, and T. There will be a premise saying that if something is the case then there are two other things that cannot be the case together. Another premise will allege that one of those two things is predicted in some object or other. And the conclusion will be that if that first thing is the case, then either the object does not have that thing it is predicted to have, or the object is missing the other quality of the two that cannot be the case together according to the first premise (see how much more clear it is just to jot down the structure!).

The order of the statements in the right answer might not be the same as in the main passage, but the structure will be the same. One premise will include two qualities that cannot be present simultaneously (the "not both...and"). The conclusion will include the "or" statement linking the thing in the first premise to that either/or conclusion. Complicated! In this problem the structure is particularly complex, but you must master it nonetheless, because your ability to do so is exactly what is being tested. Once you have done so, armed with a clear understanding of the pattern that you are looking for (perhaps because you have jotted it down—no need to commit it to memory), and confident that the correct answer will follow exactly the same pattern with the same number of players playing very similar roles, go to the answer choices to find the identical one.

Choice (A) is not it because there is no premise with the "not both...and" structure.

Choice (B), we see as we analyze it, does have a premise with the "not both...and" structure, but it does not include a conclusion with the "either... or" structure that the conclusion in the passage has.

Choice (C) has a premise that says "medicine then there cannot exist together both brain survival and no oxygen." Another premise says "witness says that Shaman's brain survived buried"; the conclusion drawn is that "if medicine is true, then witness wrong or brain had oxygen." This follows the same pattern: "if medicine is true (R) then it cannot be true that both brain survived (S) with no oxygen (F)." Another premise says "witness (Q) says that Shaman's (T) brain survived buried (S)," the conclusion that draws is that "if medicine (R) is true, then witness (Q) is wrong or Shaman's brain (T) had oxygen (F)." So this is the correct answer.

Choice (D) does have something like that "not both...and" part of a premise, but no conclusion with an "either... or" structure.

Choice (E) lacks both the "not both...and" structure in a premise and the "either... or" structure in the conclusion.

So it turns out that taking the time and having the patience to be exact about the structure and the passage enables you to find one correct answer with clarity. These parallel structure problems will not usually require you to make a very subtle choice between the alternatives, and that makes them often easier than they might appear to be. Look for the same number of players in the same relative logical positions and the one correct answer will become clear. The parallel will be exact. The test is evaluating your ability to discern the structure of an argument. Your patience shows the test that you can do that.

(10) Reasoning Flaw Problems

The other type of problem in the Reasoning Form Cluster directly tests understanding of valid reasoning. These are the **reasoning flaw problems**, and there are about ten of them on every LSAT, making this the type of question most frequently asked in logical reasoning sections. Reasoning flaw problems are about ten percent of the whole LSAT!

These problems announce that there is a mistake in the argument. They dare you to find it. The argument does not compel the conclusion it seems to compel or wants to compel. And it fails regardless of the truth of the premises. It fails because the premises do not relate together in a way that makes the conclusion that is drawn from them one that actually follows. Recall that in a good argument true premises combined with valid reasoning lead to a conclusion that is inescapably true. But if the reasoning is not valid, then the conclusion might or might not be true, but the argument, the premises as related to one another, simply cannot tell you. So take this example:

Some yellow fruits are lemons.

Some yellow fruits are bananas.

Therefore some lemons are bananas.

This is a flawed argument. The conclusion is not true, or at least is not something that is known to be true because of the argument. And that is the nature of an argument that is not valid: The conclusion can be false even though the premises are true. Here the premises are true, but it really doesn't matter. Because, whether they are true or not, they do not relate together to compel a conclusion about a relationship between lemons and bananas.

But this argument does compel its conclusion:

All yellow fruits have seeds.

This lemon is a yellow fruit.

Therefore this lemon has seeds.

Here the conclusion has to be true. The relationship between the premises creates a valid, and inescapable, conclusion. Because the reasoning is good, if these premises are true the conclusion is inescapably true. That is a valid argument. An argument where the premises are not related in such a way that the conclusion is inescapably true is not a valid argument. Arguments are either one or the other. Although it may be possible for something to be strengthened or weakened and thereby made more or less likely to be true (at least to our understanding), there are no degrees of validity. Some arguments are valid. All of the others are not valid.

Reasoning flaw problems present passages with arguments that are not valid. These problems give you the tremendous advantage of telling you ahead of time that they are bad. They make a mistake (perhaps more than one) in reasoning. Your task is to identify the mistake.

Here's one from Proto:

5. The radiation absorbed by someone during an ordinary commercial airline flight is no more dangerous than that received during an ordinary dental X-ray. Since a dental X-ray does negligible harm to a person, we can conclude that the radiation absorbed by members of commercial airline flight crews will also do them negligible harm.

   A flaw in the argument is its failure to consider that

   (A) there may be many forms of dangerous radiation other than X-rays and the kinds of radiation absorbed by members of commercial airline flight crews
   (B) receiving a dental X-ray may mitigate other health risks, whereas flying does not
   (C) exposure to X-rays of higher intensity than dental X-rays may be harmful
   (D) the longer and the more often one is exposed to radiation, the more radiation one absorbs and the more seriously one is harmed
   (E) flying at high altitude involves risks in addition to exposure to minor radiation

The question stem tells you right away that there is a flaw in the argument. Reasoning flaw questions always tell you that upfront, either with language asking you to identify a flaw or with language asking you to identify "questionable reasoning" in the argument. If reasoning is "questionable," it is reasoning where the premises do not compel the conclusion. And that means that it is not valid. Reasoning flaw questions are about half and half: about half use the word "flaw," and the other half ask about "questionable reasoning." So in either formulation, a reasoning flaw problem is asking you to identify a mistake in the reasoning that would allow the premises to be true but the conclusion to be false. That is the definition of an invalid argument.

Back to the problem from Proto: the question tells you that the premises do not compel the conclusion. And indeed it tells you more: the premises do not lead to the conclusion because there is a failure to consider something. The task you have is to identify that something.

Go to the passage and analyze it. Begin, of course, with the conclusion, which is pretty easy to find here because it is introduced by the phrase "we can conclude." And it is that the radiation absorbed by commercial airline flight crews does little harm. The evidence for that is contained in two premises, leading to this argument:

(p1) The radiation absorbed during an ordinary commercial air flight is no more dangerous than that received during an ordinary dental X-ray.

(p2) A dental X-ray does little harm.

(Conclusion) Radiation absorbed by flight crews does little harm.

Analysis of this relationship shows a couple of things. For one, "flight crews" is a category that appears for the first time in the conclusion. Neither premise is about flight crews. So to draw the conclusion with validity there would have to be an assumption connecting flight crews to these other premises. What would that be? It would have to be something like

The radiation into orbit by a flight crew is like the radiation absorbed by a person with dental X-rays.

But putting the missing assumption that way helps to reveal the problem: flight crews fly, and so absorb radiation, much more frequently than most people get dental X-rays. So the two cases really are not the same. They are analogous in the amount of harm done by a single exposure to the radiation, but they are not at all the same in frequency of exposures.

Your analysis shows you the problem: the situations are presented as the same when they are not the same. The question asks for something that the passage fails to consider. Well, it fails to consider that flight crews fly more frequently than people get dental X-rays. This is the mistake or the flaw. You know what the right answer has to do before you go to the answer choices. This is almost always something that you can determine pretty precisely with reasoning flaw questions. You know it makes a mistake, so find the mistake before you approach the choices.

In this case interrogate the answer choices to ask: "Does this answer choice say that the argument fails to consider that flight crews get more radiation because they fly more often than most people get dental X-rays?" The answers might do that in a variety of ways, but armed with the specific question and *insisting that the right answer do what the question asks for*, you discover that choice (D) is the answer.

Look at the others:

Choice (A) does not point to a weakness in the argument because it talks about things having to do with neither dental X-rays nor flight crews.

Choice (B) talks about health risks more broadly, but the argument is not about such risks.

Choice (C) is about the danger of other sorts of X-rays, but the argument is not about such dangers.

Choice (E) mentions the dangers of flying at altitude, something which has nothing to do with the argument before in this problem.

So having done the analysis and knowing what to look for, as is often the case, you can find the one correct answer clearly. When the question tells you ahead of time that there is a flaw then you *can* know what to look for in the right answer. Do the work to identify that flaw or reasoning mistake. Be very clear on what it is. Then find it, or find it described.

Focus on

Reasoning Flaw Problems

There *is* a mistake. What is it?

Interrogate the choices: "Does this state accurately [what the mistake is or does in the argument]?"

Look at another one from Proto:

22. Lawyer: Did Congleton assign the best available graphic artist to the project?
Witness: Yes.
Lawyer: And the best writer?
Witness: Yes.
Lawyer: In fact everyone she assigned to work on the project was top notch?
Witness: That's true.
Lawyer: So, you lied to the court when you said, earlier, that Congleton wanted the project to fail?

Each of the following accurately describes a flaw in the lawyer's reasoning displayed above EXCEPT:

(A) It takes for granted that Congleton was not forced to assign the people she did to the project.
(B) It takes for granted that the project could fail only if Congleton wanted it to fail.
(C) It ignores the possibility that Congleton knew that the people assigned to the project would not work well together.
(D) It ignores the possibility that the witness failed to infer from known facts what should have been inferred and therefore was not lying.
(E) It ignores the possibility that Congleton failed to allot enough time or resources to the project team.

The question stem makes it clear that the argument made by the lawyer in the passage is flawed. It is a little unusual to find a flaw problem with an EXCEPT question, but here is one, and analyzing it now helps to clarify the kinds of mistakes that may occur in LSAT legal reasoning passages.

So analyze the passage for its conclusion, which you find at the end introduced by the conclusion indicator, "so."

Now find the statements offered as premises leading to that conclusion:

(s1) Congleton assigned the best available graphic artist to the project.

(s2) Congleton assigned the best available writer to the project.

(s3) Everyone Congleton assigned to the project was top notch.

(Conclusion) The witness lied when the witness said that Congleton wanted the project to fail.

Indeed there appear to be many mistakes here. The conclusion is about two things that none of the premises address: the witness's lying and Congleton's wanting the project to fail. It requires multiple assumptions to connect the existing information in the premises to the conclusion. That can be seen as a flaw, or mistake: jumping to a conclusion without establishing the truth of an assumed premise.

It would be possible to detail several of the missing assumptions and to know that assuming them is likely to be a flaw brought up in the answer choices. But in this unusual case, since there are so many and since four of the five answer choices mention mistakes, it is probably best to go to the answer choices, aware of the structure of the argument, and then to ask of each of the answer choices: "Is there a mistake made here in concluding that Congleton wanted the project to fail?"

Choice (A) describes a mistake. The reasoning assumes that Congleton wanted to sign top-notch people to the project. Note that the conclusion is not about having assigned such people, but about wanting the project to fail.

Choice (B). Is this a mistake in the reasoning? There is no assumption ("taking for granted") that the project could fail only if Congleton wanted it to. Indeed, for purposes of this argument it does not matter whether the project actually failed or not. The conclusion is not about the project, but about Congleton's motives and the witness's veracity. So the information here is beside the point. This choice, then, is the one that does not present a flaw in the argument, and so this is the correct answer to the LSAT problem.

Choice (C). This describes a flaw. It assumes that a collection of top-notch people can work together, and that Congleton would know that and would expect this particular group to do so. The flaw is in making that assumption without providing evidence of its truth.

Choice (D). The mistake described in this choice is in assuming that the witness had evidence of Congleton's motives, but failed to draw the appropriate inference. Again, there is an assumption that is needed to be made here (that Congleton did want the program to fail) for which no evidence is presented.

Choice (E). In assuming that Congleton did not want the project to fail, the lawyer also assumes that Congleton did the other things that might have needed to be done for it to succeed, things in addition to having top-notch people, to make it succeed. Again, there is no evidence for that, and that is a mistake in reasoning.

The flaws in the answer choices here are instances of the particular mistake that occurs more frequently than any other in LSAT logical reasoning problems. It is an error to assume that there is only one possible explanation for a set of facts or circumstances, when other explanations are possible, and perhaps even more plausible. Sometimes the LSAT will state this as overlooking an "alternative explanation" or as "ignoring the possibility that..." In this case, for example, the witness did not realize that Congleton was not telling the truth. Note that this is the same as identifying an assumption for an assumption problem. The critical difference is that with the assumption problem you are told to make the argument good by supplying the missing premise, while with a flaw question you are asked to explain that the argument is not good because it lacks that assumption.

SOME COMMON REASONING FLAWS

There are many many different kinds of flaws or fallacies that might affect an argument. A few of those appear quite frequently in LSAT logical reasoning problems from test to test, and so it is worthwhile to note them here.

1. Overlooking Alternative Possibilities. This is the flaw that occurs more frequently than any other in LSAT logical reasoning problems. It takes a set of premises to compel a conclusion, when in fact that conclusion is only one of a number of explanations for those premises. Unjustifiably, it overlooks other possibilities. Consider this example:

Judy almost always does very well on exams.
But Judy did poorly on yesterday's Shakespeare test.
So Judy must have chosen not to study for yesterday's test.

To be sure, the premises are consistent with the possibility that Judy did not study, but they do not compel that conclusion. The premises could be true and still the conclusion could be false. There are many other possible explanations that the argument overlooks: perhaps the test was unannounced, or perhaps Judy was ill, or perhaps there was a thunderstorm knocking out the lights and Judy did not have the opportunity to study. It might be that the test was extraordinarily difficult, or that it was unfair.

A way to spot this flaw is to notice things that appear in the conclusion that are not treated by the premises. In this case, choosing to study is an item that does not appear before the conclusion. Whenever the conclusion involves something that is not treated in one of the explicit premises, there is a problem. (Be careful, for this not to say the reverse —that when the things in the conclusion are in the premises the argument must be valid. Look at the lemons and bananas above.) The problem with Judy here might be corrected by supplying an assumption, but it might also be stated simply as a flaw and that information that might be included in that assumption is missing. To say that the flaw involves overlooking alternative possibilities is to say that the gap between the premises and the conclusion might be filled in a variety of ways, and the argument does not make clear that there is only one way.

2. Confusing Things That Are Necessary and Things That Are Sufficient. A very important category of reasoning mistake, a kind of mistake that appears often in several places on every LSAT exam, involves confusing something that is needed to make something else happen with something that is enough to make something else happen. That means confusing the necessary and the sufficient (the LSAT does not use technical logic language, but it does sometimes use these terms and expects that you know what they mean and what the distinction between them is). Consider this statement:

Whenever a Democrat is elected president, the voters have voted.

The statement establishes a conditional relationship between a Democrat being elected and voters voting. If a Democrat is elected, then the voters voted. So that means that in order for a Democrat to be elected it is necessary that the voters have voted. But it does not mean that whenever the voters vote a Democrat is elected! So how can you sort that out? In this example the Democrat's being elected is sufficient enough for us to know that voters voted. And voters voting is necessary, or required, for a Democrat to be elected. *But you cannot reverse those things!* And that is where the mistake comes in. For this statement does not mean that we know that if the voters voted then that is enough to tell us that a Democrat won. We do not know that it is necessary for a Democrat to win whenever the voters vote. Making this mistake is very easy to do and very common. And it is often tested on the LSAT. [For a more detailed explanation of the relationship between the necessary and sufficient see the explanation of conditional statements in the analytical reasoning section of this book.]

3. Cause and Correlation. Another common mistake involves confusing a correlation with a causal relationship. When two things tend to happen together, it is tempting to conclude that one of them must be responsible for the other. But that is not necessarily the case. A correlation occurs when things happen at the same time. A cause happens when one thing makes another happen. There can be a correlation without a cause. Consider this observation:

Have you noticed that every time Zelda is in the library the lights are on in the reference room!

The statement establishes that a correlation exists between Zelda's being in the library and the lights being on. But can we conclude any more than that? Do we know that Zelda turns on the lights or causes them to be on? Do we know that the lights somehow magically or hypnotically draw Zelda to the library? In the absence of further evidence we know neither of those things. All we know is that they seem to go together.

When thing J and thing K always seem to happen together, there are at least four possible explanations:

1. **It might be that J causes K to happen.**
2. **It might be that K causes J to happen.**
3. **It might be that some other thing, perhaps thing L, causes both J and K to happen.**
4. **It might be simple coincidence.**

The mistake is usually to assume that one of the two things that are correlated causes the other to happen. It is one to be alert for.

4. No Evidence as Evidence. The fact that no one has been able to prove that something does not exist does not mean that it does exist. It is a mistake to take the absence of evidence against something as positive evidence for it. Consider this:

No one has been able to offer any evidence to prove that my client was not in Denver on March 4.
Therefore we know that my client was in Denver on that day.

Well, no one has produced evidence that the client was not in Seattle or Montréal or Jakarta as well, but none of that means that the client was in those places either!

This mistake is one that appears frequently on LSAT exams, though not on every one. It is worthwhile to be alert for it.

5. Misleading percentages. 40% of the things in group A need not be more than 20% of the things in group B. If group A is the United States Senate, for example, with its one hundred members and in group B is the population of New York City at about eight million, then the 20% of group B is a whole lot more in actual numbers than the 40% of group A. So it is a mistake to assume that a larger percentage means a larger actual number. For that to be the case that percentage and the number of things have to refer to exactly the same category. So when you see a movement from actual number to percentage or ratio in an LSAT problem, be alert and be careful for misused percentages.

A Variation: Parallel Flaw

Every LSAT includes either one or two reasoning flaw problems that require you to identify a flaw in an argument and then to find the one of the five answer choices with an argument that shows exactly the same flaw. These are similar to parallel reasoning structure problems except that they are less interested in mirroring the exact structure than in making the exact same mistake. Here it is the mistake that is important.

Here's one from Proto that exemplifies the flaw of confusing necessary and sufficient conditions:

15. People who are good at playing the game Drackedary are invariably skilled with their hands. Mary is a very competent watchmaker. Therefore, Mary would make a good Drackedary player.

The flawed pattern of reasoning in the argument above is most similar to that in which one of the following?

(A) People with long legs make good runners. Everyone in Daryl's family has long legs. Therefore, Daryl would make a good runner.
(B) People who write for a living invariably enjoy reading. Julie has been a published novelist for many years. Therefore, Julie enjoys reading.

(C) All race car drivers have good reflexes. Chris is a champion table tennis player. Therefore, Chris would make a good race car driver.
(D) The role of Santa Claus in a shopping mall is often played by an experienced actor. Erwin has played Santa Claus in shopping malls for years. Therefore, Erwin must be an experienced actor.
(E) Any good skier can learn to ice-skate eventually. Erica is a world-class skier. Therefore, Erica could learn to ice-skate in a day or two.

The question challenges you to find the choice that shows the same mistake in reasoning. You need to know the mistake. So begin by analyzing the passage to find its conclusion and then its premises. Analyze the relationship between those things and identify the mistake that the argument makes. There is one (at least), so identify it. Remember that this is not about the content of the passage or the answer choices, but about the reasoning form only.

The conclusion here is announced with the strongest of conclusion indicators, "therefore." It is that Mary would make a good D player. Here is how the argument claims to reach that conclusion:

Major premise: Whenever people are good at D they are good with their hands.
Minor premise: Mary is a skilled watchmaker (and so skilled with her hands).
Conclusion: Mary is good at D.

The minor premise involves an implicit argument that goes like this:

Watchmakers are skilled with their hands.

Mary is a watchmaker.

So Mary is skilled with her hands.

There is nothing improper about this subsidiary argument, it seems, and so the mistake is not here.

Analyze the passage until you find the mistake. Here the mistake is in taking something that is needed for another thing to be the case as being enough to guarantee that that other thing will be the case. If it is the case that D needs F, it does not follow that F is enough to produce D. Here, just because in order to be good at D one has to be good with one's hands, it does not mean that everyone who is good with his or her hands is a good D player. Good hands are necessary to be a good D player, but perhaps not enough, not sufficient, to be a good D player. (Maybe one also needs to know the rules, strategy, or something like that.)

Now that you know the mistake, be very clear on it, and know that exactly one of the five answer choices will make exactly the same mistake. Now move to an analysis of each, asking each: "Do you confuse a necessary with a sufficient condition?"

Choice (A) does not make a mistake. It says that having long legs is sufficient to make one a good runner and that Darryl has long legs. Therefore the conclusion is compelled that Darryl would make a good runner. This is valid.

Choice (B) also reaches a valid conclusion. Writing for a living is sufficient to guarantee enjoying reading. Julie writes for a living, so the conclusion must follow that Julie enjoys reading.

Choice (C) is the one that makes the same mistake. It says that being a race car driver is enough to have good reflexes. Then it says that Chris has good reflexes (through a good subsidiary argument). It then concludes that Chris is a good race car driver, which does not follow. Having good reflexes is needed to be a good race car driver, but it is not enough to make one into a good race car driver. Being good with one's hands is needed to be a good D player, but it may not be enough to make one a good D player. It is the same mistake. Exactly.

Choice (D) does not make the same mistake. Its mistake is moving from a claim that something is "often" the case to a conclusion that could be properly made only if that something were "always" the case. Other than the correct answer, this is the only one of the answer choices that actually has a flaw in its reasoning, but the flaw is a different one from the one in the passage.

Choice (E) is a valid argument. Being a skier is enough to mean that one can ice skate. Erica is a skier. Therefore Erica can learn to ice skate.

As is the case with so many LSAT logical reasoning problems, this problem is difficult because understanding the reasoning is difficult. But once that difficult analysis is done, finding the one correct answer involves simply interrogating the answer choices and insisting on the one that does what analysis shows the one correct answer must do. Once you know what you're looking for, and insist on it, the actual task of answering the question can be accomplished.

CHAPTER 2

READING COMPREHENSION

Take a look at what you are doing right now.

You are probably working to gain admission into law school so that you can study law and earn a law degree. As part of that effort toward admission, you are learning about a test, called the Law School Admission Test, which you must take as part of the process of being admitted to law school. The score you earn on that test seems to be an important factor in law school admission, so you are trying to learn about it. Let's review some things we know about that test:

On the LSAT

The LSAT is one of the things that law schools use to determine a prospective law student's ability to do the work in law school. It is designed to provide a measurement of the skills that are needed for success in law school, skills in reading and analyzing complex texts and arguments and in reasoning carefully about those arguments. The test can be very important for determining which, if any, law schools someone might be offered admission into. Admissions decision makers take the test results into account as a key indicator of whether a particular person is someone they should admit to their school.

The LSAT measures sophisticated reasoning skills with a test that is not especially long: it includes five multiple-choice sections, each thirty-five minutes long, and a sixth thirty-five minute section that is written in form. The actual LSAT score that is reported to the law schools is based upon performance on four of those five multiple-choice sections. The sections are of three different types, and the official score always includes results from performance on two sections of logical reasoning problems, one section of analytical reasoning problems, and one section on reading comprehension.

Together the four multiple-choice sections on which the LSAT score is based include about 100 actual questions. That score is reported on a scale of 120 to 180, and it reflects, most of all, the number of correct answers to those approximately 100 multiple-choice questions that the test taker has submitted. Each correct answer is equal in value to every other correct answer. Doing very well on the LSAT, then, means answering many questions correctly on each of the three kinds of sections included among the four sections that comprise the graded test.

Doing well on these multiple-choice sections is quite difficult and challenging because of the nature of the test. The LSAT helps to draw distinctions between highly successful students from various institutions of higher education across the country. Students with the same basic range of grades—usually high ones—will often score quite differently on the LSAT, and insofar as those scores are reliable indicators of those test takers' analytical abilities, the test helps law schools decide which among their academically accomplished applicants are more likely to succeed with the work they will be asked to do in the first year of law school.

So an individual who wants to go to law school should try to do well on the LSAT, and, in particular, on the three kinds of problems that make up the scored test. The purpose of this book is to explain what those three sections do specifically, to clarify what kinds of things the questions and problems are about, and then to help the prospective test taker understand something about how to work with those problems and questions so as to answer them correctly rather than incorrectly.

Think about how you just read the preceding passage. You tried to learn from the information it contains about what you want to do in approaching the LSAT and preparing for it as part of an overall project of gaining admission to law school. The passage represents a communication by its authors to you and many other actual and prospective readers about that test. You read and paid attention to the passage's paragraphs not to criticize them or find some hidden agenda or anything of that sort, but to learn about the test and to add to the store of information that you have to make judgments about your future behavior. You can gain this information because of your ability to read the passage accurately and to appreciate what it means to say. You don't want to read anything into it and you don't want to tear apart its reasoning. You want to understand what it explains.

That ability to read things and to appreciate what they mean to say is crucial for human beings as we seek to share and develop information. It is especially so for lawyers who need to comprehend particular circumstances, issues, laws, court cases, and disputes in order to consider and analyze particular circumstances and to make judgments and arguments about what has happened and ought to happen in those circumstances. The reading comprehension section of the LSAT measures a prospective law student's ability to comprehend what is going on in a particular situation. It is about understanding the presentation of complex material and ideas so as to be able to make judgments from and about that information.

Careful reading is different from logical analysis. Well-developed reading skills enable people to appreciate what the author or authors of the text are expressing or advancing. Logical analysis involves judgments about whether what that writing advances is something that is the result of sound reasoning. But careful reading and logical analysis are related: before Chris (for example) can make a judgment about whether Terry is logically entitled to say that something is the case, Chris must be clear on what exactly Terry is trying to say. Chris needs to be clear on what the point is, and how particular bits of information fit within that larger whole. Reading comprehension is about that whole: what is it that the author or the text is saying, and how do the particular pieces in the text contribute to that overall theme.

In "On the LSAT" above the author is saying that someone who wants to get into law school needs to be able to do well on the LSAT. Doing well on the LSAT, more specifically, means doing well on three different kinds of questions testing skills that are important for success in law school. Knowing what those sections and skills are can be useful in enhancing performance on the LSAT and, therefore, on gaining admission into law school.

The reader can then take that information and act on it, focusing on details that seem useful. Or the reader might compare it to other information from other sources, or analyze its internal presentation to see whether, in fact, it can know what it claims to know as thoroughly as it claims. But any one of those analytical uses requires comprehension of what the passage actually says! Using information, discounting information, adding information to other information, analyzing the validity of information, discovering assumptions that lie behind information—these are all things that require, first, appreciating precisely what the information is that is being communicated. The reading comprehension section tests the ability to do that.

READING COMPREHENSION AND LOGICAL REASONING

In approaching the reading comprehension section, take a look at the differences between the logical reasoning section of the LSAT and what it tests compared to the reading comprehension section and what it tests. The reading comprehension section tests accuracy about what is being said. It assesses the ability to read clearly and accurately without bias and to report what is said and, in terms of the passage being read, why it is said. The logical reasoning section, on the other hand, tests the reasoning included in the parts or pieces that contribute to the whole passage. In the case of the box **On the LSAT**, for example, the reading comprehension section might test the understanding that there are five multiple-choice sections on the test and that the test score is made up of a number of correct answers on four of those five sections. The logical reasoning section, on the other hand, might test the reasoning leading to the conclusion that each of the sections, or kinds of questions, is equally important in determining the LSAT score: is that claim really compelled by the evidence?

So then, reading comprehension is about accurately identifying the things, the data, presented in a passage, while logical reasoning is about understanding what those data assume and what inferences can be drawn from them. Performance of the logical reasoning task requires, first, good performance of the reading comprehension task. Analysis of the evidence cannot be good unless you know accurately what the evidence is. As the saying goes, Garbage in, Garbage out!

Look at the directions at the beginning of the two sections. The reading comprehension section says that its questions are to be answered "on the basis of what is stated or implied in the passage." Something that is "implied" is something that is indicated or suggested by the passage, without being explicitly stated. The test directions emphasize that this section is about what the passage says. The logical reasoning sections, on the other hand, say at the outset that their questions "are based on the reasoning contained in brief statements or passages." While the reading comprehension is about what is there, the logical reasoning is about the reasoning that lies behind and follows from "what is there." The reading comprehension section challenges you to report accurately on what a passage says. The logical reasoning section challenges you to analyze what that passage says for what it assumes and allows you to infer.

Look at it this way: when you're doing a reading comprehension section, you are a **reporter**. When you're doing a logical reasoning section, you're an **analyst**. The reporter's job is to report with accuracy and perceptiveness what is there. The reporter leaves it to the reader of his or her report to take the information about what is there and to draw inferences about what it means. The analyst depends upon the raw data reported in order to be able to make judgments about what those data assume and about what else might follow from the data. The virtue of the reporter is to tell accurately and without bias what is actually there. The reporter takes pride in making a report that is thorough and exact enough to permit meaningful analysis. Without that faithfulness to the unvarnished truth, the analyst does not have at his or her disposal the true premises from which the valid reasoning might allow true conclusions to be drawn.

Take this example of two reports of a courtroom trial event. The event is the testimony of a defendant, named Socrates, at his trial in Athens. According to Plato, Socrates is saying these remarks as part of testifying about how the nearly universal prejudice against him in the community was created:

Transcript:

"Chaerephon went to Delphi and dared to consult the oracle and ... asked whether there was anyone wiser than I. The Pythian replied that no one was wiser.... Now consider why I say these things: I am going to teach you where the slander against me has come from. When I heard these things, I pondered them like this: "What ever is the god saying, and what riddle is he posing? For I am conscious that I am not at all wise, either much or little. So what ever is he saying when he claims that I am wisest? Surely he is not saying something false, at least; for that is not sanctioned for him." And for a long time I was at a loss about what ever he was saying, but then very reluctantly I turned to something like the following investigation of it. I went to one of those reputed to be wise, on the ground that there, if anywhere, I would refute the divination and show the oracle, "This man is wiser than I, but you declared that I was wisest." So I considered him thoroughly—I need not speak of him by name, but he was one of the politicians—and when I considered him and conversed with him, men of Athens, I was affected something like this: it seemed to me that this man seemed to be wise, both to many other human beings and most of all to himself, but that he was not. And then I tried to show him that he supposed he was wise, but was not. So from this I became hateful both to him and to many of those present."

Two people, Gamma and Delta, are sent to the courtroom to report back on the day's events. These are their reports on the testimony:

Gamma's Report:

Socrates says his service to the god is what led to the slander against him. He began to question politicians in public because of what the god said through the oracle at Delphi. The oracle led him to try to show that others were wiser than he was. And it was that activity that began to make people hate him.

Delta's Report:

When the oracle at Delphi said there was no one wiser than he, Socrates says he went out to try to refute the oracle by questioning others in the community to find someone wiser than he so that he could prove to the god that such a person existed. He says his effort to find such a person through his questioning is what made people hate him.

Now consider the difference between the two reports. Both enable the reader of the report to gather the impression that Socrates suggests that he does what he does in response to something said by the god. The report from Gamma does not allow the reader to go further, since Gamma's summary is based on Gamma's conclusion that that's all there is to the testimony. But Delta's report is more precise, including the information that Socrates says that "he went out to refute the oracle." Delta's report gives data to the analyst, accurate and descriptive detail that the analyst can use as a premise in making the inference that Socrates is willing to question accepted opinion about the gods. Gamma's report allows only the overall impression that Socrates is pious.

Delta's report offers grounds for that impression, but also includes specific data that enable the analyst to show that the data support doubt about that impression. So Delta's is a better report. Delta's report is more based on what was actually said than Gamma's report. Gamma's report is more based on what Gamma feels Socrates meant, whereas Delta's report is less of what Delta feels Socrates meant and more of what Socrates actually said. Neither report presents an analysis, for that is not what the reporters were charged to do, but the higher accuracy of Delta's report allows for better analysis of the accuracy of the impression created by the testimony that Socrates is simply a believer in the Athenian gods.

This skill of observing things with openness and perceptiveness, without bias or previous expectation, is important and difficult to master. To use it takes great discipline. This skill is tested on the reading comprehension section of the LSAT.

THE READING COMPREHENSION TASK

Each LSAT Reading Comprehension section includes four tasks. Each of these tasks is a passage followed by five to eight questions that ask you to describe what the passage is about. Each passage is in one of four broad topic areas, and any LSAT includes one passage from each of the four. They are humanities (including literature and fine arts), social science, science, and law. Some of the specific topics might be familiar, but many probably will not be. Prior familiarity is not required, and perhaps not even beneficial in dealing with the task well. As always with the LSAT, the test is not about the things that you know, but about the things that you are able to do. It will give you all of the information you need in the task itself for you to show your ability to read with precision, accuracy, and attentiveness.

The questions that follow the passage test your ability to read the passage carefully and to report accurately on what it says. Remember, with a reading comprehension section your job is to ***report*** what is there, and the questions challenge you to do it accurately. The questions test your reporting ability by asking you

(1) about the passage as a whole, and
(2) about some particular part or detail within the passage.

These two sorts of questions have much in common: they are questions about what is going on in the passage. What is the author saying and why is the author saying it?

Go back to the passage **On the LSAT**. Suppose you are recommending the article to a friend. You might explain what it is about like this:

"It's describing a particular test that people take as part of the application to law school. It explains how the test is made up and what a test taker can expect. It includes some details about the specific parts of the test, if you care about that. And that detail includes the fact that the test is made up of six sections, and that four of those count in the scoring. The test, the passage mentions, is especially difficult because of the group of students whom it targets and because of its purpose to distinguish between those students and to show the different levels of their analytical skills. The author has written a passage to describe the test to readers who might be interested."

That is pretty much the kind of thing that the questions will test your ability to see and to articulate. ***What is the passage about?*** Notice that it includes no judgmental language, and neither does the passage. The author is not intending to be persuasive or to support or criticize the test (although authors of passages in reading comprehension tasks may adopt any of those perspectives).

All of the questions in a reading comprehension task are about what is in the passage. They are the things a reporter should notice and be able to report. The questions do not include questions about the reasoning in the passage. There are no questions about assumptions, principles that might guide the author, or paradoxes that might be included. There are no questions that ask you to describe the method of reasoning that a passage follows and there are no questions about reasoning flaws. If there are flaws within any passage, the questions will not ask you about them, and identifying them as flaws will not be required or rewarded. Your job is not to analyze or critique the passage; it is to describe it and to explain what it says!

THE IMPORTANCE OF THE MAIN IDEA

The questions in a reading comprehension task never, never, never ask you to identify the main conclusion of the passage. Conclusions are the critical part, the completion, the main idea of arguments. But the passage in a reading comprehension task is not presented to you primarily to advance an argument, or to convince or persuade the reader of something. Its purpose is not to go through a reasoning process to move from the things you know to the things you did not know, but rather to explain or clarify the something that you know. It seeks to inform rather than to persuade. The passage describes something—perhaps an approach to autobiography or an architectural difficulty, or the mechanism by which some insect reproduces, or the way some legal system works, as compared to some other. It is descriptive. Even on those relatively rare occasions where the passage does present an argument, the goal of the passage is not to convince you of the conclusion in the argument but to explain about the argument and to describe its existence to you. It is not to make the argument, but to describe the argument.

So while the reading comprehension tasks are never about the main conclusion in the passage, they are always, always, always about the "main idea" of the passage. There is almost always a question (usually the first question) asking for the "main idea" of the passage. And the main idea is simply: what is it about?

And knowing the main idea is important also for the questions that are not directly about it. Questions that ask about some detail or other also are not about reasoning in the passage, but about pieces, or details, mentioned in the course of making the main point. For example, a detail question on the **On the LSAT** passage might be the following:

According to the passage, the LSAT includes sections on each of the following, except:

(A) logical reasoning
(B) grammatical structure
(C) reading comprehension
(D) writing
(E) analytical reasoning

Of course the answer here is (B) and the question is about a part of the passage that contributes to the main point of the passage with some particular information about the specific makeup of the LSAT. Most of the time the details make sense in terms of the overall main point that the passage seeks to describe. A good reporter will be able to explain those details and their relevance in light of that main point. So you might take the information about the specific content of the sections and ask "why are we talking about this?" And the answer would lead back to the main point.

So, just as the conclusion figures in every type of question or operation in a legal reasoning problem, so the main idea figures in everything that goes on in a reading comprehension task. That means that your effort to answer the questions that ask you to describe the passage in a reading comprehension task is made easier if you can put them in the context of the main idea. So it is a good idea to make certain that you know what the main idea is.

One effective way to approach a reasoning comprehension task is to read the passage to be clear on that main idea, much as you might read a magazine article on an unfamiliar subject to learn about what it describes about its topic. Each task will include questions about details and some questions about the whole. For the questions about details, the context of the whole is often important; you will probably return to the passage and look up particular details anyway. But questions about the main idea are things that you need a comprehension of the whole passage to answer. Therefore, one suggestion is to read for that.

Reading for the Main Idea

It turns out that reading the passage in a reading comprehension task for the main idea is difficult. One reason for this is that most of the passages include plenty of detail used in explaining the main idea. It is easy to get wrapped up in that detail, and in so doing to lose sight of the main idea. This possibility is exacerbated, ironically, by working to improve your performance on the logical reasoning section. There, improvement requires very careful attention to the details in the argument. But here, focusing on the details of the argument can distract from the main idea and leave you less able to answer both sorts of questions well! Again, the reporter and the analyst do different things, and it is useful to remind yourself that with a reading comprehension task you are a reporter.

Focus on

Main Idea

Reading for the main idea of the passage, not for the reasoning.

Remember: The challenge is to be a good reporter: accurate, thorough, unbiased.

When reading for the main idea, it is useful to focus paragraph by paragraph on what each paragraph does to contribute to the passage's main idea. This focus is very broad, not mastering detail in the paragraph, but rather, asking why the detail is there.

Go to a reading comprehension task from test Proto for an example of this.

The passage has five paragraphs. Take them one at a time.

Paragraph 1:

By the time Bentham turned his interest to the subject, late in the eighteenth century, most components of modern evidence law had been assembled. Among common-law doctrines regarding evidence there were, however, principles that today are regarded as bizarre; thus, a well-established (but now abandoned) rule forbade the parties to a case from testifying. Well into the nineteenth century, even defendants in criminal cases were denied the right to testify to facts that would prove their innocence.

What does this paragraph do? It tells us that common-law evidence principles were sometimes bizarre. (It is not about Bentham or about the 18th-century, though both of those are mentioned.)

Paragraph 2:

Although extreme in its irrationality, this proscription was in other respects quite typical of the law of evidence. Much of that law consisted of rules excluding relevant evidence, usually on some rational grounds. Hearsay evidence was generally excluded because absent persons could not be cross-examined. Yet such evidence was mechanically excluded even where out-of-court statements were both relevant and reliable, but the absent persons could not appear in court (for example, because they were dead).

What does this paragraph do? It says that there was often irrational exclusion of evidence.

Paragraph 3:

The morass of evidentiary technicalities often made it unlikely that the truth would emerge in a judicial contest, no matter how expensive and protracted. Reform was frustrated both by the vested interests of lawyers and by the profession's reverence for tradition and precedent. Bentham's prescription was revolutionary: virtually all evidence tending to prove or disprove the issue in dispute should be admissible.

> Narrow exceptions were envisioned: instances in which the trouble or expense of presenting or considering proof outweighed its value, confessions to a Catholic priest, and a few other instances.

What does this paragraph do? It says that somebody named Bentham suggested admitting nearly all evidence. (It includes a counter example, but mainly it establishes that Bentham [and you don't need to know anything about Bentham for this] proposed this alternative rule.)

> **Paragraph 4:**
>
> One difficulty with Bentham's nonexclusion principle is that some kinds of evidence are inherently unreliable or misleading. Such was the argument underlying the exclusions of interested-party testimony and hearsay evidence. Bentham argued that the character of evidence should be weighed by the jury: the alternative was to prefer ignorance to knowledge. Yet some evidence, although relevant, is actually more likely to produce a false jury verdict than a true one. To use a modern example, evidence of a defendant's past bank robberies is excluded, since the prejudicial character of the evidence substantially outweighs its value in helping the jury decide correctly. Further, in granting exclusions such as sacramental confessions, Bentham conceded that competing social interests or values might override the desire for relevant evidence. But then, why not protect conversations between social workers and their clients, or parents and children?

What does this paragraph do? It details a problem with Bentham's proposal, that it could allow misleading evidence.

> **Paragraph 5:**
>
> Despite concerns such as these, the approach underlying modern evidence law began to prevail soon after Bentham's death: relevant evidence should be admitted unless there are clear grounds of policy for excluding it. This clear-grounds proviso allows more exclusions than Bentham would have liked, but the main thrust of the current outlook is Bentham's own nonexclusion principle, demoted from a rule to a presumption.

What does this paragraph do? It says that modern evidence law follows Bentham's basic idea.

Some people find it helpful to jot down a very brief indication of what each paragraph does beside the paragraph. Doing that indicates our basic reading up to this point:

By the time Bentham turned his interest to the subject, late in the eighteenth century, most components of modern evidence law had been assembled. Among common-law doctrines regarding evidence there were, however, principles that today are regarded as bizarre; thus, a well-established (but now abandoned) rule forbade the parties to a case from testifying. Well into the nineteenth century, even defendants in criminal cases were denied the right to testify to facts that would prove their innocence.

Common-Law on Evidence bizarre

Although extreme in its irrationality, this proscription was in other respects quite typical of the law of evidence. Much of that law consisted of rules excluding relevant evidence, usually on some rational grounds. Hearsay evidence was generally excluded because absent persons could not be cross-examined. Yet such evidence was mechanically excluded even where out-of-court statements were both relevant and reliable, but the absent persons could not appear in court (for example, because they were dead).

Irrational exclusion

The morass of evidentiary technicalities often made it unlikely that the truth would emerge in a judicial contest, no matter how expensive and protracted. Reform was frustrated both by the vested interests of lawyers and by the profession's reverence for tradition and precedent. Bentham's prescription was revolutionary: virtually all evidence tending to prove or disprove the issue in dispute should be admissible. Narrow exceptions were envisioned: instances in which the trouble or expense of presenting or considering proof outweighed its value, confessions to a Catholic priest, and a few other instances.

Bentham: admit everything

One difficulty with Bentham's nonexclusion principle is that some kinds of evidence are inherently unreliable or misleading. Such was the argument underlying the exclusions of interested-party testimony and hearsay evidence. Bentham argued that the character of evidence should be weighed by the jury: the alternative was to prefer ignorance to knowledge. Yet some evidence, although relevant, is actually more likely to produce a false jury verdict than a true one. To use a modern example, evidence of a defendant's past bank robberies is excluded, since the prejudicial character of the evidence substantially outweighs its value in helping the jury decide correctly. Further, in granting exclusions such as sacramental confessions, Bentham conceded that competing social interests or values might override the desire for relevant evidence. But then, why not protect conversations between social workers and their clients, or parents and children?

Difficulty: Misleading evidence

Despite concerns such as these, the approach underlying modern evidence law began to prevail soon after Bentham's death: relevant evidence should be admitted unless there are clear grounds of policy for excluding it. This clear-grounds proviso allows more exclusions than Bentham would have liked, but the main thrust of the current outlook is Bentham's own nonexclusion principle, demoted from a rule to a presumption.

Current Main thrust= Bentham

Now add together what the paragraphs do to clarify what the passage as a whole does. It is about evidence law and the change from common-law evidence law that was highly exclusionary to modern evidence law that follows a proposal from Bentham, somewhat modified to take into account its difficulties, to allow nearly all evidence to be heard. Each paragraph includes some more detailed information or example to make its point, but, looking at the function of each paragraph shows what the passage as a whole is about. Armed with this critical information, go to the questions about the passage and show your ability to report accurately on what it says:

The first of the six questions in this task is this:

23. Which one of the following is the main idea of the passage?

    (A) Bentham questioned the expediency of modern rules of legal evidence.
    (B) Bentham's proposed reform of rules of evidence was imperfect but beneficial.
    (C) Bentham's nonexclusion principle should be reexamined in the light of subsequent developments.
    (D) Rules of legal evidence inevitably entail imperfect mediations of conflicting values and constraints.
    (E) Despite their impairment of judicial efficiency, rules of legal evidence are resistant to change.

The question asks simply and directly for the main idea of the passage. About 90% of the regular reading comprehension tasks include a question like this, and it is usually the first of the questions in the task. It is a good idea consciously to read the passage with the purpose in mind of answering this question correctly—of identifying the main idea accurately—without returning to the passage after the initial reading. There will, of course, be plenty of cause to return to the passage to look at specific things, but that process will be easier if you already have the context of and know the main idea. And, again, the question asks for the "main idea," not for a "conclusion." In fact this passage, like most, does not have a conclusion. It is not making an argument or even describing an argument, but describing some things about evidence law. It elaborates on some things that we know.

Go to the question with the main idea in mind as you have already formulated it: It is about evidence law and the change from common-law evidence law that was highly exclusionary to modern evidence law that follows a proposal from Bentham, somewhat modified to take into account its difficulties, to allow nearly all evidence to be heard. Approach the answer choices just as you did in the logical reasoning sections: be in charge; know what the one correct answer has to do and insist on finding the one that does that. Do not approach the answer choices with a disposition to allow them to sell themselves to you. Know what you need, and insist on finding it.

Here the answer that best restates the main idea as you know it is in choice (B). Consider also what the wrong answers do to clarify how these questions work and the kinds of mistakes they encourage you to make in identifying the main idea. Choice (A) simply mistakes Bentham's point, which does not question modern evidence law but earlier evidence law. Choice (C) involves a misstatement of why the author presents the passage, which is not to encourage some reexamination, but to describe the change to modern evidence law in terms of Bentham's proposal. Choice (D) is something that can be found in the passage, but is not the passage's main idea. And choice (E) takes a detail from the passage about a particular period of evidence law and offers it as a main idea. In this case the incorrect answers are not even close to the actual main idea. Knowing that main idea makes for answering the question efficiently.

Here is the second question in the task:

24. The author's attitude toward eighteenth-century lawyers can best be described as

(A) sympathetic
(B) critical
(C) respectful
(D) scornful
(E) ambivalent

The question asks for the attitude of the author of the passage about a detail mentioned in the passage. You recall that 18th-century lawyers are brought up in the course of discussing 18th-century evidence law, and so return to the passage to find the exact place where that discussion is. Knowing that it will be in the second or third paragraph, you find it in the third. Now look for exactly what the author says about 18th-century lawyers. You should not attempt to draw conclusions or inferences about what the author brings up about those lawyers, but look to exactly what the author says. Here it is:

contest, no matter how expensive and protracted. Reform was frustrated both by the vested interests of lawyers and by the profession's reverence for tradition and precedent. Bentham's prescription was revolutionary: virtually all evidence tending to prove

The author says that the lawyers frustrated reform both from their own interests and from the nature of their profession. So the author is critical of the lawyers. You may respect lawyers, or be ambivalent about them, but this is not about you! Your job is simply to report on the author's attitude, and that is accurately stated in choice (B).

The third question also asks about a specific detail:

25. The author mentions "conversations between social workers and their clients" (lines 49–50) most probably in order to

(A) suggest a situation in which application of the nonexclusion principle may be questionable
(B) cite an example of objections that were raised to Bentham's proposed reform
(C) illustrate the conflict between competing social interests
(D) demonstrate the difference between social interests and social values
(E) emphasize that Bentham's exceptions to the nonexclusion principle covered a wide range of situations

It asks you to identify the purpose of a particular phrase. So go back to the passage as the question directs you to and reread the portion that begins a sentence before the quoted phrase and ends a sentence after the quoted phrase to put it in context:

granting exclusions such as sacramental confessions, Bentham conceded that competing social interests or values might override the desire for relevant evidence. But then, why not protect conversations between social workers and their clients, or parents and children?

Despite concerns such as these, the approach underlying modern evidence law began to prevail soon after Bentham's death: relevant evidence should be admitted unless there are clear grounds of policy for excluding it. This clear-grounds proviso allows more exclusions than Bentham would have liked, but the

Attentive reading for what is actually there reveals the answer to the question, for line (51) tells you that the phrase presents a "concern" about a drawback or limit to Bentham's proposal, one that, according to line (47) Bentham conceded. Again, this is not finding a missing assumption or asking for something that is "most strongly supported," but being open and alert for what is actually there and reporting it accurately. Now that you know that the phrase represents a problem or limit to Bentham's proposal, find the one answer choice that captures that. Of course it is choice (A). There is no discussion of "objections" mentioned in choice (B). The phrase does not illustrate a conflict as choice (C) says. There is nothing here about a difference between social interests and values (choice (D)). And it is not about the breadth of Bentham's proposal (choice (E)) but about a problem with it. With the reading comprehension task you answer the question correctly in most cases simply by finding what the passage actually says!

> ***The Questions***
>
> **Find what is actually said in the passage.**
>
> ***Interrogate the choices:*** Find the only choice that accurately reports what is there.

The fourth question in the evidence law task returns to the whole passage:

26. Which one of the following statements concerning the history of the law of evidence is supported by information in the passage?

    (A) Common-law rules of evidence have been replaced by modern principles.
    (B) Modern evidence law is less rigid than was eighteenth-century evidence law.
    (C) Some current laws regarding evidence do not derive from common-law doctrines.
    (D) The late eighteenth century marked the beginning of evidence law.
    (E) Prior to the eighteenth century, rules of evidence were not based on common law.

The question asks you for something that "is supported" by the information in the passage. But remember this is not analytical; it is reporting. Do not try to draw a conclusion or other inference from what the passage says, but rather clarify what the passage says. So remind yourself of the main idea: It is about evidence law and the change from common-law evidence law that was highly exclusionary to modern evidence law that follows a proposal from Bentham, somewhat modified to take into account its difficulties, to allow nearly all evidence to be heard. The specific answer to this question might be as broad as that main idea or it might be something about evidence law that is mentioned in the course of describing that idea. Do not go outside the passage, but report on what the passage says.

Here you probably cannot predict exactly what the right answer will be, but you can predict what it will do. It will be some form of restatement of the main idea, or statement of something that is mentioned in the course of developing the main idea. Firm in your determination not to stray from what the passage says, go to the answer choices and ask *"Does the passage as a whole say this?"*

The passage does not say that evidence law has been replaced by "principles" but by altered evidence law, so choice (A) is not in the passage. The passage does seem to say that modern evidence law is less rigid than eighteenth century law, as in choice (B)—indeed that is in the main point—and if you wish to confirm that, review the first paragraph and the last paragraph where the point is made. This does not require identifying assumptions and drawing their consequences or careful analysis of what the passage actually says to determine what we know in addition, but it does require accurately restating what the passage says. The point made in choice (C) is not to be found anywhere in the passage. While the passage begins its description with the 18th century, it certainly does not say what choice (D) says, that evidence law itself began then. Similarly, it says that 18th-century evidence rules were based in common law, but does not say that they were not so based before that, as choice (E) wants you to infer. Don't do it! You have done the job when you report accurately on what the passage says or does. (As a general rule, if something feels just "too easy" it is likely to be correct. Don't reject the correct answer just because you have gotten good at finding it!)

The fifth question in this reading comprehension task also asks for a report on the passage as a whole:

27. The passage is primarily concerned with which one of the following?
    - (A) suggesting the advantages and limitations of a legal reform
    - (B) summarizing certain deficiencies of an outmoded legal system
    - (C) justifying the apparent inadequacies of current evidence law
    - (D) detailing objections to the nonexclusion principle
    - (E) advocating reexamination of a proposal that has been dismissed by the legal profession

This is yet another way of asking: "What is the passage about?" This time the particular form of the question asks "Why did the author present the passage?" So review the main idea with a focus on the author's objective. Is it to argue something; to advocate something; to criticize something; to explain or to describe something? In this case it is to explain or describe the change in evidence law in terms of Bentham's nonexclusion proposal. Don't be talked out of that! It is easy on a question like this to want the passage to try to do more than it actually does. Resist that temptation, and report on the actual—often quite limited or simple—purpose of the passage.

With that determination in mind, interrogate the answer choices. Immediately choice (A) seems close to what you need because, well, the purpose *is* to discuss the advantages and limitations of the reform of evidence law as suggested by Bentham. The purpose goes beyond choice (B) in that the passage does more than just to summarize the deficiencies of the 18th-century model. Neither is its purpose to excuse or justify whatever inadequacies there might be in current evidence law, as choice (C) states, but to explain the differences between current evidence law and the laws that it replaced. To be sure the passage does what choice (D) says, but that is only in the course of accomplishing its overall purpose, which is explaining the change in evidence law. Choice (E) is way beyond the purpose of the passage as you can see from the very first word of the choice. The purpose of the passage is to explain, and not to advocate. Choice (A) does what you are looking for, and it is the only one that comes close. The others are just wrong.

The final question in this task is about a detail:

28. According to the fourth paragraph of the passage, what specifically does Bentham characterize as preference of ignorance to knowledge?

(A) uncritical acceptance of legal conventions
(B) failure to weigh the advantages of legal reform
(C) exclusion of sacramental confessions
(D) refusal to allow the jury to hear and assess relevant testimony
(E) rejection of exceptions to Bentham's nonexclusion principle

The question asks you simply to identify something in the fourth paragraph. As simple as it sounds, this task can be challenging. Go to the fourth paragraph and find the something that is characterized as a preference of ignorance to knowledge. Find the phrase—the actual language will be there—and then read a sentence on either side of it to establish context to be able to answer the question.

28. According to the fourth paragraph of the passage, what specifically does Bentham characterize as preference of ignorance to knowledge?

One difficulty with Bentham's nonexclusion principle is that some kinds of evidence are inherently unreliable or misleading. Such was the argument underlying the exclusions of interested-party testimony and hearsay evidence. Bentham argued that the character of evidence should be weighed by the jury: the alternative was to prefer ignorance to knowledge. Yet some evidence, although relevant, is actually more likely to produce a false jury verdict than a tru2e one. To use a modern example, evidence of a defendant's past bank robberies is excluded, since the prejudicial character of the evidence substantially outweighs its value in helping the jury decide correctly. Further, in granting exclusions such as sacramental confessions, Bentham conceded that competing social interests or values might override the desire for relevant evidence. But then, why not protect conversations between social workers and their clients, or parents and children?

So a "preference of ignorance to knowledge" is involved in preventing the jury from hearing testimony and deciding for themselves how much weight to give it. That is what the passage says and that will be in the answer choices. Again, it is not about assumptions or inferences, but about "what specifically" Bentham characterizes. And once you accept that challenge and formulate accurately what is said, you realize that the answer is exactly choice (D). Report it.

THE QUESTIONS

In a logical reasoning section there is one question for each passage, and that question requires you to demonstrate your analytical ability by identifying the parts of the argument in the passage and, sometimes, by doing something to one of those parts, or by explaining the relationship between the parts and any flaw that might be included. The differences in the types of questions are quite important in the logical reasoning problems because different analytical operations performed on the same passage will lead to very different answers. Consider this passage for example:

> We read more and more stories in the newspaper about mountain lions in the suburban city of Hurleyville. Lions are rummaging through the garbage, climbing on the slides in the park, snarling traffic at the town's major intersection by begging on the street corners, startling sunbathers by swimming in public pools, and scaring pet rodents because of their carnivorous ways. The number of mountain lions, therefore, is increasing in Hurleyville and we might wonder where the increase will lead.

In a logical reasoning problem this passage might be followed by a question about the conclusion, an assumption, strengthening the argument, weakening the argument, or a flaw. Each of those possible questions would have a very different answer, based upon what the question was asking you to do with the relationship between the premises and the conclusion.

But in a reading comprehension section the question will never ask you "to do" anything with the passage. It will not ask about argument, and so it will not ask about premises and conclusion. It will not ask about flaws or about the reasoning process. Only in extremely rare cases (not even one per LSAT) will it ask about strengthening, weakening, or assumptions, and even then the purpose will not be to demonstrate skill in analyzing how and how well an argument reaches a conclusion, but to report on what the passage describes the argument as being about.

A logical reasoning problem on the lion passage will focus on whether one really knows that the number of mountain lions in Hurleyville is increasing. What are the premises leading to that conclusion? Are they true? And do they in fact compel the conclusion? In a reading comprehension section, on the other hand, the task will be to identify what is actually said: describe the content; don't try to say whether it is sound. Be clear on the fact that the statements are saying that there are more mountain lions and that there are specific mountain lion sightings in a variety of settings.

This does not mean that the questions in one section or the other are easier, but only that they are different. Consciousness of those differences is crucial for performing well on the reading comprehension section.

There are other important differences between the questions in logical reasoning sections and the questions in reading comprehension tasks. First, a single reading comprehension task will include one passage and several questions about that same passage. Second, where questions in logical reasoning problems ask you to do different things with regard to the reasoning in the passages, each of the questions in a reading comprehension task asks you to do basically the same thing, which is to report what is said in the passage. While there are different types of questions, then, those differences are not fundamental but rather are ways to draw your attention either to the whole of the passage or to particular parts or pieces of the passage.

So the most useful distinction in reading comprehension questions is between just two basic types:

(1) questions that ask about the main idea of the passage
(2) questions that ask about some piece or detail within the passage

Main Idea Questions

About 40%, or ten to twelve, of the questions in any reading comprehension section ask about the passage as a whole. What is it about and why is it there? Among the ways the questions are asked about the passage as a whole are these:

- **Main Idea.** Nine out of ten regular reading passages include a question that asks directly about the main idea in the passage.
- **Primary Purpose.** These ask for the reason the author presents the passage. The purpose will be to describe something, to advance something, to dispute something, to argue something, to praise something, or the like.
- **Organization.** Sometimes questions ask about the organization of the passage. For example with the lions: an assertion is made; details are listed about the thing asserted; a conclusion is drawn from the details; and a question is raised about the future.

Detail Questions

The remaining 60%, or fifteen to eighteen, of the questions in a reading comprehension section address details in the passage. The most common forms of detail questions are these:

- **Explain a Detail.** Identify and clarify the meaning of some detail in the passage. For example, question 28 in the exclusion of evidence passage asks you to clarify what Bentham characterizes as a preference of ignorance to knowledge. There are several of these in any reading comprehension section.
- **Thing Mentioned.** These questions are frequent (several in any reading comprehension section) and ask simply for what is there, or perhaps what is not, in the passage.
- **Attitude about Detail.** Often questions ask for the attitude of the author of the passage or of someone the author discusses in the passage about something. Based on what the passage says, what does the author think about this or that?
- **Purpose of Detail.** Some questions ask about the role of some detail, some statement or some fact, in a passage, or some portion of the passage. Question 25 in the exclusion of evidence passage, for example, asks why an author presents a particular phrase.

- **Agrees With.** Two to four questions in a reading comprehension section ask for something that the author or someone that the author describes would agree with. This is asking what the passage says the person in question believes or feels. It does not require you to identify assumptions or principles that lie behind the belief of opinion being identified, but only to find it.
- **Inference.** It is common for a reading comprehension question to ask for an "inference." This is also one of the major question types found in the logical reasoning section, but the nature of inferences sought in the two sections tends to differ. In logical reasoning sections, the focus of an inference is on something that must be true from the premises, or something that is the strict logical consequence of premises. In the reading comprehension section, consistent with its overall goal to test the ability to read objectively and precisely for what is there, an inference question typically is testing clarity on what the passage says about the author or someone that the author discusses. In a reading comprehension section inference questions are usually qualified, asking for what can "most reasonably be inferred," or saying that it can be inferred that something is "most likely" to be the case. This is different from the "must be true" characteristic of the logical reasoning section. In the reading comprehension section the goal is not to see whether you can take given premises and analyze them for conclusions they compel, but rather whether you can accurately report on what those stated premises actually are.
- **Analysis of Detail.** A very few questions, not even one per test, ask you for something that will strengthen or weaken a belief or opinion described in the passage. These are closer to analysis than most questions in reading comprehension tasks, but even here the analysis involved is less rigorous and more focused on correct identification of what is actually there—what is actually being strengthened or weakened—than on adding new evidence or questioning the truth of a stated premise.

The particular sort of detail question is not of critical importance in a reading comprehension section since they all ask "what is there?" Your approach does not change, and what you need in the correct answer does not change. Be attentive and disciplined to find what is there.

A Challenging Example

Several of these question types appear in the most difficult of the reading comprehension tasks in test Proto. As you begin reading it, remind yourself that after you read the passage the first time you want to be able to answer the question about the main idea correctly and without rereading the passage. You might even remind yourself to focus there by looking at the first question stem (but do not look at the answer choices yet; 80% of them will misdirect you!):

> 15. Which one of the following best states the main point of the passage?

Now read the passage by paragraphs, asking what each does as you finish it:

Experts anticipate that global atmospheric concentrations of carbon dioxide (CO_2) will have doubled by the end of the twenty-first century. It is known that CO_2 can contribute to global warming by trapping solar energy that is being reradiated as heat from the Earth's surface. However, some research has suggested that elevated CO_2 levels could enhance the photosynthetic rates of plants, resulting in a lush world of agricultural abundance, and that this CO_2 fertilization effect might eventually decrease the rate of global warming. The increased vegetation in such an environment could be counted on to draw more CO_2 from the atmosphere. The level of CO_2 would thus increase at a lower rate than many experts have predicted.

One thing that sometimes makes reading comprehension tasks on the LSAT as difficult as they are is that the passages do not include clear introductions, telling you what is coming in the passage and why. In reading about something, in that case, you just jump right into it without knowing what the "it" is into which you are jumping. The preceding example is an instance of that. So just read the paragraph for what it does. It talks about carbon dioxide and global warming. It introduces some research that carbon dioxide increases may actually decrease the rate of global warming and not just contribute to its increase. Note that the word "however" seems to indicate the key point about the paragraph. So *what does the paragraph do?* It says that some research says carbon dioxide increases may decrease the rate of global warming. You might note that quite briefly.

Now on to the second paragraph:

However, while a number of recent studies confirm that plant growth would be generally enhanced in an atmosphere rich in CO_2, they also suggest that increased CO_2 would differentially increase the growth rate of different species of plants, which could eventually result in decreased agricultural yields. Certain important crops such as corn and sugarcane that currently have higher photosynthetic efficiencies than other plants may lose that edge in an atmosphere rich in CO_2. Patterson and Flint have shown that these important crops may experience yield reductions because of the increased performance of certain weeds. Such differences in growth rates between plant species could also alter ecosystem stability. Studies have shown that within rangeland regions, for example, a weedy grass grows much better with plentiful CO_2 than do three other grasses. Because this weedy grass predisposes land to burning, its potential increase may lead to greater numbers of and more severe wildfires in future rangeland communities.

What does it do? Again a key is the "however" at the beginning, which signals a disagreement with, or perhaps complication from, what has come before. And the point of the paragraph seems to be that CO_2 increases could result in decreased agricultural yields. There are details in there involving discussions of different kinds of plants, and there is a presentation of research with the names of the researchers. These details might be important, and there might be occasion when you will need to master them and learn, for example, which plants fall into some category or other. But that is not the goal now. And getting wrapped up in the details now could distract from the immediate goal of just learning what the passage is about. So the details are there, but *what are they for?* They are for making the point that CO_2 increases may mean decreased agricultural yields. That's what you want to know for now; if you need to explain something about the details, you know where to find them! So now that you know what the paragraph does, jot it down beside the paragraph, and go to the next one.

It is clear that the CO_2 fertilization effect does not guarantee the lush world of agricultural abundance that once seemed likely, but what about the potential for the increased uptake of CO_2 to decrease the rate of global warming? Some studies suggest that the changes accompanying global warming will not improve the ability of terrestrial ecosystems to absorb CO_2. Billings' simulation of global warming conditions in wet tundra grasslands showed that the level of CO_2 actually increased. Plant growth did increase under these conditions because of warmer temperatures and increased CO_2 levels. But as the permafrost melted, more peat (accumulated dead plant material) began to decompose. This process in turn liberated more CO_2 to the atmosphere. Billings estimated that if summer temperatures rose four degrees Celsius, the tundra would liberate 50 percent more CO_2 than it does currently. In a warmer world, increased plant growth, which could absorb CO_2 from the atmosphere, would not compensate for this rapid increase in decomposition rates. This observation is particularly important because high-latitude habitats such as the tundra are expected to experience the greatest temperature increase.

This paragraph begins by confirming that the previous paragraph is to make the point that CO_2 increases do not mean agricultural abundance. It goes on to suggest what this third paragraph does. It claims that the increases in CO_2 will not decrease the rate of global warming. The paragraph presents details, evidence about peat and something about tundra and some researcher named Billings, but the goal here is not to master such detail but to learn what those things do, and what they do is to make the point that research shows that increases in CO_2 do not mean the decrease in the rate of global warming forecast in the first paragraph.

So take the three paragraphs together and the information about what each does to get to the main idea of the passage as a whole.

Experts anticipate that global atmospheric concentrations of carbon dioxide (CO_2) will have doubled by the end of the twenty-first century. It is known that CO_2 can contribute to global warming by trapping solar energy that is being reradiated as heat from the Earth's surface. However, some research has suggested that elevated CO_2 levels could enhance the photosynthetic rates of plants, resulting in a lush world of agricultural abundance, and that this CO_2 fertilization effect might eventually decrease the rate of global warming. The increased vegetation in such an environment could be counted on to draw more CO_2 from the atmosphere. The level of CO_2 would thus increase at a lower rate than many experts have predicted.

CO_2 might decrease global warming

However, while a number of recent studies confirm that plant growth would be generally enhanced in an atmosphere rich in CO_2, they also suggest that increased CO_2 would differentially increase the growth rate of different species of plants, which could eventually result in decreased agricultural yields. Certain important crops such as corn and sugarcane that currently have higher photosynthetic efficiencies than other plants may lose that edge in an atmosphere rich in CO_2. Patterson and Flint have shown that these important crops may experience yield reductions because of the increased performance of certain weeds. Such differences in growth rates between plant species could also alter ecosystem stability. Studies have shown that within rangeland regions, for example, a weedy grass grows much better with plentiful CO_2 than do three other grasses. Because this weedy grass predisposes land to burning, its potential increase may lead to greater numbers of and more severe wildfires in future rangeland communities.

But CO_2 could decrease agr. yield

It is clear that the CO_2 fertilization effect does not guarantee the lush world of agricultural abundance that once seemed likely, but what about the potential for the increased uptake of CO_2 to decrease the rate of global warming? Some studies suggest that the changes accompanying global warming will not improve the ability of terrestrial ecosystems to absorb CO_2. Billings' simulation of global warming conditions in wet tundra grasslands showed that the level of CO_2 actually increased. Plant growth did increase under these conditions because of warmer temperatures and increased CO_2 levels. But as the permafrost melted, more peat (accumulated dead plant material) began to decompose. This process in turn liberated more CO_2 to the atmosphere. Billings estimated that if summer temperatures rose four degrees Celsius, the tundra would liberate 50 percent more CO_2 than it does currently. In a warmer world, increased plant growth, which could absorb CO_2 from the atmosphere, would

Not reduce warming by making more CO_2

> not compensate for this rapid increase in decomposition rates. This observation is particularly important because high-latitude habitats such as the tundra are expected to experience the greatest temperature increase.

Adding together what the three paragraphs do, we get the main idea: **Some research suggests that more CO_2 could actually mean a decrease in the rate of global warming. But more CO_2 would not mean agricultural abundance and more CO_2 would not decrease the rate of global warming.** The rest of the detail is there because it contributes to this theme.

Knowing what the passage is about, go to the questions. (There are eight!)

The first is the usual initial question:

> 15. Which one of the following best states the main point of the passage?
>
> (A) Elevated levels of CO_2 would enhance photosynthetic rates, thus increasing plant growth and agricultural yields.
> (B) Recent studies have yielded contradictory findings about the benefits of increased levels of CO_2 on agricultural productivity.
> (C) The possible beneficial effects of increased levels of CO_2 on plant growth and global warming have been overstated.
> (D) Increased levels of CO_2 would enhance the growth rates of certain plants, but would inhibit the growth rates of other plants.
> (E) Increased levels of CO_2 would increase plant growth, but the rate of global warming would ultimately increase.

You have prepared for this question by learning the main idea. Do not let the answer choices make suggestions to you about what the main idea might be, but take your knowledge of the main idea and find the one that states it accurately. The statement may not be exactly as you formulated it, but it must contain the same primary content. And that content here is in choice (C). Look at what the wrong answers do: Choice (A) takes an assertion from the first paragraph and makes it into the main idea. Choice (B) may seem close, but it is restricted to agricultural productivity and not to global warming, which is what the passage is about. Choice (D) is also partial, repeating a point made in the second paragraph that contributes to, but is not all of, what the passage is about. Similarly, choice (E) takes a point from the final paragraph as the main idea, when it is one point made in the passage to contribute to the main idea. Getting too wrapped up in the details in either the second or third paragraphs might easily have led to a misunderstanding of the main idea and a mistaken selection of one of the last two answers.

The second question's stem is a lengthy way of asking you to identify a detail in the passage:

16. The passage suggests that the hypothesis mentioned in the first paragraph is not entirely accurate because it fails to take into account which one of the following in predicting the effects of increased vegetation on the rate of global warming?

(A) Increased levels of CO_2 will increase the photosynthetic rates of many species of plants.
(B) Increased plant growth cannot compensate for increased rates of decomposition caused by warmer temperatures.
(C) Low-latitude habitats will experience the greatest increases in temperature in an atmosphere high in CO_2.
(D) Increased levels of CO_2 will change patterns of plant growth and thus will alter the distribution of peat.
(E) Increases in vegetation can be counted on to draw more CO_2 from the atmosphere.

Carefully sort out what the question is asking. It says the first paragraph—stating that CO_2 might decrease the rate of global warming—is inaccurate because of something about the increased vegetation and its effects on global warming. The question is about plant growth and global warming, which is what the third paragraph is about. So to answer this detail question, review the third paragraph. You find the "increased vegetation" mentioned there in line 45.

It is clear that the CO_2 fertilization effect does not guarantee the lush world of agricultural abundance that once seemed likely, but what about the potential for the increased uptake of CO_2 to decrease the rate of global warming? Some studies suggest that the changes accompanying global warming will not improve the ability of terrestrial ecosystems to absorb CO_2. Billings' simulation of global warming conditions in wet tundra grasslands showed that the level of CO_2 actually increased. Plant growth did increase under these conditions because of warmer temperatures and increased CO_2 levels. But as the permafrost melted, more peat (accumulated dead plant material) began to decompose. This process in turn liberated more CO_2 to the atmosphere. Billings estimated that if summer temperatures rose four degrees Celsius, the tundra would liberate 50 percent more CO_2 than it does currently. In a warmer world, increased plant growth, which could absorb CO_2 from the atmosphere, would not compensate for this rapid increase in decomposition rates. This observation is particularly

16. The passage suggests that the hypothesis mentioned in the first paragraph is not entirely accurate because it fails to take into account which one of the following in predicting the effects of increased vegetation on the rate of global warming?

The sentence that follows explains that warming resulted in increased vegetation, but also in more decomposition and, so, more CO_2. No inferences are required here! Your assignment is to locate a place in the passage where it talks about what the question talks about. So now find the answer choice that tells what the passage says about the increased vegetation with more CO_2. The correct answer is choice (B). Choice (A) brings up the detail from the second paragraph that is not explicitly related to global warming. Choice (C) is something that is not discussed in the passage. A reading question will not require you to make inferences outside of the passage. It will not ask you to analyze, but to describe. Choice (D) deals with "distribution of peat," something that is not mentioned in the passage. Choice (E) says something that is not asserted in the passage. So on a question like this asking about a detail, find the discussion of the detail and stick close to the text. The question is not: "can you analyze the passage for its assumptions and inferences and then identify one of those?" The question is: "can you find and correctly state what the passage actually says about this?"

Focus on

Reading Comprehension Detail Questions

Find where the detail is mentioned in the passage.

Interrogate the choices: Find the only choice that accurately reports what the passage says about the detail.

The next question is a **purpose of detail question**, and it asks you about something that you have already considered: What does the third paragraph do?

17. Which one of the following best describes the function of the last paragraph of the passage?

    (A) It presents research that may undermine a hypothesis presented in the first paragraph.
    (B) It presents solutions for a problem discussed in the first and second paragraphs.
    (C) It provides an additional explanation for a phenomenon described in the first paragraph.
    (D) It provides experimental data in support of a theory described in the preceding paragraph.
    (E) It raises a question that may cast doubt on information presented in the preceding paragraph.

Before going to the answer choices, review what the third paragraph does so that you will know what to look for and so you will not permit yourself to be talked into anything by one of the wrong answers. The third paragraph claims that increased CO_2 will not decrease the rate of global warming (as had been suggested in the first) and it explains a reason why. The question does not ask about the detail in the third paragraph. So stay away from it and keep in mind how that third paragraph contributes to the main idea. Now find the answer choice that states that, and it is right there in Choice (A).

Note what the wrong answers do, and how easy it might have been to be talked into one of them. Choice (B) speaks of the solution to a problem, but there is no problem presented in the other paragraphs. Choice (C) says it is an explanation of a phenomenon, but there is no phenomenon presented to be explained in the passage. Choice (D) says it provides experimental data, which is not what the detail here does, and that it offers that data in support of a theory, but there is no such theory presented in the previous paragraph. Choice (E) says the passage raises a question, but it does not do that. All are fine things for paragraphs to do, but not what this one does.

Notice that this question was about a part of the passage, but it was *knowing the main idea* that made it possible to address it easily and accurately. Again, then, you are rewarded for not giving in to the temptation to attempt to master all the detail as you read. You might know less at this point in your life about some person named Billings and about the temperature of something called "peat," but you know the answer to question 17!

The next question is a good example of an **agrees with question**:

18. The passage suggests that Patterson and Flint would be most likely to agree with which one of the following statements about increased levels of CO_2 in the Earth's atmosphere?
    (A) They will not increase the growth rates of most species of plants.
    (B) They will inhibit the growth of most crops, thus causing substantial decreases in agricultural yields.
    (C) They are unlikely to increase the growth rates of plants with lower photosynthetic efficiencies.
    (D) They will increase the growth rates of certain species of plants more than the growth rates of other species of plants.
    (E) They will not affect the photosynthetic rates of plants that currently have the highest photosynthetic efficiencies.

The question asks for something that Patterson and Flint would agree with. When reading the passage for its main idea, we did not linger on Patterson and Flint, but only noticed that they offered evidence on agricultural yields. So now return to the second paragraph and find the discussion of Patterson and Flint. It begins in line 25. They show that important crops may experience yield reductions with increased CO_2 because certain weeds would grow more. There should be no need to try to penetrate that for assumptions or to try to carry it further for inferences. Take what the passage says about Patterson and Flint and interrogate the answer choices to find the one that they clearly agree with. There it is in choice (D).

18. The passage suggests that Patterson and Flint would be most likely to agree with which one of the following statements about increased levels of CO_2 in the Earth's atmosphere?

    (A) They will not increase the growth rates of most species of plants.
    (B) They will inhibit the growth of most crops, thus causing substantial decreases in agricultural yields.
    (C) They are unlikely to increase the growth rates of plants with lower photosynthetic efficiencies.
    (D) They will increase the growth rates of certain species of plants more than the growth rates of other species of plants.
    (E) They will not affect the photosynthetic rates of plants that currently have the highest photosynthetic efficiencies.

rich in CO_2. Patterson and Flint have shown that these important crops may experience yield reductions because of the increased performance of certain weeds. Such differences in growth rates between plant species could also alter ecosystem stability. Studies have shown that within rangeland regions, for example, a weedy grass grows much better with plentiful CO_2 than do three other grasses. Because this weedy grass

Someone who believes that weeds will grow at a faster rate than other plants will certainly agree that some species will have higher growth rates than others. Choice (A) deals with "most species of plants," which the discussion of Patterson and Flint does not reach. Choice (B) also speaks of "most crops": which is beyond what it says about Patterson and Flint. Choice (C) is more sweeping than what the passage says about Patterson and Flint. And choice (E) speculates about photosynthetic rates, something which Patterson and Flint are not presented as addressing at all. As a reporter, take pride in being clear and accurate about what is actually there, and you can be certain of the answer.

The next question is about both a detail and the main idea:

19. The author would be most likely to agree with which one of the following statements about the conclusions drawn on the basis of the research on plant growth mentioned in the first paragraph of the passage?

    (A) The conclusions are correct in suggesting that increased levels of CO_2 will increase the photosynthetic rates of certain plants.
    (B) The conclusions are correct in suggesting that increased levels of CO_2 will guarantee abundances of certain important crops.
    (C) The conclusions are correct in suggesting that increased plant growth will reverse the process of global warming.
    (D) The conclusions are incorrect in suggesting that enhanced plant growth could lead to abundances of certain species of plants.
    (E) The conclusions are incorrect in suggesting that vegetation can draw CO_2 from the atmosphere.

This is another good example of an **agrees with question**. It requires you, as reporter, to know what is said in the first paragraph about research on plant growth and then to know the main idea the author explains in the passage as a whole. Beginning in line 6, what is mentioned is that higher CO_2 could enhance photosynthetic rates and result in agricultural abundance, decreasing the rate of global warming. Now ask what the author believes about that. Turning to the second and third paragraphs, the author believes that part of this is correct, in that plant growth will be enhanced, but the author does not believe that the increase will extend to all plants or that the rate of global warming will decline, as you know from the main idea. In fact, we know this from the previous question in that the author presents the work of Patterson and Flint positively. So now, based upon these things from the text, find the answer choice that is consistent with them. Choice (A) certainly is. It does not go too far, but grants what the author observes that indeed plant growth would be enhanced (line 16). Choice (A) does not mention everything that the author might agree with, but it does mention something. That is all you need. Choice (B) goes further than the author does with the words "guarantee" and "important." Choice (C) does not take into account the main idea of the passage. Choice (D) is the opposite of what is in Choice (A) and is clearly not what the author says (again, reading comprehension is about what is said!) at the beginning of the second paragraph. And choice (E) is simply incorrect in that the author does not deny that vegetation draws carbon dioxide.

Next is a question that asks you to **explain a detail**:

20. The passage supports which one of the following statements about peat in wet tundra grasslands?

(A) More of it would decompose if temperatures rose four degrees Celsius.
(B) It could help absorb CO_2 from the atmosphere if temperatures rose four degrees Celsius.
(C) It will not decompose unless temperatures rise four degrees Celsius.
(D) It decomposes more quickly than peat found in regions at lower latitudes.
(E) More of it accumulates in regions at lower latitudes.

Find and review the things said about peat in tundra. That is in the third paragraph, so return to that paragraph now to go through what it says about that detail, a detail you need not have mastered in reading for the main idea. Find the beginning of that treatment in line 43 and continue with it through most of the rest of the paragraph. The facts developed are these:

- In these grasslands the level of CO_2 increased.
- Plant growth increased because of warmer temperatures and more CO_2.
- But also more peat began to decompose, liberating more CO_2.
- According to Billings, if summer temperatures rose 4°, the tundra would liberate 50% more CO_2 than now.

Now having reviewed these, do not attempt to analyze them, but find an answer choice that repeats one of them.

Choice (A) does, quite simply, repeat the last one in the list. None of the others does. Choose (A) to report accurately on what the passage has to say about peat in wet grasslands.

The next question is more complex in the way it requires you to report clearly on yet another detail. This is an example of one of the relatively rare **analysis of detail questions**.

21. Which one of the following, if true, is LEAST consistent with the hypothesis mentioned in lines 22–25 of the passage?
    (A) The roots of a certain tree species grow more rapidly when the amount of CO_2 in the atmosphere increases, thus permitting the trees to expand into habitats formerly dominated by grasses with high photosynthetic efficiencies.
    (B) When grown in an atmosphere high in CO_2 certain weeds with low photosynthetic efficiencies begin to thrive in cultivated farmlands formerly dominated by agricultural crops.
    (C) When trees of a species with a high photosynthetic efficiency and grasses of a species with a low photosynthetic efficiency were placed in an atmosphere high in CO_2, the trees grew more quickly than the grasses.
    (D) When two different species of grass with equivalent photosynthetic efficiency were placed in an atmosphere high in CO_2, one species grew much more rapidly and crowded the slower-growing species out of the growing area.
    (E) The number of leguminous plants decreased in an atmosphere rich in CO_2, thus diminishing soil fertility and limiting the types of plant species that could thrive in certain habitats.

The detail that the question is about is a hypothesis in lines 22–25. Start by going to find it and be clear on what it means. That is what the question is about. The hypothesis is that some important crops could "lose their edge" in an atmosphere with more CO_2. What exactly does that mean? (This is the crucial step that will enable getting the correct answer!) It means that some crops, like corn, that grow now more efficiently than others would not continue to have that advantage in the different climate. This question is more difficult than most in that it asks you not only to be clear on that hypothesis, but to apply it, and then to apply *it in the negative* by identifying the answer choice that does *not* go along with it.

So being clear on what the hypothesis is—that some plants that now have a competitive advantage because of their "photosynthetic efficiency" (because they grow especially well in the current climate) would no longer have that advantage with more CO_2. Ask each answer choice whether it goes along with that, that some plants that now have an advantage would lose that advantage, or does it conflict with that claim? There will be exactly one that conflicts—that is not consistent with the hypothesis—and that is the correct answer.

Choice (A) depicts plants that do not do as well as those with higher photosynthetic efficiency as doing better with more CO_2. That is what the hypothesis says.

Choice (B) shows plants which now have lower photosynthetic efficiency prospering with more CO_2. That is consistent with the hypothesis.

Choice (C) gives the example of a species of tree with currently higher photosynthetic efficiency over the one with lower photosynthetic efficiency that would actually increase its advantage with more CO_2. That is the opposite of what the hypothesis predicts! This is the answer.

Choice (D) is about plants with equal photosynthetic efficiency, and so is neither especially consistent nor inconsistent with the hypothesis.

Choice (E) speaks of plants that are not in the categories discussed by the hypothesis and so is neither especially consistent nor inconsistent with the hypothesis.

So complex as it was—and this is about as complex as a question in a reading comprehension task will get—the question still is testing whether you can find the hypothesis that is stated in the passage and understand it accurately by finding the one example that is inconsistent with it.

The final question in this task is another **explain a detail question**:

22. According to the passage, Billings' research addresses which one of the following questions?

    (A) Which kind of habitat will experience the greatest temperature increase in an atmosphere high in CO_2?
    (B) How much will summer temperatures rise if levels of CO_2 double by the end of the twenty-first century?
    (C) Will enhanced plant growth necessarily decrease the rate of global warming that has been predicted by experts?
    (D) Would plant growth be differentially enhanced if atmospheric concentrations of CO_2 were to double by the end of the twenty-first century?
    (E) Does peat decompose more rapidly in wet tundra grasslands than it does in other types of habitats when atmospheric concentrations of CO_2 increase?

What does Billings's research address? Go to the final paragraph and review beginning at line (43). There are a number of points here, a number of details and any one of them might be the one the question will use. Be sure to continue with the exposition of Billings's research until it has finished:

- Billings' research is on global warming conditions in wet tundra and the level of CO_2.
- If summer temperatures rise four degrees, the tundra will liberate 50 percent more CO_2.
- Plant growth would increase in the warmer world but would not compensate for amount of CO_2 liberated by decomposition.

One of the answer choices will restate one or another of them. Report what you find in the passage (note the language of the question: "According to the passage..."). Choice (C) does exactly the job.

This CO_2 task is more difficult than most. It involves eight questions on unfamiliar things (when was the last time you had an extended discussion that included talk about peat in wet tundra?). That makes comprehending the passage and its details challenging. But the material is there to do so, and patience and accuracy in finding that material in the passage enables you to identify the one right answer to each question.

A VARIATION: COMPARATIVE READING

Since June of 2007 exactly one of the four reading comprehension tasks presents a "comparative reading" passage. Here, instead of having a single passage to read and answer questions about, there are two shorter passages. Together the two are about as long as the single passage in the other reading comprehension tasks. In these comparative reading tasks the two passages will be about the same topic, broadly, but will approach it somewhat differently from one another. One passage might be broader; one might offer an example of the other; they might conflict with each other; or they might be parallel. Generally, however, the comparative reading tasks are basically like the other reading comprehension tasks. The challenge is to report accurately what goes on in the passages. The questions with comparative reading will be similar to the questions in other reading comprehension exercises, except that often they will involve comparing what is in one of the passages to what is in the other.

The passages in a comparative reading task might be similar to this:

Passage A

The principal argument against absolute moral rules concerns the possibility of conflict cases. Suppose it is held to be absolutely wrong to do A in any circumstances and also wrong to do B in any circumstances. Then what about the case in which someone is faced with having to do either A or else B? This kind of case seems to show that it is *logically* untenable to hold that moral rules are absolute.

Do such circumstances ever actually arise? It is not difficult to find real-life examples that make the same point. During the Second World War, Dutch fishermen regularly smuggled Jewish refugees to England in their boats, and the following sort of thing sometimes happened. A Dutch boat, with refugees in the hold, would be stopped by a Nazi patrol boat. The Nazi captain would call out and ask the Dutch captain where he was bound, who was on board, and so forth. The fishermen would lie and be allowed to pass.

Now it is clear that the fishermen had only two alternatives, to lie or to allow their passengers (and themselves) to be taken and shot.

Now suppose the two rules "It is wrong to lie" and "It is wrong to permit the murder of innocent people" are both taken to be absolute. The Dutch fishermen would have to do one of these things; therefore a moral view that absolutely prohibits both is incoherent.

Passage B

A case of contradictory moral requirements is presented in two dialogues from Plato. In the *Apology,* Socrates claims that no matter how many laws are passed by the Athenian majority prohibiting philosophy, he will continue his life of philosophic inquiry. This moral requirement for philosophy comes from Socrates' judgment that the greatest good for human beings is to develop the mind. Accordingly, Socrates' judgment seems plain that living as one ought, or living according to the dictates of morality, may at times require disobedience of the law.

Yet in the *Crito,* a conversation set just a few days after Socrates' trial, Socrates argues that it is always wrong to break the law. Breaking the law might encourage others to do so as well, thereby destabilizing the law and the community and harming, at least potentially, the people whom the law helps. The argument of the *Crito* makes it clear that the laws help everyone, or nearly everyone, including Socrates by providing for their birth and for whatever education they receive.

A hypothetical law against philosophy, then seems to require obedience according to the argument of the *Crito* and disobedience according to the argument of the *Apology*. Yet further reflection shows that the contradiction is only apparent. The problem is not a contradictory moral principle, since the moral principle behind both judgments is the same: it is wrong to harm people (including oneself). The problem would be the imperfect law against philosophy which, because of that imperfection, would necessarily entail violating that basic moral principle in one way or another.

Approach the comparative reading passage as you would the others, by reading each of the two passages to identify its main idea. Here the main idea of Passage A is that: It does not make sense to say that there are absolute moral rules because circumstances can arise where such rules conflict, making it impossible for both to be absolute. And the main idea for Passage B is that: Apparent conflicts in moral rules indicate a still more basic moral rule that allows the other two to make sense simultaneously.

The questions might include questions about the main idea of either or both passages:

1. Which of the following questions best expresses a main issue discussed in both passages?
   (A) Under what conditions may people decide to sacrifice one moral principle to another?
   (B) Do human beings sometimes face situations where moral principles do not offer conflicting direction?
   (C) Under what conditions does it make sense for human beings to risk their lives or the lives of others for moral principle?
   (D) Do competing moral principles inevitably result in conflicting information about how a human being should act?
   (E) Can a commitment always to abide by the law be consistent with moral beliefs?

The question asks for a "main issue" discussed in both passages. The two have different main ideas, but those ideas are linked by their common subject matter dealing with moral rules. This question asks for something that the two discussions of moral rules have in common. So review the main idea from each and interrogate the answer choices to ask each choice if it is an issue in Passage A and in Passage B.

Neither passage raises the question in choice (A), since the two deal with apparently competing moral principles differently. Choice (B) raises a question that is similar to the issue in either passage, but has the important difference of addressing not the circumstance where moral rules seem to conflict—the issue in both passages—but the possibility of situations where they do not conflict. Choice (C) mentions an issue that is raised to some degree in Passage A, but is not an issue with the two passages. An understanding of the main ideas of the two passages allows ready agreement that choice (D) does present an issue discussed in both. The difference between the two is about how to resolve an apparent conflict between moral rules. So this is the answer since it describes both passages. Choice (E) does not, though it does raise an issue mentioned in Passage B.

Another question that deals with both passages is a good example of an **inference question** in a reading comprehension task:

2. It can be inferred that the authors of the two passages are most likely to agree that

   (A) There are sometimes circumstances where moral principles taken to be true require seemingly contradictory actions.
   (B) Telling falsehoods is wrong in any circumstance
   (C) The requirements of morality are always clear, and in cases of apparent conflict the problem is likely to be that the moral principle is poorly understood.
   (D) Because it benefits people in the community by leading to their moral and intellectual development, the law is always valuable and worthy of support.
   (E) The value of saving life is greater than any other value that human beings face and so is a more important moral principle than any other moral principle.

Notice here that the question stem qualifies the "inference," as it most often does when a reading comprehension task asks for an inference, and is unlikely to do when a logical reasoning problem asks for one. So here find something on which the two authors "are most likely" to agree. In order to find that, look for something that each of the two authors believes, based upon what the two authors say. Indeed, the basic formula for making an inference in the reading comprehension task is this: since the author believes this, the author would almost certainly think that as well. An example: since Erica likes all dogs, Erica most likely likes golden retrievers. In fact, inference questions in reading comprehension sections are much more like "agrees with" questions in reading comprehension sections than they are like inference questions in logical reasoning sections. The reading comprehension ones are much more "common sense" inferences than the strict logical consequences asked for in inference questions in logical reasoning.

So here what can you infer is most likely to be something on which the two agree? The answer is in choice (A). Although they disagree about how the apparent contradiction might be best resolved, the authors of the two passages do agree that circumstances can and do arise where moral rules seem to result in contradictory requirements. This is clear and plain. The other choices are not things on which agreement would be clear. Indeed, choice (B), choice (D), and choice (E) are all things that the author of Passage A would be unlikely to see as absolute rules, since that author disputes the existence of such rules. And the point in choice (C) is one that the author of Passage B might make, but not Passage A.

FOCUS on

Reading Comprehension Inference Questions

Find what the passage says the author thinks.

Interrogate the choices: Someone who thinks this is likely to think what else?

It is surprising that we could do ten reading comprehension questions (since reviewing the types of questions) without doing a single **thing mentioned question**, for they are more common than that, with about four appearing in any section. Here is an example from the comparative reading task:

3. Which of the following is not something mentioned in either passage as a moral rule or principle?
   (A) The murder of innocent people is wrong.
   (B) Since the laws help people, it is wrong to disobey them.
   (C) It is a great good for human beings to develop their minds.
   (D) A moral rule requires people to educate one another.
   (E) A moral rule says that it is wrong to lie.

In this case the question is made a little more complicated by being in the negative. It asks for the one thing in the list of five choices that is not mentioned in either one of the passages. In a thing mentioned question it will be just that: the right answer, or in this case the four wrong answers, will be explicitly mentioned somewhere in the passage. It might be anywhere: in a list in the discussion of an experiment, in a set of objections, or in examples in any paragraph. The challenge is to find it, and the discipline is to make certain that the thing is actually and explicitly mentioned. It can be quite a treasure hunt, or almost like a hidden picture puzzle, because while the thing will be mentioned explicitly, it can be difficult to spot and easy to pass over.

In this case, review the five things in the answer choices and simply look in the passages for places where they are mentioned. You may recall some of them, which will make it easy to eliminate those choices. Confirm that there is exactly one that is not mentioned. And that is the answer. This is not a process of reasoning or deduction, but one of careful and attentive reading. Here are the answer choices and where the four that are discussed are mentioned in the passages:

England in their boats, and the following sort of thing sometimes happened. A Dutch boat, with refugees in the hold, would be stopped by a Nazi patrol boat. The Nazi captain would call out and ask the Dutch captain where he was bound, who was on board, and so forth. The fishermen would lie and be allowed to pass. Now it is clear that the fishermen had only two alternatives, to lie or to allow their passengers (and themselves) to be taken and shot.

Now suppose the two rules "It is wrong to lie" and "It is wrong to permit the murder of innocent people" are both taken to be absolute. The Dutch fishermen would have to do one of these things; therefore a moral view that absolutely prohibits both is incoherent.

Passage B

A case of contradictory moral requirements is presented in two dialogues from Plato. In the *Apology,* Socrates claims that no matter how many laws are passed by the Athenian majority prohibiting philosophy, he will continue his life of philosophic inquiry. This moral requirement for philosophy comes from Socrates' judgment that the greatest good for human beings is to develop the mind. Accordingly, Socrates' judgment seems plain that living as one ought, or living according to the dictates of morality, may at times require disobedience of the law.

Yet in the *Crito,* a conversation set just a few days after Socrates' trial, Socrates argues that it is always wrong to break the law. Breaking the law might encourage others to do so as well, thereby destabilizing the law and the community and harming, at least potentially, the people whom the law helps. The argument of the *Crito* makes it clear that the laws help everyone, or nearly everyone, including Socrates by providing for their birth and for whatever education they receive.

3. Which of the following is not something mentioned in either passage as a moral rule or principle?
   (A) The murder of innocent people is wrong.
   (B) Since the laws help people, it is wrong to disobey them.
   (C) It is a great good for human beings to develop their minds.
   (D) A moral rule requires people to educate one another.
   (E) A moral rule says that it is wrong to lie.

While education is mentioned in Passage B, there is no mentioning of any moral rule requiring people to educate one another. And so choice (D) is the correct answer.

Like many questions in a reading comprehension task, the thing mentioned question seems like it would be easier than it is. In fact it takes patience, discipline, and alertness to find what needs to be found in the passage and to answer the question correctly. In this, then, these questions are highly representative of the reading comprehension section of the LSAT as a whole.

CHAPTER 3

ANALYTICAL REASONING

The logical reasoning section of the LSAT tests the human faculty of argument, or of moving from the things that we know to things that we did not know. The reading comprehension portion of the LSAT tests one component of that argument process: the ability to appreciate and to state accurately and precisely the things that we know. The analytical reasoning portion of the LSAT tests a different part of that argumentation process: the "moving" part. With the reading comprehension we seek clarity on what it is that we know. With the analytical reasoning section we seek clarity on the inferences that the things that we know enable us to draw. With the reasoning comprehension section what matters most is the content, and the test taker's job as reporter is to explain with precision what the content is. But with the analytical reasoning section, the specific content is utterly unimportant. What matters is how the things that we know relate together to reveal that we also know, or do not know, other things.

The analytical reasoning section tests analytical ability with a set of four situations. Each of the four begins with a list of things about some situation which are known. Those things are not to be discovered, and they need not be determined or clarified on the basis of interpretation of some text. They are just what is known. The language in analytical reasoning situations has exactly one meaning. There is to be no controversy, no uncertainty, and no ambiguity. The question here is never "what are the things that we know?" Instead it is "we know these things, so what follows?"

But we never know everything! A key to recognizing the challenge involved in working with analytical reasoning situations is to appreciate that they never include enough things that we know to produce a single, simple, clear outcome or conclusion. The things that we know will enable us to deduce some things about the situation but not everything about the situation. Assessment of the situation as explained by the facts means appreciation of both what we do know—or what must follow from those known facts—and what we do not know—or questions that analysis of the known facts cannot answer simply.

Here is a situation, for example:

A chain reaction accident involving four cars has occurred on Tuesday on a fog drenched highway. The four cars are numbered consecutively from one to four, and each of the four is painted in a single color. Each of cars 2, 3, and 4 has run into one other vehicle. Car 2 has run into the rear end of car 1. Car 3 has run into the rear end of car 2. Car 4 has run into the rear end of car 3. Two witnesses, Alex and Nicky, report accurately about the chain reaction as follows:

> Alex: Car 1 is red. Car 2 is silver or green. Car 3 is not blue.
>
> Nicky: Car 2 is green or gold. Car 3 is black or purple or blue, Car 4 is red or orange.

The scenario spells out exactly what we know about the situation to start with. There is no doubt that there was an accident, that there were four cars involved, that each of the first three was rear-ended by exactly one of the others, and that each of the four cars involved is painted a single color. Furthermore, there is no question about the truthfulness of the testimony of each witness. There are no discrepancies or assumptions to be identified or accounted for. There is no challenge to strengthen or weaken the testimony of one of the witnesses. There is no faulty reporting of what they say, and what they say is not based on erroneous reasoning. What they say is simply the case. Our job is not the reading comprehension task's job of reporting clearly on what the situation is. Instead the presentation of the situation here is the clear report. Our job is cold and clinical analysis. The reporter has told us what the case is. The task now is to answer the question ***"SO WHAT?"***

Taking the things that we know together and analyzing them we realize that we know more about the situation than either Alex or Nicky taken alone tells us.

- We know that car 1 is red.
- Since both witnesses are accurate, we infer (that is, the conclusion is compelled, or it simply must be true) that car 2 is green.
- Car 3 is either black or purple.
- Car 4 is red or orange.
- We cannot deduce exactly what color car 3 is or what color car 4 is. But in the case of each of those two we can narrow it down to two possibilities.

And that is what we know about the situation. Knowledge of the situation means knowledge of both **what we know** (for example that car 2 is green and that car 3 is either black or purple) and **what we don't know** (for example the exact color of car 3 or the exact color of car 4). An analytical reasoning situation on the LSAT might ask questions requiring us to prove both what we are certain about and what we remain uncertain about.

Because they do not tell us or enable us to deduce everything about a situation, LSAT analytical reasoning situations are complex. They are not games or problems with a simple outcome, but situations where some things are the case; some things are possible; and some things are not possible. Accurate understanding of the situation requires embracing all of that, and realizing through accurate and careful analysis both what you know and what you do not know. It means reasoning well to infer what else you know from the stated facts, and it means not misusing logic to conclude wrongly that you know things when the facts do not permit you to make those inferences.

THE ANALYTICAL REASONING SITUATION

Each LSAT includes exactly one analytical reasoning section that is included in the score. And that analytical reasoning section includes exactly four situations. Each situation includes between five to seven questions testing your mastery of what you know and do not know about that situation. Together the four situations will have a total of twenty-two to twenty-four questions. This makes the analytical reasoning section the least important of the sections that contribute to the LSAT score in that overall score. Nonetheless, points earned here count just as much as points earned on the other sections, so although it makes no sense to focus on analytical reasoning to the exclusion of the other sections, it is worthwhile to learn to do these questions as effectively as you can in order to earn as many points as you can during the thirty-five minutes allotted to this part of the test.

Working a section as effectively as possible means doing the analysis well. That is exactly what each section is designed to test your ability to take a set of premises or things that you know and to use logic to infer what you can from those things. Accurate analysis does not claim that conclusions are valid that are not, and the section tests whether you know the difference between things that follow logically from a set of facts and things that do not. The best way to do well on this section is simply to do this analysis well.

There are a number of approaches that might be taken to maximize the number of right answers on the analytical reasoning section. The goal of using any such approach should be to make it easier to do the analysis that needs to be done to understand the situation. No approach will substitute for good reasoning and no approach will compensate for faulty or incomplete analysis. Keeping in mind that understanding a situation requires knowing what is the case and knowing where there is uncertainty, it is important not to adopt an approach that is designed to lead to more certainty than is possible in these situations.

One approach is a simple five-step procedure that enables you efficiently, effectively, and openly

- to be as clear as you can be on what you know about a situation.
- to be as clear as you can be on what you don't know about a situation.
- to use the knowledge of what you do and don't know about a situation to answer questions about it correctly.

The five steps are these:

Step 1: Identify the TYPE

About 90% of LSAT analytical reasoning situations can be understood in terms of these three categories:

(1) Ordering
(2) Grouping
(3) Placement

Typically the scenario for a situation presents a collection of things or items. These items then have to be sorted out according to a set of rules or regulations that govern the situation. That sorting out usually means doing one or more of three things: putting the items in order, collecting items in groups, or placing items in particular containers. Usually in working to appreciate what you know and don't know about the situation you will realize that one or another of these actions predominates in your analysis. Knowing the type helps you know what logical operations to perform to understand the situation.

Step 2: Draw the DIAGRAM

Second, organize what the setup tells you about the situation clearly so that you can learn what else valid reasoning reveals about the situation and so you can see what remains unknown or unsettled about it. Drawing a basic diagram helps you to conceptualize the problem by building a basic structure to represent the situation.

It is useful to make a diagram as large as the available space on the page in the test booklet permits. As you work with the situation you will add or remove information as particular questions lead you to do. The flexibility a big diagram allows will be quite helpful. Build the diagram not to find a particular answer—because *there isn't one*—but to enable yourself to see and to work with a range of possibilities. Remember: appreciating that range as range is quite important (for example, that car 3 in the chain reaction situation could be either black or purple, and that it must be one of those two but it cannot be said which of those two).

In order to let the diagram help you understand what you don't know as well as what you do know, avoid a matrix where you can. A matrix can be a rigid diagram designed to zero in on the one single solution to a logic problem. But LSAT analytical reasoning situations are not logic problems with one single solution. They are situations with a range of possibilities. Success with them means understanding the range; it means appreciating both where there is certainty and where there is not, and you do not want a diagram that hides the uncertainty or attempts to force certainty when it isn't there.

Step 3: SIMPLIFY and Symbolize the Conditions

An analytical reasoning situation includes a basic description of the scenario and a list of particular conditions or rules that govern what goes on in that scenario. The description and the conditions are stated in precise, unambiguous language. But that doesn't mean that the language is not complex or difficult. Sometimes it is very plain, while at other times it takes careful reading to determine its precise meaning. This step in working the situation is to make sure that you know exactly what each part of the scenario and each of the rules means.

Rewrite each of the conditions in the situation in short and clear symbols. Using symbols leads you to determine precisely what each rule means and lets you access it easily as you work with the situation. Some of the rules might give information that can be applied directly to the diagram you have created. In those cases, simply add the information to the diagram, being clear to represent it as something that must be true.

As you work with LSAT analytical reasoning situations, develop a set of symbols with clear and unambiguous meanings to you. We will do that here as we go along and make the meaning of the symbols we are using clear, so it may be useful to adopt the same usage. But remember there are no points for style here: writing the symbols is not a goal in itself, but a step in analyzing the situation that you take because it helps you understand the situation, do that analysis, and then answer questions about it efficiently and effectively.

Step 4: DEDUCTIONS

Now do the real analysis. From the previous step, the facts in this situation are clear. These are the things that we know. The next step in analysis—this is what analysis is all about—is to determine what else you know, using logical reasoning on the things that you know about the situation. Move from what is known to what is not known. Each inference then provides additional information, or something else that is known, that can be connected with the other things that are known to allow for still more inferences or deductions. The questions included in an analytical reasoning situation are testing your ability to do these deductions, or testing that you know what can and cannot be inferred from a particular set of known things. So in the chain reaction example, the point is not simply to see that you can read the statements correctly to determine what they say about the cars, but more especially to show that you know that the information presented compels the conclusion that car 2 is green as well as the conclusion that the facts are consistent with car 3 being one of two colors, but only those two.

Step 5: WALK AROUND IT

Making accurate deductions is what the analytical reasoning section is about. Once you are clear on what the setup tells you that you know, you can reason about it. The last step involves preparing yourself to answer questions to show that you have done valid reasoning. So before you go to those questions about the situation, take a few moments to appreciate what the questions will test: what you know and what you don't know.

"Walk around it:" look at the situation from different perspectives. Consider what pieces of information are especially critical, and what sorts of things have effects on others. Based on the rules, your diagram, and your deductions, think about things to be alert for in a particular question as that question might give you an additional piece of information or an additional constraint for the situation. What are the things to be especially aware of in working with the questions, and what things about the situation are likely to be keys in developing further deductions as individual questions might ask you to do?

This walking around a step may not take a lot of time, but it is a worthwhile exercise in thinking through what the situation is about—what you know and what you don't know—as you approach questions whose purpose it is to test whether you understand what you know and what you don't know.

Now go to the questions, and find the one correct answer for each one. Notice that in the instructions to this section there is no caveat that says that there might conceivably be more than one right answer and that you are to present the "most right" one. In this section, with these situations, it is clear and unambiguous: there is exactly one right answer! Knowing what you know about the situation enables you to determine that one right answer, often very quickly.

To summarize the five steps:

(1) Type
(2) Diagram

(3) Simplify
(4) Deductions
(5) Walk Around It

Move to the situations in test Proto to understand this approach by seeing it at work.

AN ORDERING SITUATION

Here is the first situation on the test:

> Each of seven television programs—H, J, L, P, Q, S, V—is assigned a different rank: from first through seventh (from most popular to least popular). The ranking is consistent with the following conditions:
> J and L are each less popular than H.
> J is more popular than Q.
> S and V are each less popular than L.
> P and S are each less popular than Q.
> S is not seventh.

(1) TYPE:
This situation gives a set of seven items, and it establishes a ranking between them from first to last. The rules are about where various items rank in relation to others of the items. The nature of those rules shows clearly that this is an ordering situation. A little more than 20% of the situations in LSAT Analytical Reasoning sections are ordering situations. Over 90% of the analytical reasoning sections include at least one of these. Most people find that of the three major types, the ordering situations are the easiest to work with.

(2) DIAGRAM:
When understanding the situation means deducing an order among a group of items, the diagram needs to make clear what the poles are in the order, so that there will be no confusion in setting things up and symbolizing the rules, which, in the case of an ordering situation, will be primarily rules relating items to one another. The other element to add to the diagram at this point is a list of the items involved in the situation. So the basic diagram is fairly simple:

(3) SIMPLIFY

Next, take the rules or conditions that govern the situation and interpret each one of them carefully for its exact meaning. Then restate the rule in symbolic form so that the exact meaning is clear and easily accessible. Making it clear prevents you from having to return to the words and interpret their meaning again and again while working with the situation. It keeps you from making critical mistakes with the rules, something that is especially easy in an ordering situation. Making each rule accessible helps you to remember that it is there and makes it easy to apply it together with any additional information that a particular question might add to the situation.

There are several conditions here and some of them are a bit complex:

> J and L are each less popular than H.
> J is more popular than Q.
> S and V are each less popular than L.
> P and S are each less popular than Q.
> S is not seventh.

All but one of these conditions are about relative rankings among the items in the situation. This is typical of an ordering game: the rules establish the order of things relative to one another rather than according to their absolute positions in the list. So in this case the rules do not say, for example, "P is either third or fifth," or something of the kind, but instead establish P's position only as it relates to the position of other items. Once the position of the items is determined—to whatever degree it can be—relative to one another you might be able to say something about the absolute position of some of the items.

So go to the rules. The first one is complex in that it deals with three of the items and establishes two different relationships. It is crucial to interpret it exactly for the relationships that it does, and also does not, establish. It says that each of J and L is less popular than H. In putting that into symbols it is a good idea to separate out the two different things that it says to make each of them clear. That can be done like this:

> H . . J
> H . . L

Again, the purpose of particular symbols is not to get the symbol right in and of itself, but to use a symbol to clarify exactly what a relationship is. The two dots ".." (* *)can be used precisely to establish a relative relationship, so that H..J says that in this order H is somewhere, but you don't know exactly where, to the left of J. There may or may not be things in between them. The two symbolic statements here clarify what the rule says about the three items. The rule does not establish any relationship whatever between J and L, and symbolizing it exactly helps to make that clear.

The second condition is a little bit simpler and can be represented with the same connecting symbol:

J . . Q

The third rule is like the first, only with different items. Again symbolize it to be clear on exactly what is said and what is not said. Be certain to follow the poles as represented in the diagram so that "less popular" falls somewhere to the right of "more popular" on your diagram and in your symbols:

L . . S
L . . V

The fourth rule follows the same pattern as the first and the third:

Q . . P
Q . . S

The last rule is the only one that says something about an absolute position, so make the meaning of that one clear and accessible as well:

$S \neq 7$

As you symbolize each of these rules, add it to the diagram. After you have symbolized the rules, the diagram looks like this:

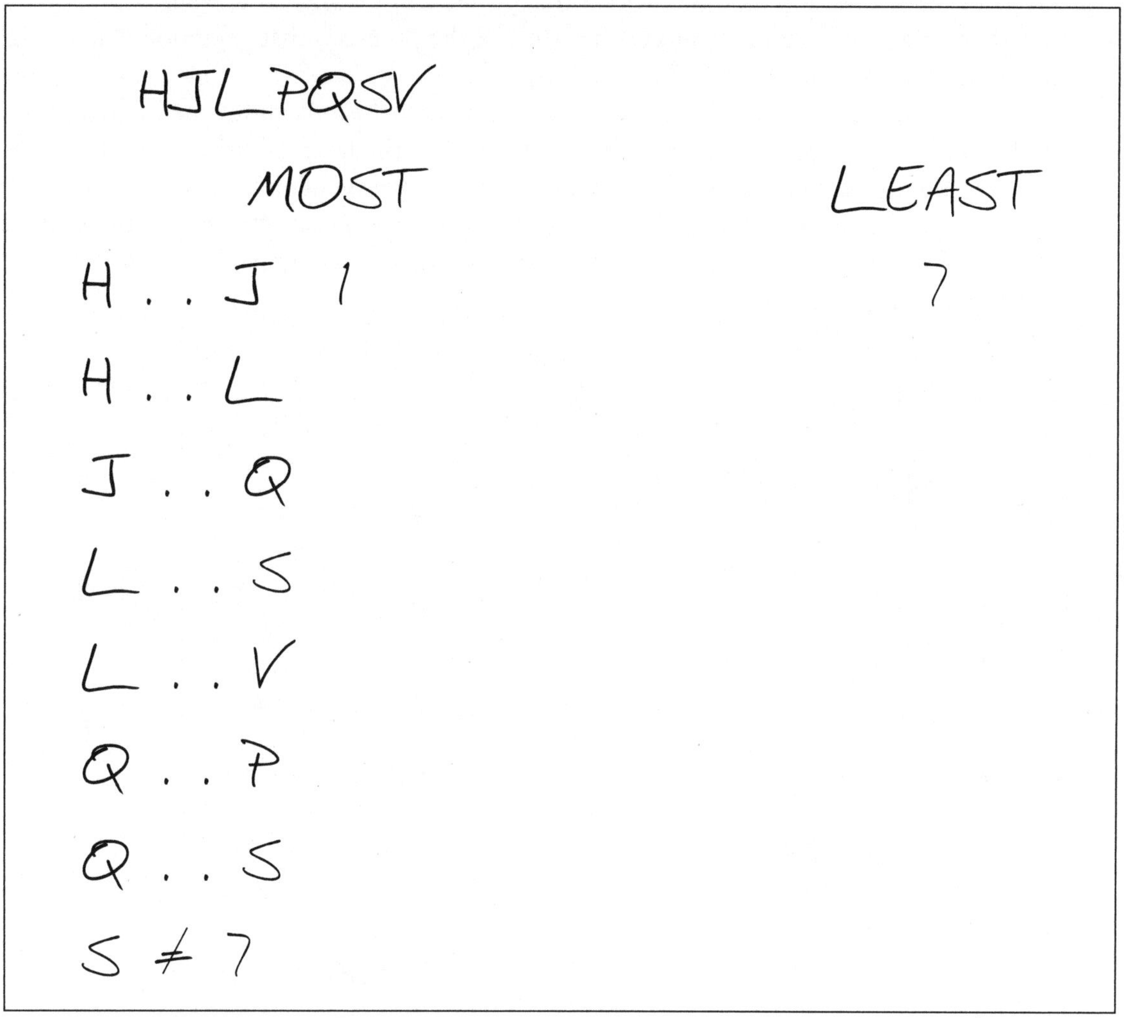

(4) DEDUCTIONS

You can now determine what you can deduce or infer from this list of rules. This is the analytical reasoning part. The conditions are premises, or the things that you know. The next step is to determine what else you know because you know these things. Take premises that involve some of the same items and look for a logically valid relationship that compels a conclusion about one or more of those items. The LSAT on this section is testing that you know when you can draw a conclusion and when you cannot. It is testing that you can do valid reasoning. The situations and conditions that you are given in the analytical reasoning section never involve flaws or reasoning errors. They merely present you with facts, or with the things that you know for sure without the slightest doubt, and questions about those things. Any flaws or reasoning errors that might creep in are going to be yours. The LSAT is testing to see whether you make any of these errors! And it will tempt you to do so.

In an ordering situation the deductions typically involve realizing that you know things about the relative order of items that are not explicitly stated in the rules, but are things that must be true, or conclusions that are compelled, by the rules that you know. Again, this is the same logical reasoning process that you use in the logical reasoning sections. But here there is a simple certainty about the truth of the premises that does not characterize the premises in the logical reasoning sections.

Use the diagram to make it easy for you to draw conclusions about the order of the items. There is a lengthy list of facts, and each entry in the list establishes the relative order of two of the items. Start somewhere, with an item; any item at all that is in the list of symbolized rules will do. It is a good idea, however, to start with one that is mentioned several times. So following that thought choose Q to start with, and simply place it in the middle of the diagram space:

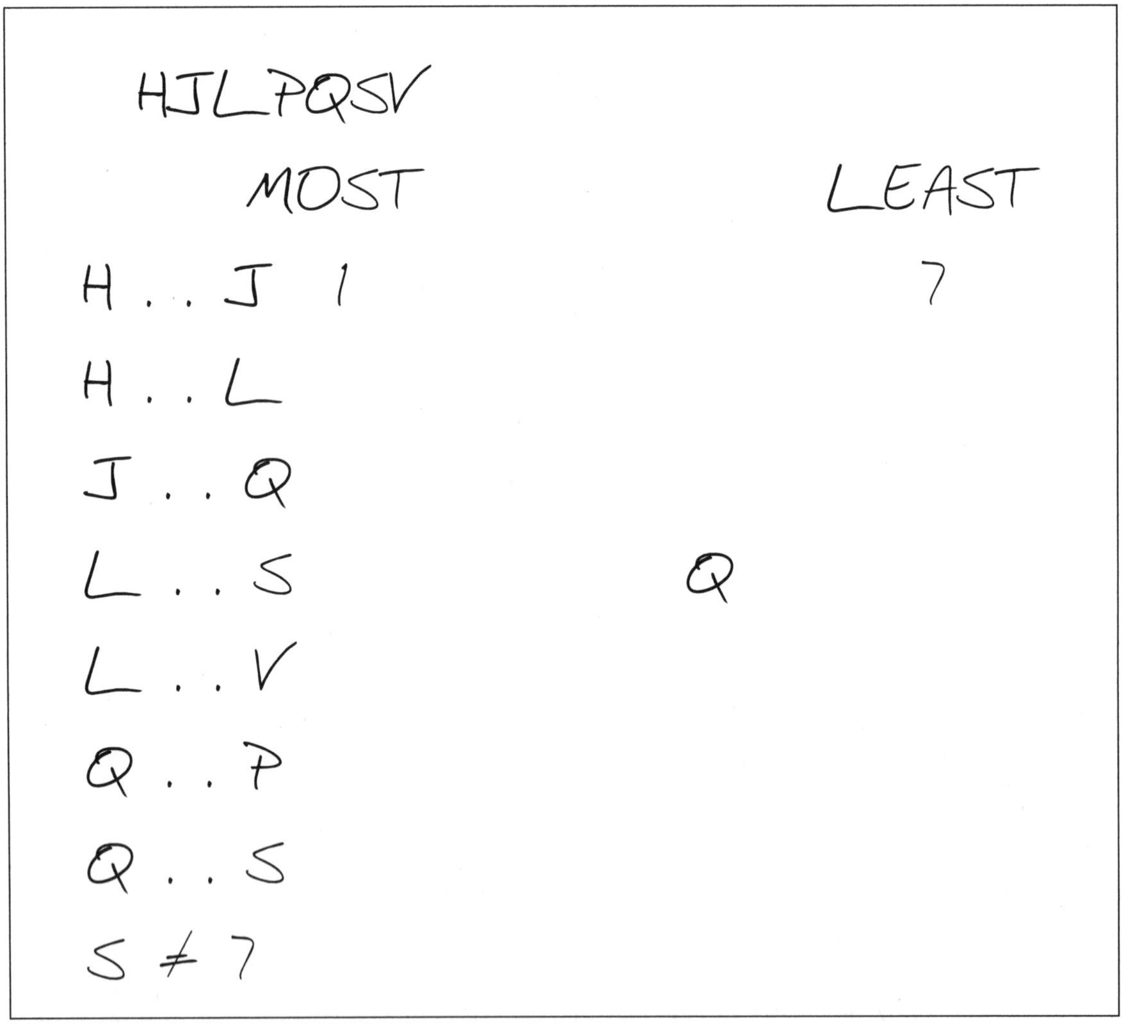

Now add what you know about the relationship between J and Q to the diagram:

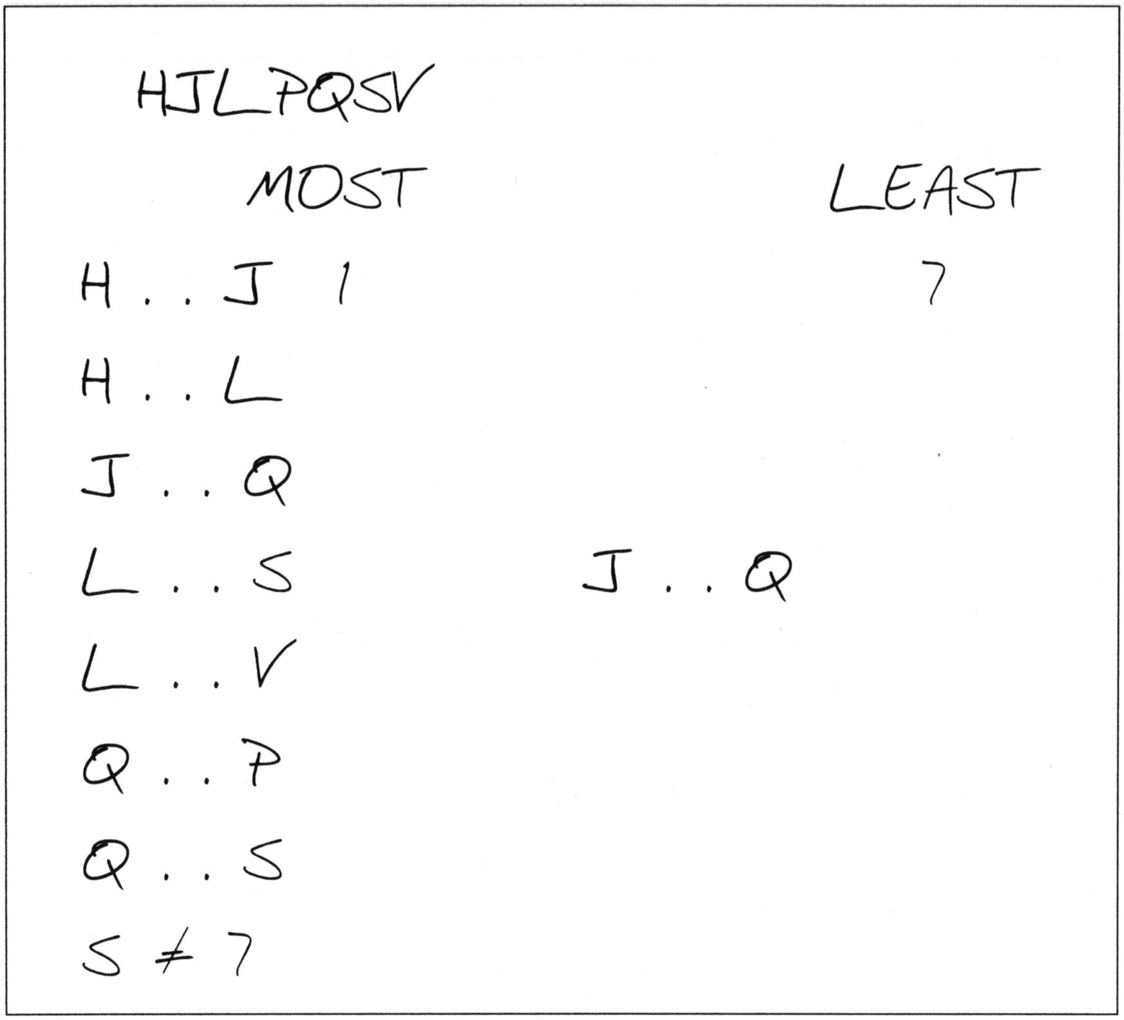

Now add the relationships between Q on the one hand and each of P and S on the other, being careful not to indicate any relationship between P and S (a mistake it is tempting you to make!):

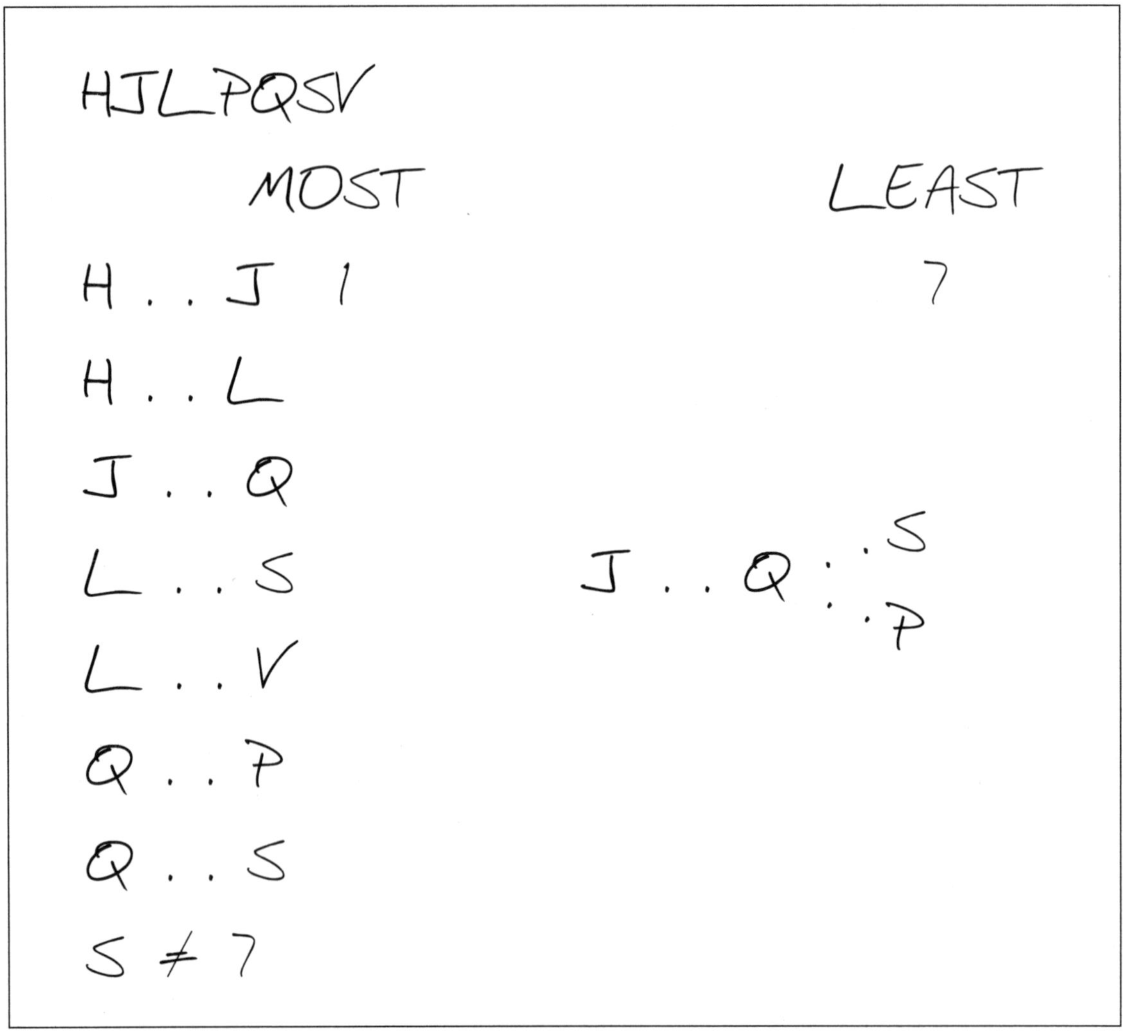

Already you have made a couple of inferences, or reached a couple of subsidiary conclusions. While none of the explicitly stated conditions relates J to S or J to P, you realize that, taken together, the premises that are stated do compel such relationships. J ranks higher than S and J ranks higher than P, and those things are just as certain—100% certain—as they would be if they were explicitly stated in the rules.

That takes care of all of the explicitly stated rules that mention Q, but there is another that mentions S, so add the information about the relationship between S and L to the diagram:

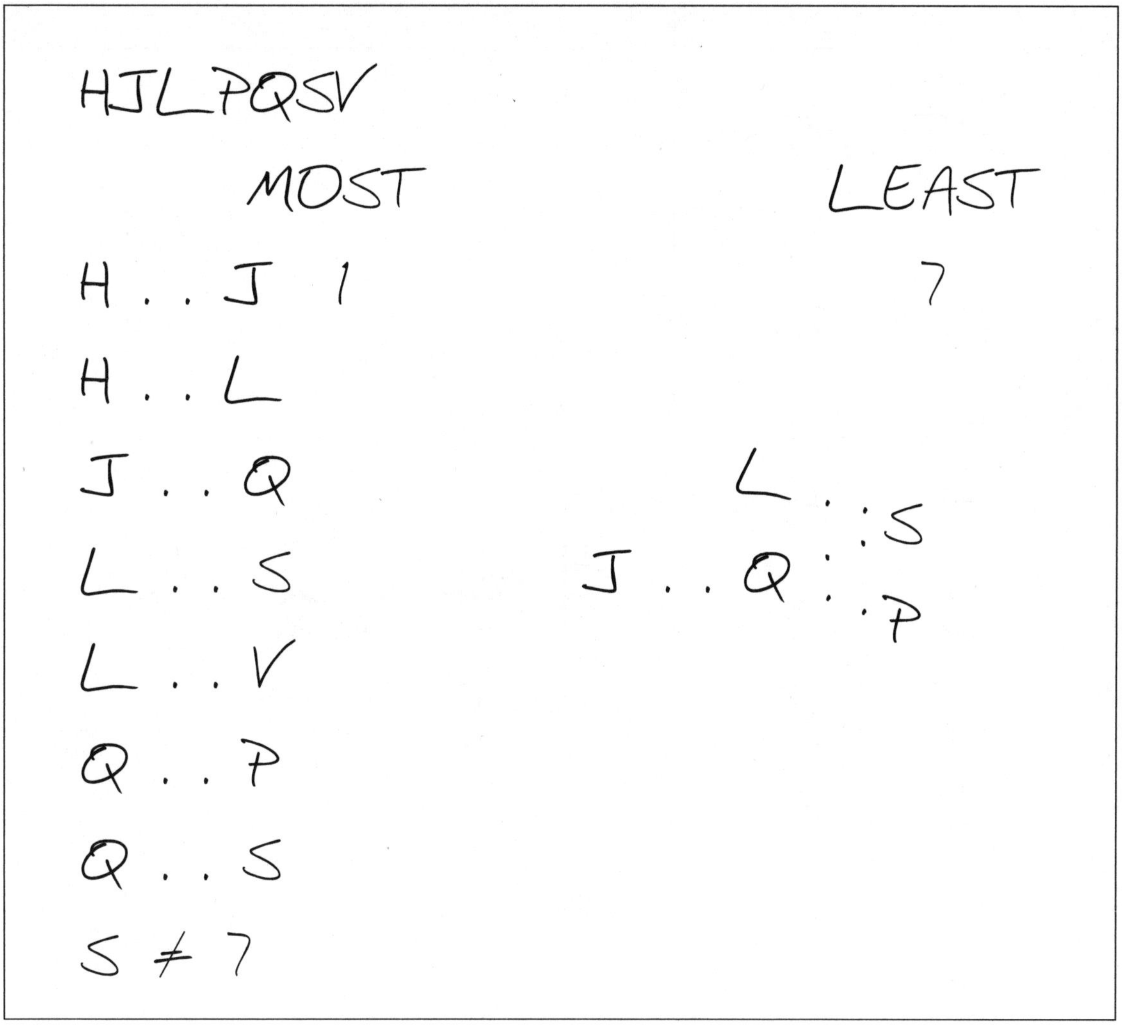

And then add the things you know about the relationship between L and V, and then about the relationship between L and H on the one hand but also between J and H on the other. Be careful to represent those facts accurately:

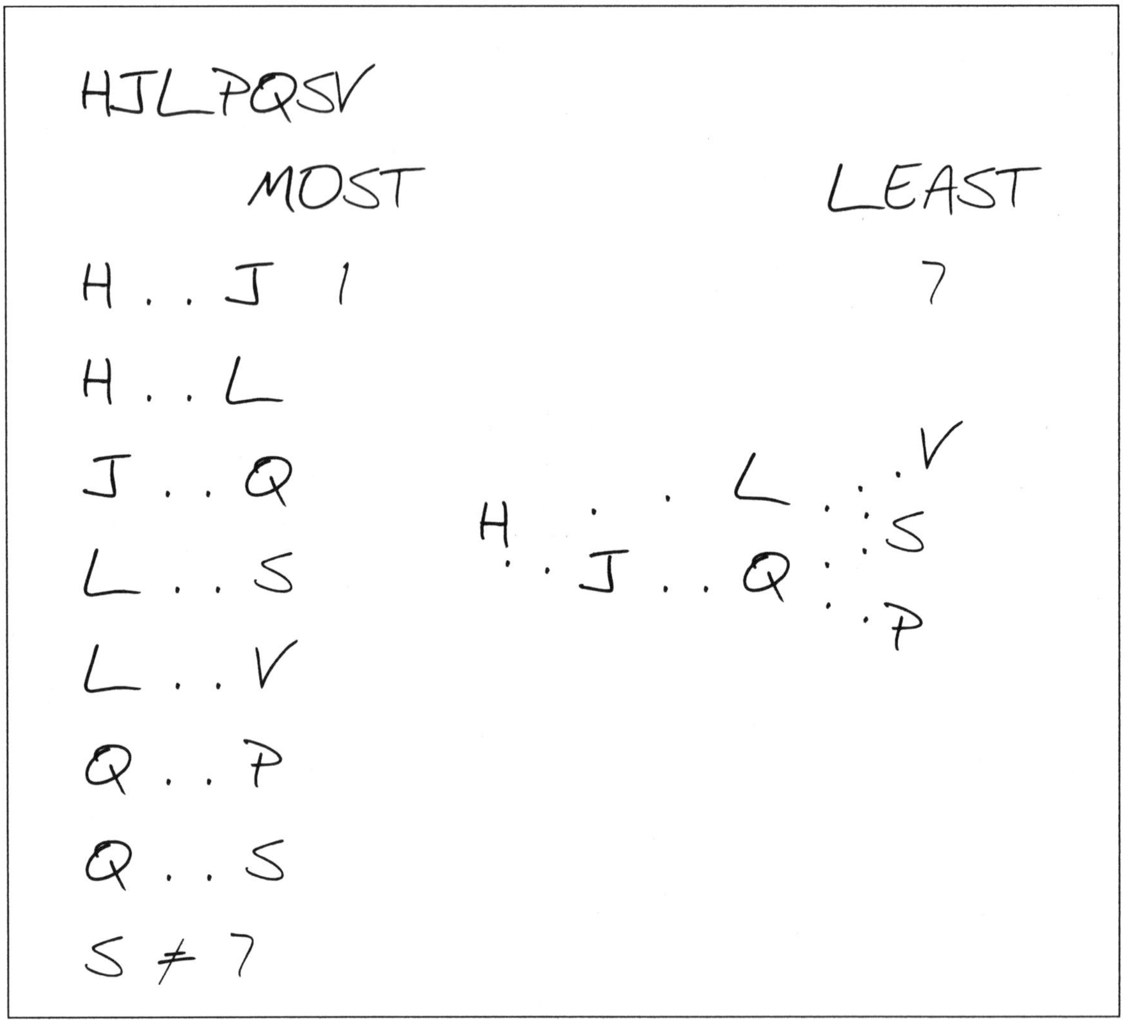

By now you have inferred a great many things that were not included in the explicit rules. Those rules, those things that we know, taken together have compelled a set of conclusions that establish certain relationships among various items. For example: H is more popular than Q or P or S or V, though none of those relationships was explicitly stated. And there are several others. The LSAT is testing your ability to analyze the things that are explicitly stated to determine accurately what other things are compelled by them.

(5) WALK AROUND IT

There are five questions that follow to assess the quality of your analysis. Before going to those questions take a moment to examine the situation as your use of logical analysis has clarified it to see what you know and what you don't know.

There are seven items that the situation deals with, and each of the seven is mentioned in at least one explicit condition, and so all seven appear in the diagram. You know something about the relative relationships of all seven.

Some things you know for certain: H must be the most popular. Remembering the other rule (that you have symbolized as part of the diagram and so have easily accessible to you) that S does not rank seventh, you know that what does rank seventh must be either P or V.

And that leads to where there is uncertainty, or to the things that you do not know about the situation. You know that the least popular is one of two, P and V, but you do not know which one. You know that the item that comes second in the list has to be either J or L, but it is impossible to say which.

Any additional fact will allow you to be more precise still about the relative order, and as you become more sure about the relative order, you can become more certain about the absolute order, or about the ranking of the specific items from one to seven.

FOCUS ON

Ordering Situations

Deducing the order of the items by moving from what you know about individual pairs of items.

Remember: Be careful to represent the order of each pair accurately.

So now that you have determined what can be deduced from the information that you have and have spent the effort to focus on what you know and do not know about the situation, move to the questions which test exactly whether you have done those things and done them well.

1. Which one of the following could be the order of the programs, from most popular to least popular?

(A) J, H, L, Q, V, S, P
(B) H, L, Q, J, S, P, V
(C) H, J, Q, L, S, V, P
(D) H, J, V, L, Q, S, P
(E) H, L, V, J, Q, P, S

This first question asks for an **"acceptable outcome."** The task is to identify an order of the items from most popular to least popular that is consistent with the conditions. About 85% of analytical reasoning situations on the LSAT begin with a question like this. Such a question requires no extensive deductions, but usually only that there be no violation of the rules. And knowing that leads to a suggestion of an efficient and useful approach. With a question like this, instead of testing each answer choice against the rules to determine whether the answer choice obeys all the rules, test the rules against the answer choices. Take the rules one by one and ask whether there is an answer choice that violates that rule. This method has these advantages:

- It gives you the opportunity to review the rules one more time to make certain that you have simplified them and symbolized them accurately.
- It enables you to get to the one correct answer quite quickly.

Use that method here. Just go down the rules as they are written in this situation:

> J and L are each less popular than H.
> J is more popular than Q.
> S and V are each less popular than L.
> P and S are each less popular than Q.
> S is not seventh.

Start with the first rule and ask: "Is there any choice that makes J more popular than H?" Choice (A) does that, and so choice (A) is simply wrong. Cross it off and consider it no more. It is out of your life. (It may be that it violates other rules, but that just doesn't matter. Once it violates one rule, it is wrong.)

> 1. Which one of the following could be the order of the programs, from most popular to least popular?
>
> ~~(A)~~ J, H, L, Q, V, S, P
> (B) H, L, Q, J, S, P, V
> (C) H, J, Q, L, S, V, P
> (D) H, J, V, L, Q, S, P
> (E) H, L, V, J, Q, P, S

Now ask whether there is any choice that makes L more popular than H? There is none. Go to the next and ask whether there is an answer choice that makes Q more popular than J. Choice (B) does that, so it is eliminated.

> 1. Which one of the following could be the order of the programs, from most popular to least popular?
>
> ~~(A)~~ J, H, L, Q, V, S, P
> ~~(B)~~ H, L, Q, J, S, P, V
> (C) H, J, Q, L, S, V, P
> (D) H, J, V, L, Q, S, P
> (E) H, L, V, J, Q, P, S

Now look for any of the remaining choices that make S or V more popular than L. Choice (D) does that and so choice (D) is just wrong. Scratch it off.

1. Which one of the following could be the order of the programs, from most popular to least popular?

   (A) J, H, L, Q, V, S, P
   (B) H, L, Q, J, S, P, V
   (C) H, J, Q, L, S, V, P
   (D) H, J, V, L, Q, S, P
   (E) H, L, V, J, Q, P, S

Keep going with the next rule. There are only two possibilities left, and ask whether either of those makes P or S more popular than Q. Since both (C) and (E) obey that rule, take up the rule that says that S is not seventh. That makes choice (E) wrong, leaving choice (C) as the one standing that does not violate a rule.

1. Which one of the following could be the order of the programs, from most popular to least popular?

   (A) J, H, L, Q, V, S, P
   (B) H, L, Q, J, S, P, V
   (C) H, J, Q, L, S, V, P
   (D) H, J, V, L, Q, S, P
   (E) H, L, V, J, Q, P, S

Follow this method for finding the answer to an acceptable outcome question. If this procedure leaves you with no correct answer or with more than one correct answer, then in all likelihood you have missed a rule. Check them again, and make certain that you have interpreted each rule correctly. This is a good way to catch an incorrect interpretation.

Next question:

2. If J is more popular than L, and S is more popular than P, then which one of the following must be true of the ranking?

   (A) J is second.
   (B) J is third.
   (C) L is third.
   (D) Q is third.
   (E) P is seventh.

As often happens, this question adds facts to the situation. (The addition is temporary. Any new facts added for a question apply only to that question.) It makes J rank higher than L, and S higher than P. It can help to show the consequences of this additional information on your diagram like this:

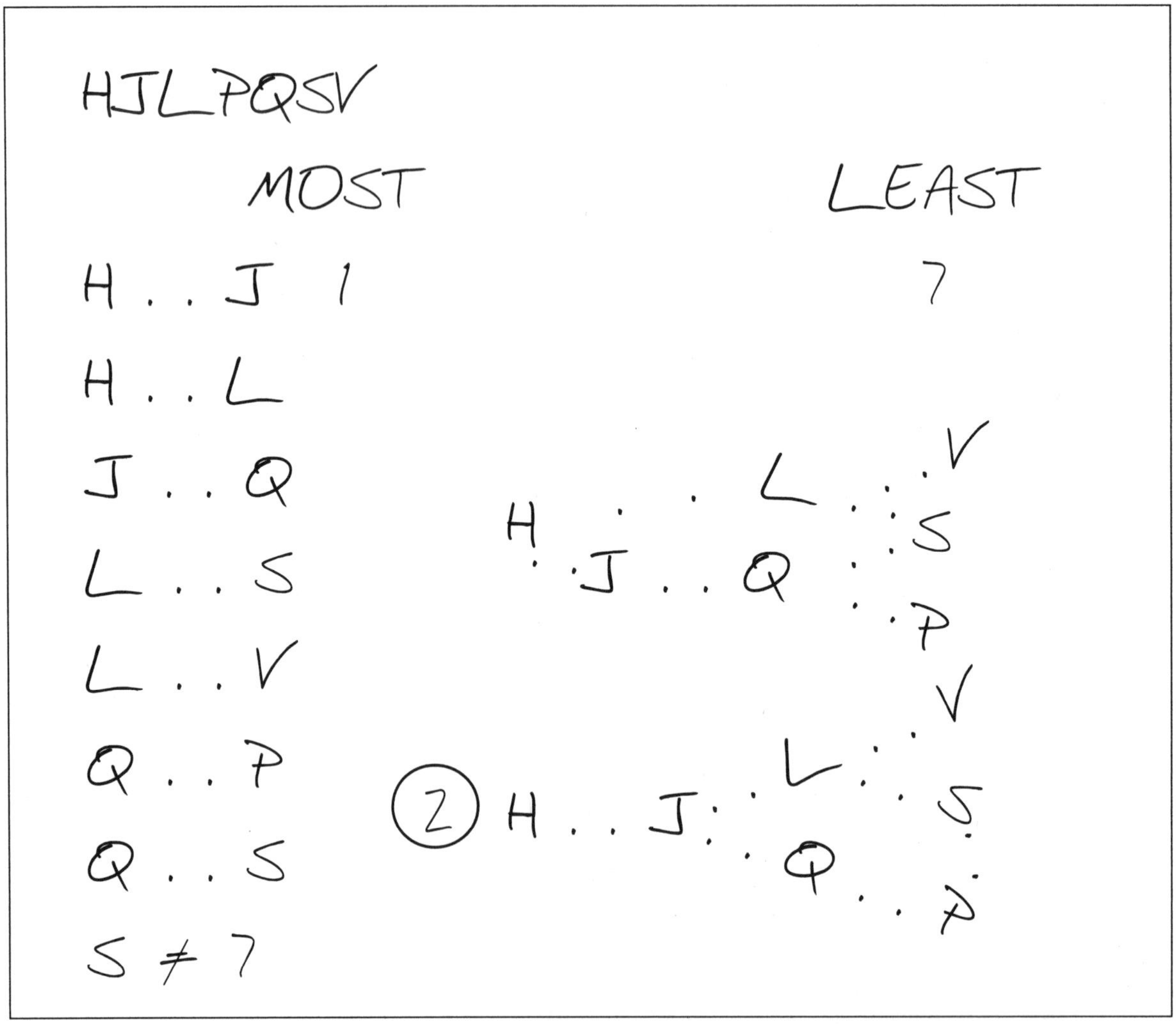

And then, having worked out the consequences of this additional information, interrogate each answer choice and ask whether it must be true. Choice (A) says that J must be second. Indeed that is true. So choice (A) is the answer. There is only one right answer, and choice (A) must be it. Test the others if you like to be certain, but once you have found the one correct answer that is all you need to do. Indeed, with the analytical reasoning section there are more questions than there are in the other sections that you can answer by finding the one correct answer and not even considering the others. This is one of those.

So, here is the next question:

3. Which one of the following programs CANNOT be ranked third?

   (A) L
   (B) J
   (C) Q
   (D) V
   (E) P

This offers no new information, so it is testing your analysis of the things included in the original list of facts. Use your diagram to determine which items in the list of five choices could be or must be third in the order. Four of the five could possibly be third, but you want the one that CANNOT be. This is asking whether you appreciate the flexibility or uncertainty about the situation, while also understanding that there are some things about the situation that must be the case or may not be the case. Test the alternatives presented in the answer choices. There are arrangements that allow for L, J, Q, and V to be third, but since P must be preceded by at least H, J, and Q, it is not possible for P to be third. In this case you have to work all the way to choice (E) to get to the one right answer.

Move on:

4. If V is more popular than Q and J is less popular than L, then which one of the following could be true of the ranking?

   (A) P is more popular than S.
   (B) S is more popular than V.
   (C) P is more popular than L.
   (D) J is more popular than V.
   (E) Q is more popular than V.

Things are added to the store of things that you know, so represent this new knowledge on the diagram:

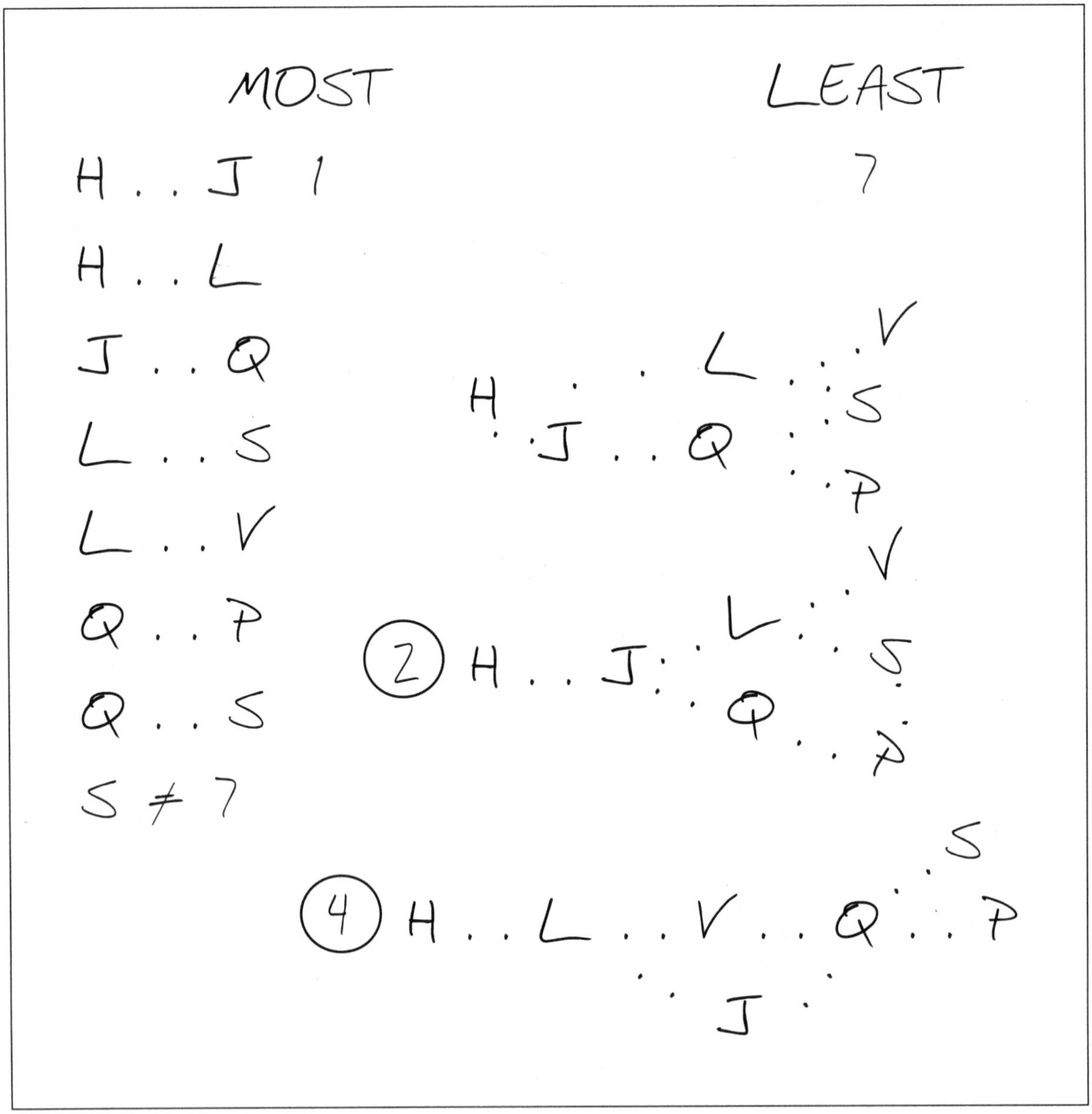

The question asks not for something that must be true, but for something that **could be true**. This is likely to focus on something that remains flexible despite these new things. (Notice that we kept the scenario worked out for question 2. This is because it is a working scenario, and there might be a question that asks for something that could be true or must be true that looking at this workable outcome might help with. So keep your work, but make it clear that it is for some particular questions.) So test the answer choices against the diagram as it has been customized for this question. Choice (A) cannot be true because in this arrangement P must be seventh. Neither can choice (B) be true since V has to be more popular than Q, which has to be more popular than S. Choice (C) must be false since P has to be the least popular. But choice (D) could be true.

Being precise about what the facts compel leaves V and J in the third and fourth positions, but they could flip-flop between one another. Your understanding of this—your maintaining your understanding that you do not know this part of the situation—is what the question is testing. So choice (D) is the answer. There is no need to, but you can confirm that by looking at choice (E) and realizing that with these facts is not possible for Q to be more popular than V.

The final question about this situation also adds a new fact:

5. If Q is more popular than L, then each of the following must be true of the ranking EXCEPT:

(A) H is first.
(B) L is fourth.
(C) V is not fourth.
(D) J is not third.
(E) Q is third.

So do a variation of the diagram with the new condition that Q is more popular than L. The result is the relative order of five of the seven items, with some flexibility remaining for P and V.

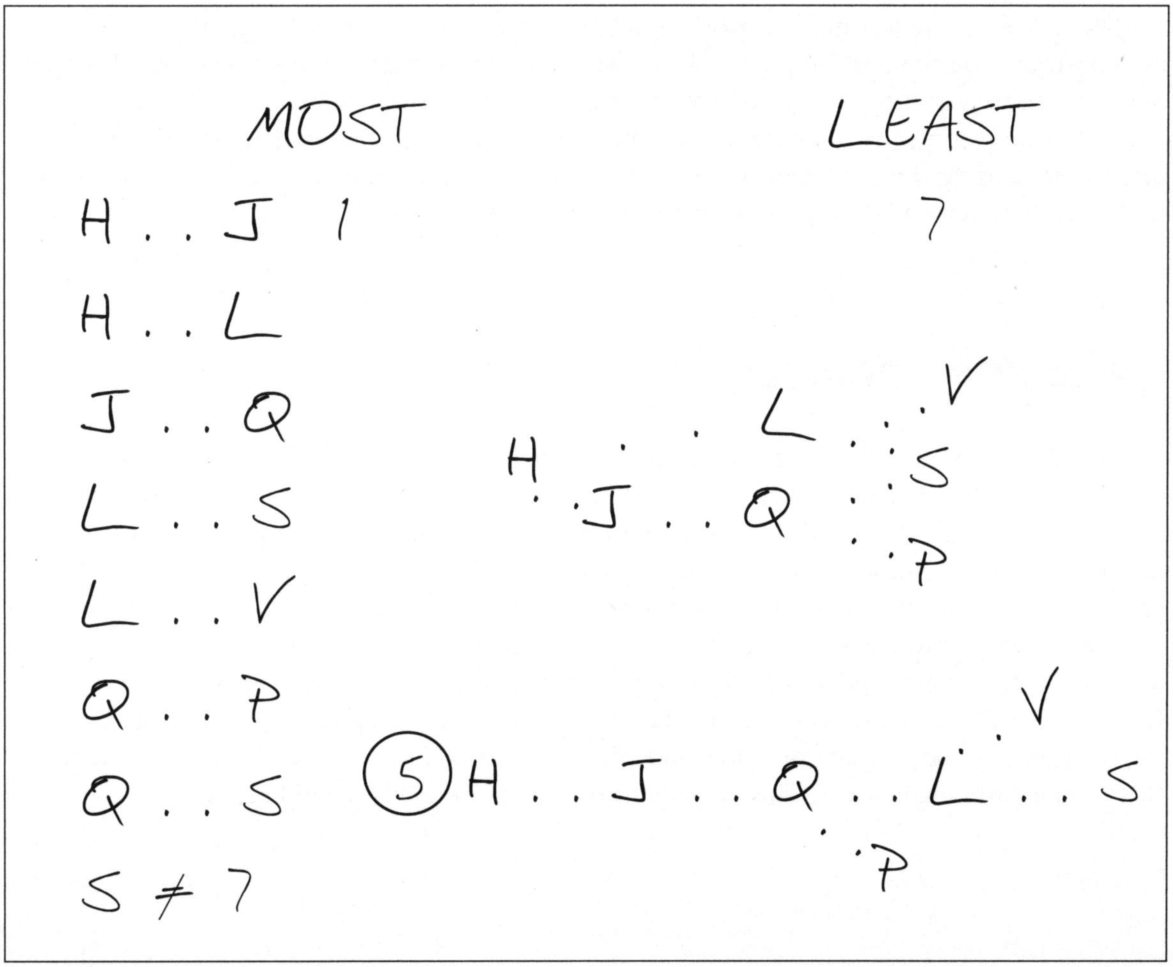

Now look at the question: it asks for something that does not have to be true and tells you that the other four of the choices are things that must be true. Do not lose the word EXCEPT! So interrogate each of the answer choices to ask whether it could be false. The one that could be false is the correct answer. Beginning with choice (A), H must always be first. Choice (B) says that L is fourth. The revised diagram shows that this clearly could be the case, but the diagram also shows that it does not have to be the case since P might come in between Q and L, which would make L fifth. So it is not the case that L must be fourth, and so choice (B) is the correct answer. You probably don't need to take the time to do so, but we can confirm that choice (C) must be true since V must have either four or five of the items preceding it in the order. Choice (D) must be true because the new rule results in J certainly being second. And, similarly, the new rule results in Q being third, so choice (E) also must be true.

What Was the Key?

Upon completing any situation that you work for practice, it is a good idea to look back and ask what was the key in answering the questions about that situation. This makes you consciously learn from your experience and focus on things that might come up in the future with other situations. It can help you to learn what to be alert for.

The situation you just finished working allowed you to learn some things and not others. It put constraints on the possibilities for the order of the items, but not much certainty. The questions tended to test that very uncertainty by adding new facts that resulted in different outcomes. Success in answering the questions came because the analysis and the diagram preserved that uncertainty and flexibility and made it easy to work with. Next time you are faced with a similar problem, then, remember to preserve clearly what you do not know.

A GROUPING SITUATION

The most common kind of situation in the analytical reasoning section requires you to collect items together in groups. Nearly 40% of the situations on the LSAT are grouping situations, and over 95% of LSATs include at least one grouping situation. These present a list of items and ask you to collect some of the items together in anywhere from one to four groups. Within each group there is unlikely to be any ranking or ordering or distinction among the items. Understanding the situation requires knowing which items are included in the group, which items are not included in the group, and which items might or might not be included in the group. Like all LSAT analytical reasoning situations, the key to working well with grouping situations is in coming to appreciate both what you know and what you don't know, and with grouping situations that can be particularly tricky. This one from Proto is an especially helpful example:

Questions 6–12

Bird-watchers explore a forest to see which of the following six kinds of birds—grosbeak, harrier, jay, martin, shrike, wren—it contains. The findings are consistent with the following conditions:

If harriers are in the forest, then grosbeaks are not.

If jays, martins, or both are in the forest, then so are harriers.

If wrens are in the forest, then so are grosbeaks.

If jays are not in the forest, then shrikes are.

Every analytical reasoning situation uses five, six, or seven questions to test whether you appreciate what you know and do not know about the situation. This one includes seven questions, suggesting that it is one of the more complicated of analytical reasoning situations. Go through the five steps:

(1) TYPE
The basic scenario says that there are six items, types of birds, and a container, a forest. Some of the items are in the container according to certain conditions. This is clearly a situation where you have to build a group that will include and exclude items. So the type is clearly grouping.

(2) DIAGRAM
This is a grouping situation with only one group. If there were two or three you would want to make that clear with the diagram, labeling the groups and giving yourself space to collect items together in them. But in this case, since there is only one group, all you really need to do is to include a list of the items and space for the conditions. Note that you can always reduce items to their first letter. LSAT situations do not include multiple items that begin with the same letter, a convenience which makes it easy to treat things in symbols.

G H J M S W

There is no reason to identify different places within the group, since there is nothing to differentiate one spot in the group from another. Neither is it likely to be helpful to do a detailed matrix like this:

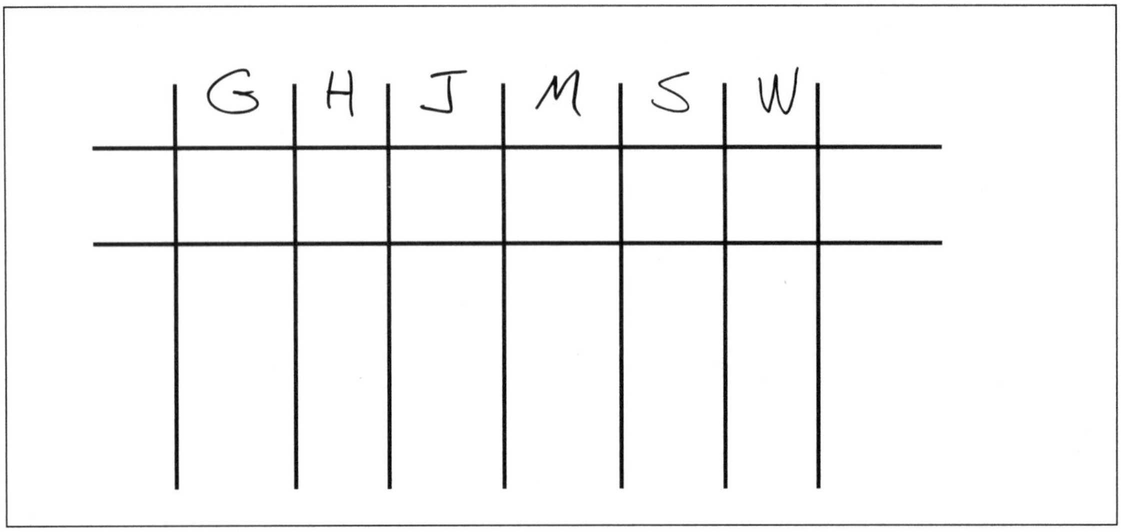

A chart like this suggests that there is more certainty available than there actually is and tends to focus your attention on a single solution. In an LSAT situation there is no single solution, but instead a situation with variables that have effects on one another. There are many scenarios that are possible in a situation like this one, and the matrix is likely to make it difficult to work with those. It is probably clearer and just easier to use the workspace to collect together items in a group as appropriate, as information is added to the situation by particular questions.

(3) SIMPLIFY

Begin to clarify the conditions that govern the situation by looking for the basic information that is contained in the situation's scenario:

- There are six items.
- There is one group to be made up of some of the six items.
- The size of the group is not fixed.

Then there are the specific rules that govern which of the items might be included in the group. In this situation the rules are all of the same type: they are conditional statements, or statements that follow the form: if A then C, or if it is Monday then Chris has Shakespeare class. Conditional statements like this figure prominently in logical reasoning sections, as indeed they figure prominently in all human thought and argument! They appear in the analytical reasoning sections especially in situations that require gathering things together in groups, like this one. *Knowing what conditional statements mean and do not mean is the single reasoning skill most tested on the LSAT.*

To understand what the conditional rules here mean and don't mean, or what they enable you to know and what they don't enable you to know about the situation, begin by clarifying what each one says and simplifying it by stating it in symbolic form.

Conditional statements like this are quite precise in what they mean and do not mean, and so it is important to be equally precise and to be consistent in clarifying what they mean in symbols. Take the example of Chris and Shakespeare.

The statement is: If it is Monday, then Chris has Shakespeare class.

Simplify "it is Monday" with the letter M, and simplify "Chris has Shakespeare class" with the letter S. (Remember, the analytical reasoning section is not about content in the slightest, but about the logical relationships among things, relationships that you can get to more easily if you get away from the content in a particular situation.)

Now the statement becomes if M then S, making it clear that it is a statement about the logical relationship between those two things.

The next step is to replace the "if... then" part with a simple arrow. Put the condition that comes after "if" and before "then" first. Then put the arrow so that it points from left to right. Then put the other condition to the right of the arrow. The statement "if M then S" thus becomes:

$M \rightarrow S$

In that form the precise meaning of the statement is clear and unmistakable. Getting it to that form, or interpreting it so that the meaning is plain might be more difficult.

So now use this technique to simplify the rules in the situation.

> If harriers are in the forest, then grosbeaks are not.

The first step makes this statement into "if H then not G." And the second step replaces the "if... then" so that the rule is stated in symbols as H → ~G, using the ~ to mean "not."

> If jays, martins, or both are in the forest, then so are harriers.

The second rule is more complex, but sorting out what it means and then restating it in clear unambiguous symbols will simplify it. It deals with jays, martins, and harriers. But when you analyze what it says, you determine that it establishes two relationships: one between jays and harriers and the other between martins and harriers. Those two relationships are accurately and simply stated this way:

$J \rightarrow H$

and

M → H

Interpreting this rule carefully and accurately shows that it establishes no relationship whatever between jays and martins, and symbolizing it as separate conditions makes that clear. Now go to the third of the rules.

If wrens are in the forest, then so are grosbeaks.

This one is comparatively straightforward and is simplified as:

W → G

And the last one says:

If jays are not in the forest, then shrikes are.

Be very careful to interpret the "not" in the statement correctly. Losing track of it would mean being exactly wrong anytime you use the rule. Using the symbol ~ to mean "not," this statement then becomes:

~J → S

So simplify each of the rules and add it to the diagram to make the rules plain and accessible.

G H J M S W

H → ~G

J → H

M → H

W → G

~J → S

As always, the next step, the actual analysis or making of deductions, is crucial to understanding what is known and not known about the situation. So before looking at that step in the context of this particular situation, consider conditional statements and what they mean and do not mean more generally.

About Conditional Statements

Deciding what can be inferred from some set of things that we know can be seen as understanding the consequences of conditional relationships among things. A conditional relationship is a relationship between two things such that when one of those things is the case, the other is the case as well. Look at some simple examples:

I can see the stars only when it is dark outside.
It is Wednesday. That means Chris has Shakespeare class today.
The car is running and so it must have fuel.
Billy must be reading *Ivanhoe* because Billy is in third grade.
All peaches have seeds.
I know that Sam does not have class right now because Sam is in the library.
Whatever Alex reads, Dale reads it first.

Each of these statements involves two things that are related to one another. And while the individual statements express those relationships in different particular language, in every case the relationship follows this form: **if** one thing is the case **then** another is the case as well. So the list of statements can be redone with each statement retaining its meaning like this:

If I can see the stars then it is dark.
If it is Wednesday then Chris has Shakespeare class today.
If the car is running then it has fuel.

If Billy is in third grade then Billy is reading *Ivanhoe.*
If it is a peach then it has a seed.
If Sam is in the library then Sam does not have class right now.
If Alex reads it then Dale has read it.

Indeed, not only is each of these in the second group an accurate restatement of the corresponding statement in the first group, but the ones in the second group are more unmistakable in their meaning than the ones in the first group. The statements in the first group assert conditional relationships, but restating them as is done in the second group makes that conditional relationship clear and the meaning of it plain.

What it does *not* mean

Two things about conditional relationships and statements:

One thing is that these **conditional relationships are not causal**. In other words, it being dark does not cause me to be able to see. Alex's reading something does not cause Dale to have read it in the past. The car's running does not cause it to have fuel. And this doesn't work in either direction: Having fuel does not cause the car to run. My seeing the stars does not cause the darkness. Of course it also doesn't mean that a causal relationship certainly does not exist, but only that a conditional relationship and a causal one are different things.

The second thing to note, and this is crucial—understanding this is in large degree what it is all about!—is that these **conditional relationships do not work both ways**.

"If it is Wednesday then Chris has Shakespeare class today" does not mean that "if Chris has Shakespeare class today is Wednesday." Chris might easily also have Shakespeare class on Monday and Friday. Or "if it is a peach then it has a seed" does not mean that "if it has a seed then it is a peach." What if it is an avocado? So when a conditional relationship is asserted, it is critically important to interpret it correctly and to put each condition in its exactly proper position in the "if... then" statement.

Maybe this example will hit home:

Anyone who makes a high score on the LSAT had a pencil to take the test.

This conditional relationship is accurately stated as:

If someone does well on the LSAT then that someone had a pencil.

But it would be woefully inaccurate to say that the reverse way:

If someone has a pencil then he or she will do well on the LSAT.

Even though it doesn't use the "if... then" formulation explicitly, the initial statement has a particular meaning, one that can be stated precisely, and one that can be misstated tragically. Again, it is critical to interpret the conditional relationship correctly and to state it accurately and precisely.

What it does mean

A conditional statement does not mean its reverse. "If it is a peach then it has a seed" is not the same thing as saying "if it has a seed then it is a peach." But a conditional statement can always be restated in one other way that means the same thing but states it differently. This other way is called the "**contrapositive.**" (This is a term that will not be used on the LSAT itself, but a term that we will use extensively here to express the relationships that exist among things.) The current example "if it is a peach then it has a seed" is the same thing as "if it does not have a seed then it is not a peach." Because if it were a peach then it would have a seed.

Other examples: "if I can see the stars then it is dark" does not mean its reverse, "if it is dark then I can see the stars" (what if it is cloudy, or what if I am indoors, or asleep?). It certainly does mean its **contrapositive**, "if it is not dark then I cannot see the stars." And again, "if the car is running then it has fuel" does not mean its reverse, "if the car has fuel then it is running," but it does mean its **contrapositive**, "if the car does not have fuel then the car is not running."

Every conditional relationship can be stated in two equivalent ways, and each is the contrapositive of the other. So "if someone does well on the LSAT then that someone has a pencil" is accurately restated as "if someone does not have a pencil then that someone does not do well on the LSAT." They mean exactly the same thing.

So remember—consciously and actively when working with analytical reasoning situations—that when you know that a conditional statement is true, you **do** know just as certainly that its contrapositive is true. But you **do not** know that its reverse is true (or that it is false—the conditional statement says nothing about its reverse).

(4) DEDUCTIONS

Now back to the situation from Proto.

Having interpreted and simplified the conditions so that the exact meaning of each is unambiguously represented in a symbol, analyze what you have.

The first thing to deduce from any conditional statement is its contrapositive, since the contrapositive is technically just a restatement of the same thing. It is quite helpful, especially with a list of conditional statements like those you have here, to include the contrapositive of each conditional statement in the rules you have symbolized on the diagram.

Deriving the Contrapositive

One reason why it is useful to write down the contrapositive is that it takes some care to state it accurately, and it will be more efficient if you do not have to reformulate it repeatedly while working with the situation. To get the contrapositive of a conditional statement **do not** simply reverse the terms in the "if... then" statement.

If it is January then it is winter does *not* mean the same thing as its reverse which is
If it is winter then it is January.
The first of these statements is true, but the second one is not.

But now get the contrapositive:
If it is not winter then it is not January.

This statement is true and means exactly the same thing as the original. So how did the original become its contrapositive restatement? To derive the contrapositive, follow this simple procedure:

(1) Flip the terms in the conditional statement.
(2) Negate them both.

So in the present example take a statement "if it is January then it is winter," and, for clarity, represent it symbolically:

$J \rightarrow W$

Now to state its contrapositive follow the two steps:

(1) Flip the terms, making $J \rightarrow W$ into $W \rightarrow J$.
(2) Negate them both, making it $\sim W \rightarrow \sim J$.

The procedure works every time: ***flip and negate.*** Neither step by itself produces an accurate result, but together, without fail, the two steps together produce an accurate restatement of the conditional statement.

Derive the contrapositive for each of the statements in the current situation:

G H J M S W

$H \rightarrow \sim G$ $G \rightarrow \sim H$

$J \rightarrow H$ $\sim H \rightarrow \sim J$

$M \rightarrow H$ $\sim H \rightarrow \sim M$

$W \rightarrow G$ $\sim G \rightarrow \sim W$

$\sim J \rightarrow S$ $\sim S \rightarrow J$

Now the things you know are clear and accessible. Treat them as premises and determine what else you know because you know them. Look for premises that deal with the same item, since a conclusion cannot introduce anything that is not in one of the premises.

Look at the very first statement: $H \rightarrow \sim G$. The same $\sim G$ appears in another of the things that you know, so try to relate them together to see if logically they compel a conclusion:

(p1) H → ~G
(p2) ~G → ~W
(Conclusion) H → ~W

To see that this works put it back in the words: if there are harriers in the forest then there are no grosbeaks. And if there are no grosbeaks, then there can be no wrens. So it follows that if there are harriers, then there are no wrens.

A syllogism like this can be accurately stated in the form of a chain: H → ~G → ~W. There are several other such chains that can be deduced here, and you can see them clearly because you have stated the contrapositives. So it is also true that W → G → ~H → ~J & ~M. You have deduced that if there are wrens in the forest you know the disposition of four of the five other sorts of birds!

Another lengthy chain starts with knowing that if there are no jays then there are shrikes, and that if there are jays, then there are harriers. The contrapositive of the first statement relating no jays and strikes is the following: if there are no strikes then there are jays. Putting that knowledge that way allows it to be combined with other premises in this deduction: ~S → J → H → ~G → ~W. So if you were to learn that there were no shrikes in the forest, then you could conclude accurately about the disposition of four of the five other types of birds. You would not know one way or the other about M, but a premise that says ~S combines with the other premises to compel conclusions of J, H, ~G, and ~W. As you do this analysis, add the deductions to the diagram. Once you have made the inferences accurately, there is no need for you to go through the same analytical process again.

G H J M S W

H → ~G   G → ~H

J → H   ~H → ~J

M → H   ~H → ~M

W → G   ~G → ~W

~J → S   ~S → J

H → ~G → ~W

W → G → ~H → ~J + ~M

~S → J → H → ~G → ~W

It turns out that since you know the things the rules state, you know quite a lot about the birds in the forest!

> **Conditional Statements**
>
> FOCUS ON
>
> **Identify the contrapositive of a conditional statement.**
>
> ***Follow two steps:*** (1) Flip the conditions around the arrow and (2) negate them both.

(5) WALK AROUND IT

Seven questions follow to test your understanding of the situation. Before going to those questions it is useful to take a moment to review that understanding. What do you know and what do you not know about the situation?

You know that you have to make a group, and you know that there are at most six items that might be included in the group. Ask: does it turn out that all six might be included? Looking at the rules and the deductions, it becomes clear that not all six could be included. H and G, for example, cannot both be there since the presence of either one requires the absence of the other. Consider the other extreme: do there have to be any items in the group? Looking at the rules and their contrapositives, you can see that at least one must be included, since the absence of J or S requires the other to be included. Indeed, the absence of S has far-reaching consequences requiring two others to be included.

Focus on the conditional statements and their restatement in contrapositive form. What they mean is clear from the symbols. But it is a good idea to review what they do not mean. It is tempting to simplify a conditional relationship and to assume it means that the items in the relationship are grouped, or that they always behave together. So it is tempting to assume, for example, that either H or G is included in the group and the other is excluded. Similarly it is tempting to think that W and G are always together, and that it must be that either both are included in the group or both are excluded from the group. But both of these things are wrong! And at this stage, looking at the situation before going to the questions, it is a good idea to remind yourself of that.

A conditional statement does not create a group, though such statements are often confused as doing so. Take this simple relationship between W and G. By rule, when W is included then G must also be included. And the other way of saying that, the contrapositive, is to say that when G is not included, then neither can W be included (because if W is there then G must be also.) But those facts do not mean that when one of W and G is included the other one must be as well. It is consistent with this conditional rule to include G but not W.

This can appear to be baffling, so to clarify the point, test it with this familiar model:

If it is Monday, then Chris has Shakespeare class.

The other way of saying the same thing, the contrapositive, is:

If Chris does not have Shakespeare class, then it is not Monday.

But, it could be that Chris has Shakespeare class and that it is not Monday. So while the conditional statement means that "Monday" and "no Shakespeare" cannot go together (since if it is Monday there is Shakespeare and if there is no Shakespeare it is not Monday), it certainly does *not* mean that "Shakespeare" and "not Monday" cannot go together (since the conditional statements here say nothing about what happens if it is not Monday or if there is Shakespeare). The point is that a conditional relationship does *not* create a simple group, but a group that exists under certain circumstances.

So in walking around the situation, review the circumstances under which the conditional items are related, and it is also a good idea is to take a moment to review the circumstances under which they are not related. The reason is quite simply this: the LSAT *will* test your understanding of that. Count on it!

For example, return to the relationship between W and G. In this situation W cannot be there without G's being there, so they must be together in the circumstance that W is included. The other way of saying the same thing is that when G is not there, neither can W be. So they are also together in the circumstance that G is excluded. But what if you know only that G is included? What does that tell you about W? The answer is: **nothing**. Just as in the model it is possible to have Shakespeare without it being Monday (but not necessary, or it not being Monday does not mean for sure that there is Shakespeare, you just don't know), so it is possible to have G without W.

When there are a lot of conditional statements as there are in this bird in the forest situation, it is a good idea during this stage of walking around and examining the situation before going to the questions to think consciously about what the conditional relationships allow in addition to what they require. That is indicated here:

G H J M S W		Could Have
H → ~G	G → ~H	~G + ~H
J → H	~H → ~J	H + ~J
M → H	~H → ~M	H + ~M
W → G	~G → ~W	G + ~W
~J → S	~S → J	S + J

In testing analytical skills, the LSAT *will* test specifically your understanding that the things in the third column in this diagram could be true while the rules of the situation are true (see questions 10 and 11 below). Many people will get these questions wrong.

Focus on

Understanding Conditional Statements

What conditional relationships do *not* require.

Think about: P → Q means also ~Q → ~P, but it also allows P and ~Q.

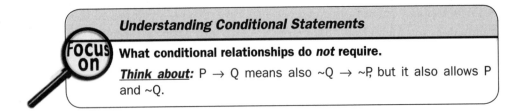

So in preparation for working with the questions on the birds in the forest, you have reviewed what you know about the situation:

- The basic makeup of the group.
- The meaning of the conditional rules.
- The contrapositives of the conditional rules.

And you have also reviewed what you do not know about the situation:

- What the conditional relationships allow but do not require.

Now that you understand what you know and do not know about the situation, prove it by answering the questions.

The first question is a twist on the usual "acceptable outcome" question:

6. Which one of the following could be a complete and accurate list of the birds NOT in the forest?

(A) jays, shrikes
(B) harriers, grosbeaks
(C) grosbeaks, jays, martins
(D) grosbeaks, martins, shrikes, wrens
(E) martins, shrikes

A more typical first question would ask for an acceptable list of the items in the group (the birds in the forest), while this question asks for a list of things *not* included in the group.

You can approach it as you would any "could be true" question and test the choices until you find one that is possible. Use the diagram and especially the contrapositives to help here, remembering that the list is a list of things **not** included.

Choice (A) is not correct—it could not be true—because of the rule that says that when one of J or S is not in the group the other must be. That makes it impossible for both to be excluded.

Choice (B) excludes H and G only, but the contrapositives show that when H is excluded, so must both J and M be. So this could not be an accurate list of those not included in the group.

Choice (C) lists G among the items excluded, but the contrapositive of the rule that says W → G requires that when G is not included in the group, W must be excluded as well (~G → ~W). That is not the case in this answer choice, and so this answer choice would violate the rule and cannot be correct. Choice (D) excludes four of the six items from the group, yet in doing so violates no rule. This could be true. Choice (E) may not seem obviously to violate a rule, but consider the relationship between G and H. It cannot be that both are included in the group, so at least one of them must be among the ones excluded. So this cannot be the correct answer.

Notice that in answering this question mastery of the contrapositives was essential. It is testing your understanding of the meaning of conditional statements.

The second question asks for something that must be true:

7. If both martins and harriers are in the forest, then which one of the following must be true?

   (A) Shrikes are the only other birds in the forest.
   (B) Jays are the only other birds in the forest.
   (C) The forest contains neither jays nor shrikes.
   (D) There are at least two other kinds of birds in the forest.
   (E) There are at most two other kinds of birds in the forest.

A "must be true" question may not require testing each of the answer choices. Begin by taking the additional information in the question, and then consult the diagram with its list of rules and deductions to determine the consequences of including both M and H.

G H J M S W		Could Have
H → ~G	G → ~H	~G + ~H
J → H	~H → ~J	H + ~J
M → H	~H → ~M	H + ~M
W → G	~G → ~W	G + ~W
~J → S	~S → J	S + J

H → ~G → ~W

W → G → ~H → ~J + ~M

~S → J → H → ~G → ~W

M produces no consequences beyond itself, but H does, as you have already deduced. So, including M and H means excluding G and W. It has no effect on the remaining two (J and S), although another rule requires that at least one of them be included as well. There are several things here that must be true, so remembering the distinction between what "could be true" and what "must be true," find the correct answer.

Choice (C) cannot be true. Each of choice (A), choice (B), and choice (D) might be true but does not have to be true. In fact, this is what the question is primarily testing about your analytical skills. Do you understand the meaning of the relationship between J and S established by the rule? The rule says that ~J →S. The first inference from that rule and its contrapositive is that one of J or S must be included, since the absence of each entails the presence of the other. But there is nothing in this rule that says that *exactly* or *only* one of the two may be included, and, indeed, the rule is consistent with including both. The question is testing whether you understand that consistency, because if you do not understand it, you will not see that "there are at most two other kinds of birds in the forest," or you would erroneously think there would be at most one other kind of bird in the forest. But knowing what this relationship means exactly, you know what must be true is choice (D). This is a difficult question that requires a sophisticated understanding.

The next question asks not for what must be true, but for something that "must be false."

8. If jays are not in the forest, then which one of the following must be false?

    (A) Martins are in the forest.
    (B) Harriers are in the forest.
    (C) Neither martins nor harriers are in the forest.
    (D) Neither martins nor shrikes are in the forest.
    (E) Harriers and shrikes are the only birds in the forest.

Take the new information presented in the question, ~J, and then ask what that compels. It turns out that it compels only one thing: that S be included in the group. Specifically, while a rule establishes a relationship between J and H, there is nothing about that relationship that results from ~J. Your understanding of that is part of what the question is testing.

Beyond including S for sure, ~J has no effect on the group, and the rest of it will be governed by the remaining rules. So really the only thing that "must be false" as a consequence of ~J is that S is not included. Being careful of the double negatives, look to see whether the question is easy enough that ~S is in one of the answers. In fact it is, in choice (D). It cannot be the case that there are neither M nor S. (This is a bit crafty in the way it is stated, for if there are neither M nor S, then there are no S. And it cannot be the case that there are no S.).

Once you have the correct answer—you know that it must be false that S are not included—there is no need to linger over the other answer choices, and you can move on to the next question about the situation:

9. Which one of the following is the maximum number of the six kinds of birds the forest could contain?

    (A) two
    (B) three
    (C) four
    (D) five
    (E) six

This question tests your understanding of the situation by asking precisely what you know and do not know about the number of items that could be included in the group. Start by asking whether it could be all six. That would not be possible because of the relationship between H and G, which means that both cannot be included. Now go a step further: does including either H or G require excluding something else? The contrapositives make clear that including G means excluding not only H, but also J and M. Since the question is asking for the maximum number that could be included, it looks like including G is not the way to go.

So how about including H? How many others might be included then? Again the contrapositive of including H requires excluding G and W. So with H there might be a maximum of four. Does anything else reduce the number further? Put another way, would it be possible to include everything but G and W with H? J and M could be included, but what about S? Again, it turns out that it is testing your understanding of the situation and specifically your understanding that both J and S could be included, since the rule establishing a relationship between those two means only that both cannot be excluded. So, indeed, an acceptable group could include H, J, M, S. The answer is choice (C).

Each of questions 8 and 9 has required an accurate and sophisticated understanding of the relationship between J and S. So does the next one:

10. Which one of the following pairs of birds CANNOT be among those birds contained in the forest?

(A) jays, wrens
(B) jays, shrikes
(C) shrikes, wrens
(D) jays, martins
(E) shrikes, martins

This question is asking directly whether you understand what you know about J and S. Many people will answer choice (B) to this question, taking the rule on J and S to mean not only what it does, that both cannot be excluded, but also something that it does not, that both cannot be included. Accurate analysis, combined with reflection on the situation in the "Walk Around It" step (where you focused consciously on what the conditional relationship did not mean, knowing that you would be tested on the point!) prepares you to know that both J and S can be included, so choice (B) is not the correct answer.

So once you have not fallen for the trap that the question is designed for you to fall for, what is the answer? In fact you have prepared for that as well introducing the chains that you deduced:

H → ~G → ~W

W → G → ~H → ~J + ~M

~S → J → H → ~G → ~W

Review those deductions. Look first for whether the list in question 10 includes a choice of H with either G or W. That is not there. Now look at W. It cannot be included with H, J, or M. Is W there? It is, and in Choice (A). So Choice (A) is the correct answer. There is no need to test the others. Move on.

11. If grosbeaks are in the forest, then which one of the following must be true?

    (A) Shrikes are in the forest.
    (B) Wrens are in the forest.
    (C) The forest contains both wrens and shrikes.
    (D) At most two kinds of birds are in the forest.
    (E) At least three kinds of birds are in the forest.

This is another "must be true" question testing your understanding of the conditional relationships. In particular, this one is about conditional relationships involving G. Review the diagram to see what you do know, and not know, when G is included.

G H J M S W		Could Have
H → ~G	G → ~H	~G + ~H
J → H	~H → ~J	H + ~J
M → H	~H → ~M	H + ~M
W → G	~G → ~W	G + ~W
~J → S	~S → J	S + J

H → ~G → ~W

W → G → ~H → ~J + ~M

~S → J → H → ~G → ~W

Again, the question tempts you to misinterpret the relationship between W and G. Many people will incorrectly choose choice (B) based on that relationship. But the rule that says W → G does not work in reverse—as none of them do!—and so it is not the case that if G is included, W must also be. Not only did you know that, you also knew (having focused on the during the "Walk Around It" step) that you would be asked to prove that you know it. Prove it now, and do not select choice (B).

But knowing that choice (B) is incorrect doesn't say which is correct. What does the diagram show must be when G is included?

W → G → ~H → ~J + ~M

Regardless of W, G forces ~H, ~J, and ~M. Review the remaining answer choices and see whether that is enough information to get you to the right answer. It is not. So go another step and review the rules and contrapositives for consequences of ~H, ~J, and ~M:

~J → S

There is one: if J is not included, then S must be included. Is that an answer choice? It is, and choice (A) is the right answer.

That was a difficult question. It required, first, that you be clear and confident about what a conditional statement means and does not require. Then it made you draw deductions from the conditions and the contrapositives. And then it took yet one more deduction from the first set of subsidiary conclusions you drew. Earning a right answer to this question indeed shows sophisticated analytical skills.

Occasionally the final question on an analytical reasoning situation changes a rule. This is such a case:

12. Suppose the condition is added that if shrikes are in the forest, then harriers are not. If all other conditions remain in effect, then which one of the following could be true?

(A) The forest contains both jays and shrikes.
(B) The forest contains both wrens and shrikes.
(C) The forest contains both martins and shrikes.
(D) Jays are not in the forest, whereas martins are.
(E) Only two of the six kinds of birds are not in the forest.

This is never done with any question except the last one in a situation, and when it is done it usually does not result in a very difficult question. The challenge lies in accepting the change in a situation that you have been working with for several questions. In this case the change is easily added to the diagram:

G H J M S W		Could Have
H → ~G	G → ~H	~G + ~H
J → H	~H → ~J	H + ~J
M → H	~H → ~M	H + ~M
W → G	~G → ~W	G + ~W
~J → S	~S → J	S + J
S → ~H		
H → ~G → ~W		
W → G → ~H → ~J + ~M		
~S → J → H → ~G → ~W		
S → ~H → ~J + ~M		

It doesn't have the effect of altering any of the existing conditions, but only of adding one more. But that one has consequences since ~H requires ~J, and so on. The question then asks for something that "could be true," which means something that is consistent with the rules as now enhanced. So approach it as you would any "could be true" question, and test each answer choice against the rules until you find one that does not violate anything.

Choice (A) is not possible with the new rule because now S entails ~J (something it did not do before this question). Testing choice (B) against the information you have developed on the diagram, however, shows no difficulties. W does not require ~S, and S does not require ~W. So this could be true, and choice (B) is the answer. It would not be necessary to do so in testing conditions, but for information here continue with the other choices to see that each of them cannot be true. Choice (C) is impossible under the new rule since, as you deduce, S now requires ~M. Choice (D) follows through on that same thought, since M and S now cannot be in the group together, when M is in the group it will have to be with J. Neither could choice (E) be the case any longer, since, as the deductions with the new rule now show, each of S and ~S requires that three must be left out of the group. So, again, working with this final question required patiently accepting the new rule, and its application turned out to be fairly straightforward.

What Was the Key?

Again, after practicing any analytical reasoning situation it is a good idea to review what you have done and what enabled you to succeed, or made it especially difficult to succeed, in understanding the situation. This was an especially difficult situation because of all the conditional statements and the importance of understanding them in a very precise way. These keys were fundamental:

- knowing what a conditional statement means and does not mean
- deriving and spelling out the contrapositives of conditional statements
- understanding that a conditional relationship between two things does not make them into a group

A PLACEMENT SITUATION

The remaining type of situation commonly found in the analytical reasoning section requires you to place items into discrete, well-defined containers or slots. About 20% of the situations on the LSAT are placement situations, and about nine out of ten LSAT tests include at least one of these. These situations present a list of items and then carefully and precisely define the places into which those items are to be put. A placement situation does not require collecting items together, as a grouping situation does; neither does it require putting items in order relative to one another, as an ordering situation does. Here you are concerned with the items relative to the containers or slots into which they are to be placed. Think of a mail carrier placing mail in the boxes in an apartment complex mailroom. It's not the mail relative to other pieces of mail, and it's not so much collecting it together, but it is all about putting it in the right slot. That is the case here. The places are well defined, and the question becomes which item goes into which place?

The fourth situation in test Proto is one of these placement situations:

Questions 19–23

There are exactly ten stores and no other buildings on Oak Street. On the north side of the street, from west to east, are stores 1, 3, 5, 7, and 9; on the south side of the street, also from west to east, are stores 2, 4, 6, 8, and 10. The stores on the north side are located directly across the street from those on the south side, facing each other in pairs, as follows: 1 and

2; 3 and 4; 5 and 6; 7 and 8; 9 and 10. Each store is decorated with lights in exactly one of the following colors: green, red, and yellow. The stores have been decorated with lights according to the following conditions:

No store is decorated with lights of the same color as those of any store adjacent to it.

No store is decorated with lights of the same color as those of the store directly across the street from it.

Yellow lights decorate exactly one store on each side of the street.

Red lights decorate store 4.

Yellow lights decorate store 5.

(1) TYPE

The scenario here identifies ten stores and makes it clear that each of the ten is a discrete location. It then identifies three colors of lights and indicates that the task is to place one color of lights in each of the ten stores. Where the stores are and the fact that they are distinct from one another are both carefully set out. The task is to place individual items in each of those particular stores. So this is a placement situation.

(2) DIAGRAM

Having identified the type as a placement situation, proceed to build a diagram that makes the containers or slots as clear as they can be, since in a placement situation they are constant and rigid, and what changes or remains uncertain is which items are to be placed in which slots. Here it is appropriate, even necessary, to do something that is a bad idea with ordering situations and grouping situations, and that is to make a matrix. With the other types it is important to maintain the uncertainty in the situation and not to draw a diagram that tends to obscure or suppress what you do not know. In a placement situation, however, you do know the places. They do not change. And so it is important to identify them clearly, leaving space for what does change or what is unknown about the situation.

The places of the stores are well-defined by sides of the street and order on each side of the street. Draw a diagram that clearly and accurately shows that placement:

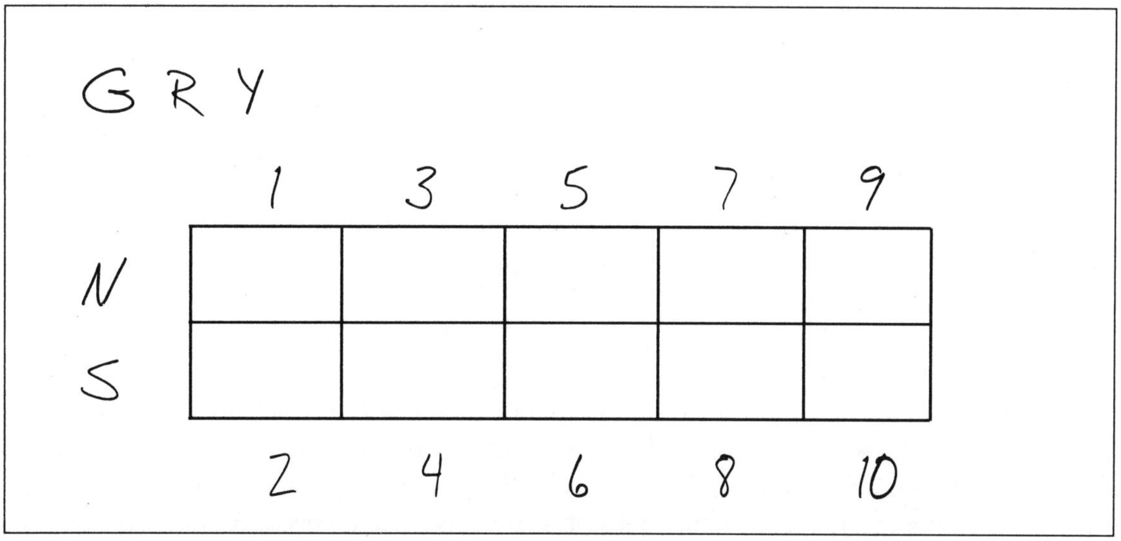

The scenario spells out the placement of the stores, or slots, with great care and precision. This is clearly represented on the diagram indicating which containers are adjacent to one another and which ones are across from one another.

(3) SIMPLIFY

The next step is to clarify the rules and add them to the diagram. Begin by noting the very important rules that slots beside each other (that is what "adjacent" means) and slots across from each other cannot contain identical items. Those rules are going to be very limiting. They also show the importance and utility of drawing the diagram precisely.

Note the next rule that there's exactly one Y on each side of the street, and finally the two rules that fill in two of the slots with their items. Now the diagram looks like this:

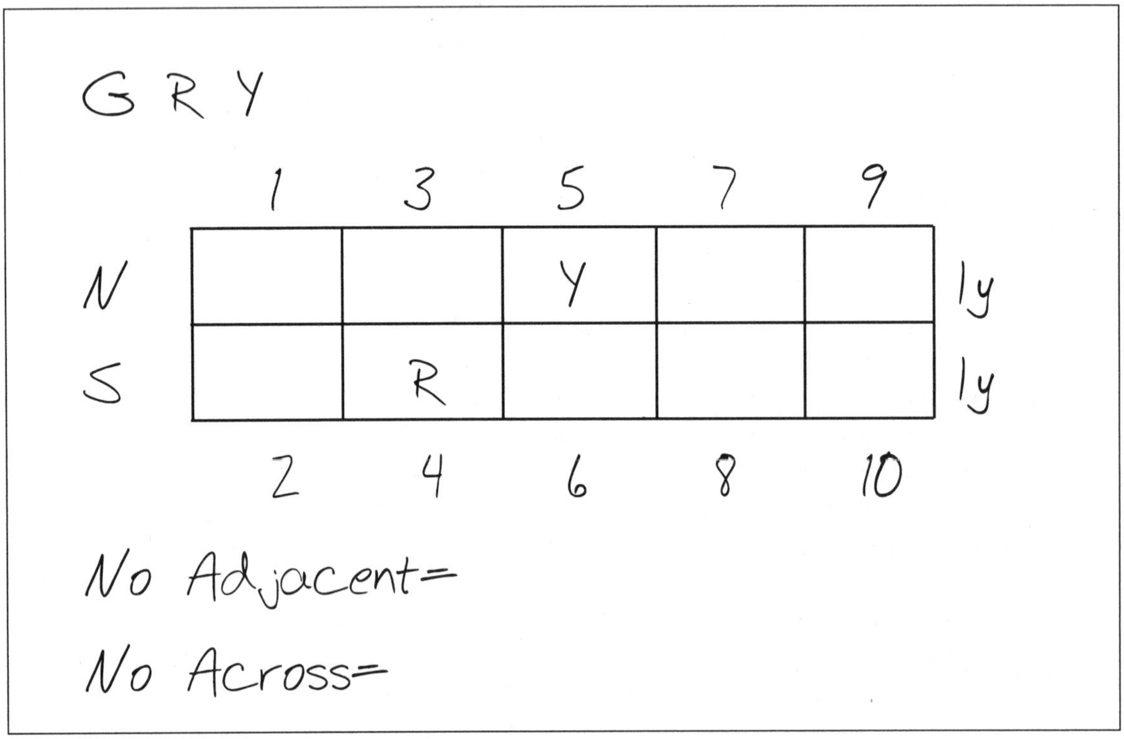

(4) DEDUCTIONS

Now, for the all-important analysis. Take the things that you know as premises and draw conclusions that can be drawn. Make arguments like this (spelling out the reasoning here step by step to show the analysis):

(p1) If slot 5 has a Y, then slot 3 must be either G or R.
(p2) Slot 5 does have a Y.
(sc1) So slot 3 has a G or an R.

(p3) If slot 4 contains an R then slot 3 cannot contain an R. (Which actually follows from this syllogism: If slots across from one another cannot contain the same item, then if slot 4 contains an R, slot 3 cannot contain an R. And slots across from one another cannot contain the same item. So if slot 4 contains an R, then slot 3 cannot contain an R.)

(p4) And slot 4 does contain an R.
(sc2) So slot 3 cannot contain an R.

(sc1) If slot 3 is not an R, then slot 3 contains a G.
(sc2) Slot 3 does not contain an R.
(c1) So slot 3 contains a G.

So the first major conclusion that comes from analyzing the things that you know enables you to fill slot 3 with a G. This conclusion is compelled—it must be true because the other things are true.

The analytical process is exactly the one used in the logical reasoning section, and that, of course, is the point of the test. The difference here is that there can be no doubt about the truth of the premises, and what is being tested is the reasoning that you are able to do with those premises. The deduction phase here is collecting together premises about the same thing and drawing conclusions that are compelled by valid logical reasoning. Each of those conclusions or subsidiary conclusions can then become premises as well, leading to further conclusions. Spell out another step to see exactly that point, a step that starts from the conclusion that slot 3 contains a G. That is now one of the things that we know, and it now figures in another argument as p6:

(p5) If another slot on the north side has a Y, then slot 1 must be either G or R.
(p2) Slot 5 does have a Y.
(sc3) So slot 1 has a G or an R.

(p3) If slot 3 contains a G, then slot 1 cannot contain a G.
(p6) And slot 3 does contain a G.
(sc4) So slot 1 cannot contain a G.

(sc3) If slot 1 is not a G, then slot 1 contains an R.
(sc4) Slot 1 does not contain a G.
(p2) So slot 1 contains an R.

Valid logic combined with true premises reveals additional things that we know. So slot 1 contains an R and slot 3 contains a G.

Similar reasoning leads to the conclusion that slot 6 must contain a G. It also leads to the conclusions that slot 2 must contain either a G or a Y, and that slot 8 must contain either an R or a Y.

Add all these conclusions to the diagram, making it clear what must be true:

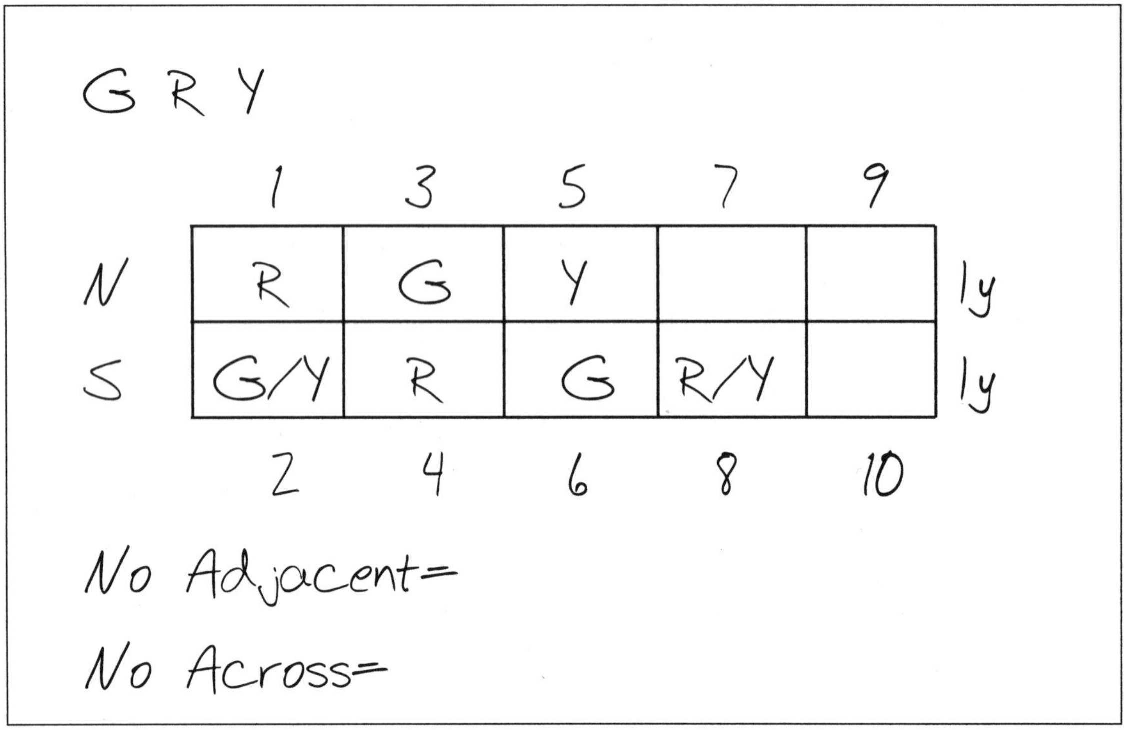

Indeed it goes further, in that since the Y allowed for the north side is used, neither 7 nor 9 can contain one, and so one must contain a G and the other an R. Which is G and which R is related to what is used to fill up slots 8 and 10. By the time you have analyzed the situation you realize that the only remaining slot that might contain any of the three items is 10!

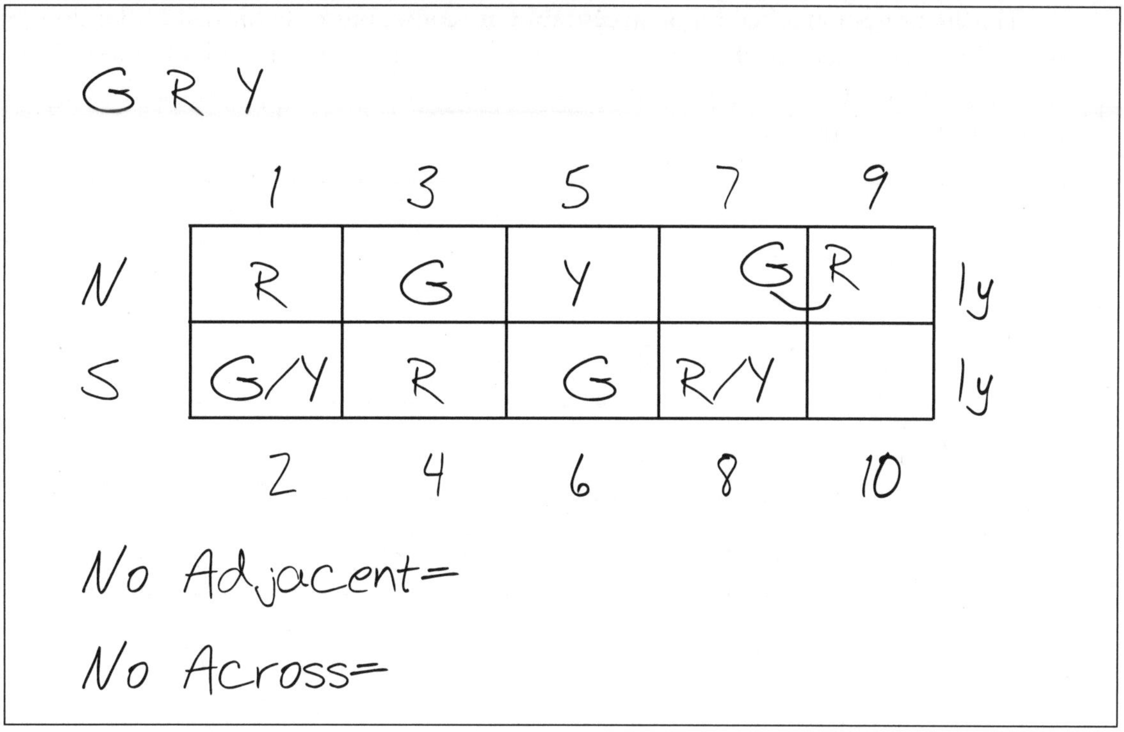

(5) WALK AROUND IT

Before going to the questions spend a little time looking at what you know and what you don't know about the situation. It turns out you know quite a lot, things you discovered by analyzing what you already knew about the situation. But there are things that you do not know as well, such as which of G and R is in 7 and which in 9. You do not know where the Y on the south side of the street is.

But if you are given any such piece of information, a "**chain reaction**" would follow giving you certainty about much of the situation. Suppose, for instance, that the question were to add the information that slot 2 is filled with a Y. That would mean these things: 8 contains an R; 10 contains a G; 9 contains an R; and 7 has a G.

Or suppose, instead, a question adds the information that 7 contains an R. That would create this chain reaction: 8 has a Y; 9 has a G; 10 has an R; and 2 has a G. What fun!

So while there is much that you do not know, realize while walking around it that it will not take much for you to know a lot more. Armed with this understanding, proceed to the questions that test your knowledge of what you know and don't know about the situation.

19. Which one of the following could be an accurate list of the colors of the lights that decorate stores 2, 4, 6, 8, and 10, respectively?

(A) green, red, green, red, green
(B) green, red, green, yellow, red
(C) green, red, yellow, red, green
(D) yellow, green, red, green, red
(E) yellow, red, green, red, yellow

This first question asked for an **acceptable outcome**, but only for half of the slots. Since which items are placed in these containers results not only from the rules but also from what is in the containers on the north side, it is most effective simply to use the diagram and to test the alternatives against it.

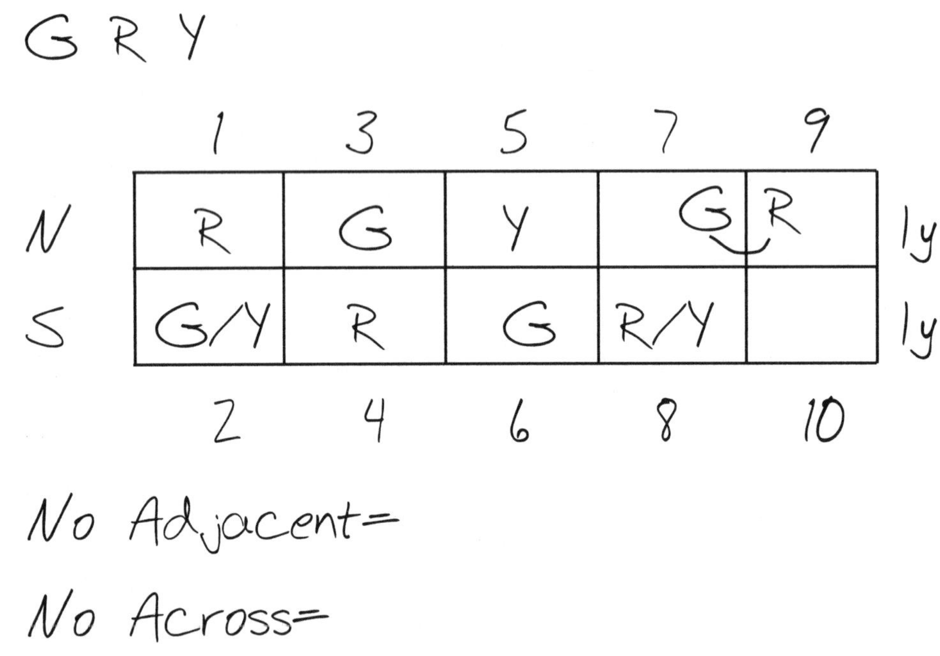

Questions that ask for what "could be true" usually require testing answer choices until you find the one, the only one, that is ***not impossible*** in the situation. So begin with choice (A). It includes no Y, and so it is impossible. Choice (B) is consistent with the diagram and presents no rule violations. It could be true, and so it is the correct answer. To demonstrate that Choice (B) is correct here (though it would probably be a waste of time in the real test) continue to test the other choices. Choice (C) makes 6 contain a Y, which it cannot do since, by rule, the one across from it has a Y. Choice (D) puts a G in 4, which must contain an R, again by rule. And choice (E) includes two Ys on the same side of the street, which violates the rule.

The next question asks you to carry through the consequences of adding additional information:

20. If green lights decorate store 7, then each of the following statements could be false EXCEPT:

(A) Green lights decorate store 2.
(B) Green lights decorate store 10.
(C) Red lights decorate store 8.
(D) Red lights decorate store 9.

Using the diagram, determine what you would know and not know with a G placed in container 7:

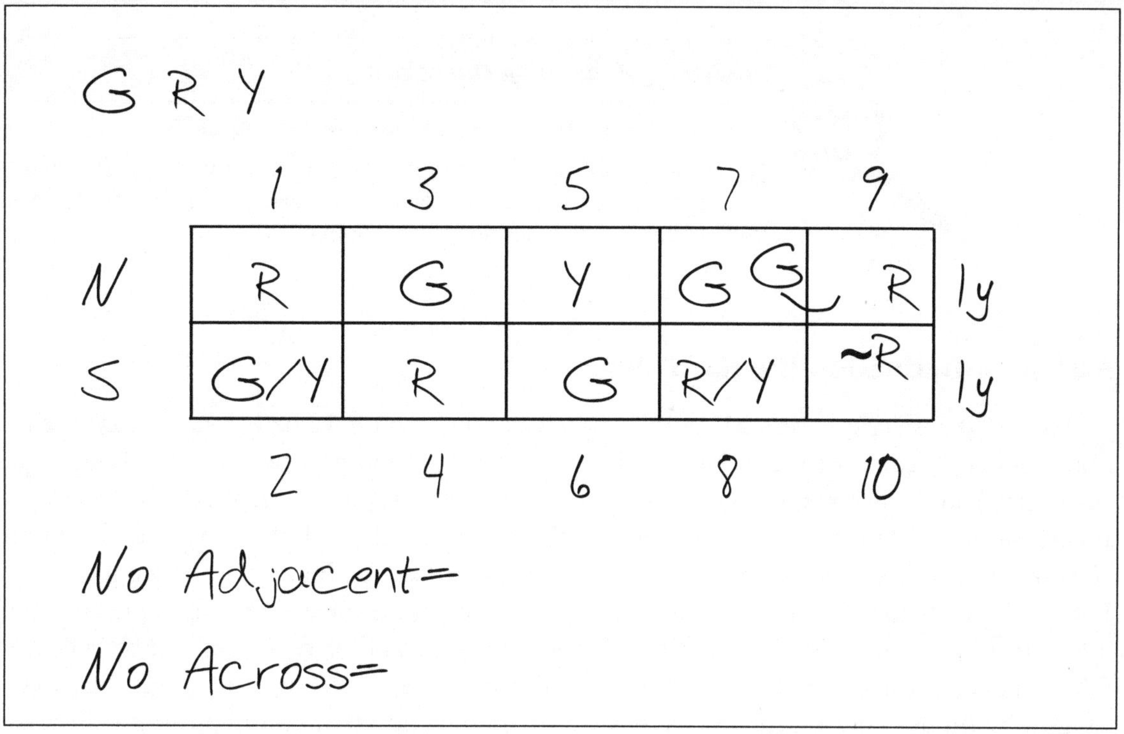

That would create certainty for 7 and 9, but still leave various possibilities for each of 2, 8, 10. The question asks for what could be false EXCEPT. Always be especially careful with "EXCEPT" questions. In asking for the one that could not be false, the question asks for what must be true. And the only thing that you have determined that must be true if 7 contains a G is that 9 contains an R. And that is in choice (D), which is the correct answer. Choice (A) and choice (E) are things that must be false, and so they certainly "could be" false. Choice (B) and choice (C) are things that could be true, but do not have to be, and so could also be false.

The next question seems more straightforward:

21. Which one of the following statements must be true?

(A) Green lights decorate store 10.
(B) Red lights decorate store 1.
(C) Red lights decorate store 8.
(D) Yellow lights decorate store 8.
(E) Yellow lights decorate store 10.

In asking for what **"must be true"** without adding additional information, the question is testing whether you have analyzed the situation well. Look for your deductions, the result of your analysis, in the answer choices. In this case you find it in choice (B), which is the correct answer. Be careful: each of the others is something that could be false but also could be true, so the question is testing whether you have gone too far and have lost the flexibility or uncertainty that is in the situation.

> ***Analytical Reasoning Questions***
>
> **Does it ask for what "must be" or what "could be"?**
>
> ***Think about:*** Not everything that "could be true (or false)" is something that "must be true (or false)." But everything that "must be true" is certainly something that "could be true."

Making a Deduction the Hard Way

We could answer question 21 rapidly and efficiently because we had already made the deduction it asks for. But what if that had not been the case? Sometimes there will be things in a situation that you do not see, despite your best efforts, until a question makes you discover them. When you have a "must be true" question with no additional conditions and you do not see the answer that is exactly the circumstance you are in, there is a deduction you have not yet made. Look at it as a help from the test: it is letting you know that you have missed that deduction, and it is assisting you in making it. Question 21, for example, could be rephrased to say "which of the following is a deduction that follows from the things that are given as true about the situation?" By giving you five choices, the test guides you to a deduction that you might not otherwise see! So if, in such a question, you do not already know the answer of what "must be true," just do it "the hard way" confident that you will come out of it having learned something new about the situation. So take this question:

21½. Which one of the following statements must be true?

(A) Green lights decorate exactly four stores on the street.
(B) Red lights decorate exactly five stores on the street.
(C) Red lights decorate exactly three stores on the north side of Oak Street.
(D) Red lights decorate exactly three stores on the south side of Oak Street.
(E) Red lights decorate exactly two stores on the north side of Oak Street.

The question asks for something that must be true without adding any additional information or premise. That means that the premises, the things that we know, that enable us to reach the conclusion that we have not yet reached, are already there. Moreover, the question tells us that the conclusion that is compelled by the information we already have is in one of these five answer choices. So we can make the deduction that we are missing by deciding which of the five answer choices is, in fact, compelled. To do that, test each of the five to see if it can be made false—not whether it can be made true, but whether it can be false. For if it cannot be false, then it must be true, and it must follow from the things that we know about the scenario.

Here are the things that we know:

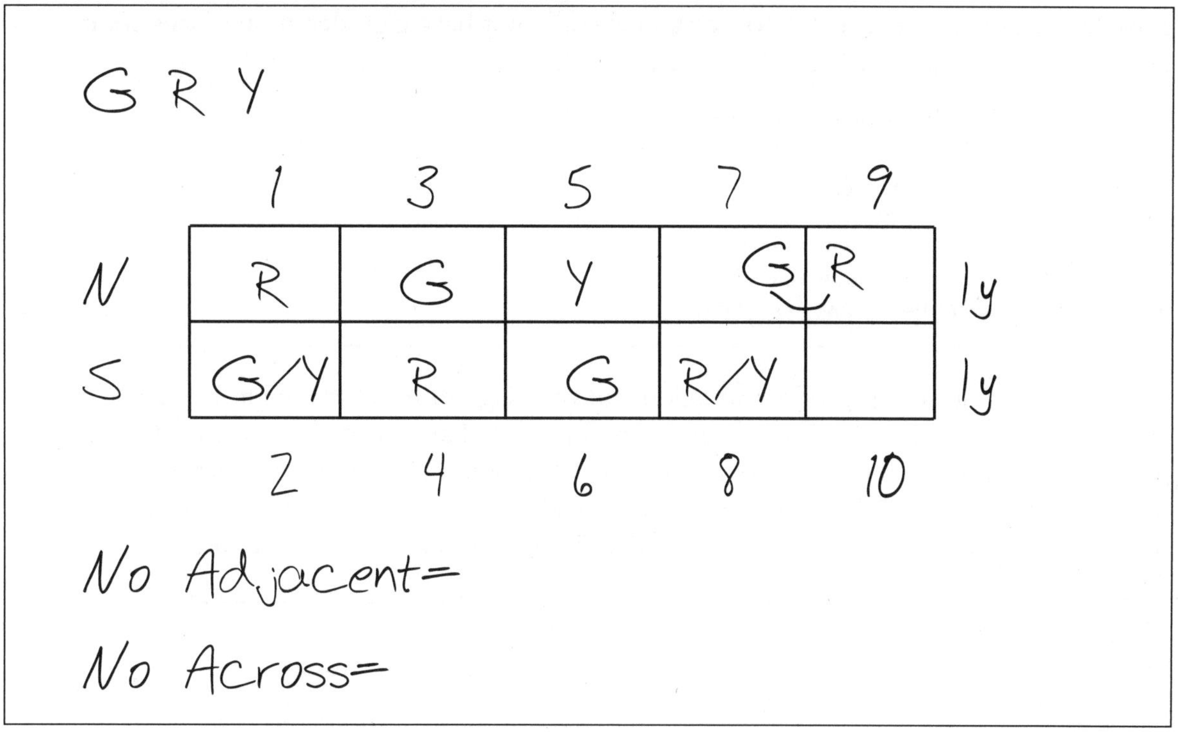

Start with choice (A). It can be true that there are four Gs, but can it be false? Analysis shows us that there must be exactly two Gs on the north side, but there could be either two (6, and either 2 or 10) or three (2, 6, 10) on the south side. This analysis shows us that choice (A) is not the correct answer, and it also reveals some things that we know about the situation that may help us get to the correct answer more quickly.

So move to choice (B). Must it be true that there are five Rs? We have just determined that it does not have to be true that there are five Gs, but have also determined that it could be true that there are five Gs. And if that could be true, then it could not be true that there *must* be five Rs because the possible five Gs and five Rs together would mean too many stores. So whether choice (B) presents something that could be true or not, it clearly does not present something that must be true.

How about choice (C)? Does what we know tell us for certain that there must be three Rs on the north side? Most certainly not. Indeed, there cannot be three Rs on the north side. So this is not the answer.

Analyze choice (D). Must there be three Rs on the south side? Looking at the diagram, it becomes apparent that there could not be three Rs on the south side, but at most, two. So not only is choice (D) not something that must be true, it is something that must be false.

So we are left with choice (E), and if we understand the situation, choice (E) will have to be the correct answer. Is it? In fact looking at the diagram shows that it is the case that there must be exactly two Rs on the north side: 1 and either 7 or 9. Choice (E) is indeed the answer.

So the result of working this question "the hard way" is actually to learn much more about the distribution of Gs and Rs on the street. These are conclusions, especially in choice (E) and choice (A), that may turn out to be helpful with other questions.

Returning to the questions on the stores and lights from Proto, the next question asks you to consider a possibility that you almost certainly would not have considered up to this point:

22. If green lights decorate five stores on the street, then which one of the following statements must be true?

    (A) Green lights decorate store 9.
    (B) Red lights decorate store 2.
    (C) Red lights decorate store 7.
    (D) Red lights decorate store 10.
    (E) Yellow lights decorate store 8.

Use your understanding of the situation and the diagram to determine how it could be that five of the slots contain Gs. There is no room for more than two on the north side, so the remaining three Gs would need to go in 2, 6, and 10. Would that have any further effects—would it cause a chain reaction? It would since there would be only one slot remaining for the Y on the south side, and that is 8. So you determine that five Gs would come out like this:

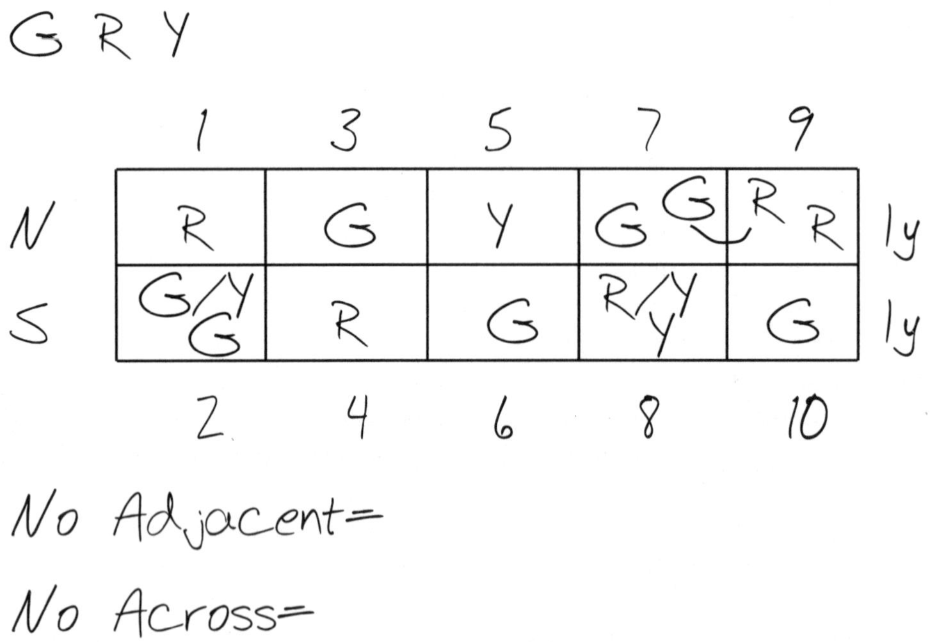

And now the question is for something that "must be true." Look at what you have determined and look at the choices. The right answer is choice (E). In fact, when you have done the analysis, the question turns out to be fairly simple, since all of the other choices are things that must be false! This question is testing just how thoroughly you understand the situation. Will you remember and implement the Y rule when you have found a way to get five Gs consistent with the rules?

The final question about the situation alters a rule, as final questions sometimes do:

> 23. Suppose that yellow lights decorate exactly two stores, not just one, on the south side of the street and decorate exactly one store on the north side. If all of the other conditions remain the same, then which one of the following statements must be true?
>
> (A) Green lights decorate store 1.
> (B) Red lights decorate store 7.
> (C) Red lights decorate store 10.
> (D) Yellow lights decorate store 2.
> (E) Yellow lights decorate store 8.

The change is a small one: add a second Y to the stores on the south side. How could that be done? The two Ys must be in some combination of 2, 8 and 10. But since 8 and 10 are adjacent, they cannot both have Ys. So, the other one would have to be in slot 2. Pretty easy. The answer is choice (D). Again, when the final question in a situation alters the rules, it often turns out to be a fairly simple rule application question.

What Was the Key?

As frequently happens, answering the actual questions about the situation was not very difficult. But that was because the situation was spelled out carefully and the deductions that were possible were made, not only deductions for what had to be true, but for what was somewhat constrained. So understanding the situation required not only knowing that 3 contained a G and 1 contained an R, but also that each of 7, 9, 2, and 8 had exactly 2 possibilities. Working those out prepared the way for chain reactions that came with new information. So with placement situations, narrow down the possibilities for particular slots, even for slots you cannot fill with a single certain item.

Focus on

Placement Situations

Chain reactions.

Think about: Work out possibilities for particular slots as thoroughly as you can to be ready for chain reactions with additional information.

DISTINGUISHING SITUATION TYPES

Having worked with a situation of each of the three major types, look again at what those types are and what makes them different from one another. The differences are important not in and of themselves (no LSAT question asks what type of situation it presents!), but because recognizing the type of situation makes it easier to understand and lets you work with it more efficiently. Consider:

Hayden's Media Week:

Movies:

During a particular week Hayden sees five **movies**, P, Q, R, S, and T, and sees exactly one of them on each day from Monday through Friday. Hayden sees T sometime before seeing Q and sometime after seeing S. Hayden sees R earlier in the week than Q. Hayden sees P sometime after having seen T.

Books:

During a particular week Hayden reads five **books**, F, G, H, I, and J, and reads exactly 1 of them on each day from Monday through Friday. Hayden reads G on the day immediately before the day on which Hayden reads H. Hayden reads F on either Tuesday or Thursday. Hayden does not read I and G on successive days. Hayden does not read J on Wednesday.

Songs:

During a particular week Hayden adds five **songs**, K, L, M, N, and O to an MP3 player. Each song is added on either Monday or Friday and no other songs are added during the week. Hayden adds L on Monday and Hayden adds M on Monday. If N is added on Friday then O is not added on Friday. K and M are not added on the same day.

Suppose your task is to describe the possibilities for Hayden's media experiences on Friday. You need to determine the movie Hayden might see, the book Hayden reads, and the songs Hayden adds to the MP3 player. To do each of those things you would need to perform a different operation:

To learn which movie Hayden might see on Friday, you would take the conditions given and figure out the relative order in which Hayden sees the movies. After having determined that order, you would be able to conclude what movies are possible for Friday.

To learn which book Hayden might read on Friday, you would take the conditions given and figure out what are the possible assignments of books to days.

To learn which songs Hayden might add on Friday, you would take the conditions presented and see how the conditional relationships might work together to determine what collection of things might be possible for Friday. The order in which the songs are added on Friday (or Monday) does not matter. What does matter is which songs can be added on the same day as on another. How can these things be collected together?

So to learn about the movies, you need to establish the relative order in which the movies are seen. To learn about the books, you need to assign particular books to particular days. To learn about the songs, you need to collect groups of songs together to assign them to one of the two days. The first is an ordering situation, the second is a placement situation, and the third is a grouping situation. You know the differences in the situations from the differences in the rules, which gives you various sorts of information and so requires you to do different things to learn what more you can about each situation.

And that is the point. Identification of type of situation is useful for appreciating what you know and how to go about learning more. Once you see conditions like those on the movies, you know to look at the relative order of the items. When you see conditions like the ones on the books, however, you concern yourself more with the one-to-one relationship of days and books. And when you see conditions like the ones with the songs, you want to see how things can be collected together without worrying about any kind of order within the groups.

Analytical reasoning situations will not always be of discrete and clear types. Often a situation will have elements of two types, and as you work it you will have to see which kind of element predominates. Sometimes you will set up a situation as a particular type and will end up working it as another type, realizing that the other approach yields more conclusions. That's fine. The goal is not to identify the type correctly, but identifying the type is a means to the goal of understanding what you know and don't know about the situation.

(Incidentally, on Friday, Hayden sees P or Q; reads H, I, or J; and adds either K or M and up to two other songs to the MP3 player.)

Focus on

Analytical Reasoning Situation Types

Identify the type for efficiency in analyzing the situation.

Think about: What the rules make you do to learn more about the situation.

Look at all of this by working the remaining situation in the analytical reasoning section from Proto:

Here's what we know about the situation:

Questions 13–18

From among ten stones, a jeweler will select six, one for each of six rings. Of the stones, three—F, G, and H—are rubies; three—J, K, and M—are sapphires; and four—W, X, Y, and Z—are topazes. The selection of stones must meet the following restrictions:

At least two of the topazes are selected.
If exactly two of the sapphires are selected, exactly one of the rubies is selected.
If W is selected, neither H nor Z is selected.
If M is selected, W is also selected.

There are ten stones from three categories. A jeweler selects six of the stones in order to make six different rings.

(1) TYPE

What will we learn about the six selected stones based on the conditions (the things that we know)?

- Is it important or possible to determine the order in which the jeweler selects the stones? There is nothing about that point.
- Is it important or possible to place particular stones in particular rings (for example, "ring three has either a topaz or H")? The rules do not give information about the stones relative to the numbers of the rings, so such numbers, if they exist, do not appear to be important.
- Is it about simply identifying what the six stones are? That is what the conditions deal with. They are rules about collecting together a group of six. The order in which they are selected is irrelevant, and there is no attempt to place particular stones in individual rings. There is a collection of six, and within the six no particular order or particular placements. So understanding the situation means making a collection. This is a **grouping** situation.

(2) DIAGRAM

Designing and drawing the diagram both reflects and clarifies the type.

If this were an ordering situation, like the problem of Hayden's movies, a diagram that focuses on order would help:

In clarifying an ordering situation a diagram would show the beginning and end of the order. But here the poles of "first" and "last" would be of no use since there are no rules that establish the relative order in which the stones are selected.

And if it were a placement situation where the individual stones were to be matched with individual rings, like the situation with Hayden's books, a useful diagram would separate out those slots into which the stones are to be placed:

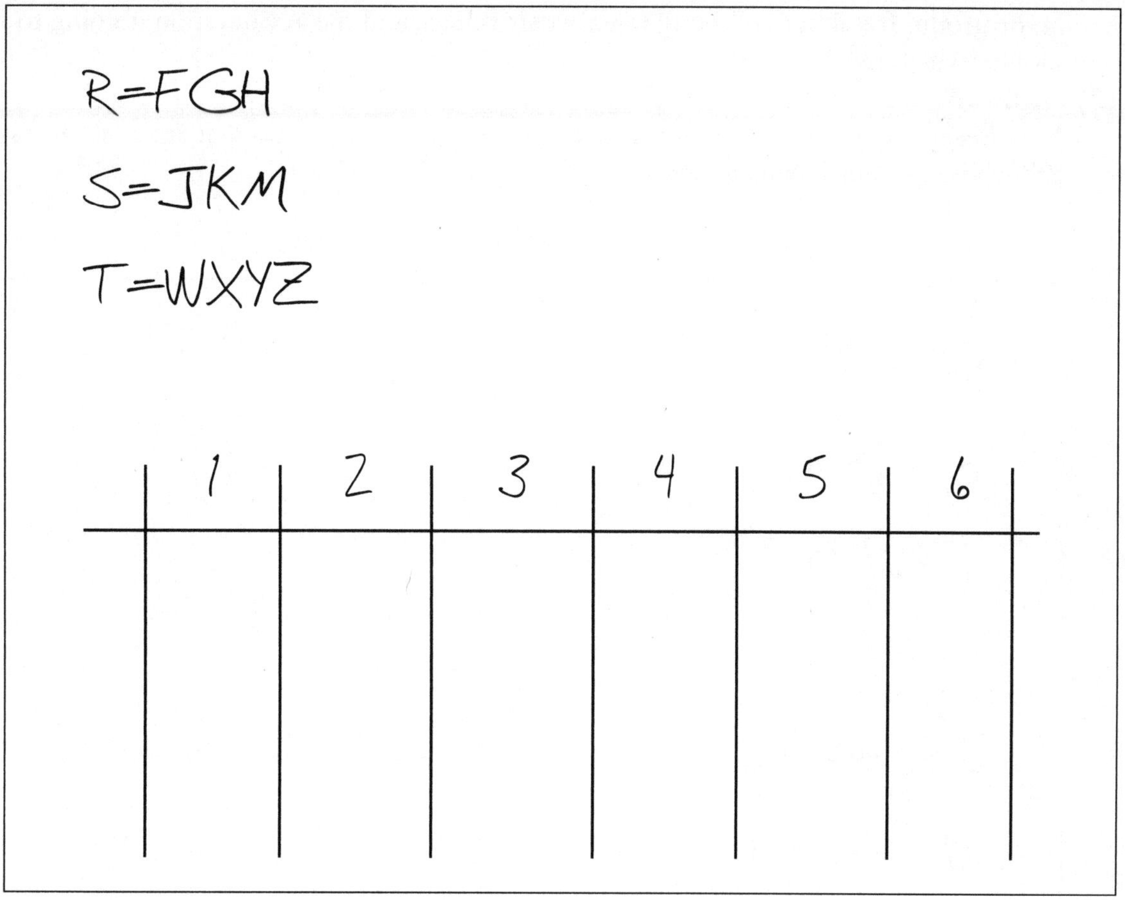

But reviewing the rules shows that this would not be helpful for this situation. There is no identification of particular rings, and an attempt to make one would be a frustrating failure. It is not what the situation is about, and far from clarifying that situation, the matrix would just get in the way.

So try drawing it simply to clarify a selection of things in a group.

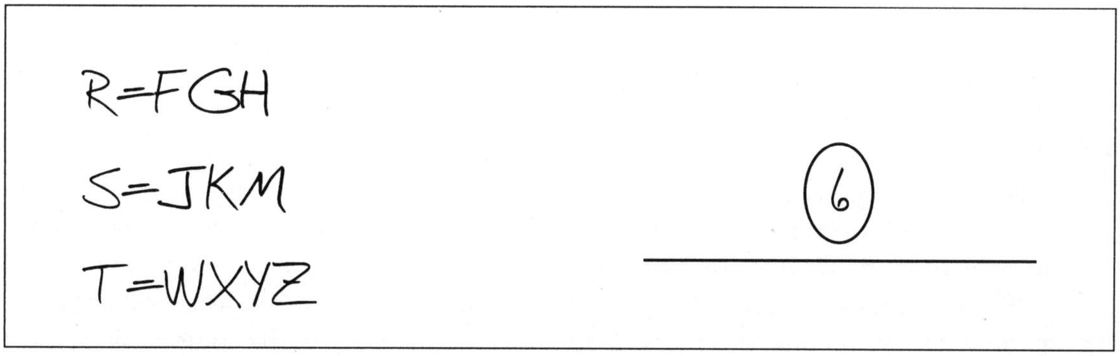

That's it! The situation is about selecting six of the ten items, and within a group of six no importance is attached to the order in which they are selected or to any particular spot in the group. It's about collecting together six things, and the key question is going to be simply "which six?"

(3) SIMPLIFY

Next clarify the meaning of each rule and restate it in clear symbols that are easily accessible and whose meaning is unambiguous:

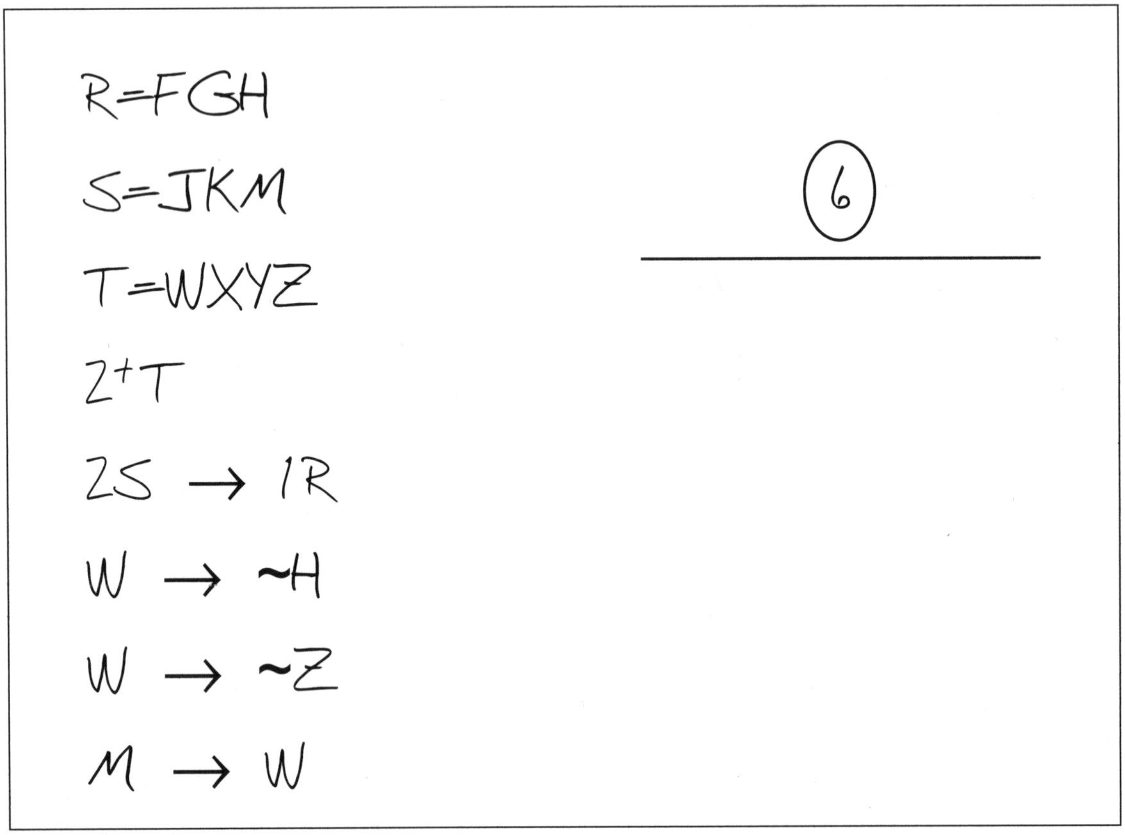

Be careful to put the conditional statements correctly. And with a rule like "if W is selected, neither H nor Z is selected," it is a good idea to separate out the items and clarify and simplify the statement by stating it as two rules.

(4) DEDUCTIONS

Now the analysis. Take the things that you know, find the statements that deal with the same item and where those are related in a logically appropriate way, draw conclusions, or infer the other things that you know.

With conditional statements a good place to start is by clarifying what you know by restating the conditional statements in their alternative form, in the contrapositive form.

Recall that the method to use to do this involves two steps:

(1) Flip the terms in the conditional statement.
(2) Negate them both.

2S → 1R	~1R → ~2S
W → ~H	H → ~W
W → ~Z	Z → ~W
M → W	~W → ~M

This restatement makes it clear that what you know about W means that if H is selected or Z is selected then M cannot be included in the group.

Consider also the relationship between W and Z in the context of the rule that says there are at least two topazes in the group. The rule and its contrapositive make it clear that both W and Z cannot be included. And so, since at least two of W, X, Y, Z must be included, any acceptable outcome must include at least one of either X or Y.

Add all of this to the diagram:

R=FGH

S=JKM

T=WXYZ

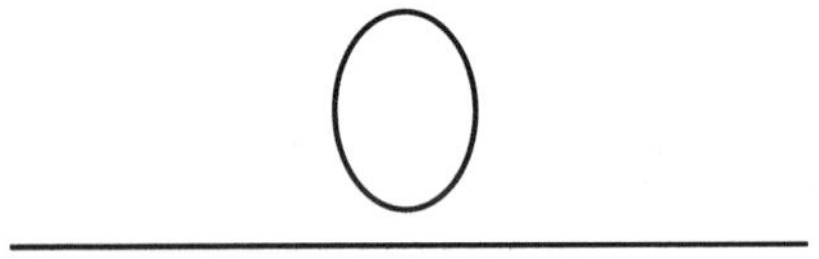

2^{+}T

2S → 1R ~1R → ~2S

W → ~H H → ~W

W → ~Z Z → ~W

M → W ~W → ~M

H → ~M

Z → ~M

NOT W+Z so X or Y or Both

(5) WALK AROUND IT

Take a moment to consider the situation. You don't know for certain even one of the six in the group, but there are many constraints that you have clarified that will affect the selection very much.

Focus on the topazes. Two must be included, and no more than three can be included as you have deduced from the relationship of W and Z. This means that either three or four of the others will be needed for the group. There is not much in the rules that affects the selection from sapphires and rubies, but the specific rule that says "if there are exactly two sapphires, then there must be exactly one ruby" will surely come into play somewhere. Note the word "exactly." It means that the rule does not apply in the case of three sapphires. Be alert for groups that use exactly two from J, K, and M.

Once you're comfortable with what you know and do not know about the situation, move on to the questions.

The first question is a typical **"acceptable outcome"** first question:

13. Which one of the following could be the selection of stones?

    (A) F, G, H, M, X, Y
    (B) F, G, J, K, M, W
    (C) F, G, J, K, W, X
    (D) G, H, J, X, Y, Z
    (E) G, H, K, W, X, Z

The correct answer will be the choice that violates none of the rules. Take each rule and look for answer choices that violate it. The first rule, that at least two topazes are selected, is violated by choice (B), and so choice (B) is eliminated from further consideration. Next look for a group that has exactly two sapphires but not exactly one ruby. Since choice (C) violates that rule, it is eliminated. The rule that when W is included neither H nor Z is included is violated by choice (E), leaving only two choices. And choice (A) violates the remaining rule by including M but not W. So choice (D) is the correct answer.

Go to the next question:

14. Which one of the following must be true?

    (A) G is selected.
    (B) J is selected.
    (C) X is selected.
    (D) Of at least one of the three types of stones, exactly one stone is selected.
    (E) Of at least one of the three types of stones, exactly three stones are selected.

It asks for something that **"must be true."** And since it adds nothing to the situation, it is asking for a deduction. So, first see if it can be answered with deductions you have already made. Is there an answer choice that says that either X or Y must be included? Reviewing the choices, you find none (choice (C) goes too far).

So, there is a deduction here that you have not made. Make it now **"The Hard Way"**: test each answer choice for whether it must be true. There is no reason to suppose that either G or J has to be selected, and so you can be pretty certain that the correct answer must be either choice (D) or choice (E).

So consider choice (D). Is it possible to make a group of six without including all three types of stones? On reflection, it seems so. Three topazes might be included, say X, Y, and Z, and with those three, all three rubies. In the alternative, if W, X, and Y are included, so might all three sapphires be included. So in fact there are two acceptable outcomes with only two of the types of stones.

So what of choice (E)? Here is the answer. Go back to the rule that when exactly two sapphires are included, then exactly one ruby must be included. That means that the distribution cannot be exactly two of each of the three types of stones. And that, in turn, means that there must be three of at least one sort of stone. Focus on the fact that you have made this deduction about the distribution. You have learned something new about the situation. It may be useful in other questions as well.

The next question adds information:

15. If Z is selected, which one of the following could be true?
    (A) All three of the sapphires are selected.
    (B) Both J and M are selected.
    (C) Both K and M are selected.
    (D) None of the rubies is selected.
    (E) None of the sapphires is selected.

The question asks for what **"could be true"** rather than for what "must be true," so it is likely that it will be necessary to test the answer choices until you find one that does not violate the rules. But first consider the implications of the additional condition that Z is part of the group. You have already made the deduction—or you have already learned from considering the consequences of the things that you know—that when Z is included M cannot be. So anything that would include M is not something that could be true. Apply that inference to the answer choices, and you find it very useful!

M is a sapphire, so the knowledge that M cannot be included with Z allows you to eliminate choice (A), choice (B), and choice (C) immediately. It also allows you to calculate that three sapphires cannot be included, and since at most three topazes might be included, there must be at least one ruby. So choice (D) could not be true either. Quickly, because you did the deduction and did the analysis correctly, you arrive at the correct conclusion that choice (E) is the one correct answer. This is a small example of the unsurprising general rule that a very good way to get more LSAT questions correct is to do analytical thinking well!

The next question also adds a premise, and then asks for something that must be true:

16. If exactly two rubies are selected, which one of the following must be true?
    (A) H is selected.
    (B) J is selected.
    (C) Z is selected.
    (D) Exactly one sapphire is selected.
    (E) Exactly two topazes are selected.

With this additional premise, what can you infer? Looking at the rules and the deductions, consider what the analysis you have already done means in the case of exactly two rubies. That means that the contrapositive of the rule that says when exactly two sapphires are chosen exactly one ruby must be chosen is in effect. For according to the information with this question, it is not the case that there is exactly one ruby. And if it is not the case that there is exactly one ruby, then it cannot be the case that there are exactly two sapphires.

Now, again, perform the analytical task considering the things that you know in combination. You know that there can be at most three topazes, and you know from the question that there are exactly two rubies. There cannot be two sapphires, you have deduced. So how many sapphires are there? In order to get to six stones there must be one sapphire. And so choice (D) is the correct answer.

Here is a case where, unlike with "could be true" questions, you do not need to test every possible answer choice. When your analysis tells you that something must be true, and that thing that must be true is in the answer choices, that is all you need. The analysis took a couple of steps, and so was difficult, but once it was accomplished it led directly to the answer. The difficulty in the question lies not in the answer choices but in the analysis that it is testing.

Still another "must be true" question follows:

17. Which one of the following must be true?

(A) The selection of stones includes at least one ruby.
(B) The selection of stones includes at most two rubies.
(C) The selection of stones includes either F or Z, or both.
(D) The selection of stones includes either X or Y, or both.
(E) The selection of stones includes either X or Z, or both.

This question adds no new information, so it is testing your understanding of what you know from the basic scenario. Review the things you deduced (including the contrapositives) to see if you have already learned what the question is testing:

~1R → ~2S

H → ~W

Z → ~W

~W → ~M

H → ~M

Z → ~M

NOT W+Z so X or Y or Both

When you look to see if one of these is in an answer choice, you find it! It is not luck, and neither is it effective treasure hunting (a skill which is valuable for reading comprehension tasks)—it is knowing what you're doing and doing it well. Choice (D) must be true.

The final question in this situation again adds information:

18. If J and M are the only sapphires selected, which one of the following could be true?

    (A) F and G are both selected.
    (B) F and X are both selected.
    (C) G and H are both selected.
    (D) G and K are both selected.
    (E) Y and Z are both selected.

Since the question asks for what "could be true," you will need to test the answer choices. But first do the additional analysis of the situation to see what the additional knowledge that J and M are the only sapphires enables you to know:

- First you know that exactly one ruby must be included.
- That means that exactly three topazes must be included.
- And the topazes cannot include Z and must include W.

- Since W is in the group, H cannot be included.
- So the group is made up of W, X, Y, M, J, and either F or G (but not both).

So it turns out this new knowledge means that you know almost everything about the situation. There's not a lot that "could be true"! Realizing that, you can decide which of the answer choices is correct fairly quickly. And it is choice (B). Even with "could be true" questions, then, analyzing the situation before going to the choices can make you much more efficient in finding the one correct answer.

What Was the Key?

Reflecting on the stones and rings situation, there were three things that were especially useful in working it efficiently. The first was recognizing it as a grouping game and not treating it as a placement game. The second was making the key deduction about the topazes that at least one of X and Y had to be included. The third was the deduction that questions led us to make the hard way about the basic distribution, that it could not be two stones of each of the three sorts. The realization that it had to be three and three, or three, two, and one was very useful. Learn from that to develop the habit of checking on the distribution from categories in similar situations in the future.

On a more general level, the questions seemed fairly easy in this situation, but only because careful analysis made us as clear as we could be about what we knew and didn't know about it. And that makes sense because the section is designed to reward sound analysis.

CHAPTER 4

APPLIED ANALYSIS: THE WRITING SAMPLE

At the end of the five, thirty-five minute multiple-choice sections on which your LSAT score is based, the LSAT presents you with one more thing to do before you finish the test. That is the writing sample. This is a sixth, thirty-five minute section, but it is not multiple-choice, has no correct answer, and means nothing whatever for the LSAT score. But although it is meaningless for the score, it might mean something for law school admission, because the writing sample—a simple photocopy of it—is sent to any law school to which you apply as part of your LSAT score report.

The writing sample is meant to provide an additional measure to law schools of your analytical writing ability. It is an example of your writing that is done under time pressure without the opportunity for extensive editing. It also presents an example of analysis, or of taking a difficult situation, and embracing and explaining its difficulty.

The sixth section gives a single topic for you to write on. It describes a situation with a choice. The choice will be guided by two different principles or goals. And the choice will be between two alternatives, each of which meets the two goals to some degree, but neither of which stands out clearly as one that meets those goals while the other one does not. The choice will be between two very close alternatives, and close precisely because each meets the goals imperfectly or incompletely.

So the first thing to realize when working with the writing sample is that there is no right answer or wrong answer. It is like a combination of a discrepancy question and a principle question from a logical reasoning section. Two things are true at the same time, and you need to choose between them based on certain goals or beliefs. It is about embracing the whole situation and making a recommendation based on what the situation actually is.

There is not a lot that can be written by hand about a complex situation in thirty-five minutes, especially when it is wholly new to you and you are cautioned to spend some time thinking about it before you write. The exam will give you about one and three-quarter pages to write your essay in longhand. That will amount to somewhere between 300 and 400 words, or about the equivalent of a single double-spaced page written on computer. It is not much, and it is probably helpful for you to approach the assignment accordingly.

The instructions will tell you to present a case for one of the two alternatives. So do that. It does not matter which, for each of the alternatives will have comparative advantages and disadvantages over the other. Choose one. Announce the choice in an introduction. Explain the difficulty involved in (a) the principles or goals that are guiding the choice and (b) the pluses and minuses of the alternatives. In doing this, make no grammatical mistakes.

Put another way, in writing a brief essay for the writing sample:

(1) Do not fail to follow directions.
(2) Do not oversimplify the situation by denying one of the goals or the advantages of one of the alternatives.
(3) Do not make egregious errors in grammar or spelling.

Here is the writing prompt from the test we have worked with throughout and three essays written in response. The first two of the essays (labeled M and N) are fine writing samples. The third (labeled L) is not as good.

LSAT WRITING SAMPLE TOPIC

The mayor of Highport, a small town on the North American east coast, must decide between two development proposals, each of which precludes the successful completion of the other. The proposed projects are roughly equivalent in cost. Write an argument in support of adopting one of the proposals, with the following criteria in mind:

- New projects undertaken by the town should enhance the flow of money to the area.
- The mayor wants to maintain Highport's desirability as a tourist destination.

The first proposal is to build a light rail system connecting Highport to several nearby urban centers. Although Highport is near several major metropolitan areas, it has no public transportation system linking it to these cities, even though Highport has a large population of residents who work in the nearby cities. Highport's present infrastructure consists of old, narrow roads and while traffic congestion is usually noticeable, it is particularly bad at rush hour. In addition to providing an additional incentive for tourists to travel to Highport, having a light rail system in place would help Highport increase its tax base by attracting new residents to the town who might otherwise choose to live in urban locations more convenient to their workplaces.

The second proposal is to restore and preserve a historic military fortress that lies directly in the path of the planned light rail system. Restoration experts agree that buildings on the historic site cannot be moved and that in order to preserve the fortress the light rail project must be abandoned. Highport has a rich history of both local and national importance, and over the past decade has been successfully cultivating its attractiveness as a tourist destination, to such an extent that tourism is now Highport's largest industry. Because the military fortress is a unique piece of national history, completion of this project will ensure that Highport receives new government grants for the maintenance and preservation of national historic sites.

Essay M (an essay that is OK):

The mayor of Highport is faced with supporting either a proposal to build a light rail system for the city or a proposal to restore the city's historic military fortress. Since it is not possible to undertake both projects, the mayor should choose to support building a light-rail system. In choosing between the proposals the mayor has two primary goals in mind: one is to enhance the flow of money to the area, and the other is to maintain high points desirability as a tourist attraction. Both goals can be achieved to some degree with either proposal, but on balance the better approach is to build a light rail system.

The light rail system will do much to remedy Highport's lack of public transportation, a problem which it is inconvenient up to city residents, and that serves to prevent residential growth in the community. The difficulty that area residents have in traveling to nearby communities for work and other purposes makes people in the area less likely than they would otherwise be choose to live in Highport. But if more of the employed people of the area chose to reside in Highport, the effect would be to increase the tax base and, therefore, to enhance the flow of money into the community.

To be sure, building a light rail system would preclude the restoration of the city's historic military fortress, since the light rail system would have to go up and directly through the fortress. But that sacrifice of a tourist attraction would not necessarily mean a net loss in tourist activity or revenue. Tourism might be enhanced by the easier access to Highport's existing tourist attractions that a light rail system would grant. Moreover, while choosing not to restore the fortress would mean not receiving a government grant that would help that project, that short-term loss in revenue would be overbalanced by the longer-term permanent development of tax base and the revenue that would come for the city both from taxes and from the increased traffic.

In sum, then, while both proposals presented for the mayor's consideration have merit, and both would serve to address goals that the mayor has identified as important, building a light rail system seems to be the project that will more certainly and dependably satisfy both of those goals in the long run.

Regarding the essay above, there are a few errors: (1) Highport should be capitalized. (2) You also need an apostrophe when you say "Highport's desirability" as that is a possessive. (3) Sentence that says "a problem which it is inconvenient up to city residents…" should read "a problem which is inconvenient for city residents…."

Essay N (another essay that is OK):

There are two worthy proposals that have been recommended to the mayor for enhancing the flow of money into Highport and maintaining the city's desirability as a center for tourism. Of the two, however, the proposal to renovate the city's historic military fortress is the better one.

The competing proposal is to build a light rail system that would ease transportation concerns for city residents and, in fact, encourage population growth in Highport. These advantages are real in that residents do find themselves facing congestion problems, particularly at rush hour, and those problems discourage others from moving into the community. In the long run, however, encouraging more people to move into the community, while it would build the tax base, might just bring back the very congestion problems that the light rail system would help to alleviate. More to the point, however, is the fact that the light rail system cannot be built without going through the historic military fortress. Gaining the advantage of the rail system, then, would mean incurring the permanent disadvantage of losing that fortress.

The better proposal forgoes the real advantages of the light rail system for the comparatively greater advantages that could come from restoring the fortress. This restoration will further develop the city's thriving tourist industry while not running the risk of creating more congestion among residents. More tourists will spend more money, thus enhancing the flow of money into the city without having to build the city's own residential tax base. In fact, the government grant that the city would be able to attract to assist with this restoration would itself directly add to the community's funding.

Considering the fact that these proposals are mutually exclusive, perhaps the decisive consideration is this: if the historic military fortress is destroyed to build a light rail system that fortress cannot be re-created. But if the restoration of the fortress should prove, unexpectedly, ineffective in meeting the goals of the community, the possibility of building a light rail system will remain. And so, both because of its inherent attractiveness and because it maintains flexibility for the community, the mayor should choose the proposal to renovate the military fortress over the proposal to build a light rail system.

Essay L (an essay that is *not* OK):

The mayor of Highport should definitely choose to preserve and restore the historic military fortress and should reject the proposal to build a light train system. Building the light train system would require building in the path of the historic fortress, and that is simply unacceptable and wrong and should be rejected. You can't destroy history.

The mayor needs to think about what is good for the community as a whole. Money is not nearly as important as preservation and not destroying history. And if people don't want toac get stuck in traffic they can go at some other time. But the idea that money is as important as history is not right and needs to be rejected. If the mayor thinks otherwise then they just need to remove that mayor, because she must be motivated by private business interests.

Some people complain about traffic, but they don't know how good they have it. Besides, its not about traffic but about maintaining historic things for the future, for their children. Every citizen in Highport needs to be willing to do their part to pay taxes in the city without trying to make other people live there to pay their taxes for them. Each of Highport's people has the onerous responsibility to create posterity for the future and not destroy it for trains.

So only one proposal is worthwhile, although it can make it seem like the military is good. But destroying history for money could never be worthwhile no matter what private gain some politician might have from doing it. After all, you can't by happiness.

Avoid writing an essay that makes a critical grammar mistake or that does not follow directions, as Essay L does. Do not risk offsetting all your hard work on your analytical skills that will show on the score you earn from the multiple-choice sections with a bad writing sample. But also remember that a good writing sample will not compensate for a lower score on the multiple-choice sections. That is what matters. So now that you are acquainted with what the writing section will ask you to do, spend your time and well-focused efforts developing the analytical skills that you use for the rest of the test.

LSAT

LAW SCHOOL ADMISSION TEST

PRACTICE TEST 1

PRACTICE TEST 1

SECTION 1

Time—35 minutes
25 questions

Directions: *The questions in this section are based on the reasoning contained in brief statements or passages. For some questions, more than one of the choices could conceivably answer the question. However, you are to choose the* ***best*** *answer; that is, the response that most accurately and completely answers the question. You should not make assumptions that are by commonsense standards implausible, superfluous, or incompatible with the passage. After you have chosen the best answer, blacken the corresponding space on your answer sheet.*

1. All the teachers at Weston Academy will leave their mark on the future through influencing their students. Some of those teachers are true scientists, who bring the results of their research into the classroom. Others are artists, who inculcate in their students a love of beauty. Still others are intolerable egotists, who teach only to hear themselves talk, rather than to impart knowledge.

   If the statements above are true, which one of the following must also be true?

   (A) All true scientists will leave their mark on the future.

   (B) Everyone at Weston Academy who will leave a mark on the future is a teacher.

   (C) Some egotists at Weston Academy will leave a beneficial mark on the future.

   (D) The future will be influenced by some true scientists who are egotists.

   (E) Some teachers at Weston Academy influence students without seeking to do so.

2. The sheriff's crime prevention program uses the questionable method of inviting reformed criminals who have completed prison terms into area schools to warn students about the consequences of illegal behavior. What the students quickly realize is that the speaker has become a celebrity precisely because of those actions which he is warning them against. A better method of crime prevention would be to have citizens who have consistently avoided vice speak in the schools about the rewards of a law-abiding life. These positive role models would convince more students to avoid illegal activities.

   Which one of the following, if true, most seriously weakens the argument?

   (A) Many students identify with upstanding citizens more than with law breakers.

   (B) Students are likely to fear punishment more than to desire celebrity.

   (C) Many who have consistently avoided vice are often too busy to take time to speak in schools.

   (D) Students are unlikely to give credence to people who got caught trying to get ahead the easy way.

   (E) The sheriff's department has been sponsoring these events for years, and they have always been well received by educators.

3. The road crew includes both men and boys. All men are hateful and all boys are insubordinate. Every insubordinate person is hateful, so every person on the crew is hateful.

   Which of the following, if assumed, makes the conclusion in the argument above follow from the other statements?

   (A) Some hateful people are not insubordinate.

(B) Every hateful person is insubordinate.

(C) No member of the road crew is insubordinate and not hateful.

(D) Some members of the road crew are hateful.

(E) Anyone on the road crew who is not a boy is a man.

4. The support program for unwed mothers is currently funded through charitable donations and annual grants from the city. Private donations account for 60% of the program's budget, with the grants providing the other 40%. However, the city is experiencing its third year of budget deficits, so city grants for the program are sure to dry up. That means that the program for unwed mothers will have to reduce its operations substantially in the near future.

Which one of the following is an assumption required by the argument?

(A) The program can provide the same level of support on much less money.

(B) Charitable contributions will not increase enough to compensate for decreases in city grants.

(C) The program for unwed mothers will operate at a deficit until the city can resume its contribution.

(D) Private contributions will decrease when city grants decrease.

(E) Unwed mothers need less support now than they did in the past three years.

5. Modern life, while it has many advantages over the past, has its own set of difficulties. Many Americans claim to feel alienated from others and from the community at large. Most of these are part of a society in which people are very mobile, moving from one area to another with great frequency. Many also live in urban areas, where a person does not even know his or her neighbors. In times past most people lived their complete lives in small communities, where one person knew the other and knew about the other's family and history. Now, that is impossible. Everything is so fast paced now that most of us are doomed to remain strangers to those around us. So those feelings of alienation could be resolved only by going back to live in an earlier time.

Which of the following is an error in reasoning the passage commits in reaching its conclusion?

(A) It assumes without statistical data that earlier eras were not mobile.

(B) It compares two things that are so fundamentally different as not to be analogous.

(C) It equivocates on the meaning of a key term.

(D) It concludes without additional evidence that because two things have happened at the same time, one is the cause of the other.

(E) It generalizes about two eras without considering the possibility that other eras might offer instructive comparison.

6. The rate of inflation has risen with increased rapidity in the last six years. During the same period, the cost of labor has fallen slightly, and worker productivity has remained constant. The cause of the increase in inflation must, therefore, be the abrupt rise in the cost of oil.

Which of the following statements, if true, most strengthens the conclusion?

(A) Oil prices dropped 50% in the three-year period that ended six years ago.

(B) During the last fifty years, high inflation has tended to make oil prices increase.

(C) The price of domestic oil was regulated by the government during the last six years.

(D) During the last fifty years, when oil prices have increased for political or other noneconomic reasons, a result has been inflation.

(E) The price of oil began to rise in the last six years only as the prices of other goods and services have risen with inflation.

7. During the 1960s and 1970s in the United States, there was much reaction against "hippies," particularly men with long hair. During the same period, the voting age was being lowered in many states. In one state these two trends came together in a law that lowered the voting age to 19 for all except men with long hair. "They just don't look like citizens," a legislator explained with regard to voting in favor of the law.

Which of the following principles would most justify the legislator's reasoning?

(A) All people who reside in the community who are over 18 years old are entitled to vote.

(B) If someone in the community is entitled to vote, that someone has a responsibility to act as an appropriate role model for the young.

(C) Someone whose appearance suggests that the person does not conform to the community's values should not have a vote in determining who governs the community.

(D) Those who look like citizens in the community and who are of an appropriate minimum age should have a legal right to vote.

(E) Some people, despite their age and residence in the community, should not be trusted with the right to vote.

8. Getting good nutrition is a complex matter. You have to consider getting the right amount of a number of vitamins and minerals, the right balance of fats of different kinds, of proteins of different kinds, the right number of calories from the right sources, and much more. Yet a diet with proper nutrition is essential to being healthy and feeling good. Fortunately, PerFooD Plus, the perfect food and then some, is now available. Three designated servings a day guarantee a nutritionally balanced diet in every respect. So start on PerFooD Plus today and you will be healthy!

The reasoning in the argument is vulnerable to criticism on which of the following grounds?

(A) It bases its information on what constitutes good nutrition on the judgment of only a few experts.

(B) It fails to consider whether a well-planned diet of ordinary food costs less than PerFooD Plus, even taking planning time into account.

(C) It presupposes that a well-planned diet of ordinary food does not taste better than PerFooD Plus.

(D) It assumes that because being healthy and feeling good often happen simultaneously, being healthy causes one to feel good.

(E) It confuses something that is required for good health with something that is enough to create good health.

9. A number of apes of various species have been said to have learned to carry on at least simple conversations in a human language, American Sign Language. However, many of these claims turn out to be based on anecdotal evidence, rather than rigorous testing. What tests were conducted allowed the testers to provide (probably unconscious) cues to guide the apes' behavior to resemble conversation.

Which of the following is most strongly supported by the information in the passage?

(A) No ape has ever learned a human language.

(B) No ape has ever learned American Sign Language.

(C) No ape tested had learned American Sign Language.

(D) No ape has been shown to have learned American Sign Language.

(E) No ape could be shown conclusively to have learned American Sign Language.

10. Justin and Armand are cutting cards. The suits have been ordered as well as the cards within the suit, so each cut produces a winner and a loser and there can be no ties. Justin has won the first three cuts. Armand

decides to raise his bet considerably on the next cut, believing that it is very unlikely that Justin could win four cuts in a row.

Armand's reasoning is flawed in that Armand supposes that

(A) a random event that has turned out one way several times in succession is likely to turn out the same way the next time.

(B) something that is true of a group is likely to be true of each part of that group.

(C) a random event that turns out one of two possible ways several times in succession has a less-than-random likelihood of turning out the same way again.

(D) when a random event turns out the same way several times in succession it is likely to have been manipulated by a human being so that it is not actually random.

(E) when two things happen regularly together it is the case that one of those things is the cause of the other.

11. Environmentalist: Incineration is not a useful approach to addressing garbage problems. Incineration doesn't make garbage disappear, but converts it into poisonous gases and residue ash full of toxic heavy metals. As for recovering energy from burning garbage, so far, it's a wash. Operational problems have prevented many plants from processing their garbage at their designed capacity. The Office of Technology Assessment, Congress's analytical arm, estimates that trash-to-energy facilities generate only about 0.2% of the nation's total energy production.

Which of the following, if true, would most weaken the environmentalist's arguments?

(A) More plants than previously thought are unable to process garbage at their designed capacity.

(B) Trash-to-energy facilities represent less than 0.2% of the nation's total energy production capacity.

(C) The poisonous gases and residue ash from incinerated garbage eventually disappear.

(D) The Office of Technology Assessment usually makes accurate estimations.

(E) Some incineration plants have no operational problems.

12. Many politicians, gerontologists, and editorial writers deplore the trend toward early retirement. This trend, which began after World War II and accelerated in the 1960s and 1970s, has led to a dramatic decline in work effort and earnings among the elderly. Opponents of earlier retirement believe that keeping people in the work force longer will raise the nation's output, reduce the costs of Social Security, and improve the well-being of older Americans. In contrast, the groups most directly affected by retirement patterns—employers, labor unions, and especially older workers themselves—are not interested in reversing recent retirement trends.

Which of the following is an assumption required by the argument of the opponents of early retirement?

(A) Not all gerontologists oppose earlier retirement.

(B) People who retire early are less productive than others during their last decade of work.

(C) Labor union bosses cannot be trusted because of conflicts of interest.

(D) The Social Security system faces a crisis if trends toward early retirement are not reversed.

(E) Some older workers are wrong about what conduces to their own well-being.

13. The dream of one day becoming a professional athlete—one held widely by the boys growing up in this country—is rarely realized. The sports world is extremely hierarchical. The pyramid of sports careers narrows very rapidly as one climbs from high school, to college, to professional levels of competition. In fact, the chances of attaining professional status in sports are approximately

4/100,000 for a white man, 2/100,000 for a black man, and 3/1,000,000 for a Hispanic man in the United States. So our youth would be better off if they abandoned the dreams of athletic success and embraced other, more realistic goals.

Which of the following, if true, does the most to weaken the argument?

(A) Among professional athletes, only the few best in any sport are universally seen as successful.

(B) The effort to become a professional athlete can distract students at the high school and college levels from their academic work, thus making them less accomplished as students.

(C) Young people focused on the dream of athletic success can develop habits of dedication and hard work that serve them well in nonathletic endeavors.

(D) It is not possible to tell reliably before children are in their teen years who is likely to be more successful as an athlete in college and in the pro ranks.

(E) Many who are not successful athletes at the pro level or in major colleges might be successful athletes at smaller colleges.

14. Shannon: I used the money as a down payment on my metallic blue sports car because it was, to me, an unexpected windfall. My new accountant prepared my taxes, then concluded that my tax bill was far lower than I had anticipated and lower than it had been with similar levels of income in recent years. I'm not afraid that my tax liability will turn out to be higher because this accountant works for the most reliable accounting firm in the city. They are known for their precision and accuracy, and that is why I went to them. So, confident that the money was mine, I just spent it.

Which of the following is a flaw in Shannon's reasoning?

(A) It fails to take into account that some accountants at other firms would reach different conclusions about Shannon's tax liability.

(B) It assumes without warrant that the money that comes in any unexpected windfall ought to be spent.

(C) It takes it for granted that reliable and accurate results by accountants are caused by some expertise on the accountants' part.

(D) It assumes that the qualities that belong to an accounting firm as a whole belong also to each accountant employed by that firm.

(E) It fails to appreciate that it is possible for some accounting professional to be both reliable and inaccurate.

15. It has been commonly believed that most people's work careers follow the temporal sequence of occupational choice, preparation and training, and actually working in the occupation until retirement. However, studies reveal that most individuals do not show a strong commitment to a particular occupation during their work careers. Rather, occupational mobility is far more characteristic of most work lives than occupational stability. So it must be the case that people do not commonly make occupational choices that determine their work patterns.

The reasoning in the passage is vulnerable to criticism because it overlooks the possibility that

(A) people make conscious occupational choices after having worked in several occupations.

(B) mobility is made easy by advances in transportation over the past century.

(C) individuals respond to opportunities that develop within their occupations during the course of their careers, making them upwardly mobile.

(D) many people who make strong commitments to a particular occupation nonetheless received poor training.

(E) during the period of time of an average work life there are new occupations created.

16. After years of neglect, the poor child has come to the forefront of research in education. Studies focusing on the poor child are abundant and a thorough review of the literature would be exhausting, as well as futile. It would be futile because the literature on the poor child tends to lack imagination and focuses on a great many difficulties and issues, without ever zeroing in on the problem. The literature tends to present a hit-and-run approach to the learning needs of the poor. If we really want to address those needs, then, we must reject as faulty these studies with their multiple causes and identify and address the one true problem that poor children face in education.

The argument is flawed because it

(A) fails to take into account that some studies might be more reliable than others.

(B) offers no objective definition of the "poor child."

(C) rejects the results of studies because they do not support a conclusion which itself is assumed without evidence.

(D) accepts uncritically the results of studies with differing conclusions.

(E) takes it for granted that an issue presents a real problem only because it is taken in the popular press to do so.

17. In an analysis of the extensive poverty in the Third World, the World Bank concluded that half of the people living in poverty in the Third World are in South Asia. The other half lives in East and Southeast Asia, sub-Saharan Africa, Latin America, North Africa, and the Middle East. Roughly 80% of these poor live in the countryside, mostly as small farmers and landless laborers. Poverty is thus an essentially rural phenomenon.

Which of the following is a flaw in reasoning in the passage?

(A) Many people in South Asia whom the study classifies as being in poverty do not see themselves as being poor.

(B) A ratio of rural to urban poor that shows more rural poor is nonetheless consistent with there being a large number of urban poor.

(C) Most of the rural poverty in the world occurs in the Third World, so that the problem of rural poverty is not as great worldwide as the study might seem to suggest.

(D) Economic activities of people in Latin America are very different in kind from economic activities of people in sub-Saharan Africa.

(E) Many of the rural poor are unlikely to welcome assistance from people elsewhere in the world.

18. Sun recalls his impressions about the source of order, peace, and plenty in the West by saying "the old Honolulu post office (which delivered daily mail without fail, to his surprise) stands out in my mind very clearly." Everywhere in Hawaii he saw evidence of respect for laws which led him to believe that comfort, abundance, and progress resulted from the orderly maintenance of these laws. Admiring Americans with their "land of the free and home of the brave," he concluded that it was the American sort of stable and settled law that China wanted in order to produce its own peace and plenty.

Which statement, if true, would most weaken Sun's argument?

(A) The old Honolulu post office no longer exists.

(B) It is among the most difficult things to replace one set of laws with another.

(C) The peace and prosperity characteristic of American society are responsible for producing and maintaining stable and orderly law.

(D) It is possible to respect the law, even if the law is not maintained in an orderly fashion and does not result in abundance.

(E) Comfort, abundance, and progress result from orderly maintenance of laws in Western liberal democracies other than the American one.

19. Garage owner: I would like to raise the price of a Handy Dandy Automobile Tune-Up by 20%. I need more income, and prices have not increased at my shop in five years.

Paid consultant: My advice is to avoid raising prices. Your business has grown over those years because of your reputation for good service at a fair price. A price increase would drive some of your customers away even though it might increase your revenue during the current fiscal year.

Which of the following principles, if valid, most supports the consultant's recommendation?

(A) Increases to the price of automotive services should reflect price increases in parts used in those services.

(B) The long-term success of a service business is related above all to its having a large customer base.

(C) Many automobiles can run effectively with fewer tune-ups than their manufacturers suggest.

(D) Most auto repair prices tend to be perceived by consumers as too high.

(E) A service business that loses customers because of price can gain other customers if its reputation is for giving good service.

20. If the country of Roccolo does not agree to lower its trade barriers, we will run the worst trade deficit since World War II, domestic jobs will be lost, we will experience a worldwide economic slowdown with its attendant instability, and our European allies will stop looking to us for economic leadership. In view of these facts, we reluctantly conclude that if Roccolo does not lower its trade barriers on its own, we must use force to make it do so.

Which of the following principles supports the decision to use force as in the passage above?

(A) It is the responsibility of the government of our country to concern itself with the prosperity of the people in our country above the prosperity of people in other countries.

(B) It benefits the people in our country and our European allies for our country to assume the role of economic leader.

(C) Individual countries must have regard for the welfare of people in other countries in making their economic decisions.

(D) Economic issues must be seen as of secondary importance to military issues.

(E) The danger of instability from a worldwide economic slowdown is to be avoided if at all possible.

21. There should be no speed limits on freeways, just as in some European countries. People should be allowed to drive as fast as they wish on these modern, smoothly surfaced thoroughfares. Speed limits have the effect of telling drivers, "You are not a good judge of your own driving skills, or of how quickly you need to get somewhere." To be sure, the right of one person to drive at excessive speeds may infringe on the rights of others to be safe on the public highways, but we must try to balance these rights to afford maximum protection to each. For example, under no condition should someone be allowed to drive faster than 55 miles per hour in or near any city, even on a freeway.

The reasoning in the above passage is flawed because it

(A) contains an inconsistency about whether there should be speed limits on freeways.

(B) does not establish that citizens have a right to be safe on the public highways.

(C) takes it for granted that one right takes precedence over another right.

(D) fails to consider elements other than safety that might support speed limits.

(E) argues by analogy using cases which are more dissimilar than similar.

22. Changing your car's oil regularly, no matter what type of motor oil you use, will reduce engine wear. Scientists have concluded that regular oil changes reduce engine wear by purging the engine of dust and tiny metal fragments. So forget about buying oil with special lubricating additives: change your oil regularly and say good-bye to premature engine wear.

    Which of the following, if true, most weakens the argument's conclusion?

    (A) Some special lubricating additives have been shown to reduce engine wear when the oil is contaminated with dust and tiny metal fragments.

    (B Some special oil additives have been shown to make oil more effective in trapping engine dust.

    (C) Most people do not change their oil regularly enough to gain the greatest benefits of reducing engine wear.

    (D) Some scientists who participated in the study do not change the oil in their cars regularly.

    (E) Newer scientific studies on the effects of changing oil in engines have produced results that corrected the erroneous conclusions from earlier studies.

23. The court unanimously concluded that a 1980 law protected observations made by reporters during news gathering, in addition to undisclosed, confidential notes or tapes. But the court also ruled unanimously that the law could not be used to violate a criminal defendant's constitutional right to a fair trial, and that testimony could be compelled if there was a "reasonable possibility the information will materially assist defense."

    Which of the following is most strongly supported by the rulings taken together?

    (A) A reporter could not be compelled to testify about any observations made during news gathering.

    (B) A defendant may not have to compel a reporter to testify about confidential notes or tapes.

    (C) A reporter's observations made during news gathering are confidential, unless they interfere with a defendant's right to a fair trial.

    (D) A reporter has the obligation to reveal observations made during news gathering, unless such revelations violate the defendant's right to a fair trial.

    (E) Reporters may testify when they choose to do so, but must testify whenever a defendant demands such testimony.

24. If both Hillary and Jim come to the party, they will certainly bring that brat Mickey with them. But we just don't want Mickey to be here because he inevitably makes things unpleasant. So we can invite either Hillary or Jim, but not both.

    Which of the following exhibits a pattern of reasoning most similar to that in the passage above?

    (A) Both the sport utility vehicle and the pickup truck are comfortable, but also use a lot of fuel. Because the price of fuel has risen so much, that price for comfort would be too high. So we should not buy either the pickup truck or the sport utility vehicle.

    (B) Whenever you put Tootsie the poodle and Poofy the Pomeranian in the car together they fight. So let's just leave them both home today because we don't want a dogfight in the car.

    (C) If I take both the Italian and Russian, it will take me an extra year to graduate. But my career would be very much enhanced by mastery of both languages, so the best choice is not to avoid either Russian or Italian.

    (D) If both the representatives from Woodland and the representatives from Westview come to the conference, we are likely to learn from their interaction. That kind of learning is exactly what we want, so it is important to try to include the representatives from both countries.

(E) Don't put both artichokes and onions on my salad, please. For some reason the combination of those things gives me heartburn, something that I just want to avoid today. So either onions or artichokes is okay, but not both.

25. Israel's present system of high taxes, low wages, and a tortuous bureaucracy stifles initiative, but it also makes Israelis better fathers. Israel's inefficient economy and relative lack of economic opportunity prevent most Israelis from sacrificing family values for the material rewards of financial success. True success to an Israeli father is getting the kids out the door each morning feeling good about themselves.

Which of the following principles most helps to explain the reason why, according to the passage, Israelis are better fathers?

(A) Lack of economic opportunity allows an opportunity to focus upon family concerns.

(B) Israeli children are raised through a school system where they are taught to place great importance on their self-esteem.

(C) Human beings will tend not to focus their efforts on goals they see as impossible to reach.

(D) Economic prosperity has never been understood to be an important goal of official action in Israel.

(E) There is a natural tendency among human beings to care about their young.

STOP

If time still remains, you may review work only in this section. When the time allotted is up, you may go on to the next section.

SECTION 2

Time—35 minutes
28 questions

Directions: *Each passage in this section is followed by a group of questions to be answered on the basis of what is **stated** or **implied** in the passage. For some questions, more than one of the choices could conceivably answer the question. However, you are to choose the **best** answer; that is, the response that most accurately and completely answers the question, and blacken the corresponding space on your answer sheet.*

Restoring the seceded states to the Union was the central issue in American politics from 1865 to 1869. This was preeminently a constitutional question involving the distribution of power between the states and the federal government. Considered from a strictly legal standpoint, reunification presented perplexing difficulties. Social and economic turmoil resulting from the destruction of slavery vastly complicated the problem, if it did not make a peaceful solution virtually impossible. Behind the rhetoric of states' rights and federal supremacy, the core elements in the Reconstruction problem were the status and rights of the former Confederates, on the one hand, and the status and rights of the emancipated slaves, on the other. The task of postwar Union policy was to reconcile the demands of these conflicting groups while restoring the federal system according to Northern republican principles.

Reconstruction as a problem in constitutional politics began with the disruption of the Union in the months before Sumter and continued throughout the war. The first ideas on the subject to be given practical expression were those advanced by President Lincoln at the beginning of the war. In his message to Congress in July 1861 and in a series of executive actions in subsequent months, Lincoln held that secession was null and void, and that the so-called seceded states were, therefore, still in the Union. He admitted that the Southern states were out of their normal relationship to the other states and the federal government since they had no loyal governments and were controlled by persons in rebellion against federal authority. But the states, as political entities distinguished from their governments, still were in the Union. Hence all that was necessary for Reconstruction was the suppression of actual military rebellion, the creation of loyal state governments by loyal citizens, and the resumption of normal relations with the federal government.

Lincoln assumed that it was the duty of the federal government to assist the states in Reconstruction. The justification for this assumption he found in Article IV, Section 4, of the Constitution, by which the United States guaranteed every state a republican form of government. All subsequent Reconstruction schemes drew upon this constitutional provision as justification for federal controls.

Finally, Lincoln assumed that the president had authority to carry through a competent Reconstruction program with little congressional assistance. A principal step in the plan was the suppression of rebellion, already being accomplished under the president's war powers. Lincoln admitted that in practice Congress would have final authority to pass upon presidential Reconstruction, since it could seat delegates from southern states at its discretion.

Lincoln's plan had two great virtues. It was consistent, for it rested upon the same premise of the nullity of secession upon which the administration had prosecuted the war. And it was simple of execution and promised a rapid restoration of a normally functioning constitutional system. Its great practical weakness was that Congress could destroy it merely by refusing to seat delegates from the reconstructed states.

1. Which one of the following is the main idea of the passage?

   (A) The core element in Reconstruction from 1865 through 1869 involved the question of whether the Confederate states had ever actually been outside of the Union or whether, as President Lincoln had claimed, they always remained a part of the Union.

(B) Reconstruction is an issue that should be seen from a strictly legal standpoint involving reunification of the former Confederate states with the rest of the nation according to the constitutional principle by which each state is guaranteed a republican form of government.

(C) Early in the Civil War, President Lincoln had developed initial ideas on resolving the difficult constitutional problems that became the central political issues during the period of 1865 through 1869.

(D) A major difficulty that the nation faced during the period of Reconstruction from 1865 through 1869 was determining the roles of the president and Congress in resolving that difficult constitutional issue.

(E) Had President Lincoln lived to complete his second term as president, Reconstruction might have been accomplished under principles he developed early in the 1860s, and so might have been beset with fewer demands on conflicting groups.

2. According to the passage, President Lincoln believed that the seceded states

(A) could only rejoin the Union by petitioning Congress.

(B) were constitutionally removed from the Union.

(C) had fewer rights than other states.

(D) were under martial law and so subject to the direct rule of the president.

(E) always remained part of the Union.

3. The author of the passage refers to Article IV, Section 4 of the Constitution in order to

(A) explain Lincoln's justification for creating new state governments in these so-called seceded states.

(B) point to the tension between Congress and the president on issues of Reconstruction.

(C) detail the constitutional argument that Lincoln used against secession.

(D) describe the problem of states' rights as a constitutional political issue during Reconstruction.

(E) refer to the constitutional principle that might have made Reconstruction less controversial than it was, had Lincoln remained president.

4. Which of the following does the passage not mention as a problem involved with Reconstruction?

(A) The rhetoric of states' rights to federal supremacy

(B) Relationships of state legislatures and the national Congress

(C) Suppression of the actual military rebellion in the southern states

(D) Social and economic turmoil in the southern states

(E) The status and rights of emancipated slaves

5. Which of the following best expresses the author's overall attitude toward President Lincoln's Reconstruction plan?

(A) Well meant, but idealistic

(B) Promising and consistent

(C) Characterized by a major weakness

(D) Premature and broad

(E) Unconstitutional and problematic

6. The role of the first paragraph in the passage is to

(A) set forth the thesis that Reconstruction was primarily a social and economic issue.

(B) explain the broader context of the issues of Reconstruction to be able to put President Lincoln's proposals in context.

(C) explain the contradictions that made the issue of Reconstruction impossible to resolve.

(D) describe Lincoln's approach to war and the Union so as to be able to explain his proposed policies on Reconstruction.

(E) explore tensions between Congress, the states, and the president as they manifest themselves in a particular issue of Reconstruction.

7. The primary purpose of this passage is to

(A) criticize Congress for extremism during the period of Reconstruction.

(B) describe Lincoln's Reconstruction plan as it conflicted with the proposal from the Radicals in Congress.

(C) explain the difficulties of Reconstruction and President Lincoln's approach to them.

(D) clarify the issues after the Civil War involving emancipated slaves and states' rights.

(E) argue against federal supremacy and for states' rights.

The horseshoe crab (Limulus) was once thought to possess a primitive, simple eye that had been largely bypassed by evolution. In fact, evolution has served the crab well. Anatomical and physiological studies are showing that the 350-million-year-old animal has developed a complex, sophisticated visual system that incorporates elegant mechanisms for adapting its sensitivity to daily cycles of light and darkness.

Humans see only dimly at night, but the world of horseshoe crabs may be nearly as bright at night as during the day. Inquiry into the mechanisms by which Limulus performs this feat has added to knowledge of a most intriguing phenomenon. The brain and its sensory organs are not merely passive recipients of information from the outside world. Instead the brain actively controls those organs to optimize the information it receives.

Over the past decade researchers have begun to explore in considerable detail how horseshoe crabs adapt their visual systems. One important finding is the discovery of a 24-hour biological clock in the crab's brain that transmits nerve signals to its eyes at night. These signals work to increase the eyes' sensitivity to light by a factor of up to one million. Oddly enough, this extraordinary nighttime increase in sensitivity went undetected until the late 1970s even though the horseshoe crab's visual system is among the most thoroughly studied in the animal kingdom.

The complex interaction between the brain and the eye of Limulus is only one example of the intricate relations between the brain and the sensory organs of almost all animals. The pioneering neuroanatomist Santiago Ramon y Cajal first uncovered two-way communication between the brain and the eye of a bird in 1889; he found connections between neurons in the upper brain stem and neurons in the retina. In 1971 Frederick A. Miles of the National Institutes of Health showed these connections carry signals that change the way the retina codes spatial information and so should alter the way a bird sees its world.

Similar efferent connections have been found in many other animals, from the nerves that heighten overall sensory response in some fish to those that transmit signals from the brain to the ear in humans and other primates. Efferent (carrying signals away from the central nervous system) neural connections from other parts of the brain outnumber the afferent (carrying signals to the central nervous system) connections from the optic nerve, where the initial stages of visual processing are performed. It appears that the brain, as much as the eye, determines how people see.

People and birds are complicated, however; no one knows exactly how they see, much less how their brains modulate that vision. The work done on simpler neural systems such as Limulus may help elucidate such questions in more complicated species. Ultimately a series of ever more complex studies, founded on work on the horseshoe crab, may explain how the incomplete and unstable picture that sensory organs provide, modulated both by the brain and the environment, gives rise to such direct and incontrovertible impressions as the image of a sunset, the smell of a rose, or the sound of a Bach fugue.

8. Which of the following best expresses the main idea of the passage?

(A) The horseshoe crab has a complex, sophisticated visual system that involves the brain as an active participant in vision.

(B) Recent research has corrected the previously accepted opinion among scientists that the horseshoe crab has not evolved significantly over the past 350 million years.

(C) Studies of the relationship between brain activity and the optic nerve in humans helped to elucidate the complex visual system of the horseshoe crab.

(D) Recent studies indicate that the brain plays as large or larger a role than that played by the eye in human vision.

(E) Advances in understanding of the nighttime vision of the horseshoe crab can lead to important developments for the use of human beings.

9. According to the passage, in the decade before the passage was written, research developed a new concentration on

(A) the nocturnal activities of horseshoe crabs.

(B) the reasons for human inability to see at night.

(C) two-way communication between the eye and the brain.

(D) the primitive visual system of Limulus.

(E) adaptation in the visual system of Limulus.

10. The crab's "24-hour biological clock" in the third paragraph refers to

(A) the great age of this creature.

(B) the fact that the crab never sleeps.

(C) the way nerve signals are attuned to regular changes in light levels.

(D) the reproductive cycle of Limulus.

(E) the activity cycle of horseshoe crabs compared to birds and humans.

11. The author mentions which of the following as an important finding from the research on the horseshoe crab during the decade preceding the passage?

(A) the discovery of the active part that the crab's brain plays in its nighttime vision.

(B) the discovery of the similarities between visual systems of birds and crabs.

(C) a new understanding of how people see.

(D) the discovery that the human visual system is derived from that of the crab.

(E) a determination of the age of Limulus.

12. According to the usage of the passage, efferent connections are

(A) the stems which attach the crab's eye to its body.

(B) neural connections found exclusively in birds.

(C) a kind of timer for the crab's biological clock.

(D) connections which carry communications in a body.

(E) what causes humans to see dimly at night.

13. The author discusses the work of Ramon y Cajal and Miles in order to

(A) cite groundbreaking work on the horseshoe crab that recent research has built upon.

(B) present possible criticisms to the suggestions drawn from recent research about horseshoe crabs.

(C) place research about the visual systems of horseshoe crabs in the larger context of research about the brain and vision.

(D) indicate importance of previous connections between work on how people see and how birds see.

(E) cite initial studies detecting the nighttime vision of the horseshoe crab.

14. According to the author, the study of the visual system of horseshoe crabs

(A) may lead to greater understanding of more complex systems.

(B) is of little importance.

(C) explains why crabs have survived so long.

(D) will show why the system has not evolved.

(E) shows that the connection between the brain and the eye is simpler than originally thought.

15. The primary purpose of the passage is to

(A) criticize the lack of research on the horseshoe crab.

(B) advance a hypothesis that the brain has some control over what the eye sees.

(C) suggest similarities between the visual systems of humans and crabs as a basis for study.

(D) distinguish the types of neural connections.

(E) argue that the visual systems of crabs are more simple than once assumed.

Passage A

All of Plato's philosophical writing was done in the form of dialogues, conversations in which almost always the principal speaker is Socrates. These are the first philosophical dialogues of the Western world. So far as we know, Plato himself invented the dialogue as a literary form, apparently from his actual experience of listening to Socrates in his characteristic conversations. Socrates wrote nothing, but all the philosophy Plato wrote is attributed to him, with the result that it is impossible to disentangle with complete certainty the Socratic from the Platonic element in the dialogues. Most scholars agree that aside from the very early dialogues in which Plato was seeking to present the true teaching of Socrates in order to defend him and to honor his memory, the dialogues represent Plato's own views. Plato wrote more than 20 dialogues, many of them of fine literary quality. Since they depict actual conversations, they are open-ended, flowing, informal, very different from the tight, systematic, rigorously deductive argumentation which we will find, for example, in Descartes. The persons who take part in the dialogues become three-dimensional as Plato sketches them—the pompous, blustering Thrasymachus; the polite reasonableness of Adeimantus and Glaucon; the handsome and clever Alcibiades; and Socrates himself, master of the put-down, making fools of those who ventured to offer their opinions in response to his prodding, and making enemies of those he disagreed with in politics and philosophy.

Passage B

An example of the virtues and challenges of understanding Plato's dialogues comes with the dialogue entitled *Crito*. The argument there seems to lead to the conclusion that one should not break the law. But the student of the dialogue can understand much more than just that moral position by considering the context within which that opinion about abiding by the law is advanced. The discussion takes place between two people only, Socrates and his friend Crito. There is no one else in the room. Socrates' concern in the discussion, therefore, focuses on Crito himself and upon what Crito will believe at the end of the conversation. Close attention to the actual argument that is used to create the belief on the part of Crito that one should always obey the law reveals a more complex position. The argument in its sophistication is that it is always unjust to break the law because it is always unjust to harm people, and breaking the law harms people by destabilizing the community which benefits them to some degree. This more sophisticated argument does not contend that breaking the law is the only unjust thing, but leaves open the possibility that there might be more unjust things and greater harms involved with obeying the law in some instances. Yet this point is not made explicit to Crito, something which the careful reader must wonder about and consider both in understanding the argument about the value of all and in learning from what ought to be said and not said to ordinary and decent people like Crito. Thus, the *Crito* demonstrates both the flexibility and sophistication of the dialogue form: it can foster uncomplicated belief among some while encouraging thoughtful reflection and analysis from others.

16. Which of the following most accurately expresses a main idea of the passages considered together?

(A) Plato's use of the dialogue form is an imitation of the form that his teacher, Socrates, used in his writing.

(B) Because he writes in dialogue form, Plato cannot be said to advance any philosophical teaching of his own.

(C) Plato's philosophical writings are presented in the form of dialogues, making it difficult for readers to discern Plato's own philosophical teaching.

(D) Because he serves primarily as a chronicler of the philosophical discussions of his teacher, Socrates, Plato writes exclusively dialogues.

(E) Plato's dialogues serve to celebrate the wisdom of his teacher, Socrates, by making his opponents in dialogue look foolish.

17. It can be inferred from passage A that

(A) it is not possible to find rigorous argument presented in dialogue form.

(B) in depicting a conversation between two or more characters it is possible to convey information about physical appearance and demeanor.

(C) because they are open-ended conversations, dialogues are not carefully and rigorously written.

(D) Plato did not embrace any philosophical teaching that differed from things taught by Socrates.

(E) characters presented as physically attractive in Platonic dialogues are also presented as less reasonable than others.

18. The argument presented in passage B suggests that the author of passage B might seek to clarify passage A by

(A) replacing the phrase "they are open ended," with the phrase "they are presented as open ended."

(B) replacing the phrase "making fools of those who ventured to offer their opinions," with the phrase "making simpletons of those who ventured to offer their opinions."

(C) changing the phrase "many of them of fine literary quality," to "some of them of fine literary quality."

(D) changing the phrase "making enemies of those he disagreed with," to the phrase "sometimes making enemies of those he disagreed with."

(E) changing the phrase "all of Plato's philosophical writing," to the phrase "the bulk of Plato's philosophical writing."

19. The author of passage B would most likely agree with which of the following?

(A) Plato's philosophical teaching is that sometimes a correct understanding of justice might lead to disobedience of the law.

(B) Plato's philosophical teaching is more complex and sophisticated than that of Socrates.

(C) According to Plato's philosophical teaching, the basic requirement of justice can be summed up as "do no harm."

(D) According to Plato's depiction in the dialogue, Crito is not as reasonable as Adeimantus or as clever as Alcibiades.

(E) Plato's more important and sophisticated philosophical teachings tend to come in dialogues with fewer participants.

20. Which of the following is mentioned in passage B but not mentioned in passage A?

(A) Agreement among scholars about the content of Plato's early dialogues

(B) Consideration in interpreting a dialogue of who, in addition to the speakers, is in the room

(C) Explanation that the characters in a dialogue can become three-dimensional

(D) Opinion that the content of Platonic dialogues tends to change as they depict Socrates as nearer death

(E) Assumption that Plato's own views are sometimes presented through conversations in which Socrates is the principal speaker

21. Which of the following best describes the relationship of the passages to one another?

(A) Passage A elaborates on passage B by presenting arguments made with characters other than Crito.

(B) The two passages disagree on whether it is ever possible completely to disentangle Plato's teachings from Socrates' arguments.

(C) Passage B adds specific information to explain what makes characters in dialogues appear three-dimensional.

(D) Passage B disputes the assumption in passage A that there is such a thing as the "true teaching" of Socrates.

(E) Passage B presents an example of the use of the dialogue form described in passage A to offer a complex philosophical teaching.

The judicial branch is a coequal part of the United States government, and yet it has escaped the degree of scientific scrutiny given to the executive and legislative branches. This is not to say the judicial branch has lacked all scrutiny, only that it has traditionally been viewed from a perspective different from the other two branches of government. The executive and legislative branches have traditionally been viewed as political entities. Judges and the judicial branch have fostered the idea that they are nonpolitical arbiters of the law. In *Marbury v. Madison*, the landmark United States Supreme Court case which established judicial review under the United States Constitution, Chief Justice John Marshall rhetorically asked who should determine the meaning of the Constitution. He answered himself by pointing to the fact that members of the other two branches were politically motivated, and only judges were qualified to be truly nonpolitical arbiters of the law. These statements by Chief Justice Marshall were certainly not the beginning of what is generally known as the "cult of the robe," but they are a classic example in American jurisprudence.

Following Marshall's reasoning, the study of the judiciary has traditionally used the case analysis method, which concentrates on individual cases. Each case must be decided on the basis of cases which have preceded it. Although it may be acknowledged that each case differs from any other case in many ways, past cases must still be examined to find the general principles which are then applied to the present dispute.

This reliance on precedent, known in legal terms as stare decisis, and its accompanying detailed examination of each case, has caused legal scholars, to paraphrase Wieland, not to be able to see the forest for the trees. To get a more accurate picture of the workings of the judiciary, it is necessary to step back from the cases. One must remain cognizant of the details, but not to such a degree that they inhibit the ability to see the greater whole. This is not to say analysis of individual cases has no place in the scientific study of the judiciary. Indeed, as was pointed out by Joyce Kilmer, there is always a place to appreciate the beauty of a tree, but there are also times when we must consider the tree as a part of the greater forest.

Although judicial scholars by and large do not subscribe to the myth that judges are nonpolitical arbiters of the law, there is substantial interest in judicial biographies and case studies. Judicial biographies and case studies are certainly useful in interpreting particular judicial decisions, examining the opinions of a particular judge, or discussing specific points of law, but to optimize the results of such efforts, in terms of scientific study, such research must be viewed within the framework of a more comprehensive theory of judicial decision making.

22. Which of the following most accurately expresses the main point of the passage?

(A) Study of the judicial branch has relied largely on case study and on the application of precedent to each new case.

(B) Judicial biographies and case studies are useful approaches to understanding the role of judges as nonpolitical arbiters of the law.

(C) In order to understand better the workings of the judicial branch of the United States government, scholars would benefit from subjecting it to a kind of scientific study, viewing it, like the other branches of United States government, as a political entity.

(D) Chief Justice John Marshall in the case of *Marbury v. Madison* established the belief that has been followed ever since, that the members of the judicial branch are the ones who should determine the meaning of the Constitution.

(E) To get an accurate picture of the workings of the judiciary, it is important to look at cases as a whole and not simply at individual cases as reflections of precedent.

23. The primary purpose of the passage is to

(A) suggest that judges are political decision makers.

(B) complain that no one studies the judiciary.

(C) advocate another way of studying the judiciary.

(D) describe the case analysis method.

(E) attack the doctrine of judicial review.

24. The author uses the phrase "the cult of the robe" in the first paragraph to mean

(A) the method of interpretation of the Constitution.

(B) the approach to study of the judicial branch that concentrates on study of prior cases.

(C) the traditions of the Supreme Court of the United States.

(D) that the judicial branch ought to be viewed differently from the executive and legislative.

(E) the belief that judges are nonpolitical arbiters of the law.

25. It can be inferred from the passage that the author believes that scholars who study the judicial branch of United States government

(A) are unlikely to believe that stare decisis plays a significant role in judicial decision making.

(B) do not believe that it is actually the case that judges are nonpolitical arbiters of the law.

(C) accept that Chief Justice Marshall's decision in *Marbury v. Madison* is based upon valid reasoning.

(D) find that judicial biographies are not of any use in understanding judges or the judicial branch.

(E) seek to be cognizant of the details of particular cases.

26. The statement about the ability to "be able to see the forest for the trees" in the third paragraph is a way to

(A) advocate studies of the courts that go beyond particular cases.

(B) suggest that courts are organic entities.

(C) point out a weakness in *Marbury v. Madison.*

(D) decry the use of precedent.

(E) support the case analysis method.

27. The reference to Kilmer in the third paragraph is intended to

(A) point out the beauty of studying law.

(B) argue that individual cases are unimportant.

(C) support the courts' reliance on precedent.

(D) suggest case analysis has some merit.

(E) discourage belief in the "cult of the robe."

28. According to the author's attitude, the utility of case studies and judicial biographies in understanding judicial decision-making is best characterized as

(A) sufficient.

(B) limited.

(C) neutral.

(D) nonexistent.

(E) complete.

STOP

If time still remains, you may review work only in this section. When the time allotted is up, you may go on to the next section.

SECTION 3

Time—35 minutes
24 questions

Directions: *Each group of questions in this section is based on a set of conditions. In answering some of the questions, it may be useful to draw a rough diagram. Choose the response that most accurately and completely answers the question and blacken the corresponding space on your answer sheet.*

QUESTIONS 1–7

Julia is arranging seven books—Biology, Economics, French, Mathematics, History, Philosophy, and Sociology—on a bookshelf. The books will be arranged from left to right according to the following conditions.

French is to the left of History.
Philosophy is to the right of French.
Biology is to the left of Mathematics.
Sociology is to the right of Philosophy.
Mathematics is to the left of Philosophy.
Economics is to the left of French.

1. Which of the following is a complete and accurate list of the books, any one of which could be farthest to the right on the shelf?
   (A) Philosophy, Sociology
   (B) Sociology, History
   (C) Philosophy, History, Sociology
   (D) Sociology
   (E) History, Philosophy

2. If Economics is third from the left, which book must be first from the left?
   (A) Biology
   (B) French
   (C) Mathematics
   (D) History
   (E) Sociology

3. Which of the following CANNOT be true?
   (A) Sociology is farthest to the right.
   (B) Biology is farthest to the left.
   (C) Mathematics is farthest to the left.
   (D) History is farthest to the right.
   (E) Economics is farthest to the left.

4. If the first three books from the left side of the shelf are, in some order or other, Biology, Economics, and Mathematics, which book must be fourth from the left?
   (A) Philosophy
   (B) French
   (C) History
   (D) either French or History
   (E) either History or Philosophy

5. If Mathematics is in the fourth position from the left on the shelf, which of the following must be false?
   (A) French is to the right of Biology.
   (B) History is to the right of Sociology.
   (C) Sociology is to the left of Philosophy.
   (D) Biology is on the extreme left.
   (E) Economics is on the extreme left.

6. Which of the following could not be a possible arrangement of the books from left to right?
   (A) Biology, Economics, Mathematics, French, Philosophy, History, Sociology
   (B) Biology, Economics, French, Mathematics, Sociology, Philosophy, History
   (C) Biology, Economics, French, Mathematics, Philosophy, History, Sociology
   (D) Economics, French, Biology, Mathematics, Philosophy, Sociology, History

(E) Biology, Mathematics, Economics, French, History, Philosophy, Sociology

7. If Biology is the third book from the left, the second book from the left must be
   (A) Mathematics
   (B) History
   (C) Economics
   (D) French
   (E) Philosophy

QUESTIONS 8–13

The six sections of the village parade are filled by two bands, the volunteer fire department, the pony club, clowns, and dignitaries in open cars. The order of march must meet the following conditions:

The clowns can be neither the first nor the last group.

Neither band can be next to the pony club.

The pony club must be just in front of the dignitaries.

8. Which of the following arrangements is an acceptable order of the sections, from first to last place?
   (A) band, ponies, dignitaries, fire department, clowns, band
   (B) clowns, ponies, dignitaries, band, fire department, band
   (C) band, clowns, ponies, dignitaries, band, fire department
   (D) ponies, fire department, dignitaries, band, clowns, band
   (E) band, fire department, clowns, dignitaries, ponies, band

9. If the bands are in second and last places in an acceptable order of march, which of the following must be true?
   (A) The ponies are in third place.
   (B) The fire department is in first place.
   (C) The dignitaries are in third place.
   (D) The fire department is in fourth place.
   (E) The clowns are in fifth place.

10. If in an acceptable order of march the ponies are in second place and the dignitaries are in third place, which of the following must be true?
   (A) A band is in next-to-last place.
   (B) A band is in last place.
   (C) The fire department is in last place.
   (D) A band is in first place.
   (E) The clowns are in first place.

11. Only one order of march is possible under which of the following conditions?
   (A) The bands are in second and third places.
   (B) The clowns are in first places.
   (C) The bands are in second and fifth places.
   (D) The pony club is in last place.
   (E) The dignitaries are in first place.

12. All of the following orders of march are acceptable, EXCEPT
   (A) fire department, band, ponies, dignitaries, clowns, band
   (B) fire department, band, clowns, ponies, dignitaries, band
   (C) band, fire department, clowns, ponies, dignitaries, band
   (D) band, fire department, ponies, dignitaries, clowns, band
   (E) ponies, dignitaries, band, band, clowns, fire department

13. If there are three or more places between the two bands in an acceptable order of march, which of the following must be FALSE?
   (A) There is a band in fourth place.
   (B) Either a band or the fire department is in first place.
   (C) The ponies are in either third or fourth place.

(D) If the clowns are in second place, there is a band in last place.

(E) If the clowns are in third place, there must be a band in last place.

QUESTIONS 14–18

A four-member subcommittee must be drawn from the committee composed of G, H, I, J, K, L, and M. The subcommittee is to have equal numbers of representatives from the faculty and the administration, equal numbers of men and women, and equal numbers of representatives from the undergraduate college and the professional schools.

G, J, and L are all administrators; the others are faculty members.

G, I, and L are from the college; the others are from the professional schools.

H, I, J, and M all are men; the others are women.

14. If I is chosen for the subcommittee, which of the following must also be on the subcommittee?

    (A) G

    (B) H

    (C) J

    (D) L

    (E) M

15. Each of the following pairs of people could be chosen to be on the subcommittee together EXCEPT

    (A) G and I

    (B) G and J

    (C) G and L

    (D) H and J

    (E) H and M

16. If K is chosen for the subcommittee, which of the following must also be among those chosen for the subcommittee?

    (A) G

    (B) H

    (C) I

    (D) L

    (E) M

17. If M is chosen for the subcommittee, the subcommittee must also include which of the following pairs of people?

    (A) G and I

    (B) G and J

    (C) G and L

    (D) I and J

    (E) I and L

18. How many four-member subcommittees meeting the conditions given but differing from one another by at least one member can be formed from this list of candidates?

    (A) 35

    (B) 17

    (C) 8

    (D) 3

    (E) 2

QUESTIONS 19–24

Seated at the head table of the Fraternal Frolic Annual Banquet were, from left to right, Al, Bill, Charlie, Dave, and Ed. Each of them belonged to exactly two of five fraternal organizations—Lords, Elm, Magic, Kobra, and Old Forest. The following conditions held for the five men.

If someone was a member of the Lords, then he was not an Elm.

If someone was a Kobra, then he was not a member of Old Forest.

No person belonged to any organization to which a man sitting next to him belonged.

Bill belonged to the Magic and the Old Forest.

Ed belonged to the Lords.

19. Which of the following could be a complete and accurate list of the organizations to which the men belong?

(A) Al: Lords, Kobra; Bill: Magic, Old Forest; Charlie: Lords, Elm; Dave: Magic, Old Forest; Ed: Lords, Kobra

(B) Al: Kobra, Lords; Bill: Magic, Old Forest; Charlie: Elm, Old Forest; Dave: Magic, Elm; Ed: Lords, Kobra

(C) Al: Kobra, Elm; Bill: Magic, Old Forest; Charlie: Lords, Kobra; Dave: Magic, Elm; Ed: Lords, Kobra

(D) Al: Kobra, Magic; Bill: Elm, Old Forest; Charlie: Lords, Kobra; Dave: Elm, Magic; Ed: Lords, Old Forest

(E) Al: Lords, Kobra; Bill: Old Forest, Magic; Charlie: Elm, Kobra; Dave: Magic, Lords; Ed: Old Forest, Elm

20. Which of the following must be true?

(A) Al is an Elm.

(B) Charlie is a Lord.

(C) Charlie is a Kobra.

(D) Dave is an Old Forest.

(E) Ed is an Old Forest.

21. If exactly one of the men is both a Magic and either in Kobra or Old Forest, which of the following must be true?

(A) No more than two of the men are Lords.

(B) No more than two of the men are Elms.

(C) No more than two of the men are in Kobra.

(D) No fewer than two of the men are both Magic and in either Lords or Elm.

(E) No fewer than two of the men are Old Forest.

22. Which of the following is a possible combination of memberships for Dave?

(A) Elm and Magic

(B) Magic and Kobra

(C) Lords and Old Forest

(D) Kobra and Lords

(E) Elm and Kobra

23. If Charlie is an Elm, which of the following must be true?

(A) Charlie is an Old Forest.

(B) Dave is an Old Forest.

(C) Dave is a Magic and neither an Old Forest nor in Kobra.

(D) Ed is a Magic and neither an Old Forest nor in Kobra.

(E) Ed is an Old Forest.

24. If Frank sat down just to the right of Ed, and Frank was in the Magic and Kobra, but the same conditions continue to apply to men at the table, which of the following must be true?

(A) Charlie is a Lord and a Magic.

(B) Charlie is an Elm and in Kobra.

(C) Dave is an Elm and a Magic.

(D) Dave is an Elm and an Old Forest.

(E) Ed is a Lord and in Kobra.

STOP

If time still remains, you may review work only in this section. When the time allotted is up, you may go on to the next section.

SECTION 4

Time—35 minutes
24 questions

Directions: *The questions in this section are based on the reasoning contained in brief statements or passages. For some questions, more than one of the choices could conceivably answer the question. However, you are to choose the* ***best*** *answer; that is, the response that most accurately and completely answers the question. You should not make assumptions that are by commonsense standards implausible, superfluous, or incompatible with the passage. After you have chosen the best answer, blacken the corresponding space on your answer sheet.*

1. The causes for intellectual alarm about the generally accepted understanding of the formation of the universe began in the second half of the 1980s. In 1987, the Big Bang theory received a shock when a probe sent up by U.S. and Japanese researchers found distant energy emissions that suggested a series of secondary Big Bangs. The previous year, it was first noted that in addition to the uniform outward expansion of the universe, there seemed to be a gravitational pull toward a vast region subsequently named the Great Attractor. Then in April 1989, an Italian group identified another giant agglomeration of galaxies three times farther away.

   Which of the following is most strongly supported by the passage?

   (A) Astronomical discoveries, including secondary Big Bangs, have demonstrated the falsity of the Big Bang theory.

   (B) U.S. and Japanese researchers respect the validity of one another's astronomical discoveries.

   (C) There is a uniform outward expansion of the universe that makes it difficult to understand the Great Attractor.

   (D) Prior to the late 1980s the Big Bang theory was generally accepted as the correct understanding of the formation of the universe.

   (E) Japanese discoveries of the secondary series of Big Bangs are inconsistent with Italian discoveries of a giant agglomeration of galaxies.

2. Since it is very important to control inflation, a more aggressive prosecution of antitrust cases is needed. Even when no one company enjoys a total monopoly, a tendency toward monopoly still results in decreased competition. This reduces production and increases prices. Thus, a tendency toward monopoly is a principal cause of inflation.

   Which of the following is an assumption required by the argument?

   (A) Inflation is harmful because it stifles economic growth.

   (B) Prosecution of antitrust cases can control monopolistic tendencies.

   (C) Monopolistic tendencies cannot provide benefits in any industry.

   (D) Antitrust prosecution does not itself cause unemployment.

   (E) Increased competition in the industry keeps inflation low.

3. Whether or not you can tell a person's level of intelligence by the excellence of his grammar is not clear to me. Is someone who asks, "Who did you vote for?" definitely going to be less intelligent than someone who asks, "For whom did you vote?" Whatever the answer, most people do believe that better grammar means more intelligence.

   If the statements in the passage are true, which of the following can be inferred from them?

(A) If someone believes that an intelligent person uses poor grammar, that someone is probably not in the majority.

(B) Someone with poor grammar is less intelligent than someone with good grammar.

(C) Someone with poor grammar will be perceived by some as being no less intelligent than someone with good grammar.

(D) Someone with good grammar will be believed by most people to be more intelligent than someone with poor grammar.

(E) Someone who is perceived as being more intelligent by most people will be assumed to be using good grammar by those people.

4. Tiffany: Well, I'm not surprised that she was offered a scholarship, since in none of the volleyball games in which I have played has Lisa ever made a mistake.

John: But that's not true. Lisa made several mistakes in the game on Tuesday night, although you played only briefly. Still, when she's good she's very, very good.

Tiffany and John disagree on which of the following?

(A) Lisa should have been offered a scholarship.

(B) Lisa is a good volleyball player.

(C) Lisa has made mistakes in some volleyball games that Tiffany has played in.

(D) Tiffany has played in every game that Lisa has played in.

(E) Lisa has played in every volleyball game that Tiffany has played in.

5. Studies show that life expectancy of persons in positions of authority is greater than that of the general population. For example, look at how many members of Congress exceed the average life expectancy. One study in particular showed that military personnel at the rank of colonel or above have a greater than average life expectancy. This is surprising, since other studies also show that people in authority are much more likely to feel job-related stress, and stress is a well-known cause of heart attacks.

Which of the following most helps to explain the apparently paradoxical results of the studies cited in the passage?

(A) Studies on stress also show that unemployment causes people to feel great stress.

(B) People in positions of authority tend to be people who were successful before taking those positions.

(C) Because they tend to have higher incomes, people in positions of authority have easy access to good nutrition and health care.

(D) The number of people with positions of authority represents a very small percentage of the total population.

(E) There is no major occupation or life condition that guarantees absence of stress.

6. A Canadian cold front will hit Eureka in about four hours. Precipitation results from about 75% of such fronts in the Eureka area. Moreover, the current season, winter, is the time of year in which Eureka is most likely to encounter snowfall.

Which of the following, in addition to the information above, would be most helpful to know to assess the likelihood that Eureka is to get snowfall in the next several hours?

(A) The percentage of snowfalls that occurs in Eureka in the winter, as opposed to the fall

(B) The percentage of time that precipitation in the Eureka area is in the form of snowfall

(C) How many Canadian cold fronts hit the Eureka area, on average, in a year

(D) The percentage of wintertime Canadian cold fronts hitting the Eureka area that cause snowfall

(E) Whether Eureka has more or fewer snowfalls during the winter than do nearby towns

7. Writing beautiful operas requires a talent for music composition and a flair for the dramatic. Bach, however, was the greatest of all composers. But he did not have a flair for the dramatic, which would have made him excel at writing operas.

Which of the following contains a reasoning error that most closely resembles the reasoning error in the passage?

(A) The question is whether Angela could be the author of this short story. The episode described as occurring on the night of September 10 is like nothing she has actually experienced, so we can eliminate her as the author.

(B) It is true that it is necessary to feel great passion in order to be a true artist. However, Friedmann has a very vivid imagination, so she could be a true artist without feeling great passion.

(C) Whenever I talk to Lynn on the phone I enter it in my phone log. I did not enter a conversation for last Thursday in the log, so I know that I did not talk to her on the phone that day.

(D) Only if I can make my payment before next week can I prevent foreclosure on the property. However, I cannot possibly get the money for the payment together this week, so I cannot prevent foreclosure.

(E) Only the brightest senior designers deserve to be on the advisory committee. Sally is clearly among the brightest, but she is not a senior designer. If she were, then she would deserve to be on the committee.

8. Even employers who are among the least caring about the well-being of their employees should realize that their desire for profit maximization should make them support continued increased wages for overtime. Of course, if you abolish increased wages for overtime, workers would find that their take-home pay has decreased. But it is also the case that if you abolish increased wages for overtime, employers would find that increases in production have disappeared.

Which of the following, if assumed, allows the conclusion to be properly drawn from the information in the passage?

(A) If overtime work were abolished, employers can save money that would otherwise be paid for overtime.

(B) The best workers are those who would be willing to work overtime for regular pay.

(C) Losing the prospect of increased pay for overtime would cause workers to be less productive during the regular workday and, so, threaten the profitability of companies.

(D) Increased wages for overtime can make workers working overtime shifts as productive on those shifts as they are during regular work hours.

(E) Workers must be at least as productive when working overtime as they are during regular work hours.

9. Nutrition as a discipline examines the interaction of nutrient ingestion, metabolism, and utilization with the health and behavior of the organism. Human ingestion of nutrients is initiated by a complex array of factors, only some of which are directly related to the body's physiological need for food. The sensory qualities of available foods can be a powerful factor in eating behavior. Everyone is occasionally induced to eat beyond physiological need in response to a delicious taste or aroma. For some individuals, however, sensory factors assume primary importance in guiding intake, and this sensory dominance may lead to improper nutrition.

Which of the following is an assumption relied on in the passage?

(A) Sensory qualities can help to determine availability of foods.

(B) Nutrition as a discipline examines the interaction of nutrient ingestion.

(C) Everyone is occasionally induced to succumb to improper nutrition.

(D) Satisfying sensory desires is not a physiological need for human beings.

(E) Acting according to physiological needs can result in improper nutrition.

10. There are many attempts, primarily among theologians, to ascertain the contribution which Whitehead's process philosophy might make to social and political theory, but they must be judged as inadequate. The reason for this is that a serious study of Whitehead's own social and political thought has been largely neglected. This neglect is no doubt due in part to the fact that Whitehead never produced a systematic political theory.

Which of the following, if true, would most weaken this passage's argument?

(A) Whether or not Whitehead's process philosophy has made a substantial contribution to social and political theory is not yet understood.

(B) There are no studies of why Whitehead's own social and political thought has been largely neglected.

(C) Many important and instructive contributions to political and social theory have been made in nonsystematic ways.

(D) It is not necessary to understand Whitehead's own social and political thought in order to appreciate how process philosophy might contribute to other social and political theory.

(E) Determination of Whitehead's political beliefs is not difficult even though they are not presented in a systematic way.

11. In a trend that must remind historians of publishing in the 1950s, the news media are criticizing the adult orientation of comic books, especially the increase in violence and sexual themes. An article in a major news magazine questioned the judgment of comic book publishers, noting that "comics have forsaken campy repartee and outlandishly byzantine plots for a steady diet of remorseless violence." And a major cable news show went a step further, explicitly linking violence in comic books with a rise in juvenile delinquency. This commentary is long overdue and will lead mainstream publishers to think about cleaning up their comic book act.

Which of the following, if assumed, allows the conclusion to be properly drawn?

(A) Contemporary criticism of comic books is in fact similar in tone to 1950s criticism.

(B) Respected newspapers follow the lead of major news magazines in criticizing comic book makers.

(C) Publishers of comic books are likely to change their products in response to criticism from mainstream news outlets.

(D) Comic book publishers are driven above all by the profit motive and readily take advice about how to improve profitability.

(E) Comic books producers prefer to have campy repartee and outlandishly byzantine plots.

12. Meat substitutes tend to be lower in protein than their real-meat equivalents, which is one unexpected reason why opting for a fake burger over a real one can be a healthy practice. Excess protein can stress the kidneys because protein is hard to digest. It can also stretch the waistline, since many meat sources of protein are high in fat calories.

Which of the following is not a premise in the argument in the passage?

(A) A fake burger might have less protein than a real one.

(B) Protein sources can be fattening.

(C) Too much protein can harm the kidneys.

(D) Protein can be hard to digest.

(E) A fake burger can be healthier than a real one.

13. Politics is a subject difficult to pin down, though discussions of politics have a long and venerable history. No less a figure than Aristotle propounded his views in a book called *Politics* more than 2,000 years ago. Of course, politics certainly predated Aristotle, manifesting itself, for example, in events reported in the Bible. To further complicate the subject, the politics of the 21st century are vastly different in scope and substance, if not in form, from the politics of the ancients. Thus, it is not unreasonable to be

perplexed about the meaning of politics. So the meaning of politics remains mysterious and confounding.

The reasoning in the passage is vulnerable to which of the following criticisms?

(A) It rests its claims on the authority of a single person.

(B) It fails to consider relevant distinctions between communities that are more than 2,000 years removed from one another.

(C) It assumes that the definition of "politics" is both known and not known.

(D) It fails to recognize that both the Bible and Aristotle are of ancient origin.

(E) It presupposes that a large difference in years that could lead to fundamental differences actually does lead to such differences.

14. There is no need to spend much time demonstrating that Molière had contact with, and was affected by, Italian forms of comic theater. That such influences were constantly available to him is a commonplace rather than a point of contention. Let just two facts stand for a host of others, so that we may dispose of the point. From 1658 to 1660 Molière's company shared its acting space with a resident Italian troupe. Secondly, his personal acting style was seen by contemporaries to have been modeled to some extent on that of Tiberio Fiorilli.

Which of the following statements, if true, would most weaken the writer's argument?

(A) Molière's company shared acting space with a resident Italian troupe until 1665, not 1660.

(B) There were several forms of comic theater in Italy.

(C) The space Molière's company shared in 1659 was so small that groups using the same space could not avoid frequent contact with one another.

(D) Italian comic theater was not much respected during the seventeenth century.

(E) Tiberio Fiorilli was born and raised in Argentina.

15. Something many people actually see is visible to anyone with at least an ordinary sense of sight. Something that many people actually hear is audible to anyone with at least an ordinary sense of hearing. So something that many people desire is desirable to anyone with at least ordinary desires. And many people desire the release from physical or emotional pain that comes with death. So death is desirable.

An error in reasoning in the passage is that it

(A) fails to consider that many visible things are not seen by all people.

(B) treats something that is proven to be necessary for something to be desirable as being enough by itself to guarantee desirability.

(C) concludes incorrectly that something that is true of each component of a group is true of the group as a whole.

(D) overlooks important differences between things treated as similar.

(E) generalizes from a sample that is likely to be unrepresentative.

16. Locke: By the fundamental law of nature, man being to be preserved as much as possible, when all cannot be preserved, the safety of the innocent is to be preferred; and one may destroy a man who makes war upon him, or has discovered an enmity to his being, for the same reason that he may kill a wolf or a lion; because such men are not under the ties of common-law of reason, have no other rule, but that of force and violence, and so may be treated as beasts of prey.

The statement "for the same reason that he may kill a wolf or a lion" serves what role in Locke's argument?

(A) It is an example of a circumstance where people may assume that others are motivated to harm them and so may be destroyed without additional evidence of intent.

(B) It exemplifies the reasoning that distinguished human beings from beasts of prey.

(C) It is the analogy that is the principal evidence in the argument leading to the conclusion that the safety of the innocent ought to be preferred.

(D) It is an example of a circumstance where people tend to assume that others are motivated to harm, but should not act until some overt act on the part of the lion or wolf makes the motive clear.

(E) It shows an exception to the law of nature that may allow action against the innocent when a greater good is at stake.

17. A parapsychologist investigating "lucky guesses" found that close to 30% of the major winners in state lotteries she interviewed had chosen their winning numbers as a result of some kind of "flash"—a dream or an inner voice, for example—rather than on more explainable grounds, like a loved one's birthday or some system. She concluded that these data demonstrate that some people possess clairvoyance, albeit often in an indirect and uncontrolled way.

Which of the following would be most important to know in proving or disproving the parapsychologist's claim?

(A) The percentage of lottery players she interviewed who picked each particular number

(B) The percentage of players who are winners in the state lotteries

(C) The exact meaning of "major winner" in her survey

(D) The percentage of lottery players who chose their numbers on the basis of a "flash"

(E) The percentage of the population who play the state lotteries

18. Henry: Capitalism and environmentalism are mutually exclusive. Therefore a corporation cannot both make profits and protect the environment simultaneously.

Alice: But aren't many corporations doing precisely that? The REO Corporation has made a nifty profit for the last several years, and at the same time it has spent millions of dollars on reforestation and reclamation of dead lakes in its vicinity. Its advertising even tries to lure customers by celebrating the fact that it is a "green" corporation. So, even though it puts primary emphasis on profits, this corporation simultaneously helps protect the environment.

Which of the following best describes Alice's argumentative strategy?

(A) She demonstrates that corporate profits make protection of the environment possible.

(B) She uses the word "environmental" in a different sense than Henry does.

(C) She reinterprets the data of Henry's own premise to prove the opposite conclusion.

(D) She uses an example to show the falsity of Henry's conclusion.

(E) She invokes a relevant analogy to demonstrate the absurdity of Henry's reasoning.

19. I think that it is improper for a nation to put up monuments to its famous men and women. Even though a citizen spends a lifetime in service to the country, he or she does not deserve to be deified. We scientists should imitate Prometheus, whom the ancient Greeks said brought fire down from Heaven to give to the superstitious and ignorant men of his time. We should teach that reason must displace myth, and that worthless idolatry must be abandoned.

The main conclusion of the passage is based on which of the following assumptions?

(A) Reverence for the nation's heroes ought not to be expected from scientists.

(B) Idolatry is based only in ignorance and superstition.

(C) Scientists should help educate the public not to deify national heroes.

(D) A community cannot build a monument to a famous citizen without deifying that citizen.

(E) Prometheus was not himself a mythical figure.

20. Family members have a responsibility to each other. In a crisis each member should be prepared to endure some self-sacrifice to preserve the well-being of every other member. A corporation is like a giant family. Thus, each employee of a corporation should be willing to endure some hardship for the sake of fellow employees.

Which of the following assertions, if true, most seriously weakens the argument above?

(A) Membership in the corporation is based on self-interest, whereas membership in the family is based on mutual love.

(B) Corporations experience few crises which require self-sacrifice on the part of employees.

(C) One is first a member of a family before being an employee of a corporation.

(D) Some members of some families do not sacrifice for one another, but see other family members as people to be taken advantage of.

(E) Many corporations are larger than most nuclear families, but not larger than many extended families.

21. I used to like Go East Airline, and though it is no longer in business, I think some of its pilots are flying this plane. You see, I know that all pilots who used to fly for Go East Airline are bitter about the outcome of the merger with Gone South Airlines, and some of the pilots on this flight are clearly bitter about that merger, since I just overheard them complaining.

Which one of the following most closely parallels the flawed reasoning used in the argument above?

(A) Well, I know that all the children at the family reunion are playing croquet. But that person playing croquet looks like Uncle Wilbur. No, it can't be Uncle Wilbur because he's an adult, and all the children are playing croquet.

(B) I don't care what you say; it is just the case that rich people have fun. Maybe not all of the time, but some of the time rich people have fun. So don't believe Bridget when she tells you she never has any fun, because, of course, she's a lawyer, and all lawyers are rich.

(C) There is just no way that that funny-looking thing is properly called a car, no matter what the magazine says. It's a bicycle. You know as well as I do that all bicycles have two wheels, but no cars have two wheels. And that funny-looking thing has two wheels.

(D) Just remember this: all birds have beaks. So if the animal that you have to identify in your zoology lab exam has a beak, then it is a bird. It's just that simple.

(E) Not everything with the word *ball* in it is really a ball. A basketball is a ball. Balls are round, and so is a basketball. But footballs are not round, so despite their name, footballs are not balls.

22. If our students are to keep up with academic achievement of students in the rest of the world, a program is needed that will release teachers from classroom responsibilities for a time each week that can be used to train them on new technologies. The full utilization of technology as a tool to enhance learning will depend largely on how skilled our teachers are in its use. Many teachers have embraced the use of technology to enhance learning; however, it is increasingly clear that as powerful technologies and software proliferate, teachers will need to learn more about these new tools on a continuous basis. Experience shows that this learning can happen only when learning about technology is a part of the regular work-week for teachers.

Which of the following is an assumption that the argument depends on?

(A) Many teachers have already embraced the use of technology to enhance learning.

(B) All teachers have at least a basic level of technological skill before they begin teaching.

(C) Powerful technologies and software will continue to proliferate in the future.

(D) The utilization of technology as a tool to enhance learning is required for our students to keep up with students in the rest of the world.

(E) There are not any teachers with the technological sophistication to learn new technologies on their own and outside of school time.

23. A top expert on Native Americans lectured on the topic of early American mythology on the Yeti. During his lecture he said, "Native Americans had a deep reverence for the Yeti, which we know as Bigfoot. Drawings have been discovered on cave walls which depict encounters with the creature. Also, stories were passed down from one generation to the next, describing the creature as shy and intelligent." A student at the lecture concluded that the expert's findings prove Bigfoot exists.

Which of the following is most strongly supported by the information in the passage above?

(A) There is no effective way of determining whether or not Bigfoot exists.

(B) Bigfoot must exist at the present time, since it existed in early America.

(C) The expert believed Bigfoot existed in early America.

(D) Some Native Americans believed in the existence of Bigfoot.

(E) The expert's findings prove Bigfoot existed but not that Bigfoot exists currently.

24. In July 1984, Richard Leakey and colleague Kamoya Kimeu found in Nairobi an almost complete homo erectus skeleton, the first recovered that was 1.6 million years old. The skeleton was that of a boy about 12 years of age. He was about five feet four inches tall and probably would have reached a height of six feet. His bones had been scattered and trampled in a swamp. In parts and portion, they were like the human form today. Under him was volcanic material dating from 1.65 million years ago.

Which of the following is most strongly supported by Leakey and Kimeu's find?

(A) The contemporary human form developed more than one million years ago.

(B) The basic human form has not evolved over time.

(C) The body parts that Leakey and Kimeu found were probably from more than one body and deposited over many years.

(D) Because of its resemblance to the contemporary human form, the body parts were probably only recently scattered in the swamp.

(E) The basic human form as it exists currently was developed initially in Africa.

STOP

If time still remains, you may review work only in this section. When the time allotted is up, you may go on to the next section.

WRITING SAMPLE TOPIC

Time—35 minutes

Directions: *The scenario presented below describes two choices, either one of which can be supported on the basis of the information given. Your essay should consider both choices and argue for one over the other, based on the two specified criteria and the facts provided. There is no "right" or "wrong" choice: a reasonable argument can be made for either. Confine your essay to the blocked, lined area on the front and back of the separate Writing Sample Response Sheet. Only that area will be reproduced for law schools. Be sure that your writing is legible.*

During two of the previous five years, the city of Sallyville has experienced storms that resulted in significant flooding problems for the city and its residents. As a consequence, the city's Water Utilities Board has been charged to recommend a flood control initiative to the City Council to address possible future flooding problems. Present an argument as to which of two proposals the Board ought to recommend, based upon the two equally important criteria on which the Board must base its decision:

- The proposed initiative should do as much as possible to remedy future severe flooding situations.
- The proposed initiative must be paid for by taxpayers and so should be cost-effective and also cause as little disruption for city residents through construction projects as possible.

Project Purple updates the city's existing, but inadequate, flood control infrastructure that depends upon channeling storm water to certain ponding areas. Experts estimate that these changes would create a flood control system that would be adequate to solve problems created by storms at the level of those in the recent five years, but would be unlikely to address effectively amounts of storm water much greater than that. Since it would use existing systems for the most part, construction of Project Purple would be minimally invasive, and the project would require only a small increase in water fees since the project would be based upon existing infrastructure.

Project Green proposes the creation of a wholly new flood control that drains excessive flood waters to a nearby reservoir outside the city limits from which city drinking water is drawn. Experts estimate that Project Green would effectively handle flood waters at nearly twice the level experienced in recent years. Because it would involve a new infrastructure, Project Green would take at least two years to complete and would involve disruption of traffic in the city during that time. In addition, the new system would be costly to build because it would not be able to make use of the city's existing flood control system.

STOP

If time still remains, you may review work only in this section.

TEST 1 ANSWER KEY

Section 1: Logical Reasoning

1. C
2. B
3. E
4. B
5. D
6. D
7. C
8. E
9. D
10. C
11. B
12. E
13. C
14. D
15. A
16. C
17. B
18. C
19. B
20. E
21. A
22. B
23. C
24. E
25. C

Section 2: Reading Comprehension

1. C
2. E
3. A
4. B
5. B
6. B
7. C
8. A
9. E
10. C
11. A
12. D
13. C
14. A
15. C
16. C
17. B
18. A
19. A
20. B
21. E
22. C
23. C
24. D
25. B
26. A
27. D
28. B

Section 3: Analytical Reasoning

1. B
2. A
3. C
4. B
5. C
6. B
7. D
8. C
9. B
10. B
11. A
12. A
13. A
14. C
15. D
16. C
17. C
18. D
19. C
20. C
21. B
22. A
23. B
24. C

Section 4: Logical Reasoning

1. D
2. B
3. D
4. C
5. C
6. D
7. E
8. C
9. D
10. D
11. C
12. E
13. C
14. E
15. D
16. A
17. D
18. D
19. D
20. A
21. D
22. D
23. D
24. A

TEST 1 DETAILED EXPLANATIONS OF ANSWERS

SECTION 1: LOGICAL REASONING

1. **Question:** The question asks for something that "must also be true" from the statements in the passage. It is asking for an inference.

   Analysis: With an inference question it is usually not possible to know specifically what the correct answer will do, except that it is something that cannot be false if the statements in the passage are true. So be clear on what the statements mean. The first includes "all" teachers at Weston Academy and says that they will all leave a mark on the future. The next three statements are about three other categories, but each of these categories includes only "some" of the teachers at Weston Academy. Each of these three groups might or might not include some of the same teachers. You cannot tell that from the word "some" alone. But each of those three categories must identify teachers who will leave their mark on the future.

   Answer: Now look to the answer choices for one that must be true. Choice (A) goes beyond the information in the passage, which is restricted only to teachers at Weston Academy. Choice (B) requires information about nonteachers at Weston Academy, information not available in the passage. Choice (C) must be true since some teachers are egotists, and all teachers leave the beneficial mark on the future. Choice (D) could be false since it need not be that any true scientists are egotists. And choice (E) brings in a category that is not discussed in the passage. (C)

2. **Question:** The question asks for something to weaken the argument.

   Analysis: The argument's conclusion is that a method of crime prevention that would be better than the sheriff's program of using reformed criminals would be to use law-abiding citizens. The reason is that students realize that speakers who are reformed criminals have become celebrities. There is an assumption that students will want to emulate that celebrity. The conclusion will be weakened with information that would make that assumption less likely to be true.

   Answer: The information that attacks the premise that needs to be attacked is in choice (B). If it is true that students fear punishment more than they desire celebrity, then they will be unlikely to want to imitate reformed criminals who have had to serve prison sentences. (B)

3. **Question:** The question asks for something that "if assumed" makes the conclusion follow from the premises stated.

   Analysis: There will be a gap between the explicit premises and the conclusion, and the correct answer will be something that fills that gap. The conclusion to the passage is that "every person on the crew is hateful." The evidence in the premises is about "men and boys" and establishes that anyone in either of those categories is hateful. But the conclusion is broader in that it introduces the category of "persons." For that conclusion to follow there needs to be something connecting the information about men and boys to the category of "persons on the crew."

   Answer: The missing connection is in choice (E).

4. **Question:** The question asks for a "required assumption."

   Analysis: There is something that must be true, other than the explicitly stated premises, for the conclusion to follow from the information given. And we are to treat the conclusion as one that does follow, so we must supply the missing information. The conclusion is that the program for unwed mothers will have to reduce its operations. The reason is that city grant funding, which accounts for 40% of the program's funding, will disappear. For it to be true that this disappearance means that the program will have to reduce its operations it must also be true that the money lost in grant funding will not be made up by another source.

Answer: An assumption that must be true is contained in choice (B). The correct answer does not have to include everything that is required for the conclusion to follow, but something that must be true. (B)

5. **Question:** The question asks for an error in reasoning in the passage.

   Analysis: The passage concludes that the feelings of alienation that many contemporary Americans claim to have could be resolved "only by going back to live in an earlier time." Note that the word "only" is very powerful. The evidence for this conclusion is a comparison of an earlier period in which people were less mobile and lived in smaller communities to contemporary times when people are more mobile and live in larger communities. These different eras are correlated with lesser feelings of alienation in the earlier and greater feelings of alienation in the later. The error is to take this correlation between eras and feelings of alienation as a cause. Just because two things happen at the same time does not mean that one must be the cause of the other. Yet that is what the conclusion to the passage takes for granted.

   Answer: The correct answer, identifying the reasoning error, is in choice (D).

6. **Question:** The question asks for a statement that strengthens the conclusion.

   Analysis: The conclusion to the passage is that the recent increase in inflation must be caused by the abrupt rise in the cost of oil. The passage offers evidence that inflation is not due to increasing costs of labor or changes in productivity. The assumption is that there is nothing else, other than the cost of oil, that might lead to the inflation.

   Answer: A strength question usually adds more evidence, something else that we know, to make the conclusion more likely to be true. Choice (D) offers additional information to make the assumption in the passage more likely to be true. It does not make the conclusion certain, but does make it more likely that the price of oil is responsible for the inflation. (D)

7. **Question:** The question asks for a principle to justify the legislator's reasoning. This suggests that a legislator in the passage will make a subtle choice, and that the choice will make sense because of some belief or other.

   Analysis: The passage shows that the choice the legislator makes is to vote for lowering the voting age for all, except for men with long hair. The legislator has an opinion that men with long hair "don't look like citizens." That alone would not be enough to make someone conclude that these long-haired people should not be granted the right to vote. To make the choice sensible, a belief is needed that would make someone who has that opinion about long-haired people decide that those who do not "look like citizens" should not be granted the right to vote.

   Answer: The correct answer is in choice (C), which expresses the needed belief. Someone who believed that would vote as the lawmaker votes. (C)

8. **Question:** The question says that the reasoning is vulnerable to criticism, which means it makes a mistake or is not valid.

   Analysis: The conclusion to the passage is in the final sentence which says that one should "start on PerFooDPlus today and you will be healthy." The evidence in the passage is about nutritional balance, and it establishes that nutritional balance is essential to being healthy and that the product provides that balance. But the conclusion takes that necessary nutritional balance and treats it as though it were enough to ensure health. Nutritional balance is one of the things that health requires, but the passage does not establish that it is enough by itself to provide for health.

   Answer: Once your analysis has led you to identify the error, you find it stated in choice (E).

9. **Question:** The question asks for something that is "most strongly supported" by the information in the passage. This will be a conclusion, probably not the main one, that

is not explicitly stated but that the statements make true at least beyond a reasonable doubt.

Analysis: The statements in the passage note that a number of apes have been said to learn American Sign Language, but also that the evidence that in fact this has happened is not based on rigorous testing. The evidence does not support either a conclusion that the apes know or do not know American Sign Language, but precisely a conclusion that the existing evidence is inadequate to reach a determination on that point.

Answer: The correct answer to this question is in choice (D).

10. **Question:** The question says that there is a flaw, and the task is to identify it.

Analysis: The flaw lies in Armand's conclusion that the probability that a cut of the cards will turn out a particular way changes because of what has happened in previous cuts of the cards. In fact, in each case the chance is the same that either of the two players will win.

Answer: This common error is expressed in choice (C).

11. **Question:** The question asks for something to weaken the environmentalist's argument. Typically a weakened question will undermine the truth of some premise in the argument.

Analysis: The environmentalist's argument reaches the conclusion that incineration is not a useful approach to addressing garbage problems. The passage lists several reasons for that, including the dangers of poisonous gases and toxic heavy metals. The final reason is a claim that efforts to convert garbage into energy have not been successful, and the evidence is that only a very small amount of the nation's total energy production comes from incineration of garbage. This evidence on energy production would be weaker in leading to the conclusion that incineration is not useful if there were also not very many plants trying to produce energy from garbage. The evidence is about the percentage of total energy production that comes from incineration of garbage, but not about the efficiency of such programs where they actually exist. That evidence, then, would be less useful in reaching the conclusion with some additional information that might say that, where it exists, incineration of garbage is effective as an energy producer. In other words, evidence that challenges the truth of the claim that recovering energy from burning garbage is not effective would weaken the main conclusion.

Answer: The argument is weakened by choice (B), which makes it less likely that the evidence in the passage proves that incineration of garbage is not useful as an energy producer. (B)

12. **Question:** The question asks for an assumption—something that must be true to make the conclusion in the passage follow from the premises that are explicitly stated.

Analysis: The conclusion in the passage is that the trend toward early retirement is not good. The reasons, from the opponents of their retirement, involve raising the nation's output, reducing the costs of Social Security, and improving the well-being of older Americans. Yet the passage explains that those very older Americans are opposed to changing early retirement. If it is to be true, indeed, that such changes would improve the well-being of elderly people, then those people who oppose it must be wrong about what will lead to their own well-being. While this must be true, it is an assumption that might be difficult to spot just from analyzing the passage. Interrogate the answer choices by asking "does this have to be true for it to be true that the trend toward early retirement is bad?"

Answer: The interrogation question leads to the realization that a required assumption is in choice (E).

13. **Question:** The question asks you to weaken the argument.

Analysis: The argument concludes in the final sentence that the youth would be better off if they abandoned the dreams of athletic success as professional athletes. The evidence for that conclusion establishes that only a slight few are actually able to climb from high school to college to professionals in athletics, so that, for most, the goal of becoming a professional athlete is wholly unrealistic. But the conclusion, you should note, is not about whether one would be a professional athlete, but whether the youth would be "better off." The implicit premise in the argument is that if one seeks to be a professional athlete but cannot accomplish that goal, then one is not well off. The argument would be weakened by something that would weaken that major premise and offer a reason why someone might be better off seeking to be a professional athlete even though not achieving that goal. A weakened question will usually attack the truth of some premise, and that would do the job here as well.

Answer: Both the premise—that if one seeks to be a professional athlete but cannot accomplish that goal then one is not well off—and the argument are weakened by choice (C), which suggests that in fact lives might be better off with that goal even though it might be unattained. (C)

14. **Question:** The question asks for a reasoning flaw, so there is a mistake in the reasoning that can be found.

    Analysis: Shannon's reasoning is that the money her new accountant says is coming to her in tax refund is in fact correctly hers. There is evidence to the contrary, yet she accepts the new accountant's calculations based on the fact that this accountant works for the most reliable accounting firm in the city. The flaw is to conclude that the particular accountant is reliable based upon the knowledge that the firm is reliable. It is not the case that something that is true of a group as a whole is true of every individual piece of that group.

    Answer: Choice (D) accurately describes the flaw. (D)

15. **Question:** This is a flaw question that asks for the most commonly occurring kind of flaw, as it tells you that the argument overlooks some possibility.

    Analysis: The argument's conclusion is in the last sentence: people do not commonly make occupational choices. The evidence for this is that people do not follow a regular pattern of occupational choice, preparation and training, working in the field, and then retirement. Rather, the evidence shows, people tend to change occupations. But the conclusion is broader in that it claims that people do not make occupational choices. The evidence supports the claim that most people do not make occupational choices before working, but overlooks the possibility that they might make those choices at some point during their work careers. The problem here stems from the fact that the conclusion is about something—making occupational choice—that the premises about occupational mobility do not treat.

    Answer: Choice (A) is the one that expresses the possibility that occupational choice might occur at some point during one's working life. (A)

16. **Question:** The question says clearly that there is a flaw.

    Analysis: The conclusion to the passage is that studies indicating several problems having to do with poor children's learning should be rejected and we should identify and address the "one true problem that poor children face in education." The flaw here is that the evidence, as the passage details, does not support the conclusion that there is "one true problem," but rather that there are many problems. So the conclusion overlooks the evidence that is available, and offers no good reason for doing so.

    Answer: The error in reasoning is correctly stated in choice (C).

17. **Question:** The question says that there is a flaw in the reasoning, and asks the test taker to seek it out.

    Analysis: The conclusion is that "poverty is essentially a rural phenomenon." The evidence for this conclusion has to do with ratios: half of the poverty in the Third World is in South Asia, the other half in other parts of the world, with 80% of these poor living in the countryside. Apparently only the remaining 20% live in more urbanized areas, from which the passage concludes that poverty is a rural phenomenon. But that neglects the possibility that the 20% might be a significant number of people living in poverty in nonrural settings. It makes the mistake of treating a smaller percentage as an absolutely small number. Always be alert when passages deal with percentages for the way they relate those percentages to absolute numbers.

Answer: Choice (B) is the choice that expresses the flaw accurately. (B)

18. **Question** The question asks for something to weaken Sun's argument.

    Analysis: Begin by being clear on what that argument is. Sun concludes that America's stable and settled law would produce peace and plenty elsewhere, based on seeing evidence in Hawaii of respect for laws on the one hand and comfort, abundance, and progress on the other. The evidence, then, is that Sun saw a correlation between peace and plenty and American law. Yet Sun's conclusion makes one of those things, law, the cause of the other. Sun's conclusion could be weakened by evidence to suggest that the peace and plenty were responsible for the law, or that there was some third thing responsible for both. Challenge the truth of the assumed premise that if there is American law, then there is peace and plenty.

    Answer: Choice (C) presents exactly that premise to weaken the conclusion by suggesting that it is not true that American law is responsible for peace and plenty. (C)

19. **Question:** The question asks for something to support, or strengthen the consultant's recommendation.

    Analysis: The consultant's recommendation is to avoid price increases because such price increases might drive some customers away, even though it would raise revenue this year. The consultant's recommendation would be made stronger with evidence that would show that driving the customers away would result in a bigger disadvantage than the advantage of bringing in more revenue in the current year. Remember, to strengthen an argument the correct answer often adds a new premise to support the conclusion.

    Answer: Choice (B) offers the additional premise that strengthens the argument by suggesting that raising prices would do more harm than good. (B)

20. **Question:** The question asks for a principle that makes a decision make sense.

    Analysis: With a principle question like this, look for a choice that an actor in the passage makes and then a principle that causes it to make sense to choose that way. In this case the speaker notes that it is very important for the country of Roccolo to lower its trade barriers, and then makes the decision that if Roccolo does not lower its trade barriers on its own then "we must use force to make it do so." For this decision to make sense it must be that any disadvantages to using force are not as important as lowering the trade barriers and preventing the various harms that come from those barriers.

    Answer: For a decision maker who believes Choice (E), the decision to use force makes sense. If economic slowdown, one of the things that would come without lowered trade barriers, is the greatest of evils, then it would make sense to use force, or anything else, to avoid it. (E)

21. **Question:** The question says that the reasoning is flawed, and asks what the flaw is.

    Analysis: The conclusion is that there should be no speed limits on freeways. The conclusion is quite absolute. But the passage then qualifies the conclusion by saying that the rights of someone to drive at excessive speeds might infringe upon the rights of others and that those two kinds of rights need to be balanced. That statement leads to the conclusion that there might need to be speed limits on freeways, as the statements in the example suggest, thereby challenging its own conclusion. The argument is inconsistent.

    Answer: Choice (A) describes the error by explaining that the reasoning is inconsistent. (A)

22. **Question:** The question asks for something to weaken the argument's conclusion.

Analysis: The conclusion is that one should forget about buying oil with special lubricating additives since changing the oil in the car regularly can prevent premature engine wear. The premises establish the value of frequent oil changes. But the premises do not discuss additives, which appear for the first time in the conclusion. So the conclusion goes further than the premises warrant in that it assumes that the value of frequent oil changes cannot be enhanced by additives in the oil. Challenge the truth of that unstated assumption, and the result is to weaken the argument as a whole.

Answer: Choice (B) attacks the assumption, and so weakens the conclusion that additives are not useful. (B)

23. **Question:** The question asks for something that is most strongly supported by the rulings together. So the answer will be something that follows from the statements in the passage, but is not explicitly stated.

Analysis: The passage explains parts of a court ruling, one part saying that the law protects observations made by reporters during news gathering, and another part that says that the law could not be used to violate a criminal defendant's right to a free trial. The correct answer will be some statement that includes both parts of this ruling, so it is important to be clear on both in proceeding to the answer choices.

Answer: Choice (C) is the statement that includes both parts of the ruling, so it is what is strongly supported by the passage. (C)

24. **Question:** The question makes clear that this is a parallel structure question. It requires analyzing the structure of the main argument and then finding the answer choice that has exactly the same structure.

Analysis: The main passage has one premise that follows the pattern: "J and H, then M." Another premise says simply "not M." And so the conclusion follows that we should not have both J and H. The correct answer will have the same kind of valid condition syllogism involving three items in the same logical positions.

Answer: Choice (E) is the one that shares all these structural elements. (E)

25. **Question:** The question asks for a principle to help explain why Israelis are better fathers than they would be under different economic circumstances. Asking for a principle means that there must be some choice Israeli fathers make that can be explained by some belief that makes the choice sensible.

Analysis: The passage asserts that the Israelis are better fathers because of an inefficient economy and relative lack of economic opportunity. This, the passage asserts, prevents Israelis from sacrificing family values for financial success. Why would it do that? Why not devote greater energy to economic activity and less to family? The missing principle would help explain that choice, or help explain the connection between economic inefficiency and spending time on family, rather than on spending even more time overcoming the effects of economic efficiency. "If someone believed this, in these economic circumstances, then he would choose to spend more time with family."

Answer: Choice (C) offers the missing principle. If people do not focus efforts on goals they see as impossible, then it makes sense that the Israelis would not focus efforts on overcoming the economic inefficiency, and instead would focus their efforts elsewhere. (C)

SECTION 2: READING COMPREHENSION

Questions 1–7

The passage includes five paragraphs. Paragraph 1 makes the point that Reconstruction after the Civil War posed many complex legal difficulties. Paragraph 2 explains that President Abraham Lincoln had ideas about Reconstruction from early on in the war based upon the fundamental notion that the so-called seceded states remain part of the Union. Paragraph 3 makes the point that according to Lincoln it was up to the federal government to assist the states in Reconstruction. Paragraph 4 makes the point that Lincoln believed that the president had the authority to carry through a Reconstruction program without the assistance of Congress. Paragraph 5 summarizes the strengths and the weakness of Lincoln's Reconstruction ideas. Taken together these paragraphs lead to a main idea that says that Reconstruction after the Civil War was a difficult issue, one that President Lincoln had considered and made proposals about early in the Civil War.

1. The first question asks for that main idea, which is best stated in choice (C). Choice (A) makes a detail mentioned in one passage into the main idea. Choice (B) goes beyond the passage and raises an argument that is not raised as an issue in it. Choice (D) takes a weakness of President Lincoln's position that is mentioned in the final paragraph and states that as the main idea. Choice (E) speculates in a way that the passage does not. (C)

2. The question asks for something that is the case "according to the passage" about President Lincoln's view of the seceded states. This discussion is in the second paragraph where it is clearly stated that Lincoln's belief was that "these so-called seceded states were, therefore, still in the Union." This detail is repeated in choice (E), which is the correct answer. (E)

3. The question asks about the purpose of a detail, and the reference mentioned in the question is to paragraph 3 where it states that Article IV, Section 4 of the Constitution, which guarantees each state in the United States republican form of government, was the source of Lincoln's belief that it was the duty of the federal government to assist the states in Reconstruction. This function is contained in choice (A).

4. The question asks which one among five things is not mentioned in the passage as a problem with Reconstruction. Each of choice (A), choice (D), and choice (E) is mentioned in the first paragraph. Choice (C) is mentioned in the second paragraph. Choice (B) is the one that is not mentioned. (B)

5. The question asks for the author's attitude toward President Lincoln's Reconstruction plan. Reviewing the main idea, the author seems to approve of and be impressed by President Lincoln's approach, though in the final paragraph he mentions a possible weakness. Choice (B) captures that attitude, repeating the word "consistent," which the author uses in characterizing Lincoln's plan in the final paragraph. (B)

6. The question asks for the purpose of the first paragraph. Reviewing the main idea and the role of the first paragraph in it, that paragraph serves to introduce the problem of Reconstruction to establish the background and context for the subsequent discussion of President Lincoln's proposed approach to the problem. Choice (B) captures that purpose. (B)

7. The final question asks for the purpose of the passage. The author writes to explain President Lincoln's approach to the problem of Reconstruction. It is not to criticize or to argue, and it does not focus on a particular issue involving the radicals of Congress or the tension between the rights of slaves and the rights of states. The purpose is well described in choice (C).

Questions 8–15

There are six paragraphs in the passage. Paragraph 1 makes the point that the horseshoe crab has a complex visual system. Paragraph 2 explains that the horseshoe crab's visual system involves brain activity as well as sensory activity. Paragraph 3 explains that the horseshoe crab's visual system adapts to nighttime. Paragraph 4 discusses more broadly the relationship between the brain and sensory organs. Paragraph 5 discusses physical connections between the brain and sensory organs, especially the eye in various animals. Paragraph 6 asserts that research on the horseshoe crab may help to understand the interaction between the brain and sensory organs in people and birds. Taken together, these paragraphs indicate that the main point is that the horseshoe crab has a complex visual system that shows an example of the interaction between the brain and sensory organs.

8. The first question asks for that main idea, which is accurately expressed in choice (A). Choice (B) focuses on a point about evolution that is mentioned only in the first paragraph. Choice (C) states the relationship between studies on the horseshoe crab and possible understanding of human beings backwards. Choice (D) focuses on human vision rather than on the crab and the relationships between the brain and sensory organs. Choice (E) restates the point of the final paragraph, but not of the passage as a whole. (A)

9. The question asks for something that is true "according to the passage" about research from the decade before the time when the passage was written. That is discussed in the third paragraph which begins with the phrase "over the past decade," and makes the point that during that decade research has begun to explore in detail "how horseshoe crabs adapt their visual systems." This focus of research in that decade is restated in choice (E).

10. The question mentions the detail of the "24-hour biological clock," and asks what it refers to in the third paragraph. Review of that paragraph shows that the phrase refers to the crab brain's adaptation to visual signals at nighttime. This is restated in choice (C).

11. The question is about a thing mentioned in the passage as an important finding from research on the horseshoe crab during the decade previous to the article. That research is discussed in paragraph 3, where it is explained that an important finding of this research was the discovery of the 24-hour biological clock to crabs transmitting nerve signals to the eye at night. This information is repeated in choice (A).

12. The question asks for the meaning of "efferent connection." The term appears in a discussion of interaction between the brain and sensory organs, and so will appear somewhere in the final three paragraphs. Review discovers it in paragraph 5, where a parenthetical statement defines efferent connections as nerve connections carrying signals from the nervous system to the sensory organs. The correct answer, in choice (D), is not specific about the direction of the connection, but simply that they are connections which carry communications. (D)

13. The question asks about the purpose of the discussion of the work of particular researchers. Review of the passage finds the particular researchers mentioned in the question, Ramon y Cajal and Miles, in the fourth paragraph. These two are discussed as researchers who did work on the communication between the brain and the eye more generally than just in the horseshoe crab. So the purpose of introducing that research is described in choice (C).

14. The question asks for something that is true, according to the author, about the study of the visual system of horseshoe crabs. Several things are mentioned about that study by the author, including the fact that recent research has explored the newly discovered complexities in the system, and that this research might help to understand vision in people and birds. Choice (A) is the only one of the choices that describes any of these points. (A)

15. The question asks for the primary purpose of the passage, which is to explain the complexity in the visual system of the horseshoe crab and to suggest that study of that system might be useful beyond understanding that crab itself. This point is made in choice (C).

Questions 16–21

This is a comparative reading task. **Passage A** describes the writing of Plato in the dialogue form, which allows Plato to reflect the teachings of Socrates and can be contrasted to the more rigorous and systematic argumentation found in the work of other philosophers. **Passage** B is about a particular Platonic dialogue, the *Crito*, which is described in order to show both the flexibility and sophistication of the dialogue form and that it can appear to teach one thing on the surface while also offering a more sophisticated philosophical argument. Taken together, the two share this main idea: Plato wrote philosophy in dialogues, a form which can make it difficult and challenging to understand Plato's own philosophical teaching, while it focuses on the beliefs and arguments of its characters, especially Socrates.

16. The question asks for a main idea of the passages "considered together." This is best expressed in choice (C). Each of the others mentions a more restricted point that is made in only one of the two passages. Only choice (C) deals with both. (C)

17. The question asks for an inference, or for something that is true assuming the truth of the things said in the passages. It could be a conclusion or a principal idea to be drawn from the information in the passage, or it might be something more minor, or more like a side effect. It is unlikely to be the same tight analytical inference characteristic of logical reasoning problems. Here the question restricts itself to drawing an inference from passage A. Note that passage A describes the conversational form that is dialogue, but also describes appearances in the characters. For it to be able to do that it must be that the form allows the depiction of physical appearance, so the correct answer is in choice (B).

18. This question asks for something that the author of passage B might say about passage A. While there is no explicit criticism of one passage by the other, there is a difference in tone or approach. Passage B is about a rigorous interpretation of a particular dialogue, while passage A is about the description of the dialogue form. That description may seem to suggest something less rigorous than the interpretation presented in passage B does, and that difference could be captured in the change proposed in choice (A).

19. This question restricts itself to passage B and asks for something that its author would be likely to agree with. As always with a reading comprehension task, this is not asking for analysis, but for careful and attentive reporting. A review of the passage leads to the location of this statement: "this more sophisticated argument does not contend that breaking the law is the only unjust thing, but leaves open the possibility that there might be more unjust things." This possibility is repeated in choice (A). There is no mention of anything like what is in (B), nor is there a principle mentioned like that in (C). The comparisons in (D) and (E) are not supported either. (A)

20. The question asks for something that is mentioned in one of the passages. It is about details, and explicit ones. Go to the passages, find the things mentioned, and then, of those mentioned in some passage, ascertain which is in passage B only. It requires careful alertness to detail, and that alertness leads to the realization that the answer is choice (B).

21. The question asks for how the passages relate to one another. Note that they do not directly address one another, but they both deal with the same material by exploring the nature of Plato's writing in dialogues. Passage A describes that writing and its characteristics more broadly, whereas passage B describes the dialogue form in its manifestation in a particular dialogue. So the correct relationship is captured in choice (E). Neither elaborates explicitly on the other, and neither do they explicitly disagree about anything about the dialogue form.

Questions 22–28

The passage contains four paragraphs. The first paragraph explains that the judicial branch has not received the kind of scientific study given to the other branches as political entities. Paragraph 2 explains that the judiciary has traditionally been studied with case analysis. Paragraph 3 claims that case analysis prevents a more accurate scientific study of the judicial branch as a whole. Paragraph 4 explains that while there are some efforts to genuine scientific study of the judiciary as a political branch, they remain inadequate. Taken together, these paragraphs establish the main idea that the traditional focus on case analysis to study the judicial branch has prevented genuine scientific study of that branch as a whole as a political institution, something which ought to be undertaken.

22. This question asks for the main idea, which is accurately expressed in choice (C). Choice (A) states a part, but only a part of the explanation in the passage. Choice (B) restates a point from the final paragraph. Choice (D) restates a point from the first paragraph that is less complete than the main idea. Choice (E) mentions the goal of getting an accurate picture of the judiciary, but misstates what the passage says about how that might be accomplished. (C)

23. The question asks for the primary purpose of the passage, which is to urge scientific study of the judiciary. So the correct answer is choice (C).

24. The question asks for the meaning of a detail. The phrase "the cult of the robe" is used in the final sentence of the first paragraph and refers to comments of Chief Justice John Marshall discussed earlier in that paragraph. Marshall claims that the judicial branch should be distinguished from the others in that the others were politically motivated but that judges were nonpolitical arbiters of the law. This meaning is captured in choice (D).

25 The question asks for an inference about what the author believes. Scholars who study the judicial branch are mentioned especially in the first and fourth paragraphs. In the fourth it says that these scholars "do not subscribe to the myth that judges are nonpolitical arbiters of the law." If that is the case, then it can be inferred—in a reading comprehension section this tends to mean "it is most likely to be the case that"—that they do not believe that judges are nonpolitical. That content is contained in choice (B).

26. The question asks for the purpose of a detail, the phrase "be able to see the forest for the trees" in the third paragraph. Go back to that paragraph and put the phrase in context, and its purpose is described in the two sentences that follow its use. The point is that to understand the judiciary one must "step back from the cases" and be able to "see the greater whole." The purpose of this detail, then, is well expressed in choice (A).

27. This question also asks for the purpose of a detail, in this case the reference to Kilmer in the third paragraph. This reference is in the final sentence of the paragraph, and its purpose is to reinforce the point of the paragraph as a whole that to get an accurate picture of the workings of the judiciary one should step back from the particular cases and look to the whole. While there may be something to learn from particular cases, studying the whole is valuable as well. In the sentence Kilmer is said "to appreciate the beauty of a tree," and therefore is mentioned here to grant the value, however limited, of studying particular cases. The point is well stated in choice (D).

28. The question asks about the author's attitude toward the utility of case studies and judicial biographies for understanding judicial decision making. The author addresses these points in the final paragraph where the author grants that judicial biographies and case studies are "certainly useful," but also that there is more to be done in terms of scientific study. So the author's attitude is exactly described in choice (B).

SECTION 3: ANALYTICAL REASONING

Questions 1–7

This is purely an ordering situation. The following diagram simplifies the rules and shows the deductions.

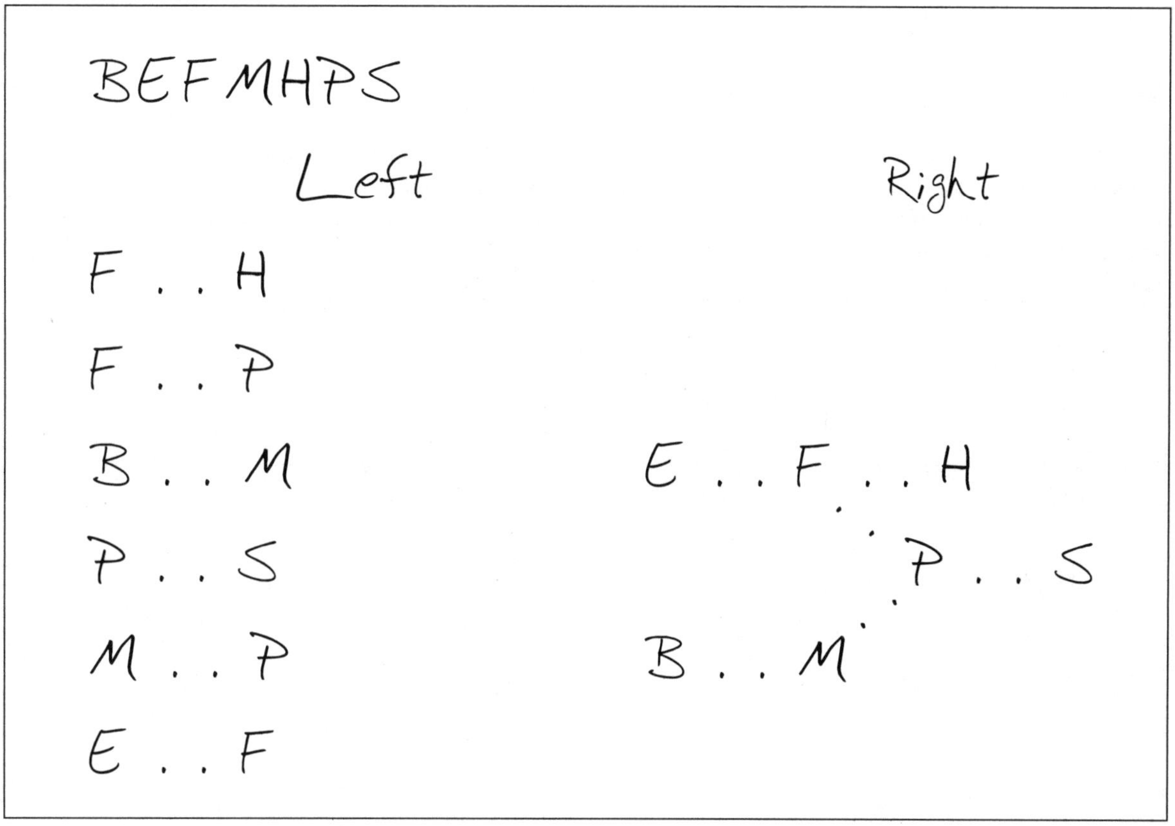

Note that the rules say something about each of the seven items, so that you know something about the relative order of each. There are exactly two of them, E and B, that might be farthest left, and exactly two, H and S, that might be farthest right. Be careful not to assume relationships that do not exist between E, F, H, on the one hand, and B and M on the other.

1. The question is testing your accurate reading of the rules and basic deductions. The answer is in choice (B).
2. The question places E third from the left, which means the first two from the left must be B and M. The answer to this question is choice (A).
3. The question asks for something that must be false, so check the five possibilities against the remaining things that are possible as shown on the diagram. The one that cannot be true is choice (C) since B must always be to the left of M. (C)
4. This question places B, E, M farthest to the left. Whatever the relative order of those three, the next one must be F, since F has to be to the left of P. The correct answer is in choice (B).

5. This question places M in the fourth position, which means that the ones to the left of it must include B, E, F, in some order. To the right are P, H, S, in some order. The question asks for what cannot be true about the remaining variables. Choice (C) would violate the rule that establishes the relative order between P and S, so it must be false. (C)

6. Four of these lists obey the rules, but one does not. That one, which violates the rule on P and S, is choice (B).

7. The question places B third from left. For that to be the case, it is necessary for the first two, in order, to be E, F, making the correct answer choice (D).

Questions 8–13

This is a placement situation. It includes six items to be placed in positions one through six. The conditions do not so much establish relative order as they do absolute placement. So we are more concerned about the placement of items relative to slots than about the placement of items relative to one another. The following diagram shows the items, the slots, and the simplified rules:

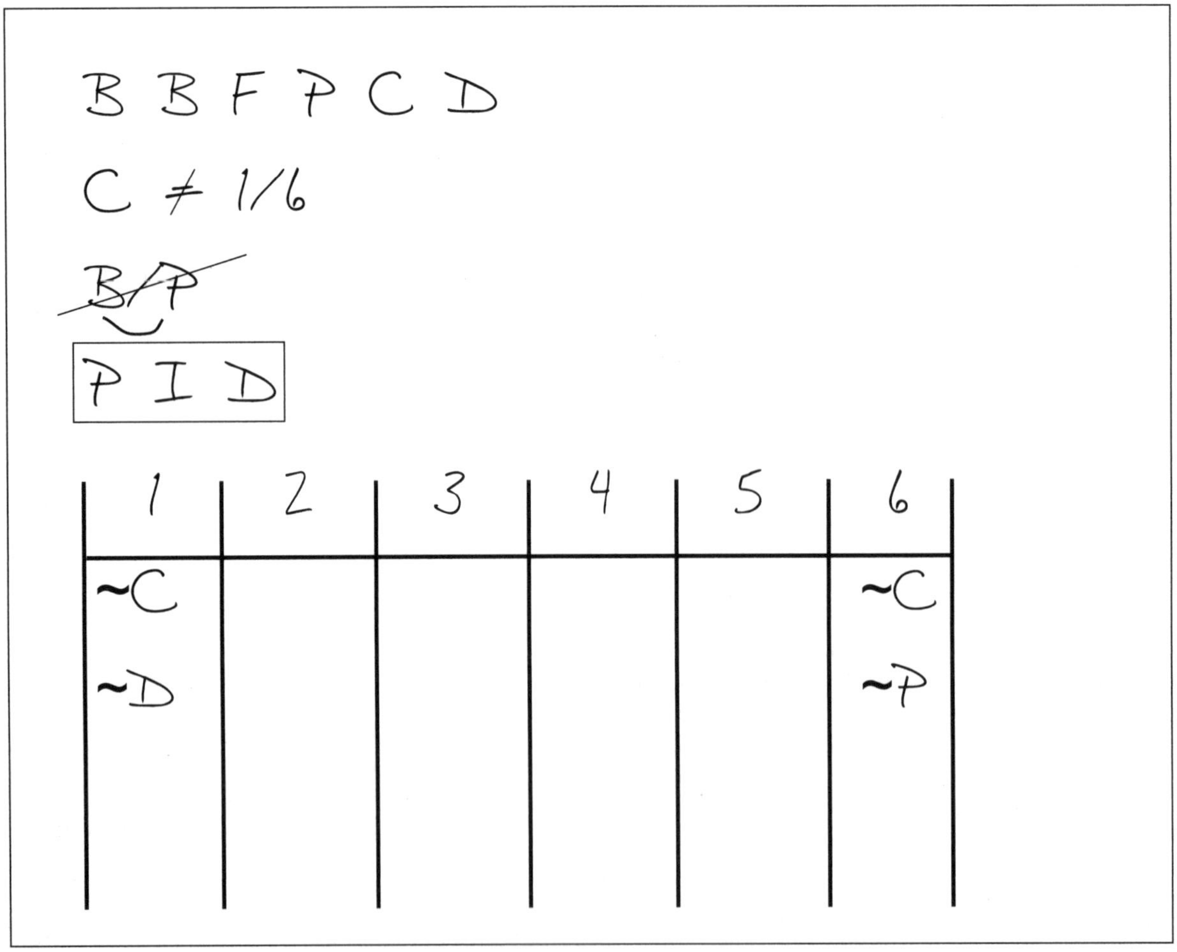

Note that the block of P and D will take up two consecutive slots, and that neither of the two Bs can be placed in the slot immediately before. So knowing the slot that any one of those four items (B, B, P, D) occupies will yield a lot of information.

8. For this "acceptable outcome" question, simply take the rules one by one and use them to eliminate answer choices that violate them. The correct answer that violates no rules is in choice (C).

9. This question places the two Bs in slots 2 and 6. Because of the rule on B and P, combined with the fact that C cannot be in 1, you can deduce the placement of all items: F, B, C, P, D, B. So what must be true is in choice (B).

10. This question places P and D in 2 and 3. In that circumstance, the only item that can be in 1 is F, and one of the Bs must be in 6. So the correct answer is in choice (B).

11. This question asks for a placement of items that makes only one outcome possible. Choice (A) does that, since it would force P and D into slots 5 and 6, requiring C to be in 4 and F to be in 1. (A)

12. This question asks for one of five choices that violates a rule. The rule on B and P is violated by choice (A).

13. This question places three or more slots between the two Bs. It must be false in that case that one of the Bs is in slot 4, since that would make it impossible to fit three in between the two Bs. So the correct answer about what must be false is in choice (A).

Questions 14–18

This is a grouping situation. It requires a group of four to be made out of seven possible items. Each of the items is either a faculty member or an administrator, and each of the items is either a man or a woman. Each is either from the undergraduate college or from the professional schools. Any acceptable group must include exactly two from each of those six categories. The simplified rules are shown in this diagram:

4 (GHIJKLM)
A = GJL
F = HIKM

C = GIL
P = HJKM

M = HIJM
w = GKL
2 EACH CATEGORY

Of course each item has two characteristics, so the key will be finding combinations that together produce the right assortment of A and F, C and P, and M and W. Individual questions are likely to involve identifying items that have particular combinations of characteristics. The situation relies heavily on the rules and on applying them in the case of every question. Notice that G and L are in the smaller category in each set of two categories. That must mean that, at a minimum, one of G and L must be included in any acceptable group of four.

14. The question includes I in the group and asks for something else that must be included as well. There seem to be many possibilities here, so find a way that will enable you to test as few as needed. If I is included, then there is exactly one other C, which must be either G or L. Test those. If G is the one, consider what this means for As. The other A could not be L, because that would mean too many Cs. So in that case the other A would have to be J. And if the second C is not G but L, then the second A could not be G because that, too, would mean too many Cs, so in that case also the second A would have to be J. In either case, then, J is an item that must be included. There may be others, but see if this one appears in the answer choices. It does, making the correct answer choice (C).

15. The question asks for a pair that could not both be in the group of four at the same time. This would be a pair that would make it impossible to meet the conditions of distribution according to the six categories. Test the answer choices to see whether each particular selection would make it possible to select two others and satisfy the rules. Choice (A), for example, would give you both Cs, one each of F and A, and one each of M and W. The remaining needs might be met with K and J, so choice (A) is a pair that could be chosen together. The pair that would make it impossible to fill out the group according to the rules is contained in choice (D).

16. The question says that K is included in the group, and asks for something else that must be as well. With K the other from category W must be either G or L. And by the same token, it would be impossible to include both G and L, since that would make for too many Ws. That means that the two As cannot be G and L, and so one of the As must be J. But J is not offered as one of the answer choices, so keep going. By similar reasoning, the two Cs cannot be G and L, and so one of the Cs must be I. This is included in the answer choices, making the correct answer choice (C).

17. This question places M in the group and asks for a pair that must also be included with M. M is in each category with four items, so its inclusion means exactly two of the items in each of the categories with three, A, C, and W must be selected. The only way to do that, while still selecting an additional item from category P, is to include both G and L, each of which is in all three of A, C, and W. So the correct answer is choice (C).

18. This question is far easier than it might at first appear. Focus on the three categories that include three items apiece. G and L are in all three, and that leaves only three basic scenarios: one including both G and L and the other two including either one of G or L along with I, J, and K. If only one of G or L is included, the remaining three items are known. If both are included, then the remaining two items would have to satisfy the requirements of the remaining categories, and only H and M can do that. So it turns out that there are only three possible groups, and the answer to the question is choice (D).

Questions 19–24

This situation has some elements of a grouping situation in that it creates five sets of two. But it also incorporates elements of a placement situation in that the groups belong to five people placed beside each other seated at a table. Both kinds of rules and deductions become important, and both are represented on the diagram below.

The diagram also shows the simplified rules and a number of deductions that are drawn from those rules.

By rule B a table has both an M and an O, and by rule E it has an L. This placement information, connected to other placement information and some grouping rules, leads to a number of deductions. One key rule is that no one belongs to a group that someone sitting next to him belongs to. So that means, for example, that neither A nor C can include either an M or an O. Since there are only five items that the two items belonging to each person come from, and since conditional statements severely restrict four of those five items, there are few choices remaining for the others sitting at the table. You know what belongs to B and to E.

Those grouping rules and their contrapositives are listed in the diagram below. And beneath that is a major deduction about what must make up the two items belonging to each of the people seated at the table.

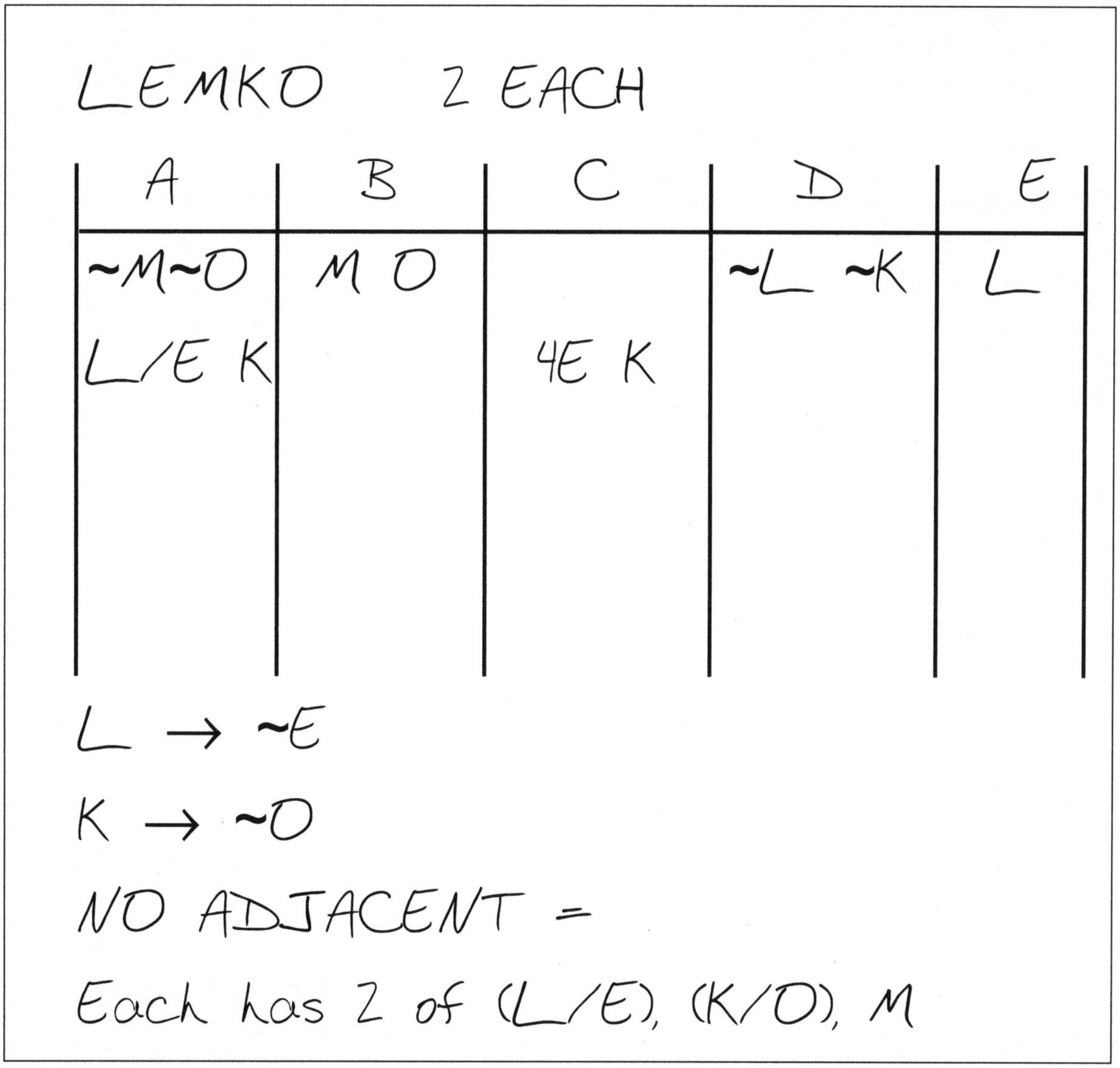
LEMKO 2 EACH
A
B
C
D
E
~M~O
M O
~L ~K
L
L/E K
4E K
L → ~E
K → ~O
NO ADJACENT =
Each has 2 of (L/E), (K/O), M

19. The first question is a typical one asking for an acceptable outcome. As always, eliminate incorrect answers by testing the rules against the answer choices until each answer choice but one has been eliminated. The one that does not violate a rule is choice (C).

20. This question asks for something that must be true, without adding additional information. And so it is asking for a basic deduction. The things that must be true include the fact that each of A and C must have a K (because neither can have one of the items that B has). That deduction is in choice (C).

21. This question adds a condition and asks for what must be true. The condition leads to a chain reaction involving several of the people. The condition that no one except B can have both M and either K or O most clearly affects D, which, if it cannot have that combination, must have E. the consequence of that is that neither C nor E can also have an E, so that at most the only other E could belong to A. So the correct answer here is to be found in choice (B).

22. The question asks for what could be true about the things that belong to Dave. The basic deduction here has already been made, that D cannot have either an L or a K. So the correct answer is in choice (A).

23. This question adds the condition that C has an E and asks for what must be true. Placing an E in C leads to a chain reaction since it means there cannot be an E in D. Since there also cannot be either an L or a K in D, D would have to contain an M and an O. So the correct answer is choice (B).

24. This question adds another person at the end of the table, an F, and places both M and K in that group. It then asks for what must be true. The first effect here is to prevent E from having either an M or a K, which means that E must have an O with his L. That, in turn, means that D cannot have an O, so D must have an M and an E. The answer is in choice (C).

SECTION 4: LOGICAL REASONING

1. **Question:** The question asks for something that is most strongly supported by the passage, or something that the passage makes true beyond a reasonable doubt.

   Analysis: The main conclusion is that causes for intellectual alarm about the generally accepted understanding of the formation of the universe began in the mid-1980s. The premises, the evidence in the passage, are about doubts about the Big Bang theory. The conclusion does not mention the Big Bang theory, and the premises do not mention "the generally accepted understanding of the formation of the universe." The passage strongly suggests that those things are connected, or that the generally accepted theory is the Big Bang theory.

   Answer: Choice (D) is the choice that provides the missing link between "Big Bang" and "generally accepted understanding of the formation of the universe." (D)

2. **Question:** The question asks for an assumption that is required by the argument.

   Analysis: The conclusion is in the first sentence, that "a more aggressive prosecution of antitrust cases is needed." The evidence in the passage has to do with the need to control inflation and with a claim that monopoly causes inflation. But "prosecution of antitrust cases" is something that appears for the first time in the conclusion. For that conclusion to follow, then, "prosecution of antitrust cases" needs to be connected to the prevention of monopoly for controlling inflation.

   Answer: Choice (B) provides the necessary connection. The other way to identify that missing assumption would be to interrogate each of the answer choices, asking, "Does this have to be true for it to be true that a more aggressive prosecution of antitrust cases is needed?" (B)

3. **Question:** The question asks for what can be inferred from the statements in the passage.

   Analysis: An inference will be something that is unstated, but that must be true based upon what the passage says. It may not be possible to know exactly what that inference will be, since there might be several, but before going to the answer choices, analyze the passage for what it means. It begins by saying that one cannot be certain that correct grammar is a sign of greater intelligence, but ends with the category of "most people" who believe that better grammar does mean more intelligence. The phrase "most people" means something definite: 50% plus one or more, and so that is likely to figure into the inference. Now interrogate the choices. Any choice that can be made false consistent with the information in the passage is not the inference.

   Answer: So ask of each choice, "Can this be false?" Choice (A) could be false, since there is nothing that says that the majority believes that intelligent people never use poor grammar. Choice (B) could be false since it deals with an individual. Choice (C) can be false as the final sentence of the paragraph indicates. Choice (D) cannot be false as it is largely a restatement of the final sentence in the paragraph: if people believe that better grammar means more intelligence, then people believe that someone with good grammar is more intelligent than someone with poor grammar. That, however, does not require Choice (E) to be true, since that choice puts the relationship the other way around. (D)

4. **Question:** The question is a structure question: it asks for something that the two discussants disagree on.

   Analysis: Often with questions like this the answer about what the two disagree on is the conclusion from the first of the two speakers. In this case, however, Tiffany and John do not disagree with Tiffany's conclusion, which is that Lisa ought to have been offered a scholarship. They do disagree, however, on the question of whether Lisa has ever made a mistake in a game in which Tiffany has also played.

Answer: Choice (C) states the disagreement. (C)

5. **Question:** This is a paradox question asking you to explain the apparently paradoxical results of studies.

   Analysis: The two sides of the apparent paradox are these: studies show that people in authority have a greater life expectancy on the one hand, yet on the other hand studies also show that people in authority are more likely to feel stress, which is a cause of heart attack. How can it be true both that people in authority are more likely to have heart attacks and that people in authority tend to live longer? The correct answer will offer additional information that allows both things to be true of the same people.

   Answer: Choice (C) adds additional information which explains how both could be true at the same time. (C)

6. **Question:** The question asks for additional information that would be helpful to have in assessing a conclusion. Ordinarily this kind of question is asking for an assumption that would need to be confirmed for the conclusion to follow from the information given. What would be helpful to know is whether that assumption is correct.

   Analysis: In this problem the conclusion is actually in the question stem, which asks whether Eureka can expect snow. The evidence in the passage says that a cold front is about to hit Eureka and that precipitation comes from 75% of such fronts. But the question is, will there be snow? Can we assume that the precipitation will be snow? And to answer that question we would want to know the likelihood of any precipitation falling being snow.

   Answer: Choice (D) correctly states the thing it would be helpful to know. (D)

7. **Question:** The question asks for a parallel flaw. The passage has a reasoning error, and one of the five answer choices has exactly the same error.

   Analysis: The passage says that if one writes beautiful opera then one has a talent for music composition and a flair for the dramatic. It then says that Bach had one of those two necessary things but not the other, and concludes that if he had possessed the other (a flair for the dramatic) he would have excelled at opera writing. The error here is to convert something that is required (to write operas well) to something that is sufficient (to write operas well). If he had been able to write beautiful operas, then he would have had a flair for the dramatic, but that does not mean that a flair for the dramatic would have been enough, together with the talent for composition, to guarantee the writing of opera.

   Answer: Analyze the answer choices for the same mistake: converting something needed for a particular result into something enough to produce that result itself. Choice (E) makes exactly the same mistake in saying that deserving to be on the advisory committee requires one to be bright and to be a senior designer. Sally lacks one of those necessary qualities, and so, it concludes, that if she had that quality she would be on the committee. Just like in the passage, the presence of the necessary qualities may not be enough to provide for presence on the advisory committee. (E)

8. **Question:** The question asks for something that, "if assumed," allows the conclusion to be drawn.

   Analysis: This is the kind of assumption that is not not required, but that fills in a gap that needs to be filled for the conclusion to follow from the information explicitly stated. The conclusion is that employers should realize that the desire for profit maximization should lead to the support of increased wages for overtime. The evidence in the passage establishes that increase in overtime wages is connected to increases in production. The evidence is about production, but the conclusion is about profit maximization. Profit maximization is something new in the conclusion which needs to be connected to the productivity that comes with increased overtime wages.

   Answer: Choice (C) offers that connection between productivity and profitability that allows the conclusion to follow. (C)

9. **Question:** The question asks for an assumption that must be true for the conclusion to follow in the passage.

Analysis: The passage is about human ingestion of nutrients, and explains that a number of factors are involved, only some of which are directly related to the physiological need for food. The passage says that sensory factors induce people to eat beyond physiological need, and that for some people these sensory factors become very important, leading to improper nutrition. The conclusion seems to be that this nutrition is improper because eating in response to sensory factors is not eating in response to physiological need. To find a missing assumption ask of each of the choices,"does this have to be true for it to be true that eating in response to sensory desires is not eating in response to physiological need?"

Answer: The information in choice (D) has to be true. (D)

10. **Question:** The question asks for something to weaken the argument.

Analysis: The argument concludes that attempts to ascertain the contribution of Whitehead's process philosophy to social and political theory must be inadequate. They must be inadequate because there is no serious study of Whitehead's own social and political thought. The unstated assumption is that such a study would be necessary to understand the contribution of Whitehead's process philosophy to social and political theory. To weaken the argument, attack that premise and make it less likely that that understanding would be necessary to understand the contribution.

Answer: Choice (D) directly challenges the assumption that a study of Whitehead's own social and political thought would be needed to understand the contribution of his process philosophy. (D)

11. **Question:** The question asks for something that "if assumed" allows the conclusion to be drawn. This says that there is a link missing between the premises and the conclusion, and asks you to supply something to make that link.

Analysis: The conclusion is in the final sentence, stating that the criticism from the media will lead mainstream publishers to think about cleaning up their act. The premise is that various news media are criticizing the adult orientation of comic books. The evidence is about the criticism, but the conclusion is that publishers will think about cleaning up their act. There needs to be a connection between those two things, a connection that does not exist in the explicit premises and, so, must be provided by an assumption.

Answer: Choice (C) provides an assumption that supplies the needed missing link between the criticism and cleaning up their act. (C)

12. **Question:** The question asks for the identification of something that is not a premise in the argument. This is a structure question, testing your ability to analyze an argument for its conclusion and premises.

Analysis: The conclusion to the argument is in the second half of the first sentence, that opting for a fake burger over a real one can be a healthy practice. The remainder of the passage includes various reasons for that being the case.

Answer: Choice (E) restates the conclusion rather than one of those premises, and so is the answer to the question here. (E)

13. **Question:** The question asks for a mistake or flaw in the reasoning.

Analysis: The conclusion is that the meaning of politics remains mysterious and confounding. But the evidence for this conclusion has to do with politics as it predated Aristotle and with the differences in politics in the 21st century. Thus the discussion of the various manifestations of politics assumes that it knows what politics is. The error in the passage, then, is that it must assume that it knows what politics is in order to conclude that the meaning of politics is not known.

Answer: Choice (C) states the error exactly. (C)

14. **Question:** The question asks for something to weaken the writer's argument.

Analysis: The conclusion is in the first sentence, that Molière was affected by Italian comic theater. The evidence is that Molière's company shared space with an Italian troupe and that Molière's acting style was seen to have been modeled after someone named Fiorilli. One implicit premise here is that if Molière as an actor modeled after Fiorilli then he was affected by Italian comic theater. One way to weaken that argument would be to challenge the truth of that premise.

Answer: Choice (E) challenges the assumed premise, and, thus, makes the conclusion less likely to be true. (E)

15. **Question:** The question asks for an error in reasoning.

Analysis: The conclusion in the passage is that death is desirable. This conclusion is reached by an analogy. Something that many people see is visible, and something that many people hear is audible. By analogy, it says, something that many people desire is desirable. But there is a difference between saying that something can be experienced through the senses and saying that something is a thing to be sought after. They are different kinds of categories, and so the analogy is very weak.

Answer: Choice (D) identifies this error. (D)

16. **Question:** The question is about the structure of the argument, asking for the role of a particular phrase.

Analysis: The passage is a quotation from Locke, who reaches the conclusion that "one may destroy a man who makes war upon him, or has discovered an enmity to his being." One may do this, according to the passage, "for the same reason that he may kill a wolf or a lion." This provides an analogy of a similar circumstance where, according to Locke, it is appropriate and right to act according to motives one assumes in another. The phrase is not evidence that the conclusion depends upon, but an example meant to clarify the conclusion.

Answer: Choice (A) correctly identifies the role of the phrase as example. (A)

17. **Question:** The question asks for something that it would be important to know in attempting to verify a parapsychologist's claim.

Analysis: The answer to this sort of question usually involves an assumption made in reaching the conclusion. The claim in the passage is that some people posit clairvoyance based upon evidence that a significant percentage of lottery winners claim to choose their numbers as a result of some kind of "flash" rather than because of some more explainable reason. But the evidence deals only with those who win, and not with those who lose. So the argument assumes that this reliance on "flashes" occurs more with winners than losers. It would help to know whether this is the case to evaluate the parapsychologist's claim.

Answer: Choice (D) states the assumption whose truth it would be useful to know accurately. (D)

18. **Question:** The question is about structure, asking for the method of argument of the second speaker.

Analysis: The first speaker concludes that a corporation cannot make profits and protect the environment simultaneously. Alice disputes that conclusion by presenting a counter example.

Answer: Choice (D) states the method of argument by counterexample correctly. (D)

19. **Question:** The question asks for an assumption on which the conclusion is based.

Analysis: The conclusion is that it is improper to set up monuments to famous men and women. The reasoning is that no citizen deserves to be "deified." For the conclusion to follow there needs to be a connection between deification and setting up monuments, or it must be the case that to set up a monument to someone is to deify that person.

Answer: Choice (D) supplies this missing piece, and would have to be true for the conclusion to follow from the explicit premises. (D)

20. **Question:** The question asks for something to weaken the argument.

    Analysis: The conclusion is that each employee of a corporation should be willing to endure hardship for the sake of fellow employees, just as family members do. This is because, according to the passage, a corporation is like a giant family. Something that would undermine the premise likening a corporation to a family would weaken the conclusion.

    Answer: Choice (A) offers information to dispute the claim that a corporation is like a family, and so serves to undermine the conclusion. (A)

21. **Question:** The question asks for a parallel flaw, or for an answer choice that exhibits the same reasoning error as the passage has.

    Analysis: The flaw in the passage is this: it moves from the claim that all pilots who used to fly for Go East Airlines are bitter to a conclusion that anyone bitter who now flies for Gone South Airlines must be one of those Go East pilots. There is a difference between saying that all Go East pilots are bitter and that all bitter people are Go East pilots. That is the mistake in the passage.

    Answer: Choice (D) is the answer choice that makes the same mistake: the fact that all the birds have beaks does not mean that all things with beaks are birds. (D)

22. **Question:** The question asks for an assumption that is necessary to the argument.

    Analysis: The conclusion is in the first sentence, stating that for students to keep up with academic achievement there needs to be a program to release teachers from classroom time to teach them new technologies. The evidence in the passage is to establish that teachers will not master these technologies and utilize them fully without such release time. But the keeping up with academic achievement of the rest of the world is something that appears for the first time in the conclusion. And so for the evidence in the passage to lead to this conclusion there must be some assumption, some unstated premise that links the utilization of technology to academic achievement.

    Answer: Choice (D) is that required premise, making the necessary link between teaching technologies and academic achievement. (D)

23. **Question:** The question asks for something most strongly supported by the information in the passage. The question is asking for something that is not stated, but that can be concluded beyond a reasonable doubt based on the statements in the passage.

    Analysis: The statements in the passage establish that Native Americans had a deep reverence for the Yeti, or Bigfoot. The passage includes information that a student concludes that Bigfoot exists, but the student goes further than the evidence does. The evidence does, however, strongly support the conclusion that some Native Americans believed that Bigfoot exists, but not more than that.

    Answer: Choice (D) expresses the conclusion that is almost certainly the case from the statements in the passage. Whether the some who believed in Bigfoot were correct to do so is not settled by the evidence in the passage. (D)

24. **Question:** The question asks for what is most strongly supported by the find of the people mentioned in the passage. Look for something not stated in the passage that follows, beyond a reasonable doubt, from the things that are stated.

    Analysis: The passage states that Leakey and Kimeu found a human skeleton that was 1.6 million years old. The bones, which were scattered in a swamp, were like the human form today.

    Answer: The information in the passage strongly supports the statement in choice (A). It does not support strongly the information in any of the other choices. Each of those would be consistent with the find described in the passage, but the find does not suggest that any of them is highly likely. (A)

SAMPLE ESSAY

Project Green and Project Purple both address the serious concerns that the Water Utilities Board must take into account in recommending an approach to address the city's flooding problem. On balance, Project Green is the better approach to recommend. After all, the reason why City Council is determined to undertake any project is the fact that the flooding problems have been devastating to city residents in recent years. Yet it is not possible to predict with certainty whether floods of similar magnitude will present themselves in the coming years or whether even greater threats might come from new storms. Project Green will dependably handle flood waters at the levels recently experienced, but more, will enable the city and its residents to rest assured that even greater problems, should they arise, will have been provided for by effective planning.

To be sure, Project Green means preparation for problems yet unseen and unpredicted and is costly and disruptive. There is no denying that this is a serious problem, one that city leaders and residents will find highly troublesome during the construction period. That trouble, however, will be seen, in retrospect, as a price that was worth paying in the event of an unprecedented storm that does not result in devastation to the city because the city planned and built ahead to prepare for such a problem. Project Purple would not entail the short-term disruption or the cost for a system that might not be needed, but it also would not provide the constant peace of mind and the actual remedy for the future flood of yet-unseen proportions.

In sum, then, it does not underestimate the difficulty of the decision to conclude that the better choice, the choice involving the most potential benefit for the city and its residents, is to undergo the short-term pain to build Project Green.

LSAT

LAW SCHOOL ADMISSION TEST

PRACTICE TEST 2

PRACTICE TEST 2

SECTION 1

Time—35 minutes
28 questions

Directions: *Each passage in this section is followed by a group of questions to be answered on the basis of what is stated or implied in the passage. For some questions, more than one of the choices could conceivably answer the question. However, you are to choose the* ***best*** *answer; that is, the response that most accurately and completely answers the question, and blacken the corresponding space on your answer sheet.*

Apprehension over the development and implementation of nuclear power plants was confirmed in the minds of critics when the media announced the fuel meltdown at Three Mile Island in Harrisburg, Pennsylvania, in 1979 and again confirmed with the accident at the nuclear plant at Chernobyl in 1986. Environmentalists who had raised serious questions preceding and after the two catastrophes continue to press for research and development of solar energy and other nonfossil sources, such as wind and geothermal.

The federal courts entered the process in the 1970s when an interest group charged the Atomic Energy Commission with unfair and inadequate procedures during a licensing process. Although the interest group convinced the United States Circuit Court of Appeals that closer judicial monitoring of the licensing process was within constitutional protections, it lost its case in the United States Supreme Court in *Vermont Yankee Nuclear Power Corporation v. Natural Resources Defense Council, Inc.* in 1978. The Supreme Court held that the agency's informal rule making was based upon technical data, and the courts should not become "Monday morning quarterbacks." Other activities of interest groups, such as Public Concern, National Audubon Society, and Worldwatch Institute, led to the demise of construction of nuclear plants with no new orders by 1978. Over the years additional concerns of interest groups and many citizens developed regarding radioactive waste disposal.

For many years nuclear scientists had great influence on industrial and political leaders, university administrator policymakers, and major professional groups. As early as the 1950s, the slogan "atomic energy for peace" led to full-scale plans for research and development which was supposed to provide safe, cheap, and unlimited sources of electricity. The bandwagon gained momentum, and the nuclear reactor program became the buzzword of the 1950s and 1960s. Enthusiasts promised that atomic energy would provide the solution for combating the greenhouse effect and for promoting industrial growth.

Problems developed when the industry failed to meet its promises. Construction costs were higher than predicted. Construction was complex and plagued by errors. The amount of time between initiation of construction and authorization by government to begin electrical generation far exceeded all expectations. Adding to the cost of construction and maintenance was the fact that plant constructions were unique, with variation from plant to plant. Cancellations of nuclear reactors by utility companies became prevalent during this period of time. At least three large plants completed construction but did not begin operation, and only about one hundred commercial nuclear plants generate electricity.

Pro-nuclear activists have gone back to the drawing board in search of new ideas which will again generate enthusiasm for nuclear energy and funds for industrial and university research projects. The high cost of nuclear energy remains the major factor in the decision-making process of managers of utilities. Over the years, stockholders became disillusioned with investment in utilities with nuclear-powered plants, and management responded accordingly. But as the price of oil increases, the relative price of nuclear energy shrinks, something that will bring it back into the energy supply conversation over time.

1. Which of the following best expresses the main idea of the passage?

   (A) Though once seen optimistically as a solution to energy problems, atomic energy fell into disrepute because of problems in the industry confirmed with accidents at Three Mile Island and Chernobyl.

   (B) Pro-nuclear activists have found themselves frustrated by events surrounding the development of nuclear power and search for new ideas to gain enthusiasm for the project.

   (C) Despite a court refusal to involve itself in the regulatory process, the nuclear energy industry has failed to grow at the same rate it grew in the 1950s and 1960s.

   (D) The fuel meltdown at Three Mile Island and the accident at the nuclear plant in Chernobyl awakened anti-nuclear activists and led them to be able to discourage future building of nuclear power plants.

   (E) Despite problems in construction at times in its history, the nuclear power industry will grow in the future as its relatively high cost becomes smaller in light of increasing energy prices elsewhere.

2. Which of the following is not mentioned as a problem that developed with the nuclear power industry?

   (A) Each nuclear power plant was unique, which made them more expensive to build and maintain.

   (B) Court regulation of the use of atomic energy slowed development of new plants and made it more costly.

   (C) Fuel meltdowns at nuclear power plants confirmed apprehension over the development and implementation.

   (D) Several active interest groups oppose the development of nuclear plants.

   (E) Construction of nuclear power plants was plagued by errors.

3. According to the passage, in the 1970s the federal courts ultimately took the position that

   (A) environmentalists had raised serious questions regarding the use of nuclear power.

   (B) the Atomic Energy Commission should be permitted to make its rules based upon technical data.

   (C) nuclear scientists should have great influence on decisions regarding the use of nuclear power.

   (D) close judicial monitoring of the nuclear licensing process was within constitutional protections.

   (E) it was appropriate for the Supreme Court to raise questions about the Atomic Energy Commission's informal rule-making process after the rules were made.

4. Which of the following best characterizes the role of the third paragraph in the passage?

   (A) It provides commentary on the court decisions discussed in the previous paragraph.

   (B) It offers historical perspective on the meltdown incidents from the 1970s and 1980s.

   (C) It puts the development of nuclear power in historical perspective by showing the early optimism toward it.

   (D) It offers an introduction to the problems that the nuclear power industry would face, leading ultimately to its demise.

   (E) It offers initial reasons for the cancellations of some nuclear reactors and for others not beginning operations once built.

5. The word *bandwagon* in the third paragraph is used probably in order to

   (A) indicate the growing consensus that nuclear power is dangerous and expensive.

(B) show that more and more interest groups in opposition to atomic energy were organizing.

(C) express the reality of increasing problems associated with the building of nuclear power plants.

(D) describe the early excitement over the possibilities of atomic energy that led to the initial growth of the industry.

(E) capture the new momentum that is developing as pro-nuclear activists generate new enthusiasm for nuclear energy.

6. The passage implies that opponents of the use of nuclear power

(A) have successfully used nonviolent protest techniques against the industry.

(B) have sought the development of energy sources that depend neither on nuclear power nor on fossil fuels.

(C) successfully shut down many nuclear power plants through their activities.

(D) succeed in persuading the courts of the problems posed by radioactive waste disposal.

(E) argue that nuclear power plants can never provide a cost-effective source of energy.

7. The primary purpose of the passage is to

(A) raise the question of the level to which the federal courts ought to be involved in regulating nuclear power.

(B) describe the demise of the nuclear power industry.

(C) advocate for the renewal of interest in generating power through nuclear energy.

(D) show the importance of interest groups and their activities in discouraging the development and implementation of nuclear power plants.

(E) argue that the initial excitement over atomic energy was misplaced and that nuclear power plants should not have been built.

8. Which of the following would be most appropriate as a title for the passage?

(A) Nuclear Power: Hopes for the Future

(B) The Power of Citizen Activists—The Case of Nuclear Power Plants

(C) Promise Unfulfilled: The Decline of the Nuclear Power Industry

(D) The Disaster of Nuclear Energy

(E) Wrongful Inaction: The Federal Courts and the Nuclear Power Industry

Passage A

Today the role of business and government in solving social problems remains a controversial topic. Children no longer work in factories. Working hours for both men and women are regulated by government. Some observers feel that New Deal legislation sponsored by President Franklin D. Roosevelt provided the major thrust for governmental regulation of private sector personnel practices that were too long within the exclusive jurisdiction of industry and business management. At first judicial independence under the system of separation of powers allowed the Supreme Court to strike Roosevelt-initiated statutes as unconstitutional.

Pressure was mounting on President Roosevelt and Congress to use the constitutional checks available to them to rein in a judicial branch that many saw as abusing its constitutional independence. Indeed the executive and legislative branches did just that, but without undertaking the unusual measures proposed by the president and under consideration by Congress. Deaths and resignations on the Supreme Court, followed by the appointment of men sensitive to the political goals of the president, led to judicial support of laws designed to deal with social ills in the country. In the 1930s and early 1940s the Supreme Court then permitted Congress to pass such legislation as Social Security, workers' compensation, and mandatory minimum wages. Congress and the Supreme Court became allies in authorizing governmental "intrusion" into the private sector's arena, allowing the country to address pressing social problems.

Passage B

By the 1950s, long-standing racial discrimination was challenged. The legislative and executive had remained too long aloof and generally ignored problems associated with inequality. The National Association for the Advancement of Colored People (NAACP) bypassed the legislative branch and took its case to the judicial branch. In a group of cases known as *Brown v. Board of Education* the NAACP brought suit challenging the constitutionality of racial segregation in public education. In a unanimous 1954 decision, the Supreme Court—several of whose justices had been appointed by President Roosevelt to be sensitive to the desires of the legislative and executive branches in the 1930s—relied heavily on social science evidence to declare that racially separate educational systems were inherently unequal and, hence, violated the Constitution.

The impact of *Brown* on public education was ultimately enormous, but its more general impact on the race relations and civil rights in the United States was even more profound. The court's political independence under the Constitution allowed it to use its moral and legal force to lead the most important social change in the twentieth century. At first many could and did disagree with the Supreme Court's position, but the court's independence under constitutional separation of powers allowed it to withstand such opposition and to use its moral and legal force to lead the country towards what was constitutionally and morally right, though, at first, politically and socially unpopular. The decision led to the massive civil rights movements of the 1960s and helped pave the way for the critically important Civil Rights Act that was passed by the legislative and executive branches in 1964.

9. Both passages are designed to do which of the following?

(A) Clarify the need for control of the judicial branch by the executive and legislative branches of government

(B) Exemplify the impact of an independent judicial branch on political issues in the United States

(C) Argue the importance of executive and legislative control of economic matters in the United States

(D) Show the origins of the contemporary judiciary in actions by the legislature and executive in the first two-thirds of the 20th century

(E) Show the primary role of the Supreme Court in bringing about social changes in the country

10. Which of the following best describes the attitude in the two passages about the Supreme Court's acting in opposition to the legislative branch?

(A) Both passage A and passage B argue that the Supreme Court's ability to remain independent of the legislature is highly limited by political reality.

(B) Passage B argues that the Supreme Court's independence is always a positive moral force, but passage A claims that the court's independence is often abused for narrow self-interest.

(C) Passage B presents a case designed to demonstrate that the Supreme Court can benefit the country through its independence, whereas passage A argues that the court can prevent social progress through its independence.

(D) Both passage A and passage B advocate the independence of the Supreme Court as a voice of wisdom to control a reckless legislative branch.

(E) Passage A asserts that the independence of the Supreme Court can result in social harm and passage B indicates its agreement, with an example to the point.

11. Which of the following most accurately characterizes the use of the word *intrusion* in the last sentence of passage A?

(A) It describes the attitude of the Supreme Court on measures regulating the economy before the court's membership was changed during the Roosevelt presidency.

(B) It reflects the opinion in passage A that neither Congress nor the Supreme Court ought to be regulating matters like minimum wage.

(C) It is used to advocate a greater role for the Supreme Court in shaping social and economic affairs in the country.

(D) It refers to the unusual measures that had been proposed by the president to control the court.

(E) It predicts that the justices appointed by President Roosevelt would become active in social change in the coming decades.

12. Which of the following is something on which the authors of both passage A and passage B would be likely to agree?

(A) The Supreme Court ought to be more actively controlled by the legislative and executive branches as it was throughout the 20th century.

(B) The actions of President Roosevelt and the Congress in the 1930s indicate the need for greater protection of judicial independence.

(C) Social change can rarely come in meaningful ways in the United States unless it is led by the judicial branch.

(D) The judicial branch should not accept a leadership role in bringing about social change that the Congress or the people do not actively support.

(E) Though it may be controllable in the long run by the executive and legislative branches, the Supreme Court can act independently of those branches to affect public policy in the United States.

13. Which of the following can be inferred from the two passages?

(A) The Supreme Court in the 1950s considered itself to be less independent than it had in the 1930s.

(B) The judicial branch is unlikely to use its independence again to restrict the legislative and executive branches on economic policy.

(C) Justices appointed to the Supreme Court by President Roosevelt were less well qualified to serve as justices than those whom they replaced.

(D) Some who had been appointed justices by President Roosevelt because he judged them supportive of congressional initiatives acted in ways that were contrary to congressional opinion in the 1950s.

(E) The legislative and executive branches are unlikely again to attempt the sorts of unusual measures to control the judicial branch that President Roosevelt attempted.

14. Which of the following is explicitly mentioned in both of the passages?

(A) Social Security

(B) segregation in education

(C) separation of powers

(D) Supreme Court Justice deaths and resignations

(E) civil rights

The intensely hot conditions that prevailed at the universe's birth probably lie forever beyond the reach of even the largest particle accelerators. Investigators of low-temperature physics, however, have long surpassed nature. In the 15 billion years since the Big Bang, no point in the universe at large has reached a temperature cooler than three kelvins (the temperature of the cosmic microwave background). In laboratories, however, temperatures measured in nanokelvins and picokelvins are being achieved. The phenomena being studied at such temperatures are not only new to physicists, they have never occurred before in the history of the cosmos.

Of all the unusual phenomena that ultralow temperatures elicit, perhaps the most spectacular are superfluidity—the frictionless flow of a fluid—and its electronic analogue, superconductivity. Superfluidity in liquid helium-4, the common isotope of helium, has been known since 1938. In 1972 Douglas D. Osheroff, Robert C. Richardson, and David M. Lee of Cornell University found that the rare isotope helium-3 could also become superfluid. Exploration of the properties of this new kind of matter has been a central project of ultralow-temperature physics in recent years.

The behavior of superfluid helium-3 can be very intricate even though its structure is that of a simple liquid, composed of identical, chemically inactive, rare gas atoms. In addition to being worthy of study for its own sake, this combination of the simple and the complex makes superfluid helium-3 an ideal substance in which to study many other condensed-matter problems, ranging from the properties of neutron stars to those of high-temperature superconductors.

Laboratory studies of the behavior of superfluid helium-3 may eventually yield insight about forms of matter found nowhere on the Earth. It is conjectured, for example, that the neutron matter (neutronium) in rapidly rotating pulsars is superfluid, even though the temperature in neutron stars is about 100 million degrees Kelvin. Neutron matter clearly cannot be studied in the laboratory, but it may be possible to mimic its behavior with superfluid helium-3 or helium-4. Neutrons, like helium-3 atoms, are fermions, and it is believed that neutronium becomes superfluid by the same mechanism operating in helium-3. Only detailed theoretical calculations can tell whether the correspondence between superfluid helium-3 and neutronium is sufficiently close for such models to yield useful results. If so, experiments will be performed on helium-3 with neutron stars in mind.

The experimental verification of such a possibility may lie far in the future because such a transition may take place only at temperatures well below those to which liquid helium can be cooled at present. Nevertheless, there is little doubt that those temperatures will eventually be reached.

15. Which of the following best expresses the main idea of the passage?

(A) Studies of helium-3 might lead to understanding of the behavior of neutron stars.

(B) The achievement of ultralow temperatures by physicists has enabled the study of new phenomena interesting both in themselves and for what they might teach about other phenomena.

(C) Helium-3 behaves in an intricate way at ultralow temperatures that makes it an interesting object of study for physicists.

(D) The achievement of ultralow temperatures in labs has allowed physicists to create new types of matter unknown in the universe.

(E) While the high temperatures achieved at the origin of the universe cannot be duplicated by physicists, the duplication of ultralow temperatures allows the study of the effects of those higher temperatures.

16. The author writes which of the following about the temperature of the cosmic microwave background?

(A) It cannot be duplicated in an experiment.

(B) It is too hot for particle accelerators.

(C) It is the temperature of the matter in neutron stars.

(D) It is unimportant to high-temperature superconductivity.

(E) It is higher than some temperatures scientists have been able to achieve in laboratories.

17. The "combination of the simple and the complex" in the third paragraph refers to

(A) helium-4 as compared to helium-3

(B) helium 3 in its gaseous and its liquid states

(C) the structure and behavior of superfluid helium-3

(D) the comparison of helium-3 to neutronium

(E) the behavior of helium-3 at ultralow and normal temperatures

18. According to the passage, superfluidity in helium isotopes

(A) has been recently discovered with the technology to produce very low temperatures in laboratories.

(B) was first treated experimentally in the work of Osheroff, Richardson, and Lee.

(C) was known in the first half of the twentieth century.

(D) can be understood as a form of neutronium.

(E) is interesting because of the technical advances it allows in superconductivity.

19. The author states that the study of superfluid helium-3 can lead to learning about

(A) superfluid helium-4.

(B) other matter found on the Earth.

(C) the Big Bang.

(D) condensed matter.

(E) the temperature of the universe.

20. The passage says that neutron matter

(A) exists at only very low temperatures.

(B) is not found on Earth.

(C) can only be produced in experiments.

(D) does not exist in nature.

(E) has been experimentally verified.

21. The primary purpose of the passage is to

(A) discuss properties of neutron stars.

(B) identify isotopes of helium.

(C) explain something interesting about ultralow temperature experiments.

(D) describe how superfluids are formed.

(E) contrast alternative theories of the temperature of the universe.

British film critic Robin Wood, in his provocative book *Hitchcock's Films,* calls *I Confess* "earnest, distinguished, very interesting, and on the whole a failure." He points briefly to some parallels with *Strangers on a Train* and then examines the character played by Anne Baxter. But in this case his analysis of Hitchcock's work—elsewhere frequently compelling—seems to me earnest, distinguished, very interesting, and on the whole a failure. *I Confess* is not flawless; but the genius which had produced *Strangers on a Train* the previous year is not entirely eclipsed in this effort. Hitchcock has expressed regret that "the final result was rather heavy-handed . . . lacking in humor." Agreed. But when he says it lacks subtlety, he is too modest. The treatment of the characters shows remarkable precision and subtlety. The structure of the film is admirable, and the sense of contrast between idealism and romantic fantasy (which lies but a hair's breadth beyond idealism) is finely delineated.

The thematic development of *I Confess* is directed toward the confession of Father Logan (Montgomery Clift) that he was once in love with Ruth Grandfort (Anne Baxter). The title of the film, in fact, refers only superficially to Keller's (O. E. Hasse) words at the beginning and at the end. Everyone in the film is forced to make a confession, an admission of feeling, if not of guilt—Father Logan most of all. Therein lies the essential irony of the tale. Logan does not confess that he had an affair, but that he is a man with feeling and emotion, traits which his manner belies. The outrage of the citizens is puritanical and self-righteous. (Only a rigidly old-world morality could be offended at the discovery that a priest has feelings!) But both the people and Logan must learn that there is a humanity underneath the black cassock—a humanity not obliterated by the ecclesiastical role a man plays. For *I Confess* to be psychically his, he must confess his humanity. (In this regard, it is interesting that his brother priests are far more relaxed, witty, and even playful. The youngest priest, for instance, has a mania for bicycle riding, which leads to humorous punctuations of rectory scenes by the bicycle's clash and clatter.) The final irony is that the priest's humanity must be established by confrontation with Ruth's unfounded romantic fantasies.

The occasional heaviness and overdrawnness of *I Confess* are due to some unfortunate casting. Clift's method acting comes across as merely wooden, and Miss Baxter, whom Hitchcock had not wanted for the role, overacts distressingly. There is too overt a use of religious symbolism. Crosses abound like birds elsewhere; Logan, walking the street reflectively, is even photographed against a foreground of a statue of Christ carrying his cross. It is all a bit too obvious to have much emotional weight or effect.

But the film on the whole is certainly not a failure. It is a minor Hitchcockian exercise in the examination of a sealed fantasy life, the analysis of role playing, and a reflection on the delicate balance necessary to achieve a healthy spiritual life.

22. Which of the following most accurately expresses the main point of the passage?

(A) *I Confess* is a Hitchcock film with an intricate plot that would have been much improved with a different set of actors.

(B) Robin Wood's provocative book *Hitchcock's Films* is incorrect in its assessment of the film *I Confess.*

(C) Alfred Hitchcock's *I Confess,* while not without flaws, is a film with many positive qualities to recommend it.

(D) While not a complete failure, Hitchcock's *I Confess* is a minor film whose flaws and weaknesses outweigh its strengths.

(E) Because it was produced by the genius Hitchcock, *I Confess* is an admirable film depicting the feelings and guilt of a variety of people.

23. The author probably mentions *Strangers on a Train* in the first paragraph in order to

(A) establish the ground of his disagreement with Wood's assessment of *I Confess.*

(B) offer an example of a film which shows, without question, Hitchcock's genius.

(C) present a case where there is no dispute that Hitchcock has produced a poor film.

(D) emphasize the disagreement between the author's perspective on Hitchcock's genius and Wood's perspective on Hitchcock.

(E) discuss the film where Hitchcock's treatment of characters is unquestionably better than it is in *I Confess.*

24. Which of the following best states the function of the second paragraph in the passage as a whole?

(A) It presents details from Wood's criticism of *I Confess* that the author then refutes.

(B) It compares plot and character development in *I Confess* to plot and character development in *Strangers on a Train.*

(C) It presents a summary of *I Confess* that is used to clarify the author's assessment of the film.

(D) It shows the general flaws in the structure of the film that prevent it from being a genuine work of genius.

(E) It details the weaknesses in the performances of the actors in the film that prevent the film from being better than it is.

25. The author uses the word *eclipsed* in the first paragraph to help to suggest that

(A) Hitchcock really was not a genius.

(B) *I Confess* was a failure.

(C) *I Confess* was better than *Strangers on a Train.*

(D) some of Hitchcock's genius shows in *I Confess.*

(E) Hitchcock had a personal interest in astrology.

26. The author criticizes *I Confess* for its

(A) thematic development.

(B) structure.

(C) character development.

(D) subtlety.

(E) casting.

27. Which of the following best expresses the author's attitude toward the work of Robin Wood?

(A) complete rejection

(B) unqualified praise

(C) qualified admiration

(D) regretful disappointment

(E) querulous disagreement

28. The primary purpose of the passage is to

(A) explore disagreements between the author and Robin Wood.

(B) examine Hitchcock's directorial style.

(C) analyze Wood's *Hitchcock's Films.*

(D) show the value and subtlety of *I Confess.*

(E) compare *I Confess* with *Strangers on a Train.*

STOP

If time still remains, you may review work only in this section. When the time allotted is up, you may go on to the next section.

SECTION 2

Time—35 minutes
25 questions

Directions: *The questions in this section are based on the reasoning contained in brief statements or passages. For some questions, more than one of the choices could conceivably answer the question. However, you are to choose the* ***best*** *answer; that is, the response that most accurately and completely answers the question. You should not make assumptions that are by commonsense standards implausible, superfluous, or incompatible with the passage. After you have chosen the best answer, blacken the corresponding space on your answer sheet.*

1. In some areas of the South, landowners practice "clear-cutting" of large areas of forest. Clear-cutting produces quicker profits in the short run because more board feet of wood can be harvested with it than with more selective harvesting procedures. However, this practice should be carefully regulated by the state governments, since it can be destructive to the environment. The erosion that is often caused by clear-cutting lessens the land's capability to produce similar resources for future generations.

   Which of the following principles makes the conclusion in the passage above reasonable?

   (A) People should not be permitted to let resources go to waste.

   (B) Maintaining a healthy and appropriately balanced environment is an appropriate goal for governmental action.

   (C) Government should regulate forest harvesting procedures to ensure the future possibility of profitable harvesting from forests.

   (D) Federal law making should be avoided where state law making can do a particular job adequately.

   (E) Landowners in the South may be regulated in the use of their land so as to ensure environmental responsibility.

2. At Barnaby's music store at least once a week, the store's manager conducted a random survey of people in the mall in which the music store was located. Of 1,000 city residents surveyed, 500 said they shopped in the store at least once a week. The manager concluded from this that half of the city's residents shopped in the store at least once a week.

   The manager's reasoning is flawed for which of the following reasons?

   (A) The number of people surveyed was too small.

   (B) The survey rejected results from some people who were likely to shop in the store.

   (C) The results of the survey were based on a sample that is unlikely to be representative of city residents as a whole.

   (D) The survey was conducted by someone who had a stake in the outcome.

   (E) The survey failed to count shoppers who might shop at the store but less frequently than once a week.

3. Two different makes of automobile, types X and Y, were each tested in different kinds of driving. Type X was shown to hold up for more miles than type Y when the driving involved fewer, longer trips. Type Y was shown to hold up for more miles than type X when the driving involved more but shorter trips. On the basis of this study, researchers recommended that drivers who take fewer but longer trips purchase type X, and drivers who take more but shorter trips purchase type Y. *Consumer Care* magazine reviewed the automobiles, the studies, and the recommendations, and strongly endorsed type Y for all motorists.

Which of the following, if true, does most to explain the magazine's endorsement?

(A) Some people's driving consists primarily of trips which are both few and short.

(B) Neither type of automobile received frequent servicing during the tests.

(C) Type X was not more expensive, comparably equipped, than type Y.

(D) More frequent and shorter trips are typically less efficient in the use of fuel than less frequent and longer trips.

(E) Crash studies showed that passengers in type Y were less likely to sustain serious injuries in accidents than passengers in type X.

4. TV ad: Brand O car wax protects your car for a year's washings! We waxed this car with Brand O and ran it through this harsh commercial car wash 52 times, and look, the wax finish still shines and the water still beads. Save your labor; save your car's finish! Get Brand O, the once-a-year car wax.

Which of the following is an assumption that the ad relies on?

(A) Brand O car wax is not difficult to apply correctly.

(B) An automobile is not washed more than an average of one time per week in any given year.

(C) An automobile is washed exactly one time each week during the year.

(D) Brand O car wax will not last for more than one year.

(E) When water does not bead on a car's finish, the wax on the car is no longer working.

5. No one can be on the baseball team who does not buy his own glove. If Nathan is not on the baseball team, Peggy will not date him. Nathan goes to the arcade and spends all his money if Peggy does not date him.

Which of the following can be inferred from the statements above?

(A) If Nathan buys a glove, he will be on the baseball team.

(B) If Nathan buys a glove, Peggy will date him.

(C) If Nathan does not spend all his money at the arcade, then he bought a glove.

(D) If Peggy dates Nathan, he bought a glove.

(E) If Nathan buys a glove, he will date Peggy.

6. It is clear that families, in some form, have always been found in human societies. Even in modern societies, with many opportunities for alternative life-styles, the family remains strong. Much has been written about the high divorce rate in the United States, and some writers suggest the American family is on the verge of extinction. Nothing can be further from the truth. The high American divorce rate is accompanied by the highest rate of remarriage in the world.

The statement about the rate of remarriage plays which of the following roles in the passage?

(A) It is a fact cited to emphasize the high divorce rate in the United States.

(B) It is cited to demonstrate that the notion of "family" in the United States is changing.

(C) It is the main conclusion that the passage seeks to advance.

(D) It is a premise presented to show that information that would seem to dispute the main conclusion in fact does not.

(E) It is a subsidiary conclusion that is combined with other information in the passage to lead to the conclusion that families are always found in human society.

7. The school newspaper's article yesterday concerning the health risks associated with eating foods cooked in animal fats had a positive impact. The cafeteria normally serves french fries cooked in animal fat, but today's

menu had baked potatoes instead. So if the author hoped to encourage more healthy eating, the article must have produced that result.

The reasoning in the passage is vulnerable to the criticism that it

(A) draws an analogy between unrelated events.

(B) generalizes from one event to another event of the same kind.

(C) takes something that would be enough to create a result as something that must have happened because the result took place.

(D) hastily assumes knowledge of the author's motives.

(E) assumes that because one event occurs before another, the first event is the cause of the second.

8. Textbooks have become the object of considerable attention in recent years and for good reason. Clearly, these packaged curricula are essential sources of information for students and teachers alike in successful public elementary schools. They outweigh all other sources in determining the day-to-day teaching and learning activities in classrooms. No other factor has a greater influence on the nature and consequences of elementary education. So, good education will not happen without good textbooks.

If the information in the passage is true, which of the following CANNOT be true?

(A) A public elementary school has adopted a well-known set of textbooks, but is not a successful school.

(B) Parental involvement has as great an influence on the nature and consequences of elementary education as do textbooks.

(C) A school district is rightly renowned for providing good elementary education, yet the district does not use textbooks.

(D) The university preparation of teachers does not play as important a role in determining day-to-day learning activities in elementary classrooms as do textbooks.

(E) The considerable attention that textbooks have come to receive in recent years is merited by their importance in promoting educational success.

9. Geoffrey: It seems to me that it is a simple matter to say that the universe cannot be eternal, since eternal things have no beginning. But the universe as a whole must have had a beginning, since it is certain that each thing in it had a beginning.

Which of the following describes the flaw in Geoffrey's reasoning?

(A) He argues from the fact that each thing began at some time, to the claim that there was some one time at which all things began.

(B) He fails to take into account the question of what could have caused the universe to begin.

(C) He argues that the whole has some property simply because each of its parts has that property.

(D) He argues that one thing is similar to another in one property just because they are similar in another property.

(E) He fails to address the fact that things last for longer or shorter times and that the universe may, thus, be the longest-lasting thing.

10. A research study found that bodybuilders who took steroids had significantly lower levels of high-density lipoproteins in their blood than did otherwise similar men who did not take steroids. The average was 50% lower for the steroid users, and the drop varied directly with the size of the steroid dose. Low levels of high-density lipoproteins in the blood are known to be correlated to high risk of heart attack. Researchers recommended that a warning be issued to athletes that steroid use may increase the likelihood of heart disease.

Which of the following most strongly supports the researchers' recommendation?

(A) The Society of Professional Personal Trainers has warned that unsupervised bodybuilding can be hazardous to the builder's health.

(B) A body that is in good physical condition can withstand the effects of heart attack better than one that is not.

(C) A two-year-old study at a Norwegian hospital suggests that in patients with heart attacks levels of high-density lipoproteins fell rapidly immediately after the onset of the attack.

(D) A study of professional athletes who were known to use and abuse steroids found that a disproportionate percentage of them had suffered heart attacks as compared with their peers who did not use steroids.

(E) Bodybuilders as a group have been shown to have a lower incidence of heart disease than the general population.

11. The phrase "public interest" or "national interest" is often used by government officials to justify their actions, but never to do things that involve helping ordinary people. Presidents refer to the national interest when they take military action abroad or call upon U.S. citizens to make sacrifices in accepting reductions in favored domestic programs. Interest groups, too, claim that their goals are in accord with the public interest. Such a claim is often heard when a business group asks for high tariffs to reduce "unfair" competition from foreign countries, or when an environmental organization asks for greater government regulation to prevent air and water pollution, or when a teachers' organization asks for increased expenditures on educational programs.

The argument above requires assuming which of the following?

(A) Public officials and interest groups are being sincere when they say they are acting in the public interest.

(B) It could not be in the interests of ordinary people to spend more on education when a teachers' organization claims the public interest requires it.

(C) There is very little doubt about what the public interest actually is.

(D) The "public interest" is a phrase without real meaning.

(E) Self-interested behavior by individuals and groups is the only motive that will guide their actions.

12. If the college does not increase tuition, it must cut back expenditures for athletics. Cutting athletics will anger the alumni. If the alumni get angry, they may reduce donations. Reduced donations will result in decreased building maintenance. However, if the college raises tuition, the students will protest.

If the statements in the above are true, which one of the following statements must also be true?

(A) Failure to increase tuition will result in decreased building maintenance.

(B) Either the students will protest, or the alumni will be angry.

(C) Reductions in donations will cause higher tuition.

(D) Increasing tuition will result in greater funding for athletics.

(E) If expenditures for athletics are cut, there is no way for the college to continue the present levels of donations for building maintenance.

13. Internships are historically common. References to apprenticeships are found as early as 2100 B.C.E. in the Code of Hammurabi. Greek and Roman sources also allude to this phenomenon. The concept was further developed in the English guilds of the Middle Ages, flourished through the 16th century in Europe, and even found its way to colonial America. Physicians' training includes a formal one-year internship after graduation. An internship experience should play a similar role in legal assistant training programs. These programs should recognize and embrace the value of an internship in

meeting the needs of the student and the internship sponsor, just as similar kinds of training activities have in the past.

Which of the following best describes the argumentative strategy the passage employs to advance its conclusion?

(A) The passage argues that history proves that internship programs are necessary for the training of successful professionals by claiming there are no cases historically in which professionals have been trained without internships.

(B) The use of internship programs to train legal assistants throughout history is offered as evidence for the continued utility of such programs.

(C) The passage indicates that well-developed internship programs are adequate training for professionals, and uses historical data to back up the claim.

(D) The passage draws an analogy between guilds in the Middle Ages and contemporary physicians to draw a conclusion about legal assistants.

(E) Evidence that internship programs have long been considered beneficial in training people for analogous professions is taken to lead to the conclusion that such programs should be used in training legal assistants.

14. According to Aristotle, through abstract thought one could discover all of the laws which govern the universe. Nor would it be necessary to check the results of one's reasoning by observation. Because of this tradition, no one until Galileo bothered to confirm the Aristotelian notion that bodies of different weights fall to the ground at different speeds. Galileo dropped balls of different weights, and found that they hit the ground at the same time. Experimentation has been the core of the modern scientific method ever since.

Which of the following is most strongly supported by the information in the passage?

(A) Aristotle did not discover all the laws of the universe through abstract thought.

(B) Since Aristotle's notions of physics were wrong, his works on logic are likely to be faulty as well.

(C) Abstract thought is not capable of learning some things that can be learned through experimentation.

(D) Skepticism is more valued by modern science than by ancient physics.

(E) Since he did not rely on abstract thought, Galileo was a better thinker than Aristotle was.

15. Historian: Understanding the dynamics of policy-making in any Communist government has always been problematic, but Castro's Cuba in the 1990s presents a particularly difficult case because so little is known of the major actors in the Cuban government. However, it is known that several Cuban government officials in the 1990s had the same titles as officials from the Communist Soviet government of the 1960s. Therefore, we may conclude that by applying descriptions of the Soviet system of the 1960s we can develop an accurate description of 1990s Cuban policy-making.

The reasoning in the historian's argument is questionable because it

(A) takes one thing that follows another to have been caused by the first.

(B) fails to consider regimes other than the Soviet regime that have been called "Communist."

(C) takes it for granted that officials with the same titles in different times and countries perform the same functions.

(D) does not consider the fact that Cuba did not become Communist until after the Soviets.

(E) overlooks the fact that, although Castro based his political structure on that of the Soviets in the 1960s, the Soviet system ultimately failed.

16. During her election campaign in Duncan City, Mayor Robinson said that city governments should not take it upon themselves to provide public assistance to the needy.

So it is surprising that now that she is mayor she praises the city's office to provide public health assistance, saying that "when a city has a high percentage of needy citizens in poor health, then obviously something has to be done, and the Duncan City plan is right on target."

Which one of the following resolves the apparent discrepancy in the mayor's views?

(A) Needs for public assistance are not as great after her election as they were during the campaign.

(B) The city office to help the needy is led by well-qualified and dedicated professionals.

(C) Public health assistance is more important than other types of public assistance.

(D) Duncan City's public health assistance office is a private charitable initiative.

(E) A city can save money in the long run by preventing health problems before they become costly to treat diseases.

17. If gasoline evaporates, it has been left in an open container. The lid for the can that Jody is using to store the gasoline he bought yesterday for his lawn-mowing business has been inadvertently left off. So the gasoline Jody bought yesterday will evaporate.

Which of the following exhibits the same flawed pattern of reasoning as the passage above?

(A) If Sam Smith is contented, he has had eight hours' sleep. Sam Smith purposefully took sleeping medication last night before going to bed. The medication was not one he had used before, but nonetheless it was effective, and he has slept for eight hours. So Sam will be content.

(B) All golfers are boors. Jack is a boor. There is nothing Jack would rather do or talk about than golf, despite his being an accomplished concert pianist.

(C) Anyone singing in public is a nuisance. Jill came out of that movie humming its theme song loudly and off key. People in the mall kept giving her really mean looks. But she was not singing, so she was not a nuisance.

(D) All musicians are talented. Miguel is a really bad computer programmer who plays the guitar in a mariachi band on weekends to pick up some extra cash. Miguel is talented.

(E) Pointing is not polite. When the ambulance came they found Genevieve waiting outside the complex pointing to the apartment where Mrs. Rivera had fallen, so the emergency medical technicians could find her. So Genevieve was impolite.

18. No matter how well written originally, the manuals that come with computer hardware frequently need to be revised. There are constant improvements in microprocessing technology, and there is the introduction of new computer software. These developments spur creation of new applications for computers in areas as diverse as animation and zoology. None of these new applications would be usable for most people without instruction on how to use them.

Which of the following is an assumption on which the argument relies?

(A) Computer manuals are outdated as soon as they are written.

(B) New software that takes advantage of new microprocessing technology is more complex and difficult to learn than existing software.

(C) Mistakes in computer manuals are due to the authors' lack of knowledge about new applications.

(D) New computer applications cannot be adequately explained in manuals that supplement the ones that come with computer hardware.

(E) Development of new applications for computers always results from improvement in microprocessing technology.

19. A low level of capital accumulation in the form of personal savings is the major cause of unemployment. A low level of personal savings is unavoidable unless government provides incentives for saving, such as keeping a lid on inflation. Otherwise, many potential savers, rather than saving, will decide to spend their money now before its purchasing power declines, and capital will not accumulate. Government failure to keep a lid on inflation is, thus, the culprit in bringing about the recession.

Which of the following presuppositions is necessary to the argument?

(A) The savings rate declines when the inflation rate goes up.

(B) Unemployment leads to recession.

(C) Recessions do not occur when government keeps a lid on inflation.

(D) Personal savings decisions are made without consideration of their effects on the broader economy.

(E) Governmental economic decisions are often based on short-term rather than long-term considerations.

20. In a recently completed test, two groups of rats were fed the same diet except that for one group the amount of vitamin E was reduced significantly below normal. As the experiment progressed, the rats receiving the feed with lowered levels of vitamin E displayed the signs of aging significantly earlier than did the rats whose diet contained normal amounts of vitamin E. The signs involved covered the range of characteristic aging—hair loss, menopause, osteoporosis, and senility, to name a few. The experimenters concluded that lowering the intake of vitamin E accelerates the aging process. These results have generated enthusiastic predictions that treatments involving many times the normal dose of vitamin E will soon be shown to slow the aging process in human beings.

Which of the following, if true, most weakens the author's prediction?

(A) Rats in experiments given only slightly less vitamin E than usual showed minor acceleration in the aging process.

(B) Other rats given a diet with higher levels of vitamin E showed no different effects than those with normal doses of vitamin E.

(C) Rats in the experiment were of widely differing ages at the time the experiment began.

(D) The experiment showing the increased signs of aging was reproduced with similar result by different scientists in a different lab.

(E) There are some signs of aging that are more marked in human beings than they are in rats.

21. Whether marijuana is a dangerous drug is not established by one claim sometimes made in arguing it is. If you accept the argument that smoking marijuana leads to using hard drugs because, even though not all marijuana smokers go on to using hard drugs, almost all hard-drug users started by smoking marijuana, then you ought also accept that drinking water leads to hard-drug use, since, although not all water drinkers go on to using hard drugs, almost all hard-drug users started by drinking water.

The argument proceeds by

(A) pointing to another argument of the same form and with equally good premises which has a clearly false conclusion.

(B) pointing out that it is faulty to conclude that since thing one causes thing two, thing two also causes thing one.

(C) pointing to an extreme consequence that might follow from an argument and treating it as the normal case.

(D) pointing out that the one argument that seems to be analogous to another in fact is not.

(E) pointing to an exception to the general claim that the original argument tries to establish.

22. Claude Bernard randomly divided a population of rabbits into two groups: one fed a vegetarian diet, the other fed meat. When he

analyzed the urine from these two groups, he found that the urine from the meat-eating group contained significant amounts of ketone, while that of the vegetarian group was free of ketone. From this he concluded that metabolizing meat caused the ketone in the urine. He then analyzed the urine of rabbits that had been deprived of food and found that the urine of starving rabbits also contained considerable ketone. From this he hypothesized that starving rabbits are also metabolizing meat—their own stomachs.

Which of the following, if true, adds the most support to Bernard's hypothesis?

(A) Rabbits whose diets included meat tended to weigh more than rabbits on purely vegetarian diets.

(B) Starving rabbits who had previously been fed only a vegetarian diet did not have considerable ketone in their urine.

(C) The meat-eating rabbits and the starving rabbits were tested in one lab, while the vegetarian rabbits were tested in a lab in another part of the country.

(D) Ketone appeared in the urine of starving rabbits regardless of whether the rabbit had previously been fed a vegetarian diet or a diet including meat.

(E) Ketone has been shown to have no substantial effect on longevity in rabbits.

23. Rodriguez's transcript from the fall semester includes Technical Writing, which indicates that Rodriguez is either a computer science major or a business major. And Rodriguez's transcript from the spring semester shows a class in accounting. Since computer science majors are not required to take accounting, but business majors are, it must be that Rodriguez is a business major.

Which of the following follows a pattern of reasoning most like that in the passage above?

(A) The drug is taken by people who have high blood pressure and high cholesterol. Both high blood pressure and high cholesterol are warning signs for heart disease, so Jenkins needs to take precautions against heart disease.

(B) Both Donnie and Michael are famous children's cartoon characters. But since cartoons are not real, neither Donnie nor Michael is real.

(C) The dictionary says that "feckless" is a word and that "feckful" is not. And we are assured on good authority that Jordan has a superb vocabulary, so Jordan may use "feckless," but will never use "feckful."

(D) Someone who is allergic to citrus will avoid oranges, but not necessarily apples. But at lunch yesterday Julienne refused the apple she was offered. So Julienne must not be allergic to citrus.

(E) Julian's order includes caldillo, which is included only on Special 3 and Special 4. And since Special 4 includes guacamole but Special 3 does not, Julian must have ordered Special 4.

24. An ancient feminist play asserts that a world where socio-religious and legal systems are governed by women would be a more humane world than the present one, which is governed by men. There would be less greed, injustice, exploitation, and warfare. There would be more concern for posterity and also for the quality of life in the here and now. Sound biological evidence supports these views. Among most mammals males do not bear responsibility for the survival of individuals other than themselves. The survival of any species really depends on the caring behavior of its females, not the aggressive behavior of its males.

Which of the following, if true, would LEAST weaken the thesis of the play discussed in the passage?

(A) Most men who control current socio-religious and legal systems were taught by women.

(B) Among a majority of mammals, males and females share the responsibility for survival of individuals other than themselves.

(C) Female behavior is often as aggressive as male behavior in most species.

(D) Greed and injustice result from instinctual human behavior.

(E) There is often dispute about what specific measures best promote the quality of human life.

25. Although the church held a virtual monopoly over marriage and divorce in medieval Russia, it did not realize that nominal authority until the eighteenth century. The reason was not lack of will but institutional backwardness: the church simply lacked the instruments—including unambiguous law and bureaucratic infrastructure—that would have enabled it to translate its formal authority into real power. As a result, matrimony was more a secular contract than a church sacrament.

The passage presupposes which of the following?

(A) If the pre-eighteenth century church had exercised real power over marriage and divorce, it would have used that power to emphasize marriage as a sacrament.

(B) Marriage should not be seen as primarily a secular contract, and the church is blameworthy if marriage is perceived that way.

(C) Had it possessed unambiguous law and bureaucratic infrastructure, the church in medieval Russia would have realized real power over marriage and divorce.

(D) Any real power in society involves the use of bureaucratic infrastructure.

(E) Whatever institutions in society have power over marriage must also have real power over divorce.

STOP

If time still remains, you may review work only in this section. When the time allotted is up, you may go on to the next section.

SECTION 3

Time—35 minutes
24 questions

Directions: *The questions in this section are based on the reasoning contained in brief statements or passages. For some questions, more than one of the choices could conceivably answer the question. However, you are to choose the* ***best*** *answer; that is, the response that most accurately and completely answers the question. You should not make assumptions that are by commonsense standards implausible, superfluous, or incompatible with the passage. After you have chosen the best answer, blacken the corresponding space on your answer sheet.*

1. The country of Quitmania demonstrates the unfortunate truth that even the most popularly responsive of governments can be overthrown by a military coup. After all, Quitmania seemed a flawless example of the very definition of bourgeois liberal democracy. Its government was a representative one, elected by the entire adult population. The votes of the various voters carried equal weight, and voters were allowed to vote for any opinion without intimidation by the state apparatus.

   Which of the following is an assumption that the argument depends upon?

   (A) Voters in bourgeois liberal democracies vote according to their true opinions.

   (B) No military coup can result in a government that is popularly responsive.

   (C) Any bourgeois liberal democracy must be popularly responsive.

   (D) If the government is not elected by the entire adult population, it cannot be popularly responsive.

   (E) All popularly responsive governments are liberal democracies of some sort or other.

2. Besides the obvious influence of Hegel, two principal influences may be discerned in Hinrich's first book. They are Neo-Platonism and, to a lesser extent, chiefly as regards the terminology filtered through Schelling and Hegel, Boehme. Hinrich is much more of a Neo-Platonist than Hegel, and these closer ties to Augustine, Pseudo-Dionysius, and Eirgena allow his religious thought to be more integrated, more systematic, more complete in itself, than Hegel's. And at the same time, by the implicit comparison, it points out certain shortcomings in Hegel's theory.

   Which of the following is most strongly supported by the statements in the passage?

   (A) Hegel's thought was not influenced by Augustine's thought.

   (B) Some Neo-Platonists' thought includes religious aspects that are not well integrated.

   (C) Schelling and Hegel used the same terminology.

   (D) In some respects Hinrich's thought represents an improvement on Hegel's thought.

   (E) The assumption that Hegel's work is superior to Hinrich's fails to take into account the religious perspective.

3. In the early ages of the world there were no wars since there were no kings. For all people being originally equals, no one by birth could have a right to set up his own family, in perpetual preference to all others forever. And though he himself might deserve some degree of honors from his contemporaries, his descendants might be far too unworthy to inherit them.

The argument relies on which of the following assumptions:

(A) The principles of right were clear to human beings in their original condition.

(B) Some worthy people might have descendents who were also worthy of preference.

(C) In every place and time where there are kings there are also wars.

(D) People who act as if people are equal are never involved in wars.

(E) Whenever there are wars, there are kings among people.

4. Human rights advocates viewed the Biological Weapons Convention of 1972 as a major and important step for protecting people against certain kinds of weapons of mass destruction. The convention forbade signatories "to develop, produce, stockpile, or otherwise acquire or retain" biological weapons—specifically, "microbial or other biological agents, or toxins whatever their origin or method of production." But then it became possible to produce various toxins synthetically in relatively easy and inexpensive ways that had the same effects as the biological agents; and these toxins are not living substances but chemicals not covered by the provisions of the Biological Weapons Convention. This development, however, did not raise much concern among the same human rights advocates.

Which best explains the seemingly paradoxical behavior of the human rights advocates?

(A) The acquisition and use of chemical weapons was forbidden by international agreements made decades before the Biological Weapons Convention.

(B) Use of chemical weapons does not involve the use of some living things to harm other living things.

(C) Chemical weapons are worse in their effects and potential widespread use than biological weapons.

(D) Human rights advocates tended to find it inconceivable that anyone would actually consider using chemical toxins as weapons.

(E) Concern about biological weapons is of longer standing than concern about chemical weapons.

5. Simmons went to a dentist and was proud of completing the session with calmness and without fear. But after the session was ended, the dentist said, "I observe that you were very much afraid of me. For I have noted that, when patients are frightened, their saliva becomes thicker, more sticky. And yours was exceptionally so."

A flaw in the dentist's argument is that it assumes without warrant that

(A) fear is essential for making human saliva sticky.

(B) sticky saliva always make people fearful.

(C) fear causes sticky saliva.

(D) sticky saliva is not the only cause of fear.

(E) most dental patients experience fear at dental sessions.

6. Graduate Student: Professor Potter claims that desire for territorial acquisition is a leading cause of war. But this cannot be right. Most wars involve ideological differences between the leadership of the warring countries. From the Peloponnesian War between aristocratic Sparta and democratic Athens, to World War II between the fascist Axis and democratic Allies, ideology has been at the root of most human conflict. So ideology, not the desire for territorial expansion, is what causes war.

Which of the following best describes an error in the graduate student's reasoning?

(A) It argues from analogy, the weakest form of proof.

(B) It takes it for granted that it is not possible for both the desire for expansion and ideology to be factors leading to the same war.

(C) It uses the term *ideology* without establishing its meaning.

(D) It bases its argument on an attack on the person making the contrary argument rather than on the content of the argument itself.

(E) It proves that ideology is the cause of war by assuming that nothing else could be the cause of war.

7. A recent survey showed that many consumers of company A's products are dissatisfied with them, believing that the products, though well-priced, are of low quality. As a consequence, to increase consumers' satisfaction with its products, the management of company A decided to undertake a campaign focused on changing consumers' beliefs regarding the quality of the company's products.

Which one of the following, if true, most supports management's decision about how to react to the survey?

(A) The dissatisfied consumers expressed a willingness to pay more for better products.

(B) Consumers who are satisfied with the products slightly outnumber those who are dissatisfied.

(C) Consumers of company A's products are more dissatisfied than consumers of the products of other companies in the industry.

(D) A recent independent study from a highly reputable consumer agency has shown company A's products to be of the highest quality in the industry.

(E) Some consumers are satisfied with company A's products, though they believe that others in the industry might be both of higher quality and more expensive.

8. Is Britain really a democracy? The question sounds absurd: 700 years of history, the vigor of the British press and television, free elections and the merciless cut and thrust of debate in the House of Commons at Prime Minister's Question Time all argue that of course it must be. But a provocative argument can be made that democracy in Britain begins and ends with national elections to the House of Commons every few years. After that, a government with a healthy majority, like those of Prime Minister Margaret Thatcher during the 1980s, can do just about anything it wants, with few formal checks or controls—just convention, precedent, and common sense, which in Britain are a more powerful balancing force than written constitutions in many other countries.

Which one of the following is an assumption relied on by the argument?

(A) A government without a prime minister is not democratic.

(B) Britain's government was established democratically.

(C) Free debate and free election ensure the presence of real democracy.

(D) A system that is really democratic does not permit officials elected duly by the majority of the voters to rule unchecked.

(E) Because Prime Minister Thatcher's government could do almost anything it wanted, it was not democratic.

9. The blood spilled in China's Tiananmen Square was the actual prelude to the great revolution of the East European peoples in 1989. The Beijing Spring provided an example to the leaders of Eastern Europe, who surrendered to the popular will. The only way to explain the mostly peaceful climate in which the events took place there is that the Tiananmen Square massacre aroused such indignation throughout the world that the governments of Eastern Europe did not dare repeat such horrors.

Which of the following is an assumption on which the argument relies?

(A) The events in Tiananmen Square led Eastern European countries to reject communism.

(B) The events in Tiananmen Square caused a peaceful revolution in Eastern Europe.

(C) Chinese democracy has led to the collapse of communist totalitarianism in China.

(D) The former rulers in Eastern Europe were aware of and concerned about international opinion.

(E) The Eastern European rejection of communism was not in response to popular will.

10. Assistant principal: Experience shows that it is surprisingly easy to change the habits of school-age children so that they will come to enjoy eating healthy foods. When the dishes children are offered are prepared well using healthy ingredients and avoiding unnecessary fats, sugars, and salt, schoolchildren, in time, come to like them. The rhubarb cobbler on today's lunch menu fits the bill, including a minimum of added sugar, no trans fats, and plenty of whole grains in the pastry. The chocolate cake, on the other hand, is full of fats and calories from refined sugar. So suggest to the cooks that they prepare many servings of the rhubarb and few of the cake, for the children will surely choose the rhubarb.

The assistant principal's reasoning is flawed because the argument

(A) does not specify the kinds of fats used in making the chocolate cake.

(B) overlooks the possibility that other desserts might be lower in calories than the rhubarb cobbler.

(C) leaves open the possibility that sometimes dishes are not prepared using healthy ingredients.

(D) assumes without warrant that because a particular set of conditions, when met, results in a particular outcome, that outcome can be produced in the absence of those conditions.

(E) fails to consider the exact definition of the term *healthy* as applied to the dietary needs of children.

11. Research suggests that analysis is frequently distorted, suppressed, or selectively represented in policy discussions. Regardless of the party in power, administration officials have ignored or distorted technical advice when it hasn't been compatible with their bureaucratic or political convenience. Similarly, analyses are cited when they bolster a particular ideological position, but sealed when they are likely to embarrass persons in power. Analysis is treated as a political instrument to be trotted out when it supports one's objectives or undercuts one's opponents, and to be suppressed, if possible, when it opposes one's objectives or strengthens one's opponent's.

Which of the following is most strongly supported by the information in the passage?

(A) Technical advice is often not compatible with bureaucratic or political convenience.

(B) Persons in power often actively suppress analyses when such analyses will be embarrassing.

(C) Analysis should not be used if it opposes one's objectives.

(D) People who wish to arrive at the truth in policy discussions will not get much help from analysis.

(E) Analysis frequently is used more as a tool in defending or critiquing policy decisions rather than in making them.

12. Some athletes are skaters. All basketball players are athletes. So at least some skaters must also play basketball.

Which of the following employs the same erroneous pattern of reasoning as the passage above?

(A) All roadsters are cars. Some cars are convertibles. So some roadsters are convertibles.

(B) Some mammals are pets, and all cats are mammals. So it must be that all cats who are pets are mammals.

(C) Some cakes are breakfast foods. Some cakes are chocolate. So all breakfast foods are chocolate.

(D) Some people from Anthony are Texans. Some people from Anthony are New Mexicans. So some Texas are also New Mexicans.

(E) All trees are plants. All plants require water. So some trees require water.

13. Only six years ago, high school students in Metropolis were more likely to commit a crime than to graduate. This was because the local culture placed too little emphasis on getting a high school diploma. But now after years of concerted effort by school board officials, parents, and community leaders to change this, students are graduating in record numbers. This is a sure sign that the local groups have been successful in changing the local culture.

Each of the following weakens the argument in the passage above EXCEPT:

(A) Employers in Metropolis are more likely to require a high school diploma for employment now than they were six years ago.

(B) The language requirements for graduation have been substantially lowered in the past few years.

(C) Parents have not been as effective in changing the local culture as community leaders have been.

(D) The state legislature passed a law five years ago which made possession of a high school diploma a requirement for obtaining a driver's license.

(E) Students entering high school in Metropolis are better prepared to do high school work than they were a few years ago.

14. In the two years since KCUS-TV dropped Lucky Silas as a regular commentator on its evening news, there have been fewer murders, assaults, and thefts, indicating that crime rates have dropped markedly in the city. It proves that those liberal views do indeed promote crime. What is even more surprising is that it proves that a TV station actually has some sense of responsibility to the community.

And it also proves, if his well-publicized failure to pay his property taxes did not already do so, that Lucky Silas's commentary is based on shoddy thinking.

Each of the following describes an error in the reasoning above EXCEPT:

(A) It challenges the truth of an argument by criticizing the person advancing it.

(B) It assumes without warrant that of two things that happen simultaneously one must be the cause of the other.

(C) It takes something that is required to produce a certain outcome as being enough by itself to produce that outcome.

(D) It takes one possible explanation of behavior to be the case without considering other possible explanations.

(E) It assumes a conclusion is false because it would have undesirable consequences if true.

15. I appreciate that in this election year news outlets have difficulty finding expert commentators who are not already committed to other news outlets, but nonetheless they do need to be careful that their so-called "experts" are in fact what they are represented to be. Take the new Satellite News channel. Their new analyst, Jeb Bayard, is a successful author whose name is connected to politics. They advertise him as a "widely read political historian." But his works are not the works of a history professor, but gossipy political thrillers: fiction based upon unlikely events and bizarre constitutional readings. Whatever interest one might have in his commentary, it is not the commentary of a prominent historian.

The criticism of the claim about the credentials of the commentator is based on which of the following errors in reasoning?

(A) It makes the unwarranted assumption that someone who is a history professor could be a professor of nothing else.

(B) It presupposes that something that would be enough to make someone a historian is required to make one a historian.

(C) It assumes that something that is true of authors as a group must be true of each individual author.

(D) It takes it for granted that because being a history professor and being an author often go together that being an author causes one to be a history professor.

(E) It takes it for granted that the network's need for a particular set of skills is sufficient to produce a set of credentials in its commentator.

16. Hinklemore: Initiative, referendum, and recall are regarded by experts as interferences outside the legislative process, but I believe they are indispensable for the people's needs because they are often the only protection against legislators' tendency to play politics with sensitive issues.

Bullfinch: I don't agree. If by "playing politics" you mean maneuvering and compromise among various factions in a legislative body, it is something necessary for making decisions that serve the long-term needs of the people in the community. Initiative, referendum, and recall, even if they are not actually used, upset the delicate balance of forces within the legislature, which makes maneuvering and compromise possible and necessary.

Hinklemore and Bullfinch disagree on

(A) whether serving the needs of the people is the appropriate goal of legislative action.

(B) the indispensability of initiative, referendum, and recall for satisfying the needs of the people in the community.

(C) the question of whether an initiative, referendum, and recall need to be actually used to be an effective protection against legislators' tendency to play politics with sensitive issues.

(D) whether politics ought to be treated as something playful, or as something taken seriously and as critical to the satisfaction of the people's needs.

(E) the meaning of the phrase "playing politics," and whether initiative, referendum, and recall promote or discourage it.

17. Designing a library to be welcoming to a wide variety of casual users is a challenging task. This is true because people who have used more than one library conclude from the venture that each library is idiosyncratic, not just in layout and collections, but in underlying logic. The same people who will go into an unfamiliar grocery, clear in their expectations of what they'll find and sure in their knowledge of how to navigate, set foot timorously in a strange library, doubtful they will come away satisfied, and uneasy about how to proceed.

Which of the following best expresses the role in the passage of the statement about the grocery?

(A) It helps to make the point that since people are comfortable with unfamiliar grocery stores, they should be comfortable with unfamiliar libraries.

(B) It is the analogy in an argument by analogy that is structured to prove that designing an unfamiliar library is a difficult task.

(C) It is an example used to clarify the problem people are said to experience when encountering an unfamiliar library.

(D) It is used to advance the argument that since groceries are idiosyncratic, libraries are likely to be idiosyncratic as well.

(E) It is designed to allay the fear of new library users and make them confident that they can navigate the library with ease.

18. There is at least one case where a collegiate sport that offers no professional prospects prevents violations of NCAA rules in that sport. Lacrosse is a hotly contested college game, but it remains an amateur sport in which successful players do not follow collegiate careers with high-paying professional

contracts. And lacrosse has been largely free of NCAA violations and the controversies concerning the academic progress of student athletes that seem so common in other sports. So here is the case of a sport that shows that the absence of any possibility of athletes' turning professional makes the sports program one that abides by the rules.

The reasoning in the passage is vulnerable to which of the following criticisms?

(A) It makes the unwarranted assumption that since two phenomena coincide, one must cause the other.

(B) It presupposes that what is true of one sport is generally true of a whole class of sports that are similar in that one regard.

(C) It takes something that is enough to create an absence of rule violations as being essential for there to be no rule violations.

(D) It takes something that is necessary to prevent rules violations as being enough, by itself, to prevent such violations.

(E) It assumes without warrant that college athletes are always driven by the lure of professional prospects where such prospects exist.

19. Even the most self-serving reports of investigations of UFOs admit that at least 8% of such reports have not been adequately accounted for in the standard "scientific" ways: as illusions or misperceived airplanes or stars. These genuinely "unidentified" flying objects must, then, be explained in some nonstandard way, such as being a remote planet, a remote time on this planet, or from a different physical or spiritual dimension.

A flaw in the argument is that it

(A) applies a general rule in a case where it is not relevant.

(B) infers that something must be the case from the fact that the opposite claim has not been proven.

(C) changes the meaning of a crucial expression during the argument.

(D) attempts to refute an argument by attacking the characteristics of those who advance it rather than its content.

(E) refutes a misleading or exaggerated version of the opposite position, rather than an accurate one.

20. It was a period of great climatic upheaval. The consensus in the scientific community that global warming due to human action was real and posed serious threats to human communities, some of which could no longer be forestalled, was joined by a political campaign season that showed a broad nonpartisan political consensus that the problem was real and worthy of immediate and most serious attention. At that very time a hugely destructive cyclone in Myanmar, a massive earthquake in China, and a series of tornadoes with a great many storms strewing massive and tragic destruction in the United States were all occurring. Yet at this moment, when nature seemed to reinforce a collaboration of science and politics, scientific meteorologists largely discounted the idea that global warming was a cause of the tornadoes.

If the statements in the passage are true, which of the following most helps to explain the position of the meteorologists discussed in the last sentence?

(A) Global warming had begun at a period far earlier than the beginning of tornado season.

(B) Scientists know that it is often erroneous to assume that because two phenomena happen in close proximity to one another, that one is the cause of the other.

(C) Scientists determined that a weather phenomenon called "la niña" that can occur with or without global warming was responsible for the extreme tornadoes.

(D) Some scientists continued to maintain that what was seen as global warming was a normal temperature fluctuation not caused by human action.

(E) The tornado season, while characterized by many strong storms, was not as destructive of human life as two others that had occurred in the past.

21. What is civilization? An old question, and definitional games are not always fruitful. In this instance, however, we can be at least partially clear. The word *civilization* ought to be used to mean something different from and more than the term *culture* of long anthropological tradition; else why have two terms? If so, it then must be something more than a set of collective norms and values of a particular group of any size in any place.

Which of the following is an assumption that the writer's argument depends on?

(A) Anthropologists have long recognized the distinction between *civilization* and *culture.*

(B) All particular groups have collective norms and values.

(C) Definitional games can be distinguished from serious attempts to understand the definitions of key terms.

(D) A civilization is larger than a culture.

(E) *Culture* refers to a set of collective norms and values of a particular group.

22. Pains and pleasures come to an end together. Good and evil do not come to an end together. The conclusion is that good is not identical with pleasure, nor evil with pain. The one pair of contraries comes to an end together and the other does not, because they are different.

Which of the following propositions, if true, would most strengthen the argument?

(A) Some actions are neither good nor evil.

(B) Some actions are neither pleasurable nor painful.

(C) No good action is ultimately painful, though it may seem to be.

(D) Some good actions are painful.

(E) Something which seems pleasant might give way to a greater pleasure.

23. Logic student: Most of my friends think that symbolic logic is useless because it does not present representations of real-life arguments. They believe that the usefulness of logic is directly proportional to the degree of realism. They are just wrong, as the following argument shows: It is a fundamental principle that only pure studies in form have true logical value. It follows that, since every symbolic argument is a pure study in form, only arguments in symbolic form have logical value.

Which of the following arguments exhibits the same flaw as the argument the student presents?

(A) Only if it is an evergreen can it be a pine. And all cedars are evergreens. Therefore, no pines are cedars.

(B) All humans are mortal. Only if it is human can something be a warrior. Therefore, all warriors are mortal.

(C) Only if it is edible to meat eaters can it be called cattle. All cattle are herbivores. Therefore, all edible animals are herbivores.

(D) That animal, named Hurley, has to be a beagle. For that animal, named Hurley, surely does howl, and only if it howls is it a beagle.

(E) No non-cats purr. But only if it meows is it a cat. Therefore, all purring animals meow.

24. President of Nadaldia: In order for arms control to have meaning and credibly contribute to national security and to global or regional stability, it is essential that all parties to agreements fully comply with them. Strict compliance with all provisions of arms control agreements is fundamental, and this administration will not accept anything less. To do so would undermine the arms control process and damage the chances for establishing a more constructive Nadaldia-Redfedria relationship.

If the statements from the president are true, which of the following could also be true?

(A) The administration accepts incomplete compliance with arms control agreements and yet the arms control process is not undermined.

(B) All parties to the arms control agreements do not fully comply, yet arms control has meaning and credibly contributes to national security and to regional stability.

(C) There is strict compliance with all provisions of arms control agreements, but the chances for establishing a more constructive Nadaldia-Redfedria relationship are damaged.

(D) Despite the fact that the administration has accepted the fact that not all parties have fully complied with arms control agreements, those agreements are meaningful and credibly contribute to national security and global stability.

(E) The arms control process is not undermined but the chances for a more constructive Nadaldia-Redfedria relationship are damaged, and the administration has accepted less-than-strict compliance with all provisions of arms control agreements.

STOP

If time still remains, you may review work only in this section. When the time allotted is up, you may go on to the next section.

SECTION 4

Time—35 minutes
24 questions

Directions: *Each group of questions in this section is based on a set of conditions. In answering some of the questions, it may be useful to draw a rough diagram. Choose the response that most accurately and completely answers the question and blacken the corresponding space on your answer sheet.*

QUESTIONS 1–6

The seven members of the Quality Control Division—Mr. Rodriguez, Ms. Unger, Ms. Queen, Mr. Singer, Mr. Thomas, Ms. Winters, and Ms. Vellars—are going to have a group photograph taken, and they will be arranged in a line in order of height, from tallest to shortest.

Ms. Queen is taller than Mr. Thomas.
Ms. Winters is shorter than Ms. Queen.
Mr. Rodriguez is taller than Mr. Singer.
Ms. Vellars is shorter than Ms. Winters.
Mr. Singer is taller than Ms. Winters.
Ms. Unger is taller than Ms. Queen.

1. Which of the following must be false?

   (A) Ms. Vellars is the shortest.

   (B) Mr. Rodriguez is the tallest.

   (C) Ms. Winters is the shortest.

   (D) Mr. Thomas is the shortest.

   (E) Ms. Unger is the tallest.

2. Which of the following could NOT be the second tallest person in the group?

   (A) Mr. Rodriguez

   (B) Ms. Queen

   (C) Mr. Singer

   (D) Mr. Thomas

   (E) Ms. Unger

3. If Mr. Rodriguez is the third tallest person in line, which of the following is the second tallest?

   (A) Mr. Singer

   (B) Mr. Thomas

   (C) Ms. Unger

   (D) Ms. Queen

   (E) Ms. Winters

4. If Mr. Singer is fourth in line, which of the following cannot be true?

   (A) Ms. Queen is taller than Ms. Winters.

   (B) Mr. Thomas is shorter than Ms. Vellars.

   (C) Ms. Winters is shorter than Ms. Vellars.

   (D) Mr. Rodriguez is the tallest.

   (E) Ms. Unger is the tallest.

5. Which of the following is not a possible ordering, from tallest to shortest?

   (A) Rodriguez, Unger, Singer, Queen, Winters, Thomas, Vellars

   (B) Rodriguez, Singer, Unger, Queen, Thomas, Winters, Vellars

   (C) Rodriguez, Unger, Queen, Singer, Winters, Thomas, Vellars

   (D) Unger, Queen, Rodriguez, Singer, Winters, Vellars, Thomas

   (E) Rodriguez, Unger, Queen, Singer, Vellars, Winters, Thomas

6. If the three tallest members of the group, in some order or other, are Mr. Rodriguez, Ms. Unger, and Mr. Singer, which of the fol-

lowing is a complete and accurate list of the people, any one of which could be next in line after those three?

(A) Ms. Winters

(B) Ms. Queen

(C) Mr. Thomas

(D) Ms. Queen, Mr. Thomas

(E) Mr. Thomas, Ms. Winters, Ms. Queen

QUESTIONS 7–12

Every Wednesday, five sales people—V, W, X, Y, and Z—check into the Dew Drop Inn. They always stay in rooms 201 through 206. Each takes a different room, but one of the rooms is not used by any of them.

W always takes an odd-numbered room.

Y always takes the third room in numerical order of those that the salespeople use.

Z always has a higher-numbered room than V, but none of the other salespeople takes a room between Z's and V's.

7. If V takes room 202, which of the following must be true?

(A) W takes room 201.

(B) Y takes room 204.

(C) Y takes a higher-numbered room than W.

(D) Z takes a higher-numbered room than W.

(E) X takes a lower-numbered room than V.

8. If W takes room 201, which of the following is a complete and accurate list of the rooms that X might take?

(A) 202

(B) 203

(C) 206

(D) 202, 203

(E) 202, 206

9. If X takes room 201, which of the following must be true?

(A) Y takes a higher-numbered room than W.

(B) V takes a lower-numbered room than W.

(C) V takes room 202.

(D) Y takes room 203.

(E) Z takes room 204.

10. If none of the salespeople takes room 201, which of the following must be true?

I. If W takes room 203, Z takes room 206.

II. If Z takes room 203, W takes room 205.

III. X does not take room 205.

(A) I only

(B) II only

(C) III only

(D) I and II only

(E) I, II, and III

11. If W takes room 203, all of the following statements must be true EXCEPT

(A) X takes a lower-numbered room than Y.

(B) X takes room 201.

(C) Y takes room 204.

(D) V takes a higher-numbered room than Y.

(E) Z takes room 206.

12. It cannot be true that Z stays in room

(A) 202.

(B) 203.

(C) 204.

(D) 205.

(E) 206.

QUESTIONS 13–18

The Basic College Council is made up of eight representatives from the departments in the three divisions. From the Science Division is one representative from each of the departments of Chemistry, Mathematics, and Biology. The Social Science Division provides one representative from each of History, Linguistics, and Economics. A representative from Philosophy and one from Rhetoric serve for the Humanities Division.

All Council Committees are made up entirely of council members.
Each committee has exactly four members.
Each committee has at least one member from each division.
The representative from Chemistry will not serve on a committee with the representative from Biology.
The representatives from Mathematics and Economics always serve on the same committees.
The representative from Rhetoric will serve only on committees on which the representative from Biology or the one from Economics serves.

13. The representatives of which of the following groups of departments can serve together on a committee?

(A) Chemistry, Mathematics, History, Economics

(B) Chemistry, Mathematics, History, Philosophy

(C) Mathematics, Biology, Linguistics, Economics

(D) Mathematics, Biology, Economics, Rhetoric

(E) Biology, History, Economics, Rhetoric

14. If both the representatives from the Humanities Division are on a committee, then the other two members of the committee can be representatives of

(A) Biology and History.

(B) Biology and Economics.

(C) Mathematics and History.

(D) Chemistry and Mathematics.

(E) Chemistry and Biology.

15. If the representative of Economics is on a committee, which is a group of three that might complete that committee?

(A) representatives of Chemistry, Mathematics, and Biology

(B) representatives of Chemistry, Biology, and Rhetoric

(C) representatives of Chemistry, Philosophy, and Rhetoric

(D) representatives of Mathematics, Linguistics, and History

(E) representatives of Mathematics, Philosophy, and Linguistics

16. If the representatives of Biology and Philosophy do not serve on a committee, representatives of both of which of the following pairs of departments must serve on that committee?

(A) Chemistry and Linguistics

(B) Chemistry and Economics

(C) Mathematics and History

(D) Mathematics and Economics

(E) History and Economics

17. Which of the following must be true?

(A) If the representatives of Chemistry and Mathematics are on a committee, the representative of Philosophy must also be on it.

(B) If the representative of Rhetoric is not on a committee, then the representatives of Mathematics and Biology must both be on it.

(C) If both Humanities representatives are on a committee, then the representative of Chemistry cannot be on it.

(D) If the representative of neither Mathematics nor Philosophy is on a committee, then the representative of Economics must be on it.

(E) If the representative of neither Biology nor Economics is on a committee, then the representative of Linguistics cannot be on it.

18. If a committee includes the representatives from History and Linguistics, which of the following is a complete and accurate list of

the departments whose representatives might also serve on the committee?

(A) Biology, Rhetoric

(B) Chemistry, Philosophy

(C) Chemistry, Biology, Philosophy

(D) Chemistry, Biology, Philosophy, Rhetoric

(E) Chemistry, Biology, Mathematics, Philosophy, Rhetoric

QUESTIONS 19–24

George, Henry, Irene, Janet, and Kay are members who may run for office if asked by the nominating committee, though none of them will run without such a request.

If George is asked to run, he will run.
If Henry is asked to run, he will run only if Kay also runs.
If Irene is invited to run, she will run, in case Janet does as well.
If Janet is asked, she will run just in case George does not.
If Kay is asked to run, she will run just in case Irene does not.

19. If all five are asked to run, how many candidates will run?

(A) 1

(B) 2

(C) 3

(D) 4

(E) 5

20. If all but George are asked to run, how many candidates will run?

(A) 0

(B) 1

(C) 2

(D) 3

(E) 4

21. If only Henry, Irene, and Kay are asked to run, which is a complete and accurate list of who will run?

(A) Henry

(B) Irene

(C) Kay

(D) Henry, Irene, Kay

(E) Henry, Kay

22. If only George, Henry, and Irene are asked to run, which of them will?

(A) George

(B) Henry

(C) Irene

(D) All of them will run

(E) None of them will run

23. Which of the following is a pair of members who could not both run?

(A) George and Henry

(B) George and Irene

(C) George and Kay

(D) Henry and Kay

(E) Irene and Janet

24. If both Henry and Janet are asked to run, which of the following is a list of people who must be asked to run?

(A) George, Henry, and Janet only

(B) Henry, Irene, and Janet only

(C) Henry, Irene, and Kay only

(D) Henry, Janet, and Kay only

(E) Henry and Janet only

STOP

If time still remains, you may review work only in this section. When the time allotted is up, you may go on to the next section.

WRITING SAMPLE TOPIC

Time—35 minutes

Directions: *The scenario presented below describes two choices, either one of which can be supported on the basis of the information given. Your essay should consider both choices and argue for one over the other, based on the two specified criteria and the facts provided. There is no "right" or "wrong" choice: a reasonable argument can be made for either. Confine your essay to the blocked, lined area on the front and back of the separate Writing Sample Response Sheet. Only that area will be reproduced for law schools. Be sure that your writing is legible.*

A subcommittee at SavoryReads Press, a company owned and managed by its 63 employees, must decide which of two competing health-care plans to adopt for company workers. Only two plans remain eligible, and one of the two must be selected as the company's only plan. The two finalists cost about the same to the company and, on average, to the individual employee. The subcommittee will focus on two key criteria of importance to SavoryReads employees in making its selection:

- It is desirable for employees to have as much flexibility as possible in choosing the physicians who treat them and the medical facilities at which they are treated.
- It is desirable that health-care program participants have prescription drug benefits that allow them flexibility in selecting brands of medication and pharmaceutical companies for filling prescriptions.

Following these criteria, make a recommendation as to which of the two following plans the committee should adopt:

Plan HealthyFolks emphasizes preventive health care by encouraging participants to visit health care providers on a regular basis at a low cost. When diseases are contracted that require serious treatment, patients may choose their physicians and health-care facilities. The plan includes a prescription medicine element that is limited to filling prescriptions through a few nationwide mail order pharmaceutical suppliers, and one that requires the use of generic drugs over brand names where possible.

Plan MediFix emphasizes flexibility on the part of patients with illnesses both in the places that they can have prescriptions filled and in the particular medications that are covered under the plan. It operates according to the principle that patients are more likely to take their medications when they can acquire them in a way that best suits the individual patient. Medifix patients may receive benefits only if they are treated by physicians on a preferred provider list, which includes exclusively physicians and medical facilities that have agreed to operate according to procedures adopted by Medifix and at rates set by Medifix.

STOP

If time still remains, you may review work only in this section.

TEST 2 ANSWER KEY

Section 1 – Reading Comprehension

1.	A	15.	B
2.	B	16.	E
3.	B	17.	C
4.	C	18.	C
5.	D	19.	D
6.	B	20.	B
7.	B	21.	C
8.	C	22.	C
9.	B	23.	B
10.	C	24.	C
11.	A	25.	D
12.	E	26.	E
13.	D	27.	C
14.	C	28.	D

Section 2 – Logical Reasoning

1.	C	14.	A
2.	C	15.	C
3.	E	16.	D
4.	B	17.	A
5.	D	18.	D
6.	D	19.	B
7.	E	20.	B
8.	C	21.	A
9.	C	22.	D
10.	D	23.	E
11.	B	24.	E
12.	B	25.	D
13.	E		

Section 3 – Logical Reasoning

1.	C	13.	C
2.	D	14.	C
3.	E	15.	B
4.	A	16.	B
5.	A	17.	B
6.	B	18.	A
7.	D	19.	B
8.	D	20.	C
9.	D	21.	E
10.	D	22.	D
11.	E	23.	D
12.	A	24.	C

Section 4 – Analytical Reasoning

1.	C	13.	D
2.	D	14.	A
3.	D	15.	E
4.	C	16.	D
5.	E	17.	C
6.	B	18.	D
7.	B	19.	C
8.	D	20.	D
9.	A	21.	E
10.	E	22.	A
11.	B	23.	B
12.	C	24.	D

SECTION 1 – READING COMPREHENSION

Questions 1–8

The passage includes five paragraphs. Paragraph 1 mentions nuclear power events that confirmed fears over development of nuclear power. Paragraph 2 explains activity by interest groups in opposition to development of nuclear power, although their efforts to persuade courts to intervene failed. Paragraph 3 explains the early optimism on the part of scientists for nuclear power. Paragraph 4 lists problems encountered by the nuclear power industry. Paragraph 5 claims that a new approach would be needed to bring back enthusiasm for nuclear power. Taken together, these paragraphs produce this main idea: Early optimism about nuclear power was met with problems in the industry, culminating in major accidents. These problems, combined with interest groups' opposition, resulted in the near demise of the nuclear power industry.

1. The main idea, capturing especially the importance of the downturn for the nuclear industry, is stated in choice (A).

2. The question asks for something not mentioned in the passage. Choice (A) and choice (E) are specifically mentioned in the fourth paragraph. Choice (D) is mentioned in the second paragraph, and choice (C) in the first. Choice (B) is the one that is not mentioned, and indeed the passage says that the courts opted not to get involved. (B)

3. The question asks for a detail about the position taken by the federal courts. This detail is discussed in the second paragraph where it states explicitly that the Supreme Court ruled that the Atomic Energy Commission was making rules based on technical data and the courts should not attempt to substitute their judgment. The correct answer is choice (B).

4. The question asks for the rule of a particular paragraph. The third paragraph explains early optimism about nuclear power and is designed to put the general idea of the demise of their power in that broader context. The correct answer is choice (C).

5. The question asks about the meaning of a detail. Go to paragraph 3 and locate the word in the third sentence. In context the word is meant to characterize increasing support and enthusiasm for nuclear power. So the correct answer is choice (D).

6. The question asks for something that passage "implies," which means something that the passage makes almost certain to be the case. The implication is contained in choice (B), and the main idea is almost explicitly stated at the end of the first paragraph. Choice (A) speaks of nonviolence, which is not discussed in the passage. Choice (C) speaks of shutting down "many nuclear power plants," which goes further than the passage does. Choice (D) is the contrary of what is stated in the passage. Choice (E) goes too far with the word "never." (B)

7. The question asks for the primary purpose of the passage. The passage is a descriptive one designed to detail the demise of the nuclear power industry. So the correct answer is choice (B).

8. This question is another way of asking for the main idea or primary purpose of the passage. The most accurately descriptive title is in choice (C).

Questions 9–14

This is a comparative reading task. **Passage A** includes two paragraphs. The first notes that New Deal legislation sponsored by President Franklin Roosevelt was the major thrust for governmental regulation of the private sector, and that at first these regulations were often struck down by the Supreme Court. The second paragraph states that with deaths and resignations from the Supreme Court, the president appointed people who supported laws designed to deal with social ills in the country, and that the Congress and the court then became allies in government regulation of the private sector. **Passage B** has two paragraphs. The first states that when the legislative and executive branches had too long ignored the problem of racial discrimination, the Supreme Court stepped in with a 1954 unanimous decision to rule that racially separate educational systems violated the Constitution. The second paragraph notes that the court's political independence allowed it to use its moral and legal force to lead the most important change in the 20th century. Taken together, the two passages focus on the independence of the Supreme Court from the executive and legislative branches and the implication of that political independence for national policy.

9. The question asks for what both passages are designed to do. Each passage shows the court acting independently and differently from the executive and legislative branches with regard to some issue of the time. The nature of the issues seems different, as does the attitude of the passages' authors on the question of whether it was good for the Supreme Court to act independently as it did. So what the passages have in common is captured in choice (B).

10. The question asks for the attitude in the two passages about the Supreme Court's opposition to the legislative branch. In Passage A the author seems to share the perspective described as that of the executive and legislative branches of the time that the court's actions were harmful. In Passage B, on the other hand, the author seems to approve of the actions enabled by the court's independence. The point is expressed accurately in choice (C).

11. The question asks about a detail, the use of the word *intrusion* in Passage A. So return to the passage to read the sentence in which the word is used and at least one sentence preceding it. In this case a key comes from the fact that the word is enclosed in quotation marks, indicating that the actors described in the current sentence do not believe that the behavior is actually intrusion, but that it would have been characterized as such elsewhere. The "elsewhere" is in the Supreme Court before its membership changed, and, therefore, the answer is choice (A).

12. The question asks for something about which the passages agree. While they have different attitudes about the independent actions of the Supreme Court that they describe, both recognize that independence and that it can be important in the United States. That common recognition is indicated in choice (E).

13. This question asks for an inference that can be made from the two passages. This will be something that is highly likely to be true based upon what both passages say, and it might be a number of things. To find the right answer, it is necessary to check the answer choices against the passages. What is true is indicated in choice (D), that some of the court's members appointed in the 1930s were still serving in the 1950s. Each of the other choices somehow mentions something that is brought up in one of the passages, but goes too far in claiming that some conclusion or true observation can be drawn. (D)

14. This question asks for a detail that is "explicitly" mentioned in both passages. Simply and alertly, check the choices against the passages and look, quite attentively, for something that is mentioned literally in both. In the list included here, separation of powers is the only such thing, so choice (C) is the answer. (C).

Questions 15–21

The passage includes five paragraphs. The first paragraph notes that physicists in laboratories have been able to produce temperatures cooler than any others that have occurred in the history of the cosmos. Paragraph 2 says that these ultralow temperatures produce superfluidity, especially using isotopes of helium. Paragraph 3 focuses on superfluid helium-3 whose study is interesting for itself and for what it teaches beyond itself. Paragraph 4 states that the study of superfluid helium-3 may help understand things found nowhere on earth, including the matter of certain stars. Paragraph 5 states that these experiments may require even lower temperatures. Taken together these paragraphs establish this as the main idea of the passage: The passage is about learning from superfluidity which can come from ultralow temperatures produced in laboratories. The study of superfluidity is interesting in itself and because it can lead to understanding of various phenomena in the universe.

15. The main idea is best stated in choice (B). Each of the other choices mentions a part, but choice (B) states the overall point of the passage. (B)

16. The question asks for something that the author says about the temperature of the cosmic microwave background. The phrase "cosmic microwave background" is located in the first paragraph, where the author makes the point that temperatures reached in physics laboratories are colder than those of the cosmic microwave background. So the correct answer is choice (E).

17. The question asks for the purpose of a phrase. Locate the phrase in the third paragraph and read on either side of it to be accurate about its context. The "combination of the simple and complex" refers to superfluid helium-3 as being a simple liquid with very intricate behavior. The answer to the question is choice (C).

18. The question asks for a detail about superfluidity in helium isotopes. That phenomenon is discussed most in paragraph 2, so review this paragraph for its details. Among the things that the paragraph says is that superfluidity in helium-4 has been known since 1938. The correct answer to the question is in choice (C).

19. The question asks for something that the author says can be learned through studying superfluid helium-3. Alertly review the details in the third and fourth paragraphs. At the end of the third, the passage states that superfluid helium-3 is useful for the study of "condensed matter problems." So the answer to the question is choice (D).

20. The question asks for something that the passage says about neutron matter. Neutron matter is discussed in paragraph 4, so review what he said there. Neutron matter is presented as an example of something "found nowhere on Earth." So the answer to this question is choice (B).

21. The question asks about the primary purpose. That purpose is to explain that the study of superfluid helium-3 might produce some interesting information. So the answer here is choice (C).

Questions 22–28

The passage includes four paragraphs. The first paragraph asserts that a Hitchcock film called *I Confess* is not without flaws, but is not the failure that a critic contends. Paragraph 2 describes *I Confess*. Paragraph 3 explains certain weaknesses in the film. Paragraph 4 gives a positive summary judgment. Taken together these paragraphs create this main idea: The Hitchcock film *I Confess* has its weaknesses, but is admirable in many ways.

22. That main idea is accurately expressed in choice (C).

23. This is a purpose of detail question, asking why the author mentions another Hitchcock film, called *Strangers on a Train* in the first paragraph. Locate that mention, and discover that the film is mentioned twice in the first paragraph. Reread those passages, and it appears that *Strangers on a Train* is presented as an example of another Hitchcock film that is considered good without controversy. So the answer to the question is choice (B).

24. The question is about the function of the second paragraph. This paragraph is a description of the film *I Confess*, explaining its plot and the meaning behind it. So the answer to this question is in choice (C).

25. This is a meaning of detail question. Return to paragraph 1 and locate the word *eclipsed*, reading the sentences before it and after it. The phrase is that Hitchcock's genius is not eclipsed, the meaning is not hidden, in *I Confess*. So the answer here is choice (D).

26. This question asks for the criticisms that the author of the passage makes about the film. Recall that the discussion of weaknesses is in the third paragraph and review it to discover that the criticism is primarily about "unfortunate casting." So the answer to the question is choice (E).

27. The question is about the author of the passage's attitude toward the work of Robin Wood. Find the reference to Robin Wood in the first paragraph as something that is used to initiate the discussion of *I Confess.* Basically paragraph 1 criticizes Wood's opinion about *I Confess,* but in the context of calling Wood's book "provocative," and saying that Wood's analysis is "frequently compelling." So the author has a generally positive attitude toward Wood, but disagrees with Wood's assessment of *I Confess.* The answer to this question is choice (C).

28. This question asks for the primary purpose of the passage, which is to present a largely positive assessment of Hitchcock's *I Confess.* So the answer is choice (D).

SECTION 2 – LOGICAL REASONING

1. **Question:** the question asks for a principle that makes the conclusion reasonable.

   Analysis: the conclusion in the passage is that the practice of "clear-cutting" should be carefully regulated by state governments. The passage states that landowners practice clear-cutting because it brings quicker profits in the short run, but also that the practice can be destructive to the environment, which, it says, could lessen the land's capability to produce similar resources in the future. A subtle choice is in favor of environmental concern over short-term profits. But in the passage those environmental concerns are motivated by the desire for the long-term capability to produce forest resources for future generations. The conclusion is reasonable with some belief that says that it is appropriatè to consider these environmental issues as well as those short-term profits.

   Answer: The correct answer will be a principle that, if believed, would lead to making the choice in the passage. Someone who believed what is in choice (C) would indeed make that choice. (C)

2. **Question:** The question asks for a flaw in the manager's reasoning.

   Analysis: The manager concludes that half the city's residents shop at the music store. The basis for the conclusion is a survey of people in the mall where the store is located. Half of those surveyed said they had shopped in a store at least once a week. The difficulty is that the survey was taken among people in the mall, but the conclusion is about people in the city, and it is unlikely that the people in the mall will be adequately representative of the people in the city as a whole.

   Answer: Choice (C) accurately states the flaw. (C)

3. **Question:** The question asks simply for something that explains the magazine's endorsement. This suggests either a paradox that needs to be resolved or a principle that needs to be employed to explain the choice, so analyze the passage to determine both the issue and its resolution.

   Analysis: The passage explains that there are two types of automobile: one, type X, recommended by researchers for drivers who take fewer but longer trips and another, type Y, recommended by those researchers for drivers who take more but shorter trips. Unlike the researchers, however, the magazine endorsed type Y for all motorists. This appears to be like a paradox: why, if the two types serve different kinds of driving more effectively, would the magazine recommend only one type.

   Answer: The correct answer will offer information making the choice of the magazine make sense. And choice (E) does precisely that by introducing another consideration that makes it make sense that the magazine "strongly" recommends only type Y. (E)

4. **Question:** The question asks for an assumption that is necessary for the passage to reach its conclusion.

   Analysis: The conclusion is that one should buy brand O car wax because it will protect the car for a year. The premise leading to this conclusion is that a car waxed with this brand car wash was washed 52 times and the wax still worked. The evidence is about 52 washings, but the conclusion is about a year. For the evidence to lead to the conclusion it must be the case that a car is waxed on average no more than once a week during a year.

   Answer: The required assumption is captured in choice (B).

5. **Question:** The question asks for an inference from the statements in the passage.

   Analysis: An inference question does not allow determination of the answer before going to the choices, except to say that the answer will be something that simply must be true based on information in the passage. The passage here states that if Nathan is not on the baseball team then Peggy will not date him. And if Peggy does not date Nathan, then Nathan will spend all his money at the arcade. These statements also mean that if Nathan does not spend all his money at the arcade then Peggy will date him, and that if Peggy does date him then Nathan is on the baseball team. The passage further states that anyone on the baseball team must buy his own glove.

Answer: The statements compel the additional statement in choice (D). None of the others accurately represents the meaning of the conditional statements. (D)

6. **Question:** The question is about structure, asking about the role of a statement in the passage on the rate of remarriage.

   Analysis: The conclusion is that families have always been found in human societies. This is supported by a statement that even in modern society the family remains strong. And the claim is that the family remains strong despite a high divorce rate, since the divorce rate is also accompanied by a high rate of remarriage. So the statement about remarriage serves to counter a possible objection to the claim that families remain important in modern society.

   Answer: The role of the statement about remarriage is accurately stated in choice (D).

7. **Question:** The question says that the reasoning in the passage is vulnerable to criticism, which means that there is a flaw.

   Analysis: The conclusion is that an article in the school's newspaper concerning health risks associated with eating foods cooked in fats had a positive impact. The evidence is that the cafeteria today did not serve french fries cooked in animal fat. The error involves moving from a correlation of two things: that the article appeared and that the cafeteria did not serve food cooked in animal fat to a conclusion that one of those two things caused the other, when in fact the occurrences could be simply coincidental or caused by some third thing. So the passage confuses correlation with cause.

   Answer: Choice (E) correctly expresses the point of confusing correlation with cause. Just because two things happen in sequence does not mean that the first was the cause of the second. (E)

8. **Question:** The question asks for what cannot be true from the information in the passage. It will behave like an inference question, except that the correct answer will not be something that must be true, but rather must be false.

   Analysis: With a question like this it is not possible to analyze the passage for what precisely the answer will involve before going to the choices. So analyze the passage for clarity on what it requires and allows so as to be able to discover an answer choice which must be false. It says that textbooks are an "essential" source of information for students and teachers, and that they outweigh "all" other sources in determining day-to-day teaching and learning activities. It claims that "no other factor has a greater influence" on the nature and consequences of elementary education. Note that this would be consistent with some other factor having an equal influence, but not a greater one, whereas nothing else could have as great an influence on determining day-to-day activities. Good textbooks, the passage says, must be there for education to be good.

   Answer: Applying the statements in the passage about the determination of day-to-day teaching and learning activities and about the influence on the consequences of elementary education, and about the necessity of good textbooks for good teaching, choice (C) is the choice that cannot be true. It must be false, given the statements in the passage that education could not be good without good textbooks. (C)

9. **Question:** The question says that there is a flaw in Geoffrey's reasoning.

   Analysis: The conclusion to Geoffrey's reasoning is that the universe cannot be eternal. That is based on the premise that if something is eternal then it has no beginning, and the additional premise that the universe had a beginning. Geoffrey's claim that the universe had a beginning is based upon the premise that each thing in it had a beginning, and so he assumes that a quality belonging to each thing in a group belongs to the group as a whole, which need not be the case.

Answer: The problem with Geoffrey's reasoning is in making the error of assuming something characteristic of each of the parts is also necessarily a characteristic of the whole, and this error is accurately expressed in choice (C).

10. **Question:** The question asks for something to strengthen a recommendation.

Analysis: The recommendation is to issue a warning to athletes that steroid use may increase the likelihood of heart disease. This recommendation is based upon a study that showed that bodybuilders who use steroids had lower levels of high-density lipoproteins in their blood and upon the knowledge that low levels of these lipoproteins are correlated to a high risk of heart attack. These premises seem to make the recommendation reasonable, and the correct answer will do even more to do so. So interrogate the answer choices by asking, "Does this make it more likely that steroid use may increase the likelihood of heart disease?" The strengthen question will typically add additional information to make that conclusion more likely.

Answer: Choice (D) offers additional information that makes it more likely that athletes using steroids should be warned of the danger of heart disease. (D)

11. **Question:** The question asks for an assumption required by the passage.

Analysis: The conclusion is that the phrase "public interest" is "never" used to do things that help ordinary people. The evidence for the conclusion is about presidents, business groups, environmental organizations, and teachers' organizations each using the phrase "national interest" when arguing for something that appears to be in their particular interest. Note the sweeping nature of the conclusion, with the word "never." Since this is an assumption question, the task is to find something that must be true for that sweeping conclusion to follow. So pose this question to the answer choices: "Does this have to be true for it to be true that the phrase 'public interest' or 'national interest' is *never* used to do things that involve helping ordinary people?"

Answer: The assumption question applied to the answer choices shows that choice (B) is correct. It must be true that what the teachers' organization asks for does not benefit ordinary people for it to be true that the use of the phrase "national interest" is never used to do things that involve helping ordinary people. (B)

12. **Question:** The question asks for an inference, or something which must be true if the statements in the passage are true.

Analysis: While it is not usually possible to anticipate the answer to an inference question precisely, discovering an inference requires a precise understanding of the statements in the passage, so undertake that analysis. The passage presents a chain of reasoning: if the college does not increase tuition it must cut back expenditures for athletics. If it cuts that spending for athletics it will anger alumni. If alumni get angry they may reduce donations (notice that it does not say that they *will* reduce donations). If donations are reduced then there will be decreased building maintenance. If, on the other hand, the college raises tuition the students will protest.

Answer: Analyze the answer choices to determine whether each could be false consistent with the information in the passage. Choice (A) could be false because it would not be certain that donations would be reduced. Choice (B) must be true since tuition either will or will not be increased. Choice (C) is not mentioned in the passage as a link. The connection in choice (D) is also not mentioned in the passage. Choice (E) need not be true because a cut and expenditures need not result in a loss of donations. (B)

13. **Question:** The question asks about the structure of the argument, specifically asking about the argumentative strategy employed.

Analysis: The conclusion to the passage is that internship experiences should be used in legal assistant training programs. The argument reaches this conclusion by providing evidence that internships are used historically, moving from ancient times to contemporary physician training, and concludes that the legal assistant programs should recognize the value of internships just as these other activities have. The conclusion, then, is based upon the historical use of internships.

Answer: Choice (E) accurately expresses the strategy used in the passage. (E)

14. **Question:** The question asks for something that is "most strongly supported" by the information in the passage.

    Analysis: With a "most strongly supported" question look for something that follows beyond a reasonable doubt from the information in the passage, but that is not explicitly stated. The passage states that Aristotle claimed that abstract thought could discover the laws that govern the universe and that it would not be necessary to check the results of such reasoning. The passage goes on to state that this led no one to check the Aristotelian claim the bodies of different weights would fall at different speeds until Galileo did so. The result of Galileo's experimentation has been to put experimentation at the core of modern scientific method. What this experiment proved is that Aristotle's claim about falling bodies was incorrect, and that is what is most strongly supported by the passage.

    Answer: Each of the answer choices tends to go too far from the evidence in the passage except for choice (A), which is shown by the passage to be the case. The most likely alternative would be choice (C), but the passage does not support the claim that abstract thought is "not capable" of learning what is learned by experimentation. (A)

15. **Question:** The question asks for a flaw in the historian's argument.

    Analysis: The historian concludes that by applying descriptions of the Soviet system of the 1960s we can develop an accurate description of 1990s Cuban policy making. The historian reaches this conclusion by noticing that the same titles held by Cuban officials in the 1990s were held by officials in the Soviet government in the 1960s. The questionable reasoning here lies in the assumption that because the titles are the same, the functions of the officials are the same.

    Answer: The error in the historian's reasoning is described accurately in choice (C).

16. **Question:** The question asks for something that resolves the apparent discrepancy in the mayor's views.

    Analysis: Read the passage to understand the mayor's views, paying special attention to the views that will appear to be contradictory. On the one hand, the mayor said that city governments should not take it upon themselves to provide public assistance to the needy. On the other hand, the mayor praises the city office that provides public health assistance. How could the mayor both praise the office that provides public health assistance and claim that city government should not provide public assistance. Embrace both sides of that question and find an additional premise that makes them make sense simultaneously.

    Answer: Choice (D) accomplishes what needs to be done. If the city's public assistance office is not a part of city government, then the mayor's positions are not inconsistent or paradoxical. (D)

17. **Question:** This is a parallel flaw question.

    Analysis: Analyze the passage for the flaw in its reasoning. The argument goes like this: If gasoline evaporates then it has been left in an open container. The container is open. So the gasoline will evaporate. The flaw lies in saying that something that is necessary for another result is enough, by itself, to create that result. That is, in the present case, you know that if the gasoline has evaporated, its container is open, but not that if the container is open the gasoline will evaporate.

    Answer: The same error of taking something that is needed for something else to happen as enough to make sure that something else will happen is made in choice (A).

18. **Question:** The question asks for an assumption on which the argument relies.

Analysis: The conclusion is in the first sentence: that the manuals that come with computer hardware frequently need to be revised. The evidence is that with improvements in technology there are new software and new applications, and that people need to be taught to use these new applications. The evidence is about new applications, but the conclusion is about revised manuals. The connection between those two things needs to be made in order for the conclusion to follow. Either look directly for that connection or ask the assumption question: "Does this have to be true for it to be true that the manuals frequently need to be revised?"

Answer: The needed assumption, making the connection between revised manuals and new applications is in choice (D).

19. **Question:** The question asks for a "presupposition" which is necessary to the argument, which means it is asking for an assumption.

Analysis: The conclusion is that government failure to control inflation is the culprit in bringing about recession. This follows from an argument that says savings will be low unless government provides incentives for saving, and low savings causes unemployment. But recession comes up for the first time in the conclusion, so for the argument to be sound, as it is taken to be in an assumption question, government responsibility for inflation and unemployment must be tied to recession. The link between unemployment and recession needs to be made.

Answer: The assumption making the required link is in choice (B).

20. **Question:** The question asks for something to weaken the author's prediction.

Analysis: The prediction is that treatments involving many times the normal dose of vitamin E will be shown to slow the aging process in human beings. This conclusion is based upon a study showing that decreasing the amount of vitamin E for rats accelerated the aging process. The assumption seems to be that the more vitamin E taken, the more aging will be retarded. To weaken the argument, provide something that makes that assumption less likely to be true, despite the results of the study.

Answer: The information in choice (B) weakens that unstated assumption that more vitamin E would mean slower aging, and so makes the conclusion less likely to be true. (B)

21. **Question:** The question asks for the structure of the argument, or how it goes about reaching its conclusion.

Analysis: The conclusion is contained in the first sentence: that it cannot be established that marijuana is a dangerous drug by one claim that is made to say it is. The passage shows that one cannot claim that marijuana is dangerous because hard-drug users once used marijuana any more than one can claim that drinking water is dangerous because hard-drug users drink water. It uses an analogous argument with a ridiculous result.

Answer: The technique used by the argument is captured in choice (A).

22. **Question:** The question asks for something to strengthen Bernard's hypothesis.

Analysis: The passage explains a study done by someone named Bernard on rabbits. One group was fed meat and the other a vegetarian diet, and the group fed meat had significant amounts of ketone in their urine. This led Bernard to conclude that the ketone was from metabolizing meat. So when the urine of starving rabbits also had ketone, he hypothesized that they were metabolizing their own stomachs. The goal here is to make it more likely that the ketone meant that they were metabolizing their own stomachs, and so interrogate each answer choice by asking exactly that: "Does this make it more likely that the starving rabbits were metabolizing their own stomachs?"

Answer: Formulating the strengthening interrogation properly leads to choice (D) as the answer. This additional information controls for whether the rabbits in question had previously been meat eaters, and says that even non-meat eaters in the past seem to show signs of metabolizing meat when starving. (D)

23 **Question:** This is a parallel structure question.

Analysis: Analyze the passage for the pattern of its reasoning. R is taking T. If T, then either CS or BUS. R also taking A. A shows that not CS, so R is BUS. The reasoning says that something can be accounted for by one of two possibilities. It then eliminates one of those two possibilities by adding another thing that shows which one of those is the case. Find the one answer choice with the same number of items in the same relative positions.

Answer: The answer choice with the same number of items in the same positions in the reasoning is choice (E). None of the others is close, something that appears only when care has been taken to sort out the reasoning in the initial passage. (E)

24. **Question:** The question asks for the answer choice which does the least to weaken the thesis of the play discussed in the passage.

Analysis: Analyze the passage for the thesis that needs to be weakened. That thesis is that a world where socio-religious and legal systems are governed by women would be more humane than one in which they are governed by men. The evidence is that most male mammals do not bear responsibility for the survival of individuals other than themselves. The passage states that the survival of any species depends upon the caring behavior of its females and not the aggressive behavior of its males. To weaken the argument ask of an answer choice, "Does this make it less likely to be true that a world where socio-religious and legal systems are governed by women would be more humane with less greed, injustice, exploitation, and warfare?" Be very alert to the fact that this is an EXCEPT question: four of the five answer choices will weaken the conclusion, and the correct answer will be the one that does not weaken the conclusion.

Answer: The primary difficulty with this question is being clear on what the correct answer must do: that it does not weaken the conclusion that a world would be more humane where women are in control. The one that least weakens that conclusion is choice (E).

25. **Question:** The question asks for an assumption.

Analysis: The conclusion in the passage is that the church in Russia did not realize its nominal authority over marriage until the 18th century. The passage says that the reason for this was that the church lacked the instruments, including the unambiguous law and bureaucratic infrastructure, that would have made its nominal power into real power. The missing assumption needs to connect these things: unambiguous law and bureaucratic infrastructure, on the one hand, to real power on the other. It must be the case that it is necessary for those things to be there for them to be real power.

Answer: The statement in choice (D) must be true for the conclusion to follow from the information in the passage. It is not the only assumption, or everything that must be assumed, but it is something that must be assumed or presupposed for the conclusion to follow. (D)

SECTION 3 – LOGICAL REASONING

1. **Question:** The question asks for an assumption on which the argument depends.

   Analysis: The conclusion is that even the most popularly responsive of governments can be overthrown by a military coup. The evidence for this conclusion is from a country called Quitmania, presented as a fine example of a bourgeois liberal democracy with a representative government elected by the entire population. The evidence is about a government that is popularly elected, but the conclusion is about a government that is popularly responsive. The notion of responsiveness appears for the first time in the conclusion. So the missing assumption will need to connect the evidence about a popularly elected bourgeois democracy to a popularly responsive government.

   Answer: The connection that is required is contained in choice (C). It must be the case that a bourgeois liberal democracy is popularly responsive for some bourgeois liberal democracy to demonstrate that popularly responsive governments can be overthrown by coups. Choice (E) appears to come close, but leaves open the possibility that there could be a liberal democracy that is not popularly responsive. (C)

2. **Question:** The question asks for something that is most strongly supported by the statements in the passage. This will be something that follows beyond a reasonable doubt from what is stated, but will not itself be an explicit statement in the passage.

   Analysis: The passage presents information about someone named Hinrich. It says that Hinrich is more of a neo-Platonist than Hegel is, and that this makes his thought more systematic and complete than Hegel's, while pointing out certain shortcomings in Hegel's theory. With these statements understood, approach the answer choices asking whether, given the information in the passage, this choice follows.

   Answer: What is most strongly supported by the passage is that there are certain superiorities to Hegel in Hinrich. And so the correct answer is in choice (D). The other choices go further than the passage supports. (D)

3. **Question:** The question asks an assumption on which the argument relies, or something that must be true for the conclusion to follow from the premises stated.

   Analysis: The conclusion is contained in the first sentence, stating that in the early ages there were no wars because there were no kings. The remainder of the passage presents reasons why there were no kings. But the passage does not provide the link between kings and wars that is needed to establish the conclusion. The missing assumption needs to say that wars require kings.

   Answer: The missing assumption is found in choice (E).

4. **Question:** The question alerts us for a paradox in the passage and asks for something that helps to explain it.

   Analysis: With a paradox question it is important to analyze the passage to clarify both items that seem inconsistent. The passage explains that human rights advocates viewed the Biological Weapons Convention as a major and important step. But subsequently developed synthetic toxins that had the same effect as the banned biological agents were not covered by that convention. This development, the passage says, did not concern the human rights advocates. The paradox is that the advocates were enthusiastically supportive of the biological weapons convention, and yet apparently unconcerned about the synthetic toxins that seemed to get around it. How could both of those things be true at the same time?

   Answer: The answer to a paradox question will typically be new information that makes the apparently inconsistent things make sense at the same time. In this case that new premise is contained in choice (A), which says that the synthetic toxins were already banned. (A)

5. **Question:** The question says that there is a flaw in the dentist's argument and that flaw involves assuming something without justification for doing so.

   Analysis: The dentist in this passage concludes that the patient was afraid of him. The reason for this, according to the dentist, is that when patients are frightened their saliva becomes thicker, and this patient's saliva was exceptionally thick. The problem with this reasoning is that the premises do not compel the conclusion that the patient was afraid, for they allow that the thicker saliva might have been explained by some other cause. The dentist assumes without justification that only fear can cause thicker saliva.

   Answer: Several of the answer choices mention saliva and fear, but choice (A) is the one that establishes the relationship that the dentist assumes without warrant. (A)

6. **Question:** The question says that there is a graduate student in the passage who makes an error in reasoning, and asks for the identification of that error.

   Analysis: The graduate student's conclusion is that a professor's claim that the desire for territorial acquisition is a leading cause of war cannot be right. The student's evidence for that is that most wars involve ideological differences, making ideology, and not the desire for territorial expansion, what causes war. But the student's reasoning is erroneous because the student assumes that it is not possible for both ideology and the desire for territorial acquisition to be leading causes of war, something that is not ruled out by the position he cites from the professor.

   Answer: The mistake in reasoning from the graduate student is described in choice (B).

7. **Question:** The question asks for something that supports or strengthens management's decision about how to react to the survey.

   Analysis: Read the passage to find a survey and management's conclusion about how to react to it. The survey shows that many of the consumers of the company's products are dissatisfied, believing that the products are of low quality. Management's decision is to undertake a campaign to focus on changing consumers' beliefs regarding the quality of the company's products. This appears something like a principle question in that the other apparent possibility would be to attempt to improve the quality rather than to change opinions about that quality. Strengthening management's decision will mean adding a reason, or a premise, that makes this choice make sense.

   Answer: The information in choice (D) strengthens management's decision by suggesting that consumers are wrong in their belief that the quality of the products is low, so that the way to address the results of the survey is not to change the quality of the products, so much as to change the erroneous opinions of consumers. (D)

8. **Question:** The question asks for an assumption that the argument relies on.

   Analysis: The conclusion in the passage is that the claim that Britain is a democracy can be seriously disputed since the government, once elected with a healthy majority, can act with few formal checks or controls and, specifically, without the controls of a written constitution. For the evidence to lead to the conclusion that there can be some doubt that Britain is really a democracy, the definition of democracy must involve some kind of constitutional checks or controls. For the evidence in the passage establishes that the British government lacks those checks, and concludes from that that it might not be a true democracy. Those two things need to be linked in the missing assumption.

   Answer: The required connection between constitutional checks and democracy is stated in choice (D).

9. **Question:** The question asks for an assumption on which the argument relies.

   Analysis: The passage deals with the revolutions in East Europe in 1989. It concludes that those revolutions were peaceful because the previous massacre in China's Tiananmen Square aroused such international indignation that the East European governments did not dare to repeat such resistance to the popular will. There may not be a plain missing assumption here, so to find one ask of each of the answer choices, "Does this have to be true for it to be true that the indignation about Tiananmen Square led the leaders of East European governments to give into popular will peacefully?"

Answer: The interrogation question reveals that the information in choice (D) is something that must be true, something on which the conclusion in the passage relies. (D)

10. **Question:** The question asks about a flaw in an argument made by an assistant principal.

    Analysis: The passage deals with dietary choices of schoolchildren. It states that when the dishes children are offered are prepared with healthy ingredients the children, in time, come to like them. From this the assistant principal concludes that given the choice between a healthy rhubarb cobbler and a less healthy chocolate cake, the schoolchildren will choose a healthier alternative. But the evidence is not about cases where children are given a choice, but about cases where the only thing they are offered is a dish with healthy ingredients. It says nothing about what happens when they are offered a dish full of sugar and fat. So the evidence does not justify the conclusion that children will choose a healthy alternative over the unhealthy one.

    Answer: The flaw in the assistant principal's reasoning is in choice (D). The assistant principal assumes that because the children eat a healthy dish when that is all that is available, they will choose a healthy dish when another alternative is also available. (D)

11. **Question:** The question asks for what is "most strongly supported" by the information in the passage. The task is to identify something that follows from the statements in the passage beyond a reasonable doubt, but something that is not explicitly stated.

    Analysis: The passage explains that research is frequently distorted or suppressed in policy discussions. Whatever party is in power will tend to distort advice that it does not find convenient, and to use analysis when it supports a previously held ideological position. Analysis is "treated as a political instrument." Clear on the meaning of the statements, then, ask whether each of the answer choices has to be true, given that information.

    Answer: Most of the answer choices go beyond the evidence in the passage, but the one that does not, the one that is true beyond a reasonable doubt, is choice (E).

12. **Question:** This is a parallel reasoning question, asking for the answer choice that shows the same pattern of reasoning involving the same mistake as the model.

    Analysis: The problem is about the structure of the reasoning and has nothing whatever to do with content. The main passage establishes a category of athletes which includes some skaters and all basketball players. But there is nothing that establishes a relationship between skaters and basketball players. Some may or may not be the same people. The passage erroneously concludes that some must be the same.

    Answer: Analyze the answer choices for the one making the same mistake. It is (A), which says that both all roadsters and at least some convertibles are cars, and that therefore some convertibles must be roadsters. (A)

13. **Question:** The question is an EXCEPT question, asking for the one of the five answer choices that does not weaken the argument.

    Analysis: The conclusion to the passage is that the actions by the local groups are responsible for the change in graduation rates. The argument compares the current rate to that of six years before when high school students in the area were more likely to commit a crime than to graduate. The passage says that this was because the culture placed too little emphasis on getting a diploma. But over the past six years those trends have changed, and also over the last six years efforts by the school board, parents, and community leaders have been undertaken to advance change. The conclusion is that it is those efforts responsible for the changing culture that are responsible for the increase in the high school graduation rate. The conclusion would be weakened by anything that suggests that there is some other cause responsible for the increase in graduation rate. So interrogate the answer choices by asking, "Does this make it less likely that the groups' efforts to change the culture are responsible for the change in graduation rate?" If the answer to that question is "yes," then the choice is one of the four that does weaken the argument, and is NOT the answer to that question.

Answer: The greatest difficulty here is in framing the problem to know what to look for. And the one of the five that does not provide some alternative explanation for the change in graduation rate is choice (C).

14. **Question:** The question is an EXCEPT question, asking for the one of the five answer choices that does not accurately identify a flaw in the argument.

Analysis: The conclusion to the passage is that the liberal views of a particular commentator on the evening news promote crime, and that the TV station is showing some sense of responsibility to the commu nity in dropping the commentator from its show, since the commentator's thinking is shoddy. Indeed there are numerous flaws in moving from the evidence that in the two years since the station dropped the commentator, named Lucky Silas, from its show that there have been fewer murders, assaults, and thefts in the city. The basic flaw is that it moves from observing a correlation to asserting that one of the correlated things is the cause of the others. Normally with a flaw question you can go to the answer choices confident that you know what the flaw is in looking exactly for it in the correct answer. In this case, because it is an except question, and because there are so many flaws in the passage, interrogate the individual answer choices asking each whether it is a reasoning error in the passage.

Answer: The one of the five answer choices that does not represent a reasoning error in the passage is choice (C). This describes an error that is frequently made in argument, but not one that is made in this argument. (C)

15. **Question:** The question is about an error in reasoning in a criticism of a claim about the credentials of a commentator.

Analysis: Analyze the argument to find the criticism mentioned in the question and then to discover the error in that criticism. The claim is that a television commentator is a widely read political historian. The criticism of that claim is that the commentator is an author of political thrillers, but not a history professor. The error in reasoning lies in assuming that only a history professor could be a "widely read political historian." It is probably true that all history professors are widely read in political history, but need not be true that all those who are widely read in political history are history professors.

Answer: The flaw is that while being a history professor would be enough to make someone an historian, one might be able to be an historian nonetheless without being a history professor. That is stated in choice (B).

16. **Question:** The passage presents an exchange between two people, and the question asks for something that they disagree on.

Analysis: Often these questions that ask for the disagreement between two people focus on the conclusion reached by the first. So analyze the two statements and identify the conclusion of the first. The two disagree on whether the initiative, referendum, and recall are indispensable. Hinklemore believes that they are because they protect citizens against legislators. Bullfinch believes that they are not indispensable, and that indeed they make the legislature less effective in representing citizens because they can upset the balance of forces which enables the legislature to work effectively. So the two disagree on the general question of whether initiative, referendum, and recall are good, and that disagreement is based on a more detailed disagreement about the rule that these things would play in the legislative process.

Answer: The answer in this case does isolate the disagreement on the conclusion reached by the first of the speakers, and that correct answer is in choice (B).

17. **Question:** The question is about the structure of the argument, asking for the role of a statement about a grocery in the passage.

Analysis: Read the passage to understand its argument, and then analyze it for the role of the statement in question. A grocery is presented as an example of something that people approach when it is unfamiliar to them, unlike the way that they approach an unfamiliar library, thus backing up the claim that designing a library to be welcoming to a wide variety of casual users is challenging.

Answer: The role of the statement about the grocery is correctly depicted in choice (B).

18. **Question:** The question asks for vulnerability, or a flaw, in the reasoning in the passage.

Analysis: The conclusion is that lacrosse is an example of a collegiate sport where there are no NCAA violations because the athletes have no prospect of turning professional. The evidence in the passage establishes that lacrosse athletes have no prospects of turning pro, and that there are no NCAA violations in lacrosse. The error lies in taking these two things that exist simultaneously and assuming, without further evidence, that one is the cause of the other. It is a case of moving from correlation to cause without appropriate justification.

Answer: Clarity regarding the flaw shows that the correct answer is choice (A).

19. **Question:** The question asks for a flaw in the argument.

Analysis: The conclusion is that since at least 8% of investigations of UFOs have not accounted for the occurrences in standard ways, these unaccounted for instances must be explained as being from a remote planet, a remote time on this planet, or from a different physical or spiritual dimension. The flaw in this is simply that it takes the lack of knowledge about some set of instances as being actual knowledge about those instances.

Answer: The choice that accurately states the flaw is choice (B).

20. **Question:** The question asks for something to help explain the position of meteorologists discussed in the passage. It suggests a paradox that needs to be resolved

Analysis: The passage does describe a discrepancy with two clear sides. On the one hand there is broad agreement that global warming is a serious problem caused by human beings, and this agreement exists at a time of especially destructive weather phenomena, including a cyclone, earthquakes, and tornadoes. On the other hand, meteorologists agree that global warming is not the cause of the tornadoes. The correct answer will embrace both of these situations: that global warming is a serious problem and that global warming is not the cause of the tornadoes.

Answer: The statement that allows both sides of the paradox to be true simultaneously is in choice (C).

21. **Question:** The question asks for an assumption on which the writer's argument depends.

Analysis: The writer in the passage concludes that "civilization" must be something more than a set of collective norms and values of a particular group. That conclusion is based upon the premise that the word *civilization* ought to be used to mean something different from and more than the term *culture*. For that information to lead to the conclusion that civilization must be more than a set of collective norms and values, it must be that "culture" is just that: a set of collective norms and values. There is the missing assumption that compels the conclusion that since culture and civilization are different from one another, civilization is different from a set of collective norms and values.

Answer: The analysis makes clear what the missing assumption is, and that assumption is found in choice (E).

22. **Question:** The question asks for something to strengthen the argument.

Analysis: The argument concludes that good is not identical with pleasure, nor evil with pain. This conclusion follows from the premises that pain and pleasure come to an end at the same time, but good and evil do not come to an end at the same time. A strengthen question will typically add additional information to make the conclusion more likely to be true, so interrogate the answer choices asking, "Does this make it more likely that good is not identical with pleasure and evil is not identical with pain?"

Answer: Choice (D) makes it more likely that the good and the pleasant, and the bad and the painful are not the same things, since some painful things are not bad, but good. (D)

23. **Question:** This is a parallel flaw problem. It asks, out of the five answer choices, for the one that suffers from the same flaw that the main passage exhibits.

    Analysis: The conclusion in the main passage is that only arguments in symbolic form have logical value. This is taken to follow from the premise that if something has logical value then it is a pure study in form. Symbolic argument is a pure study in form. But the fact that everything that has pure logical value is a pure study in form does not mean that everything that is a pure study in form has logical value. This is the error made in the passage, and it is a familiar one.

    Answer: The error is taking something that something else depends on as being enough to produce that first thing. The same mistake is found in choice (D), for the fact that an animal's being a beagle depends on its howling does not mean that because an animal howls it is a beagle. (D)

24. **Question:** The question asks for what "could be true" if the statements in the passage are true.

    Analysis: This is a kind of inference problem. It says that four of the five answer choices represent things that are inconsistent with the statements in the passage. The correct answer is the only one that could be the case if those statements are true. Like other inference questions, it will not be possible to determine ahead of time what the correct answer will contain, but you can know the meaning of the statements in the passage. These are conditional statements as follows: (1) If arms control has meaning and contributes to national security or global or regional stability, then all parties must fully comply with agreements. The administration will not accept anything other than strict compliance. (2) If the administration were to accept less than strict compliance, then the arms control process would be undermined and the chances for a more constructive relationship would be gone. According to the question, exactly one of the five answer choices will present something that is consistent with both conditional statements.

    Answer: Choice (A) violates statement (2). Choice (B) violates statement (1). Choice (C) is possible. The fact that accepting incomplete compliance will damage relationships does not mean that those relationships will not be damaged if there is complete compliance. Choice (D) violates statement (2), and choice (E) also violates statement (2). (C)

SECTION 4 – ANALYTICAL REASONING

Questions 1–6

This is a pure ordering situation. The following diagram simplifies the rules and shows the deductions:

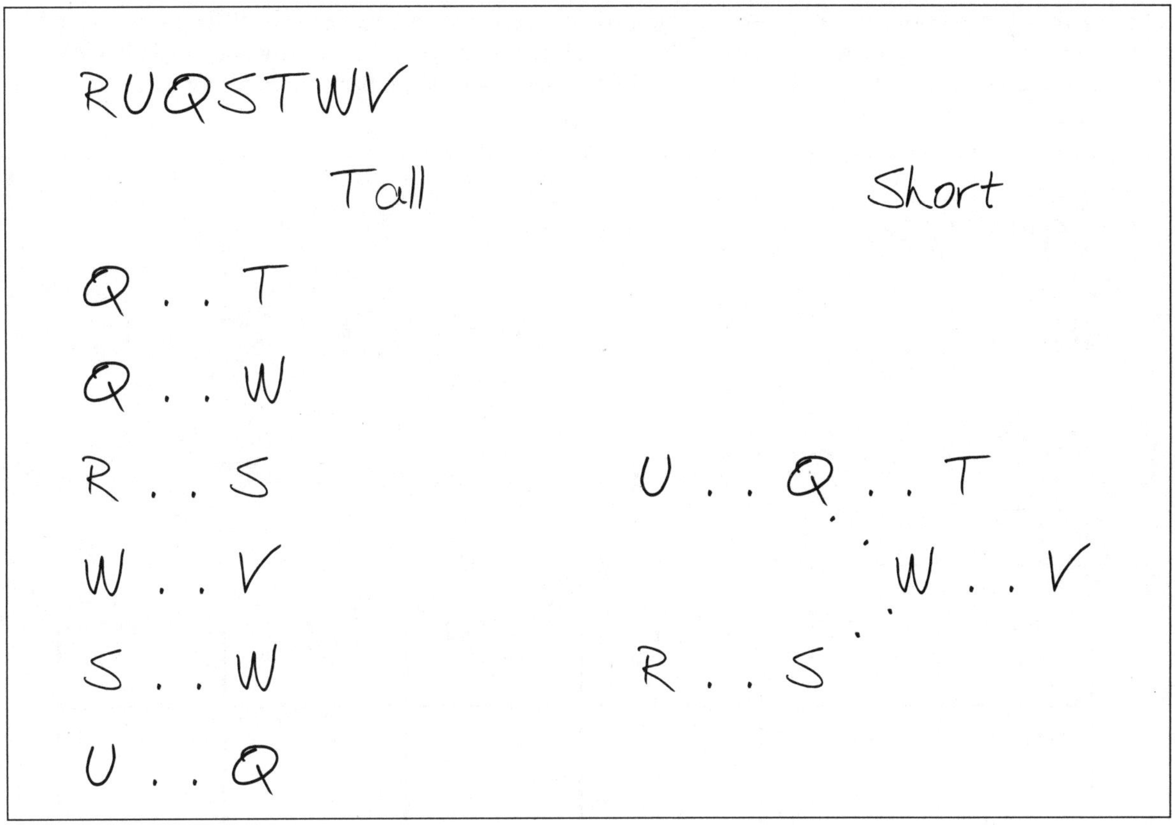

Note that something is said about the relative order of each of the seven items involved. Focusing on those relationships, there are only two items that might be the tallest, and only two that might be the shortest.

1. The question asks for something that must be false, without adding additional information. So the question is about the rules and the initial deductions from those rules. What must be false is choice (C).
2. This question asks for an item that could not be second tallest. Any item that must have at least two others taller cannot be second tallest, and each of T, W, and V must have at least two that are taller. Look in the list of answer choices and find exactly one of those three. The correct answer is choice (D).
3. If R is third tallest, then U and Q must be first and second, respectively. So the answer here is choice (D).
4. If S is fourth, then the first of three must include U, Q, and R, with R being in any position relative to the other two. Similarly, the last three must be W, V, and T, with T being in any position relative to the other two. So of the answer choices, the one that cannot be true is choice (C), which, in fact, can never be true. (C)

5. This question asks for which it is not an acceptable outcome. That means that four of the five answer choices violate no rules, and exactly one violates some rule or other. That one is choice (E), which violates the rule about the order of W and V. (E)

6. This question makes the first three, in some order or other, to be R, U, and S, and then asks what could be fourth. There is only one possibility, since Q must come before either T or W. (B)

Questions 7–12

This is a placement situation. There are five salespeople who are to be placed in six different numbered rooms. Each of the five goes into a different room, and there are no groups. So the key is to place the items into the slots, at most one per slot. The diagram below shows the basic setup along with some basic deductions:

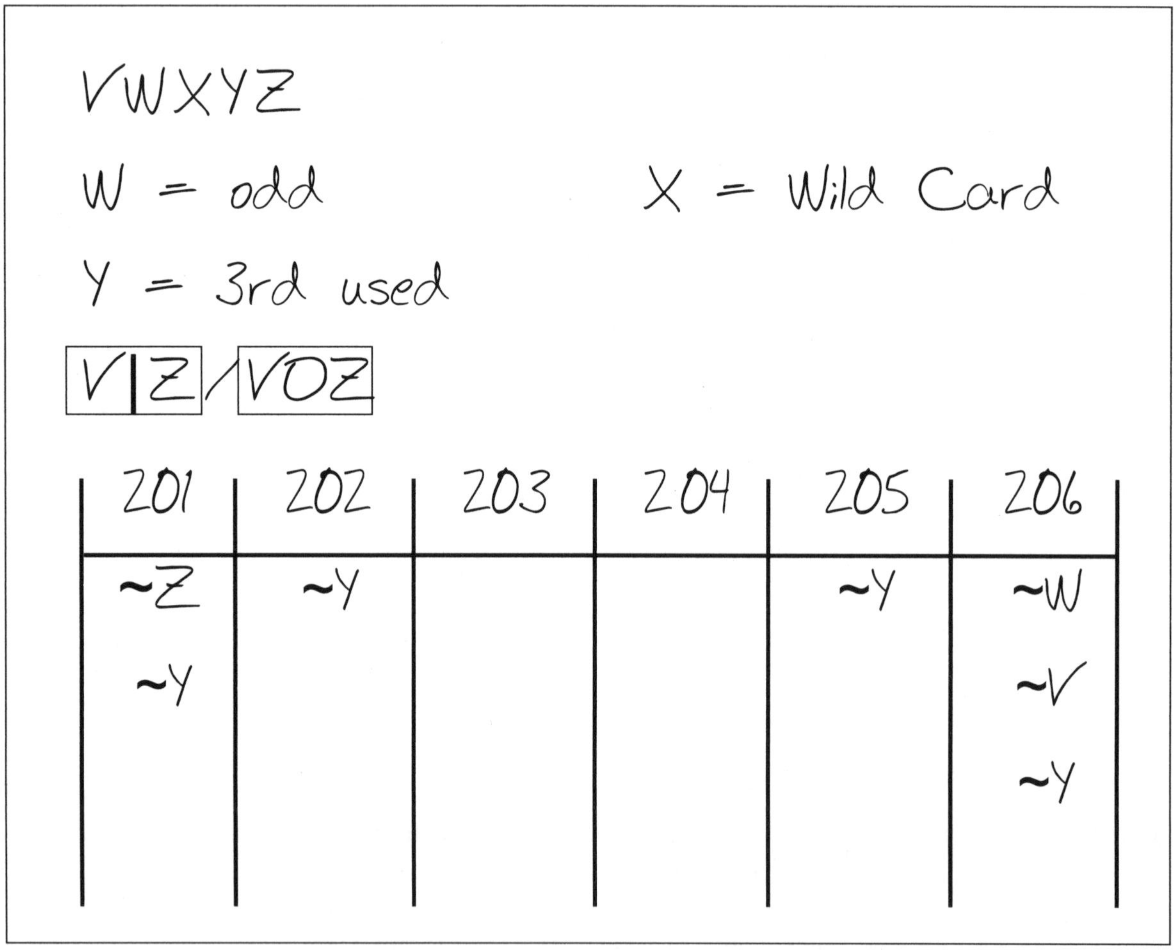

While there is no item placed with certainty, there are some very constraining rules. V and Z are adjacent and in order, although the one empty room might be between them. The rule that Y is the third of the rooms used (meaning that it is either 203 or 204, depending upon where the empty room is) will be very constraining. X is a wildcard, meaning that there are no rules that affect it directly, but it will be affected very much by what happens with the other items.

7. This question adds the information that V is in room 202, and asks what must be true. Consider the chain reaction: with V in 202 how can Y be in the third room that someone stays in? Z must follow V, so Y must

follow Z. In order to keep Y third, nothing could come before V. So the empty room must be 201, and Y must be in 204, with W in 205, and X in 206. The simple placement of V in 202 made only one placement of the items possible. And what must be true is choice (B).

8. This question places W in 201 and asks for the possible placement of X. There are no rules that mention X, but the rules affecting the others will be important. Y must be third, so V and Z must come someplace after it. X will have to be second, in either 202 or 203. The correct answer is choice (D).

9. This question places X in 201. To put Y third, W will need to intervene, but it cannot do so before 203. So then Y must be in 204 with V and Z in 205 and 206. The correct answer is choice (A).

10. If 201 is empty, what must be true? The remaining rooms must all be used, so Y must occupy 204. On one side are V and Z, and on the other are X and W, but it is not possible to say which is which, except that W must be in either 203 or 205. Now apply this information to the alternatives presented in the question to determine that the correct answer is choice (E).

11. This question places W in 203. That must mean that Y is in 204, with V and Z being in 205 and 206. X has a little flexibility, so that it could be in either 201 or 202. Therefore, the one that does not have to be true is choice (B).

12. This question adds no information and asks for something that cannot be true, so it is asking for a basic deduction. It is clear that Z cannot be in 201, but that is not among the choices. Consider the importance of the V and Z block together with the rule that Y must be third. Those two together make it impossible for Z to fit in 204. So the answer is in choice (C).

Questions 13–18

This is a grouping situation. It gives eight items that fall into three different categories and requires a group of four to be made from the eight. The following diagram simplifies the conditions:

S = CMB

SS = HLE

H = PR

(4)

Comm= 1+ Each

C → ~B   B → ~C

M → E   ~E → ~M

E → M   ~M → ~E

R → B/E   (~B + ~E) → ~R

The diagram shows the unambiguous representation of the conditional statements along with their contrapositive forms. Each of these might be a bit tricky to understand, and be especially careful with the one involving R, B, and E. Stated in the form that is used in the scenario, it becomes the following: If R, then either B or E must be present. To put that in its contrapositive form, flip the two sides of the conditional statement and negate them both (as always). The negation of the "or" statement becomes an "and" statement, so that to say that it is not the case that either B is there or E is there is equivalent to saying that it is the case that B is not there and E is not there.

It is probably also helpful to focus on what the conditional statements and their contrapositives do not mean. It is possible to have an acceptable committee that includes neither B nor C. Because of the way that the rule regarding M and E is put, they are a group and either both are included or both are excluded from a committee. Finally, it is possible to include B or E and not include R on a committee

13. The question asks for an acceptable arrangement of a committee. The correct answer is the one that does not violate any of the rules, and that is choice (D).

14. The question includes both P and R and asks what the other two members of the committee could be. The remaining two must include one from category S and the other from category SS, and also (because R is there) one each of B and E. If the latter is E, then the one from category S has to be M, but M and E are not in the list of answer choices. The pair in an answer choice that meets the requirement and does not violate a rule is in choice (A).

15. The question places E on the committee and asks what could be the other three. By the rules, one of the other three must be M. Another must be one of R and P, though it could be either or both. The fourth can be anything that involves no rule violation (so not C and B). The correct answer is choice (E).

16. The question excludes B and P and asks what must be true. If P is excluded, then R must be included, and since B is excluded according to the question, E must be included, which means that M must also be included. The correct answer is choice (D).

17. The question asks for something that must be true, and each answer choice involves a conditional statement. The one that must be true involves the same conclusion that governs question 16. If R is included, then either B or M must be included from category S, which means that C cannot be included. So the correct answer here is choice (C).

18. This question includes both H and L on a committee, and asks what might be among the others. M cannot be included because E cannot be included, for that would entail too many from category SS. Either B or C could be included along with either P or R (but in the case of R the other would have to be B). The answer is choice (D).

Questions 19–24

This is a grouping situation involving five items from which some may be selected to create a group of indeterminate number. Logically, in fact, none need to be selected, so any question will involve the choice to ask some to serve in the group. Which one is to serve is governed by a series of conditional rules, which are simplified in the diagram below:

GHIJK

G

H → K   ~K → ~H

I → J   ~J → ~I

J → ~G   G → ~J

K → ~I   I → ~K

I → ~K → ~H

G → ~J → ~I

H → K → ~I

The diagram indicates both the clarified statement of each conditional rule and its contrapositive as well. There is a rule dealing with each of the five items, though the first does not entail any consequence.

It is a good idea to reflect on what the rules, together with their contrapositives, allow but need not require. So K might be included without H; J might be included without I; it would be possible to include neither J nor G; and it would be possible to include neither I nor K.

Finally the diagram includes a few deductions, derived from interactions among the premises.

19. The question asks for the most items that could be included in a group. Since both G and J cannot be included and both K and I cannot be included, the maximum must be three. So the answer is choice (C).

20. This question excludes G and asks for the most that could be included. In fact, the same conditions apply as in the previous question, except that it is certain which of J or G might be included. So the answer is choice (D).

21. This question says that if only three—H, K, and I—are invited to be in the group, which ones would be there? At first it might seem

that there are two choices, either H and K without I, or I without K and H. But in fact that cannot be the case since I requires J. So the correct answer is choice (E).

22. This question says that only G, H, and I are asked to run, and asks which ones will. As in the previous question, I cannot be included without J. It is also true that H cannot be included without K. So here the correct answer is Choice (A).

23. This question asks for a pair that cannot both be included. It is asking for a deduction, and the correct answer is choice (B).

24. This question says that H and J are included and asks what the entire list must be. H requires K. The key is to realize that J does not require I (or anything else positive). So the correct answer is choice (D).

SAMPLE ESSAY

With health-care costs soaring nationwide, the employees of SavoryReads are fortunate to be in a position of choosing between two fine health-care provider options. But though either of the two would be beneficial, the employees would be best served by the HealthyFolks plan.

Feeling good is critically important to anyone's quality of life, and the primary goal of any health-care program is to help its members to maintain the physical health that will enable them to feel well. Preventive health-care is a critically important factor in maintaining this kind of health. The HealthyFolks program encourages preventive health-care because it takes into account the fact that different people are comfortable with different human beings as their physicians. Doctors are not merely technicians, but also human beings working with other human beings to help the patients develop and follow strategies that will be most beneficial to them in the long run. Patients are more likely to work with their health-care providers to do that if their health-care provider is someone with whom they feel comfortable.

Of course, the quality of life and the quality of health-care also require that patients who are ill follow appropriate treatments as directed by their health-care providers by taking the best medications for them and by taking them as directed. That is why convenience and selection in prescription medications is important, and that feature is surely less well provided for in the HealthyFolks system. But that system also makes it less likely that people will need prescription drugs by making it less likely that they will suffer from the kinds of illnesses that require constant medication.

The choice between the two plans requires either sacrificing flexibility in physician choice for flexibility in prescription choice, or the other way around. Since the overall goal is quality of life, although either kind of flexibility will contribute to quality of life, it seems more beneficial, when both cannot be acquired, to maintain maximum flexibility in choosing physicians. So while the selection is a difficult one, and while the employees would be well served by either program, on balance the physician choice in the HealthyFolks proposal makes it the one to choose.

LSAT

LAW SCHOOL ADMISSION TEST

PRACTICE TEST 3

PRACTICE TEST 3

SECTION 1

Time—35 minutes
24 questions

Directions: *Each group of questions in this section is based on a set of conditions. In answering some of the questions, it may be useful to draw a rough diagram. Choose the response that most accurately and completely answers the question and blacken the corresponding space on your answer sheet.*

QUESTIONS 1–5

The class is going to perform the fairy scenes from *A Midsummer Night's Dream*. The roles to be performed are Oberon, Titania, Bottom, Puck, Peaseblossom, and Cowslip. From oldest to youngest, the performers are Allie, Bobby, Cary, Donny, Eddy, and Fergie.

> The person playing Oberon is not Eddy, but is younger than the person playing Bottom.
> The person playing Titania is younger than those playing Peaseblossom and Cowslip, but older than the one playing Puck.
> The person playing Bottom is younger than the one playing Cowslip.

1. Which of the following is an acceptable arrangement of the players by role, from oldest to youngest?
   - (A) Cowslip, Bottom, Oberon, Peaseblossom, Titania, Puck
   - (B) Cowslip, Bottom, Oberon, Titania, Peaseblossom, Puck
   - (C) Cowslip, Bottom, Peaseblossom, Titania, Oberon, Puck
   - (D) Cowslip, Peaseblossom, Bottom, Puck, Titania, Oberon
   - (E) Peaseblossom, Bottom, Cowslip, Oberon, Titania, Puck

2. If the person playing Bottom is older than the one playing Peaseblossom, who must be playing Cowslip?
   - (A) Allie
   - (B) Bobby
   - (C) Cary
   - (D) Donny
   - (E) Eddy

3. If Cary plays Oberon, then Bottom must be played by
   - (A) Allie
   - (B) Bobby
   - (C) Donny
   - (D) Eddy
   - (E) Fergie

4. Which of the following CANNOT be a possible arrangement of players by role from oldest to youngest?
   - (A) Cowslip, Peaseblossom, Bottom, Oberon, Titania, Puck
   - (B) Peaseblossom, Cowslip, Bottom, Titania, Puck, Oberon
   - (C) Cowslip, Peaseblossom, Puck, Bottom, Titania, Oberon
   - (D) Peaseblossom, Cowslip, Bottom, Oberon, Titania, Puck
   - (E) Cowslip, Peaseblossom, Titania, Puck, Bottom, Oberon

5. If Eddy plays Puck, which of the following might play Titania?

(A) Bobby

(B) Fergie

(C) Donny

(D) Allie

(E) Bottom

QUESTIONS 6–12

The five-member Women's Junior Varsity Fencing Team is to be selected from a pool of five freshmen (Alicia, Beth, Carlotta, Denise, and Ellen) and four sophomores (Faith, Grace, Helen, and Irene.) Only four members of the pool have competitive experience (Grace, Helen, Ellen, and Alicia), at least three of whom will make the team. The coach, planning to build future Varsity Team members, will select three freshmen and two sophomores for the Junior Varsity Team. Unfortunately, personality difficulties make selecting the team members a bit more difficult.

Beth and Ellen will not fence on the same team.
Faith and Helen will not fence on the same team.
Grace and Carlotta will not fence on the same team.

6. Which of the following could be an acceptable list of fencers on the team?

   (A) Ellen, Faith, Grace, Alicia, Irene

   (B) Helen, Ellen, Denise, Faith, Alicia

   (C) Alicia, Grace, Ellen, Irene, Denise

   (D) Beth, Alicia, Helen, Ellen, Faith

   (E) Irene, Faith, Alicia, Denise, Beth

7. If all four fencers with competitive experience make the team, which of the following must make the team?

   (A) Beth

   (B) Denise

   (C) Carlotta

   (D) Irene

   (E) Faith

8. Which of the following fencers must make the team?

   (A) Denise

   (B) Alicia

   (C) Irene

   (D) Grace

   (E) Helen

9. If Grace does not make the team, the only decision as to team members is whether to choose:

   (A) Denise or Carlotta

   (B) Faith or Helen

   (C) Beth or Faith

   (D) Beth or Ellen

   (E) Faith or Irene

10. Which of the following is a pair of fencers who cannot both make the team?

    (A) Beth and Denise

    (B) Denise and Ellen

    (C) Ellen and Carlotta

    (D) Carlotta and Beth

    (E) Alicia and Denise

11. If Ellen does not make the team, which of the following is a fencer who also cannot make the team?

    (A) Faith

    (B) Grace

    (C) Helen

    (D) Denise

    (E) Beth

12. If Irene does not make the team, which of the following fencers will make the team?

    (A) Beth

    (B) Faith

    (C) Helen

    (D) Alicia

    (E) Carlotta

OUESTIONS 13–18

The 11 members of the Central High School Debate Team—2 freshmen, 2 sophomores,

3 juniors, and 4 seniors—are going to have a team photograph taken. The members of the team will be arranged in a line on spaces numbered 1 through 11.

The sophomores will not stand next to one another.
The juniors always stand on consecutively numbered spaces.
Neither of the freshmen will stand at either end of the line.
A junior is always at one end of the line.
No senior will stand next to a junior.

13. If a junior is standing in space 3 and a sophomore in space 10, which of the following must be true?

(A) There is a senior in space 8.

(B) There is a senior in space 11.

(C) There is a sophomore in space 4.

(D) There is a freshman in space 4.

(E) There is a sophomore in space 6.

14. If the seniors are standing in spaces 2, 3, 6, and 7, which of the following must be false?

(A) The freshmen are in spaces 1 and 8.

(B) The sophomores are in spaces 1 and 4.

(C) There is a junior in space 10.

(D) There is a freshman in space 8.

(E) The sophomores are in spaces 1 and 8.

15. Which of the following must be false?

(A) The sophomores are in spaces 1 and 8.

(B) There are juniors in spaces 9 and 11.

(C) The seniors are standing on even-numbered spaces.

(D) The freshmen are standing on odd-numbered spaces.

(E) The sophomores are standing on odd-numbered spaces.

16. If the seniors are standing together, and one of them is at one end of the line, which of the following could be true?

I. The freshmen are standing together.
II. The freshmen are standing together and next to the seniors.
III. The freshmen are not standing together.

(A) I only

(B) II only

(C) III only

(D) Both I and II

(E) Both I and III

17. Which of the following could be true?

(A) None of the odd-numbered spaces are occupied by juniors and seniors.

(B) The freshmen and sophomores are on even-numbered spaces.

(C) No freshman or sophomore is on an even-numbered space.

(D) A sophomore is on space 9 and a sophomore is on space 10.

(E) A junior is on space 1 and a freshman is on space 11.

18. Which of the following must be true?

(A) A senior is standing on space 8.

(B) A junior is standing on space 3.

(C) One of the freshmen must be standing on an even-numbered space.

(D) One of the sophomores must be standing on an even-numbered space.

(E) Either a freshman or a sophomore must be standing on an even-numbered space.

QUESTIONS 19–24

Three couples—the Ables, the Bakers, and the Carrs—have dinner together every Thursday night at Maxwell's Restaurant. To facilitate discussion, they always sit at a round table. The following rules always apply to the seating arrangements:

Mrs. Able always sits immediately to the left of Mr. Baker.
Mr. Able never sits next to Mr. Carr.
Mrs. Baker always sits directly across the table from Mr. Carr.

19. Which of the following CANNOT be true?

(A) Mrs. Able is seated directly across from Mr. Able.

(B) Mr. Able is seated next to Mrs. Able.

(C) Mr. Able is seated directly across from Mr. Baker.

(D) Mr. Carr is seated immediately to the right of Mr. Baker.

(E) Mrs. Carr is seated directly across the table from Mrs. Able.

20. If Mrs. Able is seated next to Mr. Carr, which of the following COULD be true?

(A) Mr. Able is seated directly across from Mr. Baker.

(B) Mrs. Carr is seated next to Mrs. Baker.

(C) Mrs. Able is seated directly across from Mr. Able.

(D) Mrs. Carr is seated directly across from Mrs. Able.

(E) Mr. Able is seated immediately to the left of Mrs. Able.

21. If Mr. Carr is seated immediately to the right of Mr. Baker, which of the following CANNOT be true?

(A) Mrs. Carr is seated immediately to the right of Mr. Carr.

(B) Mrs. Baker is seated immediately to the left of Mrs. Able.

(C) Mr. Able is seated directly across from Mr. Baker.

(D) Mr. Able is seated directly across from Mrs. Able.

(E) Mr. Able is seated next to Mrs. Baker.

22. If Mrs. Baker is seated next to Mrs. Able, which of the following COULD be true?

(A) Mr. Able is seated directly across from Mr. Baker.

(B) Mrs. Carr is seated next to Mrs. Baker.

(C) Mrs. Able is seated directly across from Mr. Able.

(D) Mrs. Carr is seated directly across from Mr. Baker.

(E) There is exactly one seat between Mr. Able and Mrs. Baker.

23. Which of the following must be the case?

(A) The Ables always sit next to one another.

(B) Mr. Able never sits next to Mrs. Carr.

(C) The Carrs always sit next to one another.

(D) Mrs. Able sits to the right of Mr. Baker.

(E) Mr. Carr sits next to Mrs. Baker.

24. If Mr. Able is seated directly across the table from Mrs. Able, which of the following COULD be true?

(A) Mr. Carr is seated immediately to the right of Mr. Baker.

(B) Mrs. Carr is seated next to Mrs. Baker.

(C) Mrs. Carr is seated immediately to the left of Mr. Able.

(D) Mrs. Baker is seated next to Mrs. Able.

(E) Mr. Carr is seated immediately to the left of Mrs. Able.

STOP

If time still remains, you may review work only in this section. When the time allotted is up, you may go on to the next section.

SECTION 2

Time—35 minutes
25 questions

Directions: *The questions in this section are based on the reasoning contained in brief statements or passages. For some questions, more than one of the choices could conceivably answer the question. However, you are to choose the* ***best*** *answer; that is, the response that most accurately and completely answers the question. You should not make assumptions that are by commonsense standards implausible, superfluous, or incompatible with the passage. After you have chosen the best answer, blacken the corresponding space on your answer sheet.*

1. Residential colleges often promote participation in intramural athletics as a way to help first-year students adapt more quickly to life in college. But this participation may actually have the opposite effect in some cases. Studies show that when friendships are formed among intramural team members, the students on those teams do in fact adapt more quickly to college life. However, when the team members do not develop friendships, intramural participation can actually retard the student's adaptation. The studies also show that students who do not like athletics are much less likely to make friends with intramural team members than are students who like athletics.

   Which of the following best states the main conclusion from the passage above?

   (A) Studies on the effects of participation in intramurals reach contradictory conclusions.

   (B) Participation in intramural athletics should be required for most college freshmen.

   (C) Participation in intramural athletics should not be required for most college freshmen.

   (D) Participation in intramural athletics sometimes slows students' adaptation to college life.

   (E) Participation in intramural athletics is not as important as liking or disliking athletics as a factor in helping students adjust to college life.

2. Personal income tax rates for state X are expected to rise this year. The state government is predicting a deficit for the present fiscal year at current levels of taxing and spending, but the state constitution disallows a deficit and requires the state legislature to balance the budget. Revenue from sales taxes will continue to decline in the next several months, as the economy continues to experience a downturn. Also, severance tax receipts from the coal and gas industries continue to decrease as those industries have cut back on production. So the only source available to the legislature for more tax revenue is the personal income tax.

   Which of the following is an assumption on which the argument depends?

   (A) The needed revenue could not be raised by eliminating spending on some current programs.

   (B) Income taxes in state X are already high, compared to the surrounding states.

   (C) The revenue shortfall is likely to be very small without income tax increases.

   (D) The economy will not be likely to improve in the next fiscal year.

   (E) Severance taxes account for a major percentage of state X's income.

3. Hart and Jaffa conducted experiments to test the hypothesis that there is no basic difference in the way men and women give

directions. However, these studies showed that men, in giving directions, nearly always rely on distance, as for example, "Go three blocks and turn right." Women, on the other hand, tend to give directions based on landmarks, as in "Go to the big red building and turn right."

Which one of the following is most strongly supported by the information given in the passage?

(A) Women prefer to get directions from women and men prefer to get directions from men.

(B) Men should never seek directions from women, nor women from men.

(C) The researchers who conducted the experiment were probably men.

(D) Hart and Jaffa's research did not support their hypothesis.

(E) There is no basic difference between directions based on distance and directions based on landmarks.

4. Let a person be ever so successful in business or have an income ever so large; yet without dedication to ethical behavior in all cases, the person cannot be called truly accomplished. For those lacking in dedication to ethical behavior make all decisions by their pocketbooks and give back nothing to the society of which they are a part.

The argument depends on which of the following assumptions?

(A) Unethical behavior is to be expected from the financially successful.

(B) Greed is the result of unethical behavior.

(C) To be truly accomplished one must contribute to the society of which one is a part.

(D) A person can be a benefit to society only without seeking to make a profit.

(E) Those who are financially successful are ethically deficient.

5. Robert: Striking by employees is counterproductive; while the strike goes on, the plant is effectively shut down, and the corporation loses money. This means that the employees themselves lose in the long run.

Leah: I disagree. Sometimes striking is necessary to get the attention of management. If the plant loses a little money, then management will be forced into making concessions it otherwise wouldn't, concessions that could benefit workers for years to come.

Based on the exchange above, Robert and Leah disagree on which of the following?

(A) The definition of the word *strike*

(B) Whether it can benefit employees for their corporation to lose money

(C) Whether management of companies with striking workers will make concessions to employees

(D) Whether plants with striking workers are effectively shut down

(E) Whether there is a distinction possible between the welfare of a company and the welfare of its employees.

6. Though often condemned, the loaded question is a useful device for speeding the legal process. In the classic example "Have you stopped beating your wife?," either a "yes" or a "no" answer concedes that the person has beaten his wife, thus giving a confession to an actionable offense. Similar results may be obtained generally with questions which begin, for example, "Do you regret...?," where the blank is filled with a description of the crime at issue—"murdering your grandmother," for instance.

Based on the passage, a conclusion that the loaded question ought to be used in the legal process would be most strongly supported by a belief that

(A) questioning in the legal process ought not to be guided by ethical considerations.

(B) the purpose of questioning in the legal process is to assign blame for a crime as swiftly as possible.

(C) the purpose of questioning in the legal process is to achieve justice.

(D) the purpose of questioning in a legal process is to arrive at the truth as quickly as possible.

(E) interrogations of people accused of crimes ought to be conducted by trained experts.

7. Isolationist: Current problems in the Middle East are the result of British and French interference in the breakup of the Ottoman Empire at the end of World War I. They divided the territory up to suit their national interests, without taking into account the concerns of the inhabitants of the area. So it is the British and the French, and not the United States or Russia, that ought to be concerned about a just and peaceful solution to the present conflicts in the Middle East.

Which of the following, if true, most seriously undermines the isolationist's argument?

(A) Whether it ought to or not, the Russian government is actively working for peace and justice in the Middle East.

(B) The French deny any role in creating current conditions in the Middle East.

(C) Many United States citizens actively oppose U.S. peace-keeping efforts in the Middle East.

(D) Present-day interests of many United States citizens are adversely affected by the absence of peace and justice in the Middle East.

(E) No major faction in the Middle East seeks or desires a return to the Ottoman Empire.

8. Grading Policy: "A student may request permission to submit extra credit work only if he or she has properly completed all the regular work. Regular work is properly completed only if it is either handed in on time or is handed in late with prior permission." Charles will get no better than a C on the basis of his regular work; with extra credit work he might receive a B.

According to the Grading Policy, which of the following must be the case?

(A) If he has no late regular work and does extra credit work, Charles will get a B.

(B) If he has regular work that is late without permission, Charles has no chance to get better than a C.

(C) If he has regular work that is late, but with prior permission, Charles is permitted to do extra credit work.

(D) If he has no late regular work, Charles will not get a B.

(E) If he receives a C, then Charles did not do extra credit work.

9. Of the cities and the towns in the Central Valley, none is more charged with the spirit of change than Fresno. Detractors like to point out that in a national poll taken about 20 years ago to determine the most desirable place in the country to live, Fresno placed dead last. And indeed there have been times when the city seemed to have all the ambience of a bus station. But results of the 1990 census showed Fresno to be the fastest-growing big city in the nation, having a population increase of 61% during the 1980s. Furthermore, between 1990 and 2000, Fresno County experienced a population growth rate of 19.8%, as opposed to California's 13.9% and the United States' 13.1% growth rates.

What is the role played in the passage by the sentence that offers a comparison to a bus station?

(A) It is offered as evidence that Fresno's detractors are correct.

(B) It exemplifies the main conclusion of the passage.

(C) It uses an analogy to concede a point that is contrary to the main point of the passage.

(D) It is an analogy used to emphasize the spirit of change in Fresno.

(E) It represents a subsidiary conclusion that becomes a premise in the passage's larger argument.

10. To most people who have been educated in philosophy the idea that there are things psychical which are not also conscious is so inconceivable that it seems to them absurd and refutable simply by logic. But this view is wrong. The philosophers' psychology of consciousness is incapable of solving the problems of dreams and hypnosis, phenomena whose existence necessitates the view that there are psychical things which are not conscious.

    Which of the following best states the main conclusion of the passage?

    (A) There is nothing psychical which is not also conscious.

    (B) The phenomena of hypnosis and dreams are examples of psychical phenomena which are not conscious.

    (C) The problems of dreams and hypnosis cannot be solved.

    (D) The proposition that there is nothing psychical which is not also conscious is incorrect.

    (E) The proposition that there is anything psychical which is not also conscious is refutable by logic.

11. The list of successful alumni in the room at the tenth reunion of the class of 1995 at High Point University was impressive, including lawyers, physicians, publishers, and business leaders. Yet impressive as they were, the achievements of the group are hardly surprising since, with few exceptions, they are people who had rich and successful parents, exactly the kind of parents who send their children to High Point University.

    The reasoning in the passage is vulnerable to criticism on which of the following grounds?

    (A) It reaches its conclusion on the basis of a sample that is likely to be unrepresentative.

    (B) It reaches a conclusion based upon feelings about the personal qualities of the people in the group under discussion.

    (C) It takes it for granted that because two things occurred together, that one of the things was caused by the other.

    (D) It concludes that something is true of a group as a whole because it is true of some of the component parts of that group.

    (E) It confuses something that is enough to produce a given result with something that is required to produce that same result.

12. Liz: A recent study showed that the U.S. population is now 52% female. As a result, a majority of the life insurance settlements now made go to the beneficiaries of female policyholders. Therefore, annual insurance rates should be higher for women than for men, to compensate for the greater number of claims.

    Joe: I disagree. The same study also showed that women live an average of six years longer than men, so they pay premiums for a longer period of time. When you consider the difference the six years make in the total amount paid in by the policyholder, it is clear that women's annual life insurance rates should actually be lower than men's.

    Joe and Liz disagree about which of the following?

    (A) It is appropriate that some differences between men and women be reflected in insurance rates.

    (B) There is in fact a majority of the population that is female.

    (C) What should be taken into account in calculating life insurance rates.

    (D) People who paid for life insurance policies over a longer period of time paid more in total premiums.

    (E) A female majority of the population means that most recipients of life insurance payments are female.

13. If all beliefs are not the result of rational deliberation but rather are the result of the social situation of the believer, then cognitive sociology would be self-contradictory. For if all beliefs are socially caused as cognitive sociology claims they are, rather than rationally well founded, the beliefs of

the cognitive sociologist have no relevant rational credentials and no special claims to acceptability. In other words, the thesis that all thought is socially determined and thus cannot claim to be true cannot itself claim to be true.

Which of the following best states the main conclusion of the passage?

(A) Beliefs are socially determined rather than rationally well founded.

(B) Cognitive psychology is self-contradictory.

(C) Since cognitive sociology is not self-contradictory, beliefs are the result of rational deliberation.

(D) The claim that all thought is socially determined is true.

(E) Beliefs are rationally well founded rather than socially determined.

14. Concerned about future economic development, the Alaska legislature funded a $2 million program to create an "academic-based" conference to highlight research showing that warming global temperatures and melting Arctic ice do not threaten polar bear survival. The appropriation is also to be used for a national public relations campaign to promote the findings of the conference. Critics conclude that the appropriation is a waste of state money because all of the hard scientific research points in the other direction.

The critics' conclusion relies on which of the following assumptions?

(A) Hard scientific research on global warming and polar bears is in fact accurate.

(B) The legislators know that warming temperatures and melting Arctic ice in fact do threaten the polar bear population.

(C) Many people cannot be persuaded to believe something that hard scientific research opposes.

(D) The legislators believe that warming temperatures and melting Arctic ice in fact do not threaten the polar bear population.

(E) All scientists who claim that global warming does not threaten polar bears are unable to offer any scientific evidence to back up their claims.

15. The reader knows that a story is being told by someone. Who the author is determines what is written and how the story is told, and so also determines in large measure the way in which the reader is likely to react to the story. All novels are told by an implied author who is created by the biographical author and is necessarily part of the formal experience of reading the novel. You cannot, after all, tell the dancer from the dance.

What role in the argument is played by the claim about "the dancer and the dance" in the last sentence?

(A) It is an analogy used to express the relationship between the biographical author and the implied author in a novel.

(B) It is an analogy that serves to emphasize the responsibility of the reader critically to identify the real author.

(C) It is an image meant to dispute the contention of a distinction between biographical author and implied author.

(D) It is an application of the principle of critical reading developed in the passage.

(E) It is an analogy used to clarify the main point of the passage about the readers' experience of literature.

16. Abe was a normally calm, reasonable, and well-mannered 15-year-old who threw the first blow in a fistfight outside the video rental store last month. Guthrie, Abe's school counselor, has read that neuroscientists hypothesize that when healthy teenage males who are normally calm, reasonable, and well-mannered do commit acts of violence it may be due to the influence of violent TV shows, or to nutritional imbalance, or to having a low concentration of neurotransmitters. When Abe's concentration of neurotransmitters

is tested to be adequate and his nutrition is determined to be good, Guthrie hypothesizes that the incident stems from the influence of violent media and recommends that Abe's viewing habits be monitored to prevent such incidents in the future.

Which of the following most strengthens Guthrie's recommendation?

(A) Abe's violent behavior was similar to behavior that had been observed in his older brother the year before.

(B) The person with whom Abe fought was a complete stranger who had not interacted with Abe in any way outside the video store.

(C) Abe's companions, sitting in a car in front of the video store at the time of the incident, had dared him to strike the person outside the store.

(D) The person whom Abe struck had, the day before, insulted Abe's best friend.

(E) The movies that Abe was returning to the video store at the time of the fight were rated as nonviolent and suited for a general audience.

17. The recent increase in the number of accidents involving tractor-trailer rigs is due to driver inexperience. Rising air freight costs have caused the trucking industry to expand rapidly, resulting in a great demand for truck drivers. As a result, driver training schools have shortened their training courses from six to five months, in order to turn out more graduates. This means that graduates do not get enough hands-on training before receiving their driving certifications.

Which of the following considerations, if true, most undermines the conclusion in the passage?

(A) A high proportion of the accidents involving tractor-trailer rigs involve newly certified drivers.

(B) The expansion in the trucking industry has been accompanied by much greater congestion of tractor-trailer rigs on highways, particularly in urban areas where accidents are more frequent.

(C) The expansion of the trucking industry has not been accompanied by a corresponding drop in demand for services of the air freight industry.

(D) Driver training schools have not shortened the number of hours per week of training that graduates need to spend behind the wheel in order to be certified.

(E) The demand for new tractor-trailer rig drivers continues to exceed supply despite the changes in driver training schools.

18. A free democratic political system is the best form of government there is. Therefore, it is well worth defending, and we should all be willing to do our part to preserve it. Because a free democratic system is well worth defending, it is clearly the best form of government there is.

Which one of the following illustrates the same reasoning flaw as found in the passage?

(A) A free market economy is the best type of economic system there is. It allows the distribution of wealth based on the talents and abilities that individuals bring to the market. This means that one's contribution to the health and welfare of society determines one's reward.

(B) To live a virtuous life is the best thing that there is. If one avoids vice, one is sure to be happy. Living a virtuous life surely means avoiding vice.

(C) This book is very boring. I tried to read it last night, and I almost fell asleep. Things that put me to sleep are boring.

(D) Every time I wake up the alarm clock goes off. You would almost think that I cause the alarm to ring! Therefore, when I wake up tomorrow, the alarm clock will go off.

(E) Midge love sports, and that's why she plays them all the time. She says she hopes to play sports until she's 70 years old. She certainly does play sports all the time, so Midge must really love them.

19. Some music lovers pride themselves on their knowledge of classical and baroque compositions. Some music lovers prefer the big band sound. They know the title of every tune ever played by the Glenn Miller band. Other music lovers concentrate on the works of great blues artists such as B. B. King. But even though not all music lovers can read music, they all enjoy playing and interpreting their favorite music for their friends.

If the information in the passage is true, which of the following CANNOT be true?

(A) Most music lovers do not pride themselves on their knowledge of baroque and classical music.

(B) Everyone who enjoys playing and interpreting his favorite music for his friends is a music lover.

(C) Music lovers who prefer the big band sound are more likely to memorize the names of their favorite tunes than are music lovers who concentrate on the works of blues artists.

(D) There are fewer music lovers who enjoy playing and interpreting their favorite music for their friends than there are music lovers who can read music.

(E) All music lovers who pride themselves on their knowledge of classical and baroque compositions mentioned in the passage can read music.

20. G. A. Villanova applied for and received a permit to build a large house in an old neighborhood in the city of Landsun. After the house was substantially done and more than $200,000 had been invested by Villanova in building it, it was discovered upon submission of complaints by neighbors that the city had granted a permit without obtaining the required approval from the historical commission. The historical commission refused to grant permission to build a house and ordered it razed. Villanova appealed to City Council, arguing that he had invested his money in good faith and stood to lose substantial sums. City Council, however, passed an ordinance ordering the home to be torn down. The mayor of the city of Landsun then vetoed the ordinance, thereby allowing Villanova to complete and occupy the house.

Which of the following principles, if accepted by the mayor, most helps to explain the mayor's decision?

(A) City offices should admit mistakes and attempt to correct them even when that correction causes harm or inconvenience.

(B) The historical commission in Landsun should be supported unless its decisions are overturned by City Council.

(C) Citizens acting in good faith should not be required to suffer financially for mistakes made by city offices.

(D) Effort should be made to encourage the building of new homes when such building adds to the value of neighborhoods.

(E) In a conflict between City Council and the historical commission the elected body should take precedence over the appointed body.

21. It was common to hear Cubans say in one breath, "I would give my life for Fidel," and in the next, "I don't know how we put up with all the shortages." A couple in line for ice cream echoed a refrain that has been familiar for several years: that official corruption was responsible for things working badly from ice cream distribution to the undependable buses or telephones. Yet they fervently supported Castro's rule.

Which of the following most contributes to an explanation of the apparently paradoxical opinions of the Cubans discussed in the passage?

(A) Most people believe that Castro was responsible for the shortages in the community.

(B) Most people believe that the problems in the community stem from incompetent officials and that Castro worked to chase such officials out.

(C) The buses and the telephones in Cuba are sometimes more efficient in their operation than at other times.

(D) The Cubans are unlikely to complain about inconveniences in everyday life.

(E) Cubans supported the leadership of Castro.

22. Shopping for a lawn mower, Donna knew that a lightweight one or one from an unknown brand would not be dependable for her rugged yard. The salesman showed her a sturdy model from a major national brand. Yet Donna decided that she needed to do more research to know whether the mower that the salesman showed her would be dependable for her yard.

Which of the following arguments exhibits a pattern of reasoning most similar to the reasoning in the passage above?

(A) Derek knew that if a gym had the latest equipment and was close to his apartment he would choose to do his workout there regularly. The ad made it clear that Bronze's Gym was quite close and had all of the latest equipment. Derek, however, hesitated to join because he was not sure that it was a place where he would do his workout regularly.

(B) Damien knew that if he went to class and took good notes he would pass the class. Yet he did not pass the class, and so he decided he must not have taken good notes.

(C) Doris had been told that if she was sure to lock the car and take her keys with her that her car would not be stolen. And her car was not stolen from the parking lot at the mall, so clearly Doris did lock her car and take the keys.

(D) Trying to interview well, David made sure that his suit was neat and that he was on time. So when the interview did not go well, he decided that there must be other things he should have done.

(E) Drew knew that avocados that were very green and quite hard to the touch were not ones he should buy to eat on the same day. At length in the produce department he was able to find three avocados that were not bright green and were soft to the touch. Still he was not sure whether he should buy them to eat that day.

23. Mental illness is on the rise in Latin America, according to one theory, due to the worsening national economies and the attendant instability, unemployment, and lower living standards. These economic problems, in turn, are the result of increasingly high levels of foreign debt. According to this theory, psychiatric disorders will continue to rise in the coming years, if the foreign-debt crisis is not solved.

Which of the following most supports the theory discussed in the passage?

(A) Unemployment and lower living standards among adult Latin Americans have declined in the last seven years, while rates of mental illness have increased.

(B) Unemployment and lower living standards among adult Latin Americans have risen in the last seven years, while rates of mental illness have declined.

(C) Unemployment and lower living standards among adult Latin Americans have risen in the last seven years, while rates of mental illness have remained constant.

(D) Unemployment and lower living standards among adult Latin Americans have declined in the last seven years, while rates of mental illness have remained constant.

(E) Unemployment and lower living standards among adult Latin Americans have risen in the last seven years, while rates of mental illness have increased.

24. Frustration is a result of two related factors. The first is the perception that secured rights may be lost in the future. The second is the perception that future advancement (be it economic, social, or political) is artificially limited by factors other than someone's ability or skill. This condition is the crux of Johansen's conclusion about the causes of the continuing frustration of the great mass of people in the country of Sporedia today.

Which of the following is a necessary assumption for Johansen's conclusion?

(A) A belief that a right is endangered inevitably results in frustration.

(B) There is no hope for economic advancement in the country of Sporedia.

(C) If the people of Sporedia believed they may advance through their own skills, then they would fear losing secured rights.

(D) The great mass of the people in Sporedia feel unable to advance through their own abilities or skills and feel they are about to lose secured rights.

(E) The people in Sporedia who do not feel frustration are not part of the great mass in that community.

25. Why did the metropolitan areas of the United States suburbanize so quickly? One thinks of the plentiful land around most cities, of the wealth of the nation, of the heterogeneity of the American people, of cheap energy and its inducement to decentralization, of the attractiveness of the domestic ideal, and of rapid technological advances which made long-distance commuting feasible. But those factors could not have been enough without two key government actions. Federally financed interstate highways removed the locational advantages of inner-city neighborhoods, while income-tax deductions encouraged families to buy houses rather than rent apartments.

Which of the following is most strongly supported by the information in the passage?

(A) Metropolitan areas have suburbanized as quickly as they have primarily because of plentiful land.

(B) The American people are more heterogeneous than they are often characterized to be, which has led them to seek the suburbs.

(C) Actions by the federal government caused the suburbanization of metropolitan areas of the United States.

(D) Rapid technological advances have made long-distance commuting feasible and, hence, led to the creation of the interstate highway system, which, in turn, was responsible for suburbanization.

(E) Certain governmental actions were necessary for the suburbanization of metropolitan areas of the United States to happen.

STOP

If time still remains, you may review work only in this section. When the time allotted is up, you may go on to the next section.

SECTION 3

Time—35 minutes
27 questions

Directions: *Each passage in this section is followed by a group of questions to be answered on the basis of what is **stated** or **implied** in the passage. For some questions, more than one of the choices could conceivably answer the question. However, you are to choose the **best** answer; that is, the response that most accurately and completely answers the question, and blacken the corresponding space on your answer sheet.*

Passage A

In 2006 the distant, ice-covered celestial body known as Pluto, originally discovered in the 1930s by Clyde W. Tombaugh, ceased to be a planet. The change came not because of any observed alteration in the celestial body, but because of a change in the way that scientists agreed to define the notion of "planet." Following eight days of contentious debate at the meeting, the 424 scientists who voted—comprising less than 5% of the world's astronomers—adopted the first official definition of planet and, in doing so, left Earth's solar system with eight, rather than the previously accepted nine, planets.

The definition makes a full-fledged planet an object that orbits the sun, is large enough to have become round because of its own gravity, and dominates the area of its neighborhood. It is primarily in neighborhood-dominating criterion that Pluto falls short. This is partially because it shares its neighborhood with its "moon" Charon that is about half its size. It also has not "swept up" asteroids and other celestial debris in the path of its orbit, as planets that dominate their neighborhood are expected to have done. Accordingly, Pluto is now taken to be a different kind of solar system object called a "dwarf planet." Pluto is one of at least 44 of these objects and has been expelled from membership in its previous, much more exclusive club and relegated to this larger group.

Passage B

Clyde W. Tombaugh first glimpsed Pluto in 1930 as part of a methodical photographic survey inspired by Percival Lowell, a wealthy Bostonian with a passionate interest in finding a possible trans-Neptunian planet. It was immediately evident that Pluto is an oddball in many ways. The other outer planets orbit the sun in roughly circular paths, but Pluto's highly elliptical orbit carries it from 30 to 50 times the earth's distance from the sun and, at times, brings it closer to the sun than Neptune. This was the case between 1979 and 1999.

Discoveries in the 1990s provided new insight into Pluto's complex nature. It was found to have a satellite, Charon, so large that the two objects were considered virtually a double planet. The planet has bright polar caps and a darker, mottled equatorial region. A layer of methane ice covers most of its surface. Pluto even possesses a thin atmosphere; when the planet is farthest from the sun, all or part of the atmosphere may freeze and fall to the surface as snow. Charon's surface, which appears to be quite different from Pluto's, may be a great expanse of water ice.

Pluto's size and density are much like those of Triton, the large satellite of Neptune that was recently visited by the Voyager 2 probe. These and other similarities suggest that both bodies may be leftover planetesimals, relics from the early days of the solar system that managed not to be swept up by the giant outer planets. In this scenario, Triton was captured by Neptune, whereas Pluto was able to survive as a bona fide planet because of its independent orbit about the sun.

1. A major topic in both passages is

   (A) that the definition of planet is decided upon at conventions of astronomers.

(B) that Pluto exhibits some oddities as compared to most of the planets in the solar system.

(C) that Charon's surface may be made largely of ice.

(D) that Pluto is smaller than most of the planets in the solar system.

(E) that there are many more dwarf planets than normal planets.

2. Which of the following best expresses the relationship between the two passages?

(A) Passage B disputes the factual accuracy of the findings detailed in passage A.

(B) Passage A disputes the factual accuracy of the findings detailed in passage B

(C) Though both mention Pluto, the principal topics of the two passages differ.

(D) Passage B elaborates on a point about Pluto mentioned in passing in passage A.

(E) Passage B describes action by the scientific community about discoveries discussed in passage A.

3. Which of the following is explicitly mentioned in both passages?

(A) The notion of "planet" had received no official definition among astronomers prior to 2006

(B) The relative size of Pluto's moon

(C) The name of one of Neptune's moons

(D) The approximate number of dwarf planets

(E) The path of Pluto's orbit

4. Which of the following can be inferred from one or both of the passages?

(A) The characteristics of Pluto changed in the period between the 1930s and 2006.

(B) Other celestial bodies that have been long regarded as planets in the solar system are likely to be redefined as dwarf planets.

(C) Astronomers believe that they have the authority to define the word *planet*.

(D) Charon is larger than most moons that orbit most planets in the solar system.

(E) Its size is the most important factor leading to Pluto's being classified as a dwarf planet.

5. Which of the following best describes the attitude of the author of passage B?

(A) Angry at the demotion of a familiar celestial body

(B) Eager to find new information that will lead to reclassification of bodies in the solar system

(C) Interested in the issues about Pluto raised at the scientific meeting mentioned in passage A

(D) Outraged at the astronomers taking it upon themselves to decide what is and is not a planet

(E) Advocating the importance of further research into the nature of Pluto

6. The two passages most clearly disagree about which of the following?

(A) Whether Pluto, like Triton, is a leftover planetesimal

(B) Whether Pluto was actually discovered by Clyde W. Tombaugh

(C) Whether Pluto is a bona fide planet

(D) Whether the definition of *planet* adopted at the meeting in 2006 is a valid one

(E) Whether the surface of Pluto is substantially different from the surface of Charon

As chief justice of the Supreme Court from 1801 until his death in 1835, John Marshall was a staunch nationalist and upholder of property rights. He was not, however, as the folklore of American politics would have it, the lonely and embattled Federalist defending these values against the hostile forces of Jeffersonian democracy. On the contrary, Marshall's opinions dealing with federalism, property rights, and national economic development were consistent with the policies of the Republican Party in its mercantilist phase from 1815 to 1828. Never an extreme Federalist, Marshall opposed his party's reactionary wing in the crisis of 1798–1800. Like almost all Americans of his day, Marshall was a Lockean republican who valued property not as an economic end in itself, but rather as the foundation of civil liberty and a free society. Property was the source both of individual happiness and social stability and progress.

Marshall evinced strong centralizing tendencies in his theory of federalism and completely rejected the compact theory of the Union expressed in the Virginia and Kentucky resolutions. Yet his outlook was compatible with the Unionism that formed the basis of the post-1815 American system of the Republican Party. Not that Marshall shared the democratic sensibilities of the Republicans; like his fellow Federalists, he tended to distrust the common people and saw in legislative majoritarianism a force that was potentially hostile to constitutionalism and the rule of law. But aversion to democracy was not the hallmark of Marshall's constitutional jurisprudence. Rather, its central features were a commitment to federal authority versus states' rights and a socially productive and economically dynamic conception of property rights. Marshall's support of these principles placed him near the mainstream of American politics in the years between the War of 1812 and the conquest of Jacksonian democracy.

In the long run, the most important decisions of the Marshall Court were those upholding the authority of the federal government against the states. *Marbury v. Madison* provided a jurisprudential basis for this undertaking, but the practical significance of judicial review in the Marshall era concerned the state legislatures rather than Congress. The most serious challenge to national authority resulted from state attempts to administer their judicial systems independent of the Supreme Court's appellate supervisions as directed by the Judiciary Act of 1789. In successfully resisting this challenge, the Marshall Court not only averted a practical disruption of the federal system, but it also evolved doctrines of national supremacy which helped preserve the Union during the Civil War.

7. Which of the following best states the main idea of the passage?
   - (A) John Marshall's constitutional jurisprudence exhibited strong centralizing tendencies and opposed the forces of Jeffersonian democracy.
   - (B) The key features of John Marshall's decision as chief justice of the Supreme Court indicate his distrust of the common people and his fear of legislative majoritarianism.
   - (C) John Marshall was a Lockean Republican who believed above all in the importance of property rights in conflicts between those rights and the federal or state governments.
   - (D) In the key features of his jurisprudence, John Marshall's decisions were compatible with the outlook of the Republican Party on federal authority and property rights.
   - (E) John Marshall was a Federalist chief justice of the United States Supreme Court at the time of Republican domination of Congress and the presidency.

8. According to the passage, John Marshall belonged to the
   - (A) Lockean Party.
   - (B) Republican Party.
   - (C) Democratic Party.
   - (D) Federalist Party.
   - (E) Independent Party.

9. Based upon the statements in the passage, it can be inferred that the author believes
   - (A) the Federalist party was hostile to individual property rights.
   - (B) some governmental leaders near the mainstream of American politics in the 1820s distrusted the common people.
   - (C) had John Marshall not been chief justice of the United States Supreme Court, the Civil War would have happened sooner than it did.

(D) members of the Republican Party did not support the Virginia and Kentucky resolutions.

(E) the majority of the Supreme Court did not agree with John Marshall's emphasis on federal authority versus states' rights.

10. Which of the following is not something that the passage mentions with regard to John Marshall and property?

(A) Marshall saw property as the foundation of civil liberty.

(B) Marshall held an economically dynamic conception of property rights.

(C) Marshall sided with the federal government when the state sought to invade private property rights.

(D) Marshall did not value property as an end in itself.

(E) Marshall viewed property as a source of social stability and progress.

11. The primary purpose of this passage is to

(A) describe the central features of Marshall's jurisprudence.

(B) discuss the importance of centralization to the preservation of the Union.

(C) criticize Marshall for being disloyal to his party.

(D) examine the role of the Supreme Court in national politics.

(E) chronicle Marshall's tenure on the Supreme Court.

12. According to the author, Marshall's attitude toward mass democratic politics can best be described as

(A) hostile.

(B) supportive.

(C) indifferent.

(D) nurturing.

(E) distrustful.

13. According to the author, the key features of Marshall's jurisprudence involved

(A) defending Federalist party positions against a Republican Party majority.

(B) controlling the hostility of legislative majorities to the Constitution and the rule of law.

(C) supporting Republican Party measures against a minority Federalist party.

(D) defending states rights against invasion by a Republican-Party-led federal government.

(E) a commitment to the authority of the federal government against the states.

Incrementalism is a strategy used to reduce the enormous problems of decision making and calculation arising during the budgetary process. Incrementalism assumes the calculation of each year's budget using some base as a starting point, such as the previous year's budget, and focuses attention on the marginal changes. In a broad sense, this base can be zero, as in Zero Base Budgeting. The usual case, however, is to use the previous year's budget as the base, with the expectation that the next budget will be an expansion of it.

The first test of incrementalism considers the continuity of the organization requesting the budget. Many organizations continue their activities from year to year without a great deal of fluctuation. Their requirements for funding are relatively stable, and their ongoing programs are continued as long as constituency needs are being met. Such organizations do not need to consider alternatives beyond those required to maintain their services. Only when the organization is not meeting its constituency's needs is it necessary to adapt procedures and strategies and consider new alternatives.

When new alternatives are proposed, they usually come in the form of new programs or an expansion of old programs. For the organization making a budgetary decision, the additional or expanded programs are those that will receive the greatest attention since they are the items which have not been previously discussed. The other items appearing in the request have been discussed and settled, and unless there are specific reasons for doing so, they need not be considered again. This strategy benefits those who must process large amounts of information by substantially reducing the items needing consideration. The information necessary to adequately consider even one or two programs can be enormous. Reconsideration of the entire budget on a yearly basis would make the task impossible.

The behavioral approach helps to explain why budgeting is done incrementally. The first problem facing a consideration of the entire budget is the nonintegration of the organizational goals. Each subunit of an organization can have its own goals which may not always be in line with the goals of the organization as a whole. Thus, the organization at times pursues conflicting goals. Rather than attempting to resolve this situation all at once, the goals are dealt with one at a time. This approach limits the number of decisions which must be made at a given time.

Second, in problem solving there is a tendency to look in one's own backyard first, i.e., trying something similar to what has been done previously, but different enough to solve the problem. This approach involves looking at the problem in small increments in an attempt to keep costs down. The search is not for the best solution to the problem, only an adequate one. Thus, the chances are better that small changes will adequately solve the problem at less cost than will a complete reconsideration of the problem to find the best solution.

14. Which of the following best states the main idea of the passage?

    (A) In cases where different subunits of the same organization have goals which may not be in line with the goals of the organization as a whole, incrementalism is an ineffective method to use in establishing budgets.

    (B) Incrementalism can be an effective annual budgeting strategy for stable organizations that continue their basic activities from year to year.

    (C) Incrementalism and Zero Base Budgeting represent different approaches to annual budget making that focus on different aspects of an organization's needs.

    (D) Two basic problems, conflicting goals and the tendency to solve problems with what has been done previously, must be addressed with an organization's annual budget-making process.

    (E) Annual budget making, for most organizations, is a challenging process of considering a great amount of information regarding a number of different items.

15. According to the passage, if an organization finds it necessary to consider alternatives beyond those required to maintain its existing services,

    (A) it is probably either small or quite new.

    (B) it is likely to be an organization that is not meeting its constituency's needs.

    (C) it should consider using incrementalism as an efficient way to establish its budget.

    (D) its budgetary process ought to consider implementing at least one or two new programs.

    (E) the question of whether it should use incrementalism can be decided only by taking into account the size of the organization.

16. The reference to "looking in one's own backyard" in the fifth paragraph is likely meant to indicate that

    (A) the previous year's budget is being used as the base.

    (B) organizations are continuing to find incrementalism useful.

    (C) organizations reexamine old programs before new ones are accepted.

    (D) organizations look to familiar ways to solve problems.

    (E) it is desirable to look close by for ways of keeping costs down.

17. The passage mentions each of the following with regard to incrementalism except that

    (A) it is a method for preventing the subunits of an organization from having their own goals.

(B) it helps to find small changes that will adequately solve problems at low costs.

(C) it can be a strategy that is especially effective for those who must process large amounts of information.

(D) it might use zero as a starting point in focusing on an annual budget.

(E) it allows the budgetary process to give greatest attention to the additional or expanded programs.

18. It can be inferred from the passage that which of the following is an organization most suited to the use of incrementalism as a strategy for making its annual budget?

(A) The Bass Butterfly is a small community-based opera house that each year performs three new operas and must decide each year on which three to perform, taking into account donations, ticket sales, and the operas involved.

(B) Always Talkin' is a chain of wireless phone stores whose continued profitability depends upon effective strategies of opening and closing outlets in the city as new markets open and old markets become saturated.

(C) Modems Galore is a computer products store that has been losing money increasingly over the last three years and must decide whether and how to try to continue operations in that atmosphere in the coming year.

(D) I Can Make It on My Own is a crafts store with a large inventory of arts and crafts items and a set of customers that is, as a group, very disenchanted with the store's selection and service.

(E) Pains and Gains is a successful local chain of gyms whose clientele remains basically the same but grows moderately in number from year to year and that must allocate its budget to maintain its level of services to that clientele.

19. The primary purpose of the passage is to

(A) describe two budgetary processes.

(B) indicate the limitations of incrementalism.

(C) explain the utility of incrementalism.

(D) examine the shortcomings of Zero Base Budgeting.

(E) present the behavioral approach to budgeting.

20. The author of the passage would most likely agree that

(A) Zero Base Budgeting would be preferable to incrementalism if organizations had the expertise to implement it.

(B) under incrementalism both old and new programs receive equally careful scrutiny.

(C) it would be better for a company to be the kind of dynamic enterprise that incrementalism would not work well for.

(D) incrementalism is a useful and practical budgeting approach for many successful organizations.

(E) there is no fundamental distinction that can be made between Zero Base Budgeting and incrementalism.

One response to the philosophic conflict between Heraclitus and Parmenides was that of the Sophists. The Sophists were philosophers from many different societies outside Greece who traveled about from city to city and in the fifth century B.C.E. came to Athens, where debate in the public assembly was open to all citizens. The Sophists argued that since reason produced such conflicting claims as those of Heraclitus and Parmenides, one must doubt the power of reason to lead to truth. Thus the Sophists became the first exponents of skepticism, the philosophic position of doubting the possibility of any true knowledge. Protagoras, the best known of the Sophists, appears to have made the skeptical argument that since there is no way of determining the truth about reality, reality must be said to have whatever qualities are claimed for it. Thus the Sophists threw suspicion upon all preceding Greek attempts to discover the true nature of reality.

But, more important, the Sophists may be said to have turned Greek philosophy in a new direction—away from philosophizing about the physical universe and toward the study of human beings and their moral, social, and political life. The Sophists were intellectual sophisticates who had traveled about and knew many cultures and their differing customs, morals, laws, and governments. Much to the dismay of many Athenian citizens who believed that traditional Athenian morals, laws, and democracy expressed absolute truths, the Sophists were moral relativists and argued that all moral and political principles are relative to the group which believes them. None is absolutely true.

Moreover, the Sophists claimed that the laws of cities are not natural and unchangeable but are merely the product of custom or convention. Therefore, some of the more radical Sophists argued that one is not obliged to obey the law. One should obey the law only if it is to one's advantage to do so. For example, in Book I of the *Republic,* Thrasymachus the Sophist argues that might makes right, that laws serve only to protect the interests of the powerful, the ruling party. Therefore, he concludes, only a fool obeys the law if it is against his own advantage.

Many people in the contemporary world are very close to the Sophists in their beliefs. Like the Sophists, they are skeptics, doubtful of any claims to knowledge, especially when authorities are in conflict and fight among themselves—for example, about how to teach children to read or how to stop economic inflation. Like the Sophists, many people today claim that the laws protect only the right and powerful, that they are not based upon justice and need not be obeyed; they are moral relativists who deny that morality is valid other than for the group which believes in it.

21. Which of the following best states the main idea of the passage?

    (A) A group of Greek philosophers called the Sophists can be seen as the first skeptics who began the tradition of doubting the possibility of any true knowledge.

    (B) The Sophists were a group of Greek political thinkers famous for arguing that might makes right and that the laws serve only to protect the interests of the powerful.

    (C) A powerful conflict between Heraclitus and Parmenides led to the formation of a new group to respond to both called the Sophists.

    (D) Because the Sophists were from many different places, including places outside Greece, they challenged accepted opinion especially in Athens about the validity of Athenian morals and laws.

    (E) The Sophists were a group of philosophers who turned philosophy's attention to human life and argued that moral and political principles are not absolutely true but relative to the group holding them.

22. The author mentions Thrasymachus in the third paragraph in order to

    (A) present an example of a well-known historical Sophist who argued in favor of law abidingness.

    (B) emphasize the point that Sophists knew many cultures and customs.

    (C) provide an example of the moral and political argument that was typical of some of the more radical Sophists.

    (D) clarify the disagreements between Heraclitus and Parmenides that resulted in the growth of the Sophists' movement.

    (E) emphasize that Plato was among the leading Sophists and that his work on the point is to be found especially in the *Republic.*

23. Which of the following is not something stated about the Sophists in the passage?

    (A) They claimed that laws are a product of convention.

    (B) They claimed that laws are not based on justice.

    (C) They claimed that it was foolish ever to obey the law.

    (D) They knew many cultures and customs.

(E) They were suspicious of previous Greek attempts to discover the nature of reality.

24. The primary purpose of the passage is to

(A) criticize the philosophy of Heraclitus.

(B) argue in favor of skepticism.

(C) explain the position of Protagoras.

(D) describe the philosophy of the Sophists.

(E) advocate moral enlightenment.

25. From the passage, it can be inferred that Thrasymachus would be most likely to agree with

(A) Parmenides.

(B) Protagoras.

(C) Socrates.

(D) Plato.

(E) Heraclitus.

26. According to the author, the Sophists emphasized

(A) study of the physical sciences.

(B) study of human beings.

(C) philosophy of the physical sciences.

(D) urban decay.

(E) legal structures.

27. It can be inferred that which of the following actions would be most consistent with the views of the Sophists as described in the passage?

(A) A community passes a law against polygamy from the conviction that it is wrong for a person to have more than one spouse.

(B) A community takes up a collection to build a new wing to its museum in order to house an especially beautiful painting that has been donated to it.

(C) A homeless woman turns into authorities a wallet with $4000 in it that the woman noticed was dropped inadvertently by a patron in a fast food restaurant because it is the right thing to do.

(D) A teenage thrill-seeker combats boredom by grabbing purses from elderly women who are walking between the parking lot and the mall.

(E) A citizen goes out of her way to disobey a sign that says to stay off the grass in an area of the park because she knows she can get away with the violation.

28. According to the author, Protagoras's view

(A) raised doubts about the possibility of moral ambiguity

(B) implied that the philosopher Plato was a Sophist

(C) concluded that reality must be whatever it might be claimed to be

(D) supported those who chose to disobey law

(E) sided with Heraclitus more than with Parmenides

STOP

If time still remains, you may review work only in this section. When the time allotted is up, you may go on to the next section.

SECTION 4

Time—35 minutes
24 questions

Directions: *The questions in this section are based on the reasoning contained in brief statements or passages. For some questions, more than one of the choices could conceivably answer the question. However, you are to choose the* ***best*** *answer; that is, the response that most accurately and completely answers the question. You should not make assumptions that are by commonsense standards implausible, superfluous, or incompatible with the passage. After you have chosen the best answer, blacken the corresponding space on your answer sheet.*

Questions 1–2

Since 2000, the starting salaries of those with master's degrees have failed to keep up with increased costs associated with graduate tuition, books, and fees. While it is true that the differential between the starting salaries of those who have master's degrees and those who do not is still large enough to make going to graduate school financially advantageous, the differential is now fairly small. Therefore, those who do not wish to continue their education for its own sake, should enter the workforce rather than go on to graduate school.

1. Which of the following, if true, would most seriously undermine the conclusion?
   (A) Since 2000, the percentage of people who go on to graduate school has risen sharply.
   (B) Since 2000, the number of people who go on to graduate school has fallen sharply.
   (C) Since 2000, the employment rate for those who have master's degrees has fallen more sharply than the rate for those who do not.
   (D) Since 2000, the unemployment rate for those who have master's degrees has fallen more sharply than for those who do not.
   (E) Since 2000, there are more unemployed people without master's degrees than there are with master's degrees.

2. Which of the following, if true, most strongly supports the conclusion?
   (A) Studies show that many people who do not wish to go to graduate school, but who go anyway for financial reasons, suffer emotional distress.
   (B) Studies show that those who have gone to graduate school report greater job satisfaction than those who have not.
   (C) Studies show that those with no college preparation have less difficulty landing their first job than do those with master's degrees.
   (D) Studies show that the nation's graduate schools have the capacity to enroll 10% more people in graduate studies.
   (E) Since 2000, the percentage of college graduates entering the job force has risen sharply.

3. We did not all know astrophysics, so we did know that if the professor put questions on the test about astrophysics, we would not all pass. Since half the class passed, the professor must not have put a question about astrophysics on the test.

   Which one of the following exhibits the same flaw as the argument above?
   (A) He tries so hard, but it remains a sad fact that the team always loses when Pete plays. Therefore, if the team is to win Thursday night and no one is to leave sad, the coach had better not let him play.

(B) Eating lots of those tasty hot peppers causes heartburn. But Jim did not give into temptation and did not eat hot peppers, so his ailment cannot be heartburn.

(C) If Hank had forgotten to pay a $40 fine, he would have lost his license and no one in the carpool would have had a ride to work today. But judging from the fact that they are here for all to see, Hilda and Kevin had a ride. So Hank did not forget to pay the fine.

(D) My great aunt and uncle tell me that a red sunset means good weather tomorrow. This is a red sunset, so if tomorrow's weather is not good, either my great aunt or my great uncle or both will be proven wrong.

(E) An applicant could get the job only if she had experience or an advanced degree. Emily has no experience. So if Emily gets the job it means that she has an advanced degree.

4. The Union of Compatible Countries should demand that Nabobia, one of its founding member nations, stop giving cash subsidies to farmers to influence what they do and do not produce. Nabobia's policy is designed to help its farmers, but market forces are the only reliable indicators that nations and their farmers should use to decide what to produce: which products and in what amounts. Guidance by those forces does the most good for farmers and the people of Nabobia and ultimately for all in the Union of Compatible Countries.

In making its recommendation, the passage relies on

(A) a comparison of the effects of farm subsidies in two different countries.

(B) a conclusion drawn from consideration of an analogous situation.

(C) an attempt to draw on political prejudices.

(D) application of a general principle to a particular case.

(E) persuasion that a new theory of production is preferable to an older one.

5. President: Dr. Kesler, I have been told that developing an initial climate of trust, which is the first step in building a strong and lasting relationship with our new treaty's signatory, will be impossible because we have not appointed a special team of representatives to be stationed in Edenia. Can you assure me that our relations with Edenia have not been permanently damaged by our failure to appoint such a team?

Kesler: Mr. President, our relations with this nation have not been permanently damaged by our failure to appoint such a team. An initial climate of trust between nations is not some guarantee of good and strong relations forever. In fact, such a climate of trust might give the relationship between two nations a head start, but other factors are the things needed for building a strong and lasting relationship with this nation.

The president and Dr. Kesler disagree about which of the following?

(A) Immediate actions such as one nation's appointing representatives to be stationed in the country with which it has signed a treaty might help establish good relations between those nations.

(B) It is desirable to establish good relations with the country of Edenia.

(C) A climate of trust between nations is enough to secure a strong and lasting relationship between them when they are signatories to the same treaty.

(D) Assigning a special team of representatives to a country can help to establish an initial climate of trust between the country assigning the team in the country to which the team is assigned.

(E) Establishing an initial climate of trust between signatories of the treaty is necessary for establishing strong relations between those countries.

6. Scientists have concluded that exposure to the sun is responsible for 45% of all cases of melanoma. Since last June, more reliable methods of identifying melanoma have been developed, which is why reports of melanoma have increased since last June.

The argument in the passage relies on which of the following assumptions?

(A) More than half of the increase in reported cases of melanoma are due to sun exposure.

(B) Exposure to the sun has increased dramatically since last June.

(C) The incidence of melanoma has not increased since last June.

(D) Doctors are less reluctant to report cases of melanoma than they previously were.

(E) Methods of reporting melanoma have become more convenient since last June.

7. In a recent collection of essays, *The Tempest* is twice deemed a bad, "boring" play. But this assessment is not consistent with a careful and thoughtful reading. Put in the context of English history, *The Tempest*, with its series of conspiracies, is a politically radical contribution to the vast discourse of treason that became an increasingly central response to difficult social problems in late Elizabethan and early Jacobean London. Put in the still broader context of political philosophy, the play becomes a commentary on the virtue of philosophers as rulers and on the unlikelihood of such superbly gifted and qualified people choosing to play that role.

Which of the following best states the main conclusion of the passage?

(A) From the context of the present-day reader, *The Tempest* is a bad, boring play.

(B) *The Tempest* is not a bad, boring play.

(C) Since *The Tempest* is constructed as a series of conspiracies, it is primarily a commentary on problems in late Elizabethan and early Jacobean London.

(D) *The Tempest* ought to be viewed both in historical and in philosophical context.

(E) *The Tempest* is instructive as a careful and thoughtful commentary on philosophers as rulers.

8. Leibniz's views on weakness of will should be regarded as central to his philosophical system. First, the issue of weakness of will is of considerable intrinsic interest because of its theoretical and practical aspects alike. Moreover, since for him freedom does not only involve absence of external impediments, but also, among other things, the power to will as one should, it directly conflicts with weakness of will.

Which of the following offers the most support for the argument in the passage?

(A) Other philosophers agree that freedom involves more than absence of external impediments.

(B) Weakness of will can result from a number of external and internal factors.

(C) Freedom indirectly conflicts with weakness of will.

(D) The issue of freedom occupies a prominent position in Leibniz's philosophy.

(E) Strength of will can be important in overcoming external impediments.

9. Demographic studies indicate that the number of elderly is increasing; therefore, the total cost of caring for the elderly is also increasing. At the same time, the number of wage earners is not increasing as rapidly. The funds to care for the elderly will have to come from taxes paid by the wage earners.

Which of the following is most strongly supported by the statements above?

(A) Unless average income increases sufficiently, the percentage of wage earners' incomes that must go to caring for the elderly will increase.

(B) The elderly do not receive adequate care.

(C) Health care will become increasingly costly for each elderly person in the coming years.

(D) Working people will attempt to increase tax rates in order to care for the growing numbers of elderly.

(E) Citizens should save their own money now to take care of their own needs during retirement, instead of depending on younger people to take care of them.

10. American community colleges are entering an era in which they should be especially aware of the need for new staff and their development of new skills to meet the challenges of the years ahead. Increasingly, community college leaders are examining their future staffing needs, often with some startling results. For example, in California approximately 40% of full-time faculty will be eligible for retirement in the next six years, with another 18% only a few years away. Obviously, the need to recruit and provide staff development for a substantial new cadre of faculty is upon us now.

    Which of the following offers the most additional support for the argument's conclusion?

    (A) Community colleges last needed a major addition of new staff 20 years ago.

    (B) Community college leaders are often unprepared to address their future staffing needs.

    (C) It is quite challenging to recruit and provide staff development for a new cadre of faculty while maintaining the quality and morale of existing faculty.

    (D) Most full-time community college faculty in California who become eligible for retirement do retire immediately.

    (E) The decade ahead will be challenging for American community colleges in terms of building curriculum as well as in terms of maintaining faculty.

11. *Paradise Lost* reflects Milton's view that human activity is grounded in the essential liberty that affords the individual both the freedom and the responsibility to choose among personal and public alternatives which are inherently moral in nature. The source of this liberty is virtue. Hence the poem is a moral and religious one: a guide to piety and submission, and to the supposedly appropriate relations between men and women, mortal and deity, and subject and heavenly king. So *Paradise Lost* is a political work of great sophistication that can lead to profound reflections.

    The conclusion about *Paradise Lost* is rightly drawn if which of the following is assumed?

    (A) All political texts are about morality.

    (B) Politics should adopt freedom as a goal and responsibility as a means to it.

    (C) Questions of human morality, of how people should live, are essentially political questions.

    (D) Milton hoped that the rulers of his day would learn from his treatment of the importance of piety and submission.

    (E) It rejects as artificial claims that one can separate church from state in that piety and freedom are linked.

12. The proposition is this: An action gains moral worth, not in the purpose that is to be attained by it, but in the maxim according to which the action is determined. The moral worth depends, therefore, not on the realization of the object of the action, but on the principle of volition according to which, without regard to any objects of the faculty of desire, the action has been done.

    Which of the following actions could not have moral worth, according to this argument?

    (A) An action that harms someone that was done with the intent to do good

    (B) An action performed by someone concerned primarily with acting according to proper maxims

    (C) An action done with the intent to harm that has a beneficial effect

    (D) An action intended to produce good, done incompetently and so unsuccessfully

    (E) An action done without regard to physical desires of the actor

13. Martin: Eventually, the resources of Earth will be exhausted. The air will be too polluted to breathe, the water too fouled to drink, the soil too contaminated to raise edible crops. If mankind is to survive, then, it must be on another planet. So, we must begin now to develop the means to travel to and live on other planets in large numbers.

George: Nonsense. The crude rockets and habitat equipment we have could never be used to move and support more than very small expeditions to even a very near planet. Nor do we need more, since careful pollution control rules already in force or soon to be enacted will maintain acceptable environmental quality for centuries.

George and Martin are committed to disagreeing on which of the following?

(A) Existing technology would be adequate to support travel of large numbers of people to live on other planets.

(B) There is a need for people to develop the ability to travel in large numbers to other planets.

(C) It could be possible for human beings to travel to and live on other planets.

(D) The environment on Earth will sustain human life on a large scale in the immediate future.

(E) Widespread human survival is worth the cost of developing the means to travel to and live on other planets in large numbers.

14. If the legislature does not increase appropriations for education, the teachers will strike. However, the legislature can increase education appropriations only if it cuts back on highway repair, and that may anger motorists. It seems that the legislature must either refuse to increase education appropriations, or risk the wrath of motorists.

If the above statements are true, which of the following must also be true?

(A) Increasing education appropriations will lead to motorists' being angry.

(B) Highway repair will be cut back only if the legislature increases appropriations for education.

(C) If the legislature cuts back on highway repair, the teachers will not strike.

(D) If the legislature considers increasing appropriations for education, motorists may be angry.

(E) The teachers will strike unless highway repair is cut back.

15. Latex paint often has a tendency to prematurely crack and peel when applied to wooden structures. Many homeowners who have applied a new coat of paint to their houses are shocked when, after the first summer storm followed by several hot sunny days, the paint begins to crack and peel. Professional painters cite three factors, some or all of which are to blame for the premature cracking and peeling: (1) the paint was not thoroughly stirred before application; (2) the surface was not clean and dry before application; (3) the paint was applied in one heavy coat rather than two or more light ones.

If the claims of the professional painters are true, and if the surface was clean and dry before being painted, but premature cracking and peeling still occurred, it must be true that

(A) the paint was not thoroughly stirred before application.

(B) the paint was applied in one heavy coat.

(C) either the paint was not thoroughly stirred, or was applied in one heavy coat, or both.

(D) either the paint was not thoroughly stirred, or was applied in one heavy coat, but not both.

(E) the paint was not thoroughly stirred and was applied in one heavy coat.

16. He who explores the cities of England to discover that kind of beauty in architecture which is familiar in other lands will not find it. In a satire published in London the queen reproaches her son for not taking more after his father and interesting himself in the indus-

trial affairs of the country. The poor Prince of Wales can only reply, "I've not a model-farming soul." A similar answer is all that England can return to the scoldings poured out upon her because she cannot do the work of the old Italian and Dutch masters.

Which of the following most accurately states the function in the passage of the exchange involving the Prince of Wales?

(A) It is presented as an analogy to emphasize the main point of the passage.

(B) It provides information that serves as a premise in the passage's argument.

(C) It is a subsidiary conclusion that becomes a premise to the passage's main conclusion.

(D) It is the analogy used to convince the reader of the accuracy of the conclusion that English cities are not characterized by beautiful architecture.

(E) It serves to dispute the claim that the old Italian and Dutch masters created beautiful architecture.

17. An interested and tenacious student, Nellie worked very hard not only on the coursework required for her degree in English at the university, but also in the job she needed to make the money to pay for her education. Last week she turned down a promotion at Swanson's Family Feast, where she has worked as a server and earned a decent income in tips for several years, to take a lower paying job as a hostess at Sally's Suppers and More, a large and famous restaurant in the center of town. Nellie is determined to continue working in a restaurant business only until she has worked her way through college and earned her degree.

Which of the following, if true, most helps to explain Nellie's choice to change jobs?

(A) Swanson's Family Feast is a well-known national chain that allows its servers to move from one restaurant to another if it is more convenient for them to do so.

(B) It is considered very prestigious in the restaurant business to work at Sally's Suppers and More, and so people seeking to make careers in that business very much desire to work there.

(C) The management of Sally's Suppers and More has promised to make Nellie a server there after a one-month probation, and tips at that restaurant are far higher than at Swanson's Family Feast.

(D) The management at Swanson's Family Feast is used to working with college students as servers and is willing to accommodate the needs of their class schedules.

(E) Career prospects at Sally's Suppers and More are no less attractive than career prospects at Swanson's Family Feast.

18. I love you. Therefore I am a lover. All the world loves a lover. Therefore you love me.

Which of the following follows the same pattern of reasoning as the passage above?

(A) Adam is a man. Men are homo sapiens. Therefore, Adam is a homo sapien. Homo sapiens are rational. Therefore, Adam is rational.

(B) Sam got to work on time yesterday, the day before, and for the last 50 working days. Therefore, Sam is dependable. Dependable people get raises. Therefore, Sam will get a raise.

(C) I like to talk to Pete. Therefore, I am a patient person. Everyone likes to talk to patient people. Therefore, Pete likes to talk to me.

(D) A sensible voter would care about the crime rate if it is high. The crime rate is high. Richardson promises to work to lower the crime rate if elected. Maria is a voter who is supporting Richardson. Therefore Maria is a sensible voter.

(E) Lifting weights strengthens the body. You lift weights; therefore you are strong. Strong people are happy. Therefore you are happy.

19. Government statistics claim that the per capita crime rate is down in the country's major cities as compared to 10 years ago. But it seems no safer to walk down the

streets of New York, Houston, Chicago, or Los Angeles than it was a decade ago. There are at least as many robberies, muggings, and burglaries occurring there as there were 10 years ago. So the crime rate must not be any lower than it has ever been.

The conclusion in the above passage is based on which error in reasoning?

(A) It confuses the numbers of crimes with the rate of crime.

(B) It assumes that the only major cities are New York, Houston, Chicago, and Los Angeles.

(C) It draws a conclusion about all cities from an unrepresentative sample of cities.

(D) It confuses number of crimes with number of criminals.

(E) It fails to take into account that population in cities might be lower than it was 10 years ago.

20. Public Works director: Despite the environmental damage caused in other states by strip mining of coal, we must allow the project at Grand Bank to go ahead as scheduled. The National Energy Commission has estimated that demands for electrical power will increase by 12% in the tri-state region in the next 10 years. Besides, citizens of the three states have overwhelmingly expressed their opposition to building more nuclear power plants. Any surpluses of electrical power brought about by the Grand Bank Project can always be sold to other states in the region.

Which of the following principles, if held by the Public Works director, most helps to explain the decision to allow the project to continue?

(A) It is better to overestimate than to underestimate future energy needs.

(B) Decisions to acquire energy-generating capacity need to take into account at least a 10-year period.

(C) In deciding whether to build new electrical generation plants, it is more important to be able to satisfy projected power needs than it is to avoid environmental damage.

(D) In deciding whether to build electric power plants, popular opposition on environmental or safety grounds is the most important factor.

(E) Environmental and safety issues should not be considered when a future need for electrical power is being addressed.

21. Attorney: The case against my client was as much the work of the prosecution's feverish imagination as a construction of the law. The circumstances that resulted in her arrest, trial, and imprisonment bespeak a condition of national hysteria not unlike the hysteria that seized the Massachusetts Bay Colony in the 17th century during the Salem witch trials. If the defendant was unjustly convicted, it is because we live in an age of trial by accusation. Our society at the moment is quick to condemn anybody and everybody charged, on the flimsiest of evidence, with the crime of abusing or molesting children.

The main point the attorney is attempting to support is which of the following?

(A) The defendant is not guilty of the crime for which she was convicted.

(B) The defendant was convicted of child abuse.

(C) Modern-day trials have not advanced much since the Salem witch trials of the 17th century.

(D) Society should be more tolerant of child abuse and molestation.

(E) The prosecutor acted improperly against the attorney's client.

22. Sanderson found that demand for housing in the island country of Orepsorp climbs for residents between ages 20 and 30, levels off through age 40, and then declines about 1% per year. Accordingly real estate boomed in the first decade of the twenty-first century more than in the 20 years before that decade. And the real estate market in the decade of the 2020s is forecast to be less robust than in that first decade of the century. This follows from the fact that the generation that was in its 20s in the first decade of the century is larger than the one that came before it or the one that came after it.

If the statements in the passage are true, the forecast for the real estate market depends on which of the following assumptions?

(A) The generation that will turn 20 in the 2020s will be less interested in new housing than its predecessor.

(B) Economic conditions in Orepsorp will not have a significant effect on demand for housing there.

(C) Real estate in Orepsorp boomed in the 1970s.

(D) There was a glut of housing on the market in the first decade of the twenty-first century in Orepsorp.

(E) Real estate in Orepsorp is inexpensive enough that almost anyone who wishes to purchase a home can expect to be able to do so.

23. The new film version of *Crime and Punishment* that was released this week is almost certain to be a flop. This is because important novels rarely become important or commercially successful films. The great film director Alfred Hitchcock often commented that well-crafted fiction was much harder to film than second-rate writing. Great novels—those multidimensional works which explore the interior life of their characters and offer gripping emotional development—are extremely difficult to transfer to the screen. Contrast this with popular fiction, such as the gothic romance, from which entertaining movies can be made because the audience reacts on a visceral level.

The reasoning in the argument is vulnerable to criticism because it

(A) presupposes that something true of a group of things as a whole is true of every member of that group individually.

(B) assumes that because great novels are rarely great films that it is the greatness of the novel that causes the film to be less than great.

(C) bases a broad conclusion on evidence from a single case.

(D) uses imprecise terms by not providing a definition of the word *important.*

(E) moves from evidence that something rarely happens to a conclusion that it never happens.

24. As a master chef, Browne knew that to achieve the best flavor and texture when boiling the vegetable asparagus, it was important to select stalks of a uniform and thin size; otherwise they will be undercooked on the inside or overcooked on the outside. Yet when she went to the produce market for ingredients for that evening's gourmet dinner, Browne sought out the thickest asparagus stalks she could find. She explained that she wanted to prepare asparagus that her customers would find to be delicious.

Which of the following, if true, best explains Browne's choice of asparagus stalks?

(A) When boiled for the same amount of time, thicker asparagus stalks are less cooked through than are thinner asparagus stalks.

(B) Thicker asparagus stalks are usually more mature on the plant than are thinner asparagus stalks.

(C) Asparagus is a perennial plant that grows for several years, and may be more flavorful when it is older.

(D) Cooking asparagus in a microwave oven enables thick asparagus to be cooked uniformly.

(E) Thicker asparagus stalks usually cost less per pound than the more desirable thinner stalks.

STOP

If time still remains, you may review work only in this section. When the time allotted is up, you may go on to the next section.

WRITING SAMPLE TOPIC

Time—35 minutes

Directions: *The scenario presented below describes two choices, either one of which can be supported on the basis of the information given. Your essay should consider both choices and argue for one over the other, based on the two specified criteria and the facts provided. There is no "right" or "wrong" choice: a reasonable argument can be made for either. Confine your essay to the blocked, lined area on the front and back of the separate Writing Sample Response Sheet. Only that area will be reproduced for law schools. Be sure that your writing is legible.*

Present an argument in favor of All Sports Sporting Goods Company hiring one of the following two finalists for the company's new director of personnel and public relations position. Both candidates are eager to accept the position, and their salary requirements are comparable. In light of this, two other factors should influence your decision:

- The director of personnel and public relations must be able to improve employee-management relations, which are now somewhat strained.
- The director of personnel and public relations is to strengthen national name recognition of the company and its products among the general public.

Susan Cole is a distinguished labor lawyer and professional mediator. She has served on the National Labor Relations Board (NLRB) in Washington, D.C., and is widely known in the business community, though not by the public at large. She is generally viewed as a wise and fair mediator, but some executives feel she is too quick to side with labor in disputes. While Ms. Cole has some experience in dealing with the media because of her prior position with the NLRB, she admits that her public relations skills are weak.

Henry Able is currently vice president for public relations at Save-Big, a Midwestern retail chain. Able is well known to the people of the Midwest and familiar to residents of the West Coast because of the commercials he does for Save-Big. During the 15 years he has been with Save-Big, Able has headed the company's advertising and public relations departments and been a critical player in making Save-Big the major regional retail chain it is today. Mr. Able has participated in managing employee relations at Save-Big, but his role was minor.

STOP

If time still remains, you may review work only in this section.

TEST 3 ANSWER KEY

Section 1 – Analytical Reasoning

1. A
2. A
3. B
4. A
5. C
6. C
7. B
8. B
9. A
10. D
11. A
12. D
13. B
14. A
15. C
16. C
17. B
18. E
19. B
20. C
21. D
22. A
23. C
24. E

Section 2 – Logical Reasoning

1. D
2. A
3. D
4. C
5. B
6. B
7. D
8. B
9. C
10. D
11. C
12. C
13. E
14. C
15. E
16. B
17. B
18. E
19. D
20. C
21. B
22. E
23. E
24. D
25. E

Section 3 – Reading Comprehension

1. B
2. D
3. B
4. C
5. C
6. C
7. D
8. D
9. B
10. C
11. A
12. E
13. E
14. B
15. B
16. D
17. A
18. E
19. C
20. D
21. E
22. C
23. C
24. D
25. B
26. B
27. D
28. C

Section 4 – Logical Reasoning

1. D
2. A
3. C
4. D
5. E
6. C
7. B
8. D
9. A
10. D
11. C
12. C
13. B
14. E
15. C
16. A
17. C
18. C
19. A
20. C
21. A
22. E
23. A
24. D

TEST 3 DETAILED EXPLANATIONS OF ANSWERS

SECTION 1 – ANALYTICAL REASONING

QUESTIONS 1–5

This is a pure ordering situation. It has six items to be placed in order from oldest to youngest corresponding to the letters A through F. The items, the rules, and the resulting relative order are indicated in the diagram below:

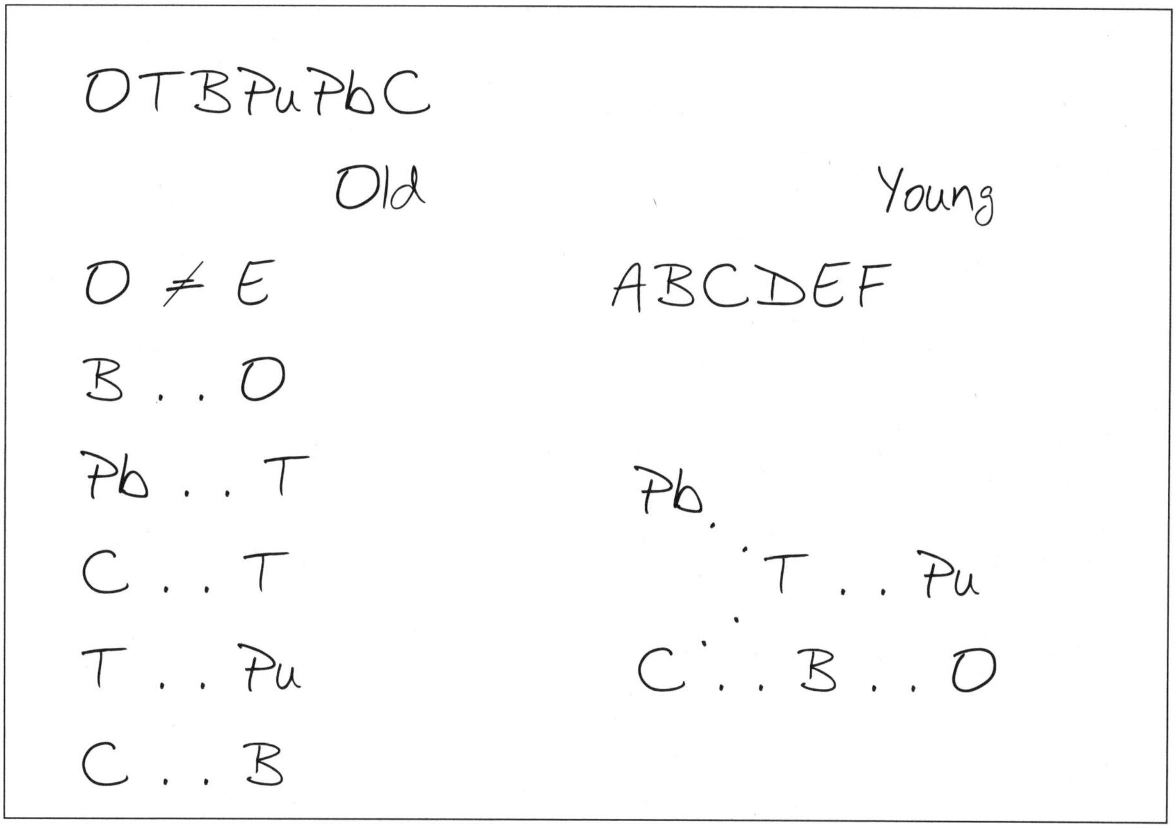

Note that while the questions might turn out to be about absolute placement (asking, for example, what character B might play), the answers to such questions will involve the relative order of the items representing the characters in the play. The order of the actors is fixed. The conditions are straightforward relative order rules, with the one exception that O cannot be played by E.

1. This is a typical acceptable outcome question, asking for the one of the five choices that violates no rule. Compare the rules against the answer choices to eliminate all but the correct one. (A)

2. The question places B as older than Pb and then asks about the placement of C. In this case, since C must be older than B, the only possibility is for C to be the oldest, and so played by Allie. (A)

3. This question puts O in the third position and asks which actor must play the role of B. Since both C and B must be older than O, they must be in positions A and B, with Bobby playing B. (B)

4. This question is like an acceptable outcome question except that it is asking for the one

unacceptable outcome. And the alternative that violates a rule does so about the relative order of Pb and T. (A)

5. This question places Pu at position E and asks who might play T. With Pu at E, O must be at F which means that T must be at either C or D. Only one of those is included among the answer possibilities, and that is the correct one. (C)

QUESTIONS 6–12

This section involves a grouping situation. There is a single group of five to be made from nine different items, classified in two different ways. The diagram shows the basic classifications and rules governing the selection of the five items. In addition, it shows some important deductions derived from those rules.

3F = ABCDE (5)
2S = FGHI
3/4 E = AEGH
B/E   B → H, G, A, ~E, ~F, ~C, D
F/H   F → A, E, G, ~H, ~B, ~C, D
G/C   C → A, E, H, ~G, ~F, ~B, I
Always A

The conditions governing the selection of the group are quite restrictive. There must be exactly three freshmen and exactly two sophomores, and within those groups either three or four must be from the category of experienced fencers as well. That category of experienced fencers includes two freshmen and two sophomores. Each of the three other conditions sets forth two that cannot be included simultaneously in the group. In each case, one of those two is among the experienced fencers, which means that with each of the pairs, if the one who is not experienced is included in the group, it has important results for the makeup of the group as a whole. Those deductions are indicated in the diagram. One key deduction that emerges from them is that in any acceptable outcome A must be among the fencers included in the group. But keep in mind that these three scenarios are not the only possible ones.

6. As is most often the case, the first question is an acceptable outcome question. The only alternative which does not violate a rule is choice (C).

7. This question places all four experienced fencers on the team, and then asks who else must make the team. With all four experienced fencers consisting of two freshmen and two sophomores, the remaining fencer must be a freshman, and from the other

rules, since both G and E are included, neither B nor C may be. So the fifth person on the team must be the only remaining freshman, D. So the correct answer is choice (B).

8. This asks for someone who must make the team, and given the restraints on experienced fencers, that someone is Alicia. So the correct answer is choice (B).

9. This question stipulates that G is not included and asks for a variable, or a decision that is to be made. G is one of the experienced fencers, so without G the group must include A, E, and H. Since that means that F cannot be included, I must be part of the group as the second sophomore. The remaining person in the group must be a freshman, and it cannot be B. So the remaining choice is whether the final freshman will be D or C. This is contained in choice (A).

10. Without adding additional information, this question asks for a pair that cannot both make the team. The key here is to remember that there must be at least three of the four from the experienced fencers, and that each of the specific conditions about pairs that cannot be included includes one of the experienced fencers in the pair. It cannot be the case that the inexperienced fencers are chosen from two or three of those pairs, for then there would not be enough experienced fencers. Choice (D) includes two of the inexperienced fencers from those pairs. (D)

11. This question adds the information that E is not on the team. That requires the remaining three experienced fencers to be included, and that means that both H and G must be included so that neither F nor C can be. One of those two appears in the list of answer choices, making the correct answer choice (A).

12. This question asks for someone who must make the team in the case that I does not. Since you have already determined that Alicia must always make the team, this question has a fairly straightforward answer in choice (D).

QUESTIONS 13–18

This situation involves 11 items that are to be placed in order on a line that numbers from 1 through 11. That sounds like it might be an ordering situation, but review of the conditions indicates that the rules do not have to do with items relative to one another so much as with items relative to the particular spots in line. Accordingly, this is a placement situation and the key question will be: in what number places are the 11 items. The diagram below includes a list of the items, the simplification of the rules, and an indication of two basic scenarios that might govern the placement of the items.

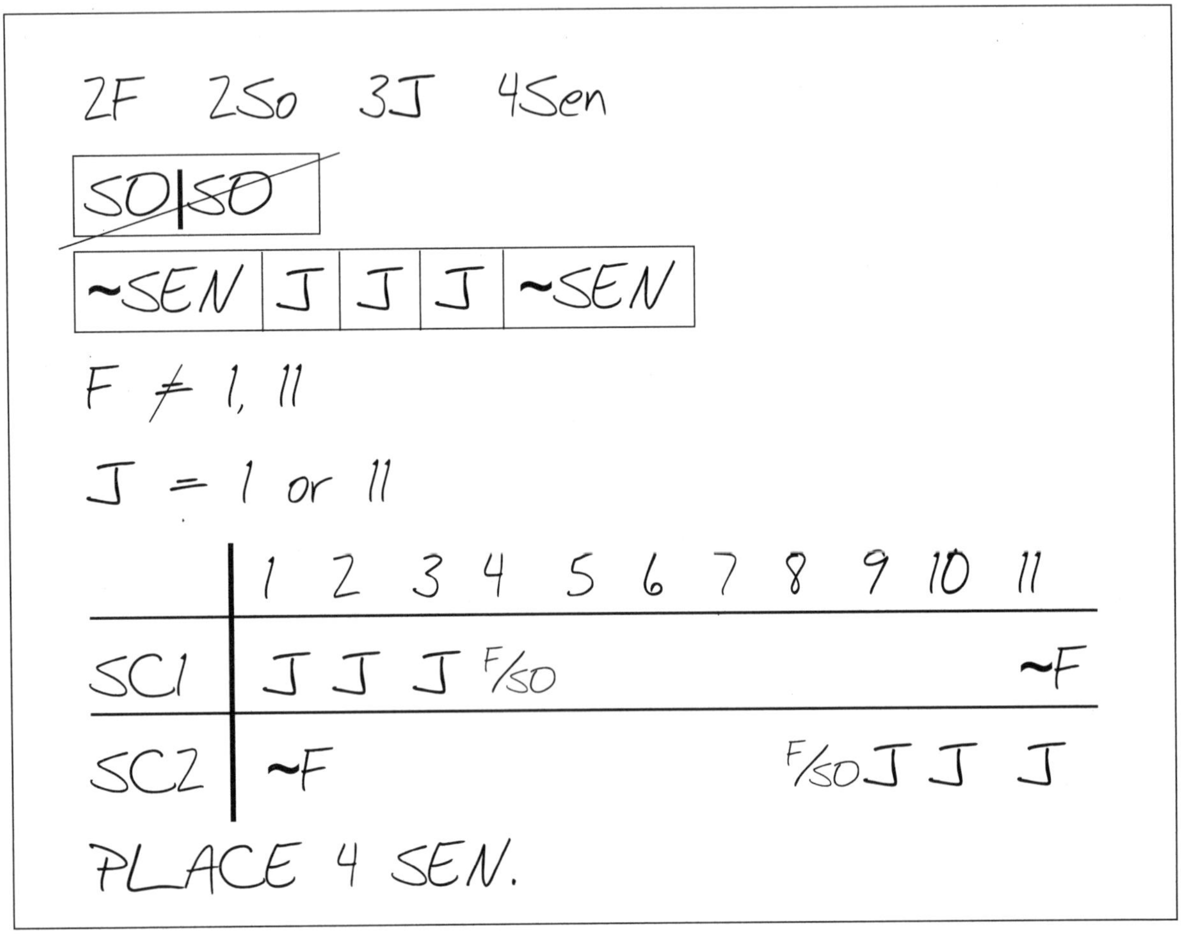

Eleven is a lot of things to place. But quickly the number becomes effectively reduced by the rule that says that the 3 juniors must stand beside each other. When that is combined with two other rules: that no senior may stand beside a junior and a junior is at one end of the line, the possibilities for placement of the items become much more limited. In effect, the juniors with the freshman or sophomore that must stand beside them take away either the first or the last 4 of the 11 slots. Seven remain, but in those 7, 4 seniors must be placed. Two sophomores must also be placed, and they cannot be beside each other. Finally the position that remains at the end of the line cannot be filled by a freshman. There will not be a lot of different ways to fulfill all of these requirements at once. The questions will test understanding of that, and perhaps add additional information that will restrain the possibilities even further.

13. The question places a junior in space 3, which puts you in scenario one on the diagram. The question then said there is a sophomore in space 10 and asks for what

must be true. By rule the sophomores cannot stand beside each other, and also by rule no freshman can be in space 11. So it follows that a senior must be in 11. (B)

14. The question places seniors in spaces 2, 3, 6, and 7 and asks for what must be false. The question puts you in scenario two in the diagram, and does not leave much to be done. The sophomores cannot be beside each other, and one of them must be in space 1. So what must be false is in (A).

15. The question asks for what must be false, without adding additional information. Testing the choices against the diagram, it appears that what must be false is choice (C). There are simply too many seniors to be placed in seven spaces numbered from 1 to 7 or from 5 to 11 to have them all on even-numbered spaces. (C)

16. The question places the seniors standing together at one end of the line. With the juniors at the other end of the line there are four places in the middle to be divided among the freshmen and sophomores. Of the three possibilities presented, the only one that could be true, and indeed it must be true, is that the freshmen are not standing together, for that would make the sophomores stand together. (C)

17. The question asks for something that could be true. To determine this you would need to develop the two possible scenarios, had you not done so already. This question makes it clear that the block of juniors constrains the possibilities for the 11 places. The only one that could be true is (B).

18. The question asks for something that must be true, without adding additional information. Testing the choices against what we know from the diagram, we discover that choice (E) must be true since no senior can be standing beside a junior, and in either scenario the place beside the block of juniors is an even-numbered space. (E)

QUESTIONS 19–24

This situation is an unusual one in that it requires you to seat people around a round table without defining specific positions at that table. Yet there are fixed positions relative to one another, and the conditions regarding the placement of the people deal with those people relative to one another. The situation is kind of a mixture between a placement situation and an ordering situation, with no beginning and end as there would be in an ordering situation and no absolute definition of slots as there would be in a placement situation. Imagine a round table and the relationships at that table, however, and the situation clarifies itself readily into two basic possibilities derived from the key rule that one of the six people always sits directly across from another. This diagram clarifies the conditions and represents the two possible outcomes:

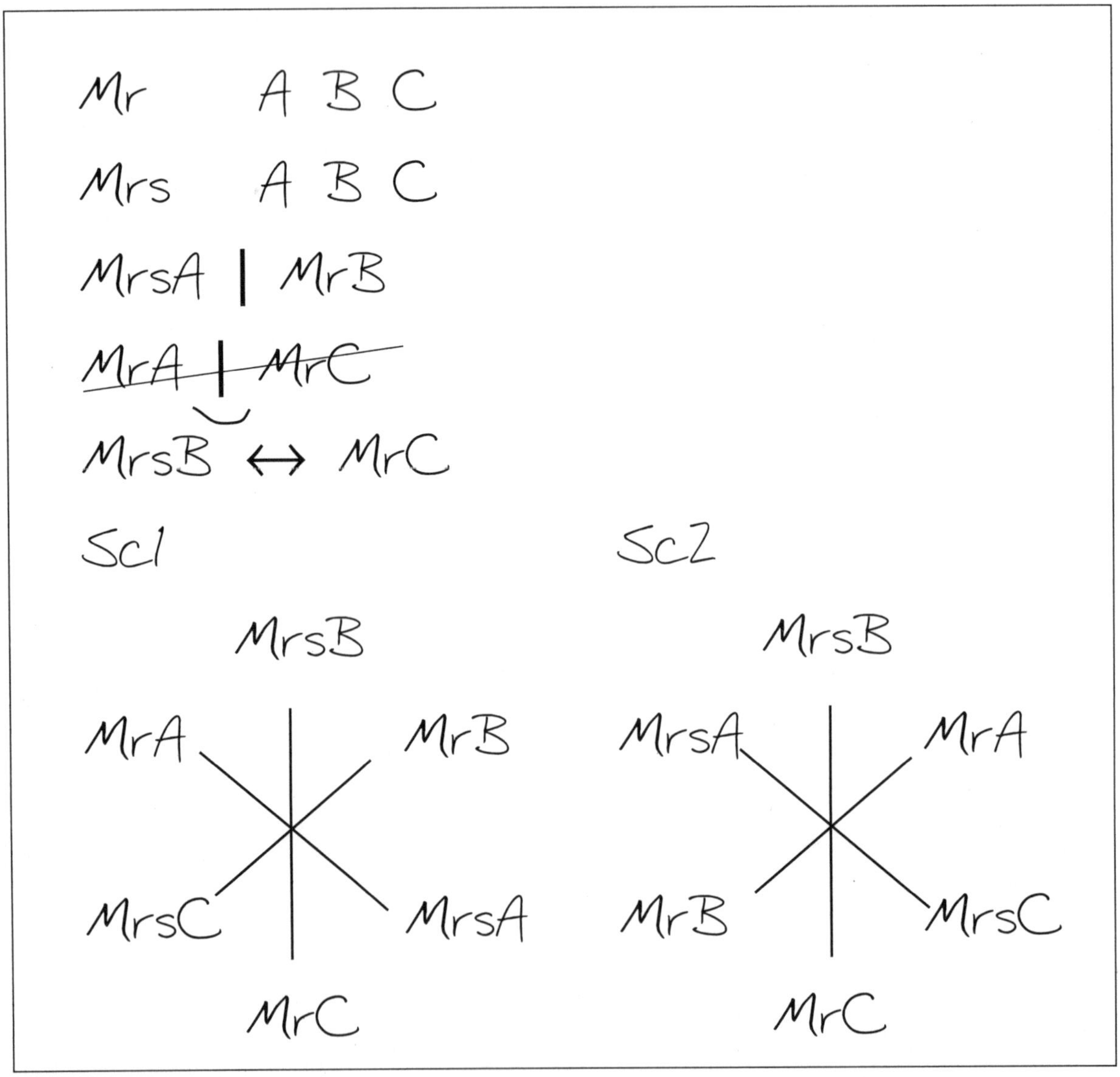

Note that while the diagram represents Mrs. B at the "top" and Mr. C at the "bottom," it could be rotated so that they would appear in a position around the circle but would always be across from one another and so the rest of the relationships would always be the same relative to Mrs. Baker and Mr. Carr. Understanding that—and understanding that is the key to this situation—you can appreciate that there are only two possibilities for seating the people around the table. That appreciation allows you to see that while you do not know which of the two scenarios will apply, that is the only thing that you do not know, because once you are in one seating situation or the other everything in that arrangement is known.

19. The question asks for something that cannot be true, which would be something that exists in neither scenario. The possibility in (A) exists in scenario 1, and the possibilities in choices (C), (D), and (E) exist in scenario 2. What cannot be true in either scenario is in (B).

20. This question places Mrs. Abell next to Mr. Carr, something which occurs only in scenario 1, and then asks for what could be true. The only one of the choices that could be true in scenario 1 is in choice (C).

21. The question places Mr. Carr immediately to the right of Mr. Baker, which occurs only in scenario 2, and then asks for what cannot be true, which, in scenario 2, is (D).

22. The question places Mrs. Baker next to Mrs. Abel, which occurs only in scenario 2, and asks for something that could be true. Of course anything that must be true is something that could be true and the only one of the choices that can be true with scenario 2 is in (A).

23. This question asks for something that must be true and therefore something that is the case in both scenarios. Examining the two against the answer choices, it becomes clear that the correct answer is in choice (C).

24. The question places Mr. Abel directly across from Mrs. Abel, an arrangement which exists only in scenario 1, and asks for what could be true. The only choice that represents something that could be true in that scenario is in choice (E).

SECTION 2 – LOGICAL REASONING

1. **Question:** The question asks for the main conclusion from the passage. This will be one of the statements in the passage, but probably not the last one and probably not introduced by a conclusion indicator.

   Analysis: The passage is about studies on participation in intramural athletics in residential colleges. The first statement is that such participation is often seen as a way to help first-year students adapt. Studies show, the passage continues, that sometimes this is the case, but also sometimes not. Each of these statements is presented as something that we know from the studies. To get to the conclusion, ask "and so?..." and the answer is that sometimes intramurals help students adapt and sometimes they don't. "And so" intramural participation may not always have the effect of helping students to adapt. The conclusion is contained in the second sentence.

   Answer: The choice that states the conclusion is choice (D). There might be a temptation to go further and select choice (C), but the passage does not do so, so that would go too far. (D)

2. **Question:** The question asks for an assumption on which the argument depends.

   Analysis: The conclusion is in the first statement: that personal income taxes will rise. The argument is that a deficit is projected at current levels of taxing and spending, but the deficit is not permitted by the Constitution. The passage says that revenue from sales taxes and other taxes will decrease, leaving the only possibility for more tax revenue as increasing personal income tax. That the only available source of more revenue is the income tax is a subsidiary conclusion that then becomes a premise leading to the major conclusion that the income tax will increase. But to get to the conclusion that in fact income taxes will rise requires another argument that uses that subsidiary conclusion. The passage supplies the premise that since the deficit cannot be permitted, if spending is not cut, income taxes must increase. And it concludes that taxes must increase, but to reach that conclusion it needs the minor premise that spending will not be cut. That is the missing assumption.

   Answer: Analysis shows that the missing assumption that must be true for the conclusion to be valid is that spending will not be cut to eliminate the deficit. The answer is choice (A).

3. **Question:** The question asks for something that is most strongly supported by the information in the passage. This will be something not stated that is true beyond a reasonable doubt because the statements in the passage are true.

   Analysis: The passage is about testing the hypothesis that there is no basic difference between the way that men and women give directions. It then includes a statement that men nearly always give directions based on distance, and another that women tend to give directions based on landmarks. So it establishes that in fact men and women do tend to give directions differently, and also that the hypothesis turns out not to be true. It does not draw this conclusion, but it is strongly supported by the findings.

   Answer: The conclusion that is strongly supported by the passage is found in choice (D).

4. **Question:** The question asks for an assumption which must be true for the argument to be valid.

   Analysis: The conclusion is that without ethical behavior a person cannot be called truly accomplished. In order to establish that the passage says that if people lack ethical behavior then they make decisions by their pocketbooks and they give back nothing to the society. What the argument lacks is a connection between giving something back to the society and being truly accomplished. Notice that the notion of being truly accomplished appears for the first time in the conclusion, but for it to be a good conclusion it must be about things that appear in some premise or other. So the missing assumption needs to connect the information about giving to society and being truly accomplished.

Answer: The missing connection that has to be there for the argument to be a good one is in choice (C).

5. **Question:** The argument asks for something on which Robert and Leah disagree.

   Analysis: Analyze the argument of each of the speakers, paying careful attention to how the second responds to the first. Often on questions like this the correct answer will be the conclusion of the first speaker. In this case Robert concludes that striking by employees is counterproductive. Leah begins by saying "I disagree," meaning that she disagrees with him about whether striking by employees is counterproductive. She believes it is not counterproductive because striking workers could gain concessions that will benefit them from for years to come, whereas Robert believes that it is counterproductive because employees lose in the long run when the corporation loses money. So there is a disagreement on conclusions that is driven by a disagreement about a key premise.

   Answer: The disagreement on the premises is captured in choice (B), or Robert asserts that employees lose when the corporation loses money, where Leah believes that the employees can benefit for years to come "if the plant loses a little money." (B)

6. **Question:** The question is an unusual one. It asks for a principle, or a belief that would lead to a conclusion that "the loaded question" ought to be used in the legal process.

   Analysis: Read the passage for what it says about loaded questions and then analyze it for a choice that would be involved in concluding that loaded questions ought to be used. The argument claims that the loaded question is useful for speeding the legal process. Yet the implicit problem is that the speed might be at the expense of truth and justice. So if someone were to conclude that using the loaded question is, nonetheless, a good idea, then that someone would need to believe that speed is more important than accuracy. Some belief or principle such as that is what the correct answer will contain.

   Answer: The difficulty with this problem is in sorting out exactly what it is asking for. Once that is done, it becomes clear what the correct answer will have to do, and that is done by choice (B).

7. **Question:** The question asks for something to undermine the isolationist's argument.

   Analysis: The isolationist concludes that the British and the French, and not the United States or Russia, ought to be concerned about a just and peaceful solution in the Middle East. The premises leading to this conclusion for the isolationist establish that the current problems in the Middle East are the result of actions by the French and British. The unstated assumption is that a country should be concerned with the solution to the problems in the Middle East only if it was responsible for that problem. One way to weaken the conclusion would be to attack that assumption and provide some of the reasons for the United States or Russia to be concerned with a just and peaceful solution.

   Answer: The information in choice (D) that interests of people in the United States are adversely affected by the lack of peace in the Middle East provides the additional premise to weaken the assumption that only those responsible for the problem should seek to solve it. So choice (D) undermines the isolationist's argument. (D)

8. **Question:** The question asks for something that "must be the case," or for an inference that follows from the statements in the passage.

   Analysis: With an inference question it is usually not possible to know precisely what the correct answer will do, but it is important to analyze the statements in the argument for exactly what they mean. The first statement here is that for someone to request permission to submit extra credit, someone must have properly completed all regular work. The statement says nothing about whether the request will be granted.

Regular work is defined as properly completed if it is on time or late with permission. The next statement is that Charles will get no better than a C on the basis of regular work, but might receive a B with extra credit. There is nothing said about whether Charles may legitimately request extra credit.

Answer: So interrogate each answer choice and ask whether it can be false consistent with the information in the passage. If it can be false, then it is not the right answer to the question. Choice (A) could be false, for if Charles does extra credit work there is nothing that compels that it would raise his grade. Choice (B) cannot be false, for if Charles has regular work that is late without permission he may not request extra credit, and the statement is that he will get no higher than a C on the basis of his regular work. Choice (C) could be false in that it provides a scenario where Charles is permitted to request extra credit, but there is nothing that says that the request must be granted. Choice (D) could be false, for in this circumstance that he has no late regular work Charles might request extra credit and might earn a B. Choice (E) could be false, for Charles might request and do extra credit work and still not earn a B. (B)

9. **Question:** The question asks about structure, and in particular about the role played by a sentence that includes a comparison to a bus station.

   Analysis: The conclusion of the passage is that no city is more charged with the spirit of change than Fresno. The evidence is census data showing Fresno to be the fastest-growing big city in the nation along with data showing the growth in the population of Fresno County. The passage also places this growth in the context of a national poll taken 20 years earlier naming Fresno as the least desirable place to live in the country. The passage then compares Fresno to a bus station, using the analogy to describe earlier impressions of the city that, according to the passage, are no longer accurate. That is the function of the bus station sentence: to grant the point about how Fresno used to be viewed.

   Answer: The role of the bus station comparison is contained in choice (C).

10. **Question:** The question asks for the main conclusion of the passage. When a question asks for this, the conclusion will usually be one of the statements in the passage, though it is unlikely to be last and unlikely to be introduced by a clear conclusion indicator such as "therefore."

    Analysis: The passage is about psychical things which are not also conscious. It begins by noting that those educated in philosophy would believe that such things are inconceivable. The passage continues, however, to note the existence of problems like dreams and hypnosis as phenomena which cannot be accounted for by this philosophical view. Taking that point and adding "and so..." after it leads to the statement that the view of those educated in philosophy is wrong. That statement is in the second sentence of the passage and it is the main conclusion, or what the passage is there to establish.

    Answer: The conclusion is expressed in choice (D).

11. **Question:** The question says that the reasoning is vulnerable to criticism. There is a flaw to be identified.

    Analysis: The conclusion in the passage is that it is not surprising that the achievements of the group of alumni at the tenth class reunion of High Point University are impressive. The reason for this is that the alumni had parents who were rich and successful as well, or those parents would not have been able to send their children to High Point University. Two things go together: the success of the parents and the success of the offspring. The passage takes it for granted that the success of the offspring is caused by the success of the parents rather than by some other cause (such as, for example, the education they received at High Point University!). It makes the common mistake of confusing a correlation with a causal relationship, or it assumes that because the two successes go together one of the successes is responsible for the other.

Answer: The accurate description of the error is found in choice (C).

12. Question: The question is a structure one, asking what the two people in the discussion disagree about.

Analysis: Notice that the first words in the second speaker's comments are "I disagree." Most likely this means that Joe disagrees with the conclusion of Liz's argument. And Liz's argument reaches the conclusion that insurance rates should be higher for women because a majority of life insurance settlements are now made to the beneficiaries of female policyholders. Joe's disagreement adds the information that women also live longer than men on average, so that women already pay premiums for a longer period than men. Because of this, Joe claims, women's rates should actually be lower than men's. So Joe does disagree with Liz's conclusion that insurance rates for women should be higher, and this disagreement on conclusions, in turn, follows from the disagreement about what factors should be taken into account in deciding whether women have higher rates.

Answer: The answer is in choice (C), which states that the two disagree about what should be taken into account. (C)

13. Question: The question asks for the main conclusion of the passage. This is likely to be something that is actually stated, but not at the end, and not introduced by a strong conclusion indicator.

Analysis: Use the "and so..." test with statements in the passage to confirm the conclusion, or the point that the author wants the reader to gain. The passage is an analysis of the claim of cognitive sociology that thought is socially determined. The problem according to the passage is that if this is the case, then it is also true of the beliefs of the cognitive sociologist, which then have no claim to be rationally correct. Whether this situation is the case or not the passage does not determine. Its purpose is to say that if beliefs are not the result of rational deliberation then cognitive sociology is self-contradictory. And so the thesis that thought is socially determined cannot claim to be true.

Answer: The answer, that it cannot be that thought is socially determined, is expressed in the choice (E).

14. Question: The question asks for an assumption on which the critics' conclusion relies.

Analysis: Begin by reading the passage to understand what the critics' conclusion is. The argument is about a program funded by the Alaska legislature to have a conference to highlight research showing that global warming does not threaten polar bear survival. The funding from the legislature is to be used to publicize the conference's findings, for public relations reasons. The critics conclude that this is a waste of money for the reason that all scientific research points to global warming's being a problem for polar bear survival. Focus on the fact that the goal of the legislature is public relations. Now ask of the answer choices: "Does this have to be true for it to be the case that this funding on public relations is a waste of money?"

Answer: The answer choice that has to be true is in choice (C). The funding is a waste of money only if people cannot be persuaded to believe something that scientific research opposes. (C)

15. Question: The question is about structure, asking for the role of a phrase in the final sentence.

Analysis: The passage is about the implied author present in any story. The suggestion is that one needs to understand who that implied author is in order to understand the experience that the reader is having with any novel. The point is clarified and emphasized in the final statement that you cannot "tell the dancer from the dance." The dancer is part of the dance just as the author is part of the experience of the novel.

Answer: The accurate description of the role of the phrase is found in choice (E). At first choice (A) might seem to be close, but it misstates the case, for the point is not about the relationship between the biographical author and the implied author, but between the implied author and the experience of the reader. (E)

16. **Question:** The question asks for something to strengthen Guthrie's recommendation.

Analysis: Begin by reading the passage to understand Guthrie's recommendation, which is that a student, named Abe, should have his TV viewing habits monitored since watching violent TV shows may be leading to violent behavior on his part. Guthrie reaches this recommendation based upon Abe's having thrown the first blow in a fight, and on research with which Guthrie is acquainted that says that such acts of violence in teenage males might be caused by one of three things. Guthrie is able to eliminate the other two, which suggests that violence on TV might be the cause and so Abe's TV watching should be monitored. This conclusion is strengthened by anything that would make it more likely—it need not make it certain—that the violence on TV is responsible for Abe's throwing the punch. So interrogate the answer choices, asking each: "Does this make it more likely that TV violence was responsible for Abe's violence?"

Answer: The information in choice (B) does make it more likely by removing a possibility that there could have been some previous incident that led Abe to strike the person in the fight. Remember, strengthen questions often add additional premises to make the conclusion more likely. (B)

17. **Question:** The question asks for a "consideration" to undermine the conclusion. The language of the question suggests that the correct answer will be additional information to weaken the conclusion.

Analysis: The conclusion is contained in the first sentence: that the number of accidents involving tractor-trailer rigs is up due to driver inexperience. The greater demand for truck drivers, according to the argument, has resulted in shortening training courses for drivers from six to five months, meaning that they do not get enough hands-on training. To undermine the conclusion find something that makes it less likely that the increase in accidents is due to inexperience, and particularly inexperience caused by shortening training courses.

Answer: The consideration that makes it less likely that the problem leading to accidents is inexperience from shortening training courses is contained in choice (B) which offers another reason for increased accidents. Remember, in a weakened question the correct answer needs to make the conclusion less likely, but may not make it certainly false. (B)

18. **Question:** The question is a parallel flaw question. It says that the passage includes a flaw in reasoning and asks for the answer choice that contains the same flaw.

Analysis: Analyze the passage for its conclusion, the premises leading to that conclusion, and the reasoning mistake that it makes. The overall conclusion seems to be in the final phrase that a free democratic system is the best form of government that there is. The reasoning begins by asserting that a free democratic system is the best form, and then draws the conclusion that it is worth defending for that reason. It then moves to saying that because it is worth defending, it must be the best form. The reasoning, then, is circular: it assumes what it sets out to prove.

Answer: Analyze the answer choices to find one that exhibits the same pattern of circular reasoning in which the proof for the conclusion is a restatement of the conclusion itself. All of the arguments present different premises and conclusions except for choice (E), which does exhibit exactly the same pattern of circular reasoning. (E)

19. **Question:** This is an inference question, but instead of asking for what must be true, this one asks for what must be false, or for something that is inconsistent with the statements in the passage.

Analysis: As with any inference question, it is not possible to say exactly what the correct answer will do, except that, in this case, it will be inconsistent with the statements in the passage. So analyze the passage to be precise on what the statements say. It begins with two categories of music lovers, each of which includes "some" music lovers. The second of these, those who prefer big bands, know the title of "every" Glenn Miller tune. There follows yet another category which includes "some" music lovers. Then the passage states that not all music lovers can read music. It concludes with something that does include "all" music lovers: that they enjoy playing and interpreting their music for their friends. Amid all the "somes" pay special attention to the "all," which would have to be inconsistent with anything that said that some music lovers do not enjoy interpreting music for their friends.

Answer: Since the task is to discover something that cannot be true, ask each answer choice, "Can this be true consistent with the passage?" The answer will be "no" for the correct answer to the problem. Therefore, choice (D) must be false since all music lovers enjoy playing and interpreting their music. (D)

20. **Question:** This is a principle question. It speaks of a decision by the mayor and a principle to explain it.

Analysis: The passage will involve a subtle choice made by the mayor, and the correct answer will be a belief that, if held by the mayor, would account for that choice, or would explain the mayor's not taking the other possible route. So read for the choice. The situation is that a citizen built a house after receiving appropriate permits, and only after the house was almost finished was it discovered that the city made an error and that the permit required acceptance from the historical commission. City Council ordered the house torn down, but the mayor vetoed the ordinance. In this case, then, the mayor chose to take the citizen's side rather than the side of the historical commission and the City Council. The question is to identify a belief that would make the mayor choose this way. Interrogate the answer choices: "If someone believed this, would that someone choose to support the citizen over the historical commission and City Council?"

Answer: The principle that explains the mayor's decision is in choice (C).

21. **Question:** This is a paradox question. It mentions Cubans discussed in the passage and asks for an explanation of their paradoxical behavior.

Analysis: The key with a paradox or discrepancy problem is to be very clear about the discrepancy: What are the things that it appears should not be true at the same time. In this case the two things are these: (1) Cuban people believed that official corruption is responsible for things working badly in their community, and (2) Cuban people fervently supported their ruler, Castro. The question used to interrogate the answer choices is, "Does this explain how they could deplore official corruption yet strongly support the ruler?"

Answer: The answer choice that enables both sides of the paradox to be true is choice (B).

22. **Question:** This is a parallel structure problem. It asks for an answer choice that uses the same pattern of reasoning as the model. It does not say that there is a flaw, but asks only for the same pattern, for the same relationship between premises and conclusion.

Analysis: Analyze the passage carefully for the way its premises lead to its conclusion. The argument describes someone shopping for a lawn mower with two conditions that had to be met. Their customer is shown a model that meets both conditions; she decides to do more research to determine whether the model is what she wants to purchase. The reasoning, then, is this: Two necessary conditions are described; an alternative is presented that meets both of those conditions, yet the would-be purchaser realizes that there might be other conditions that need to be met as well. To follow the model there should be a decision maker, two items that are necessary conditions, and the choice to put off the decision because there might be other conditions.

Answer: The same pattern is followed in choice (E): two things needed for avocados to be good for the day are present, yet the purchaser decides to do more research before buying. In choice (A) and choice (C) there are two conditions, but those conditions are presented as enough, by themselves, to make the purchaser make the choice. In choice (B) and choice (D) the judgment is that conditions have not been met. (E)

23. Question: This is a strengthen question, asking for something that supports a theory discussed in the passage.

Analysis: Read the passage to find the theory mentioned in the question. The theory is that mental illness in Latin America is on the rise because of economic problems. The economic problems, in turn, are the result of high levels of foreign debt. To find the answer, interrogate each entry choice asking, "Does this make it more likely that the economic problems are responsible for high levels of mental illness?"

Answer: The correct answer is choice (E), which states that there is a correlation between worsening economic problems over the past seven years and increased mental illness over the same period. Note that such a correlation would not be sufficient to prove that the economic problems cause the mental illness, but it can serve as evidence to strengthen such a claim. (E)

24. Question: The question asks for a necessary assumption for Johansen's conclusion.

Analysis: The argument is that frustration comes from two factors: a perception that rights may be lost in the future and a perception that future advancement is limited by things other than one's skill. From this premise that frustration comes from these factors, Johansen draws the conclusion that these factors explain the frustration of the great mass of people in the country of Sporedia. What must be the case for this to follow? Well, for it to be the case that these factors explain the people's frustration, it must be the case that these factors are present, or that most people do feel that their rights may be lost and that future advancement is artificially limited. That is the missing premise that must be true for these factors to explain their frustration.

Answer: The correct answer needs to include both of the factors that together cause the frustration, and so the answer is found in choice (D).

25. Question: The question asks for something "most strongly supported by" the things in the passage. This will be something that is not explicitly stated but that follows, and released beyond any reasonable doubt, from what is explicitly stated.

Analysis: The passage asks for what is responsible for the suburbanization of the United States. It lists a number of factors that might have been involved, but then adds two that were necessary: federally funded interstate highways and income tax deductions for purchasing houses. The key is to realize that the passage presents those federal actions as needed, though perhaps not as enough by themselves to cause the suburbanization. With that information, go to the answer choices and interrogate them, asking, "Does this have to be true given the information in the passage?"

Answer: The one that has to be true is choice (E), which states exactly the fact that these federal actions were necessary. Choice (C) might be tempting, but it goes too far in saying that the actions from the federal government caused the move to the suburbs, which goes further than saying only that they were needed for the move to the suburbs to happen. Choice (E) has to be true from what the passage says, while choice (C) could be false. (E)

SECTION 3 – READING COMPREHENSION

QUESTIONS 1–6

This is a comparative reading passage. **Passage A** includes two paragraphs. The first explains that in 2006 the notion of "planet" was redefined so that Pluto is no longer considered to be a planet. Paragraph 2 explains this new definition and applies it to Pluto. **Passage B** also has two paragraphs. Paragraph 1 explains that from its discovery it was evident that Pluto was an "oddball" as a planet. Paragraph 2 details some things about Pluto, discussing especially its satellite named Charon. The passages have in common the treatment of the planet Pluto and of the things that make it different from other planets in the solar system.

1. This question asks for a major topic in both passages, which is simply Pluto and its peculiarities, which are well described in choice (B).
2. The question asks for the relationship between the two passages. Consideration of that question leads to the conclusion that they do not disagree, and that in fact passage A describes the consequences among astronomers of the phenomena discussed in passage B. This description is reflected in choice (D) which relates the content of the second paragraph in passage A to what passage B does. (D)
3. The question asks for a detail that is mentioned in both passages. That detail has to do with Pluto's moon, and so the correct answer is choice (B).
4. The question asks for an inference from both passages, or for something that is very likely to be true in light of the content in both passages, which explains the oddities regarding Pluto and scientific reaction to that. Reviewing the answer choices, the one that is likely to be true is in choice (C), which follows from astronomers' redefinition of the word *planet.* (C)
5. This question asks for the attitude of the author of passage B. The author describes Pluto and things that make it different from the planets. There is no advocacy or argument, only description. This attitude is correctly captured in choice (C).
6. This question asks for something on which the passages clearly disagree. The first passage describes a claim that Pluto is not a planet, whereas the second passage clearly states that it is, especially in its final sentence. So the two clearly disagree on whether Pluto is a planet, which is captured in choice (C).

Questions 7–13

The passage contains three paragraphs. The first paragraph asserts that it is incorrect to view Chief Justice John Marshall primarily as a defender of the Federalist Party against the Republican Party. Paragraph 2 discusses differences and similarities between Marshall and the Republican Party, noting that the central similarities are most important. Paragraph 3 claims that the most important features of Marshall's decisions had to do with upholding the federal government against the states. Taken together, these paragraphs establish this main idea: Chief Justice John Marshall's key decisions were fundamentally compatible with the outlook of the Republican Party, particularly on issues having to do with the strength of federal authority versus the states.

7. The main idea is accurately stated in choice (D).
8. This question is about a detail about John Marshall that is to be found in the first paragraph, and clearly confirmed in the second where Marshall is likened to his "fellow Federalists." So the answer is choice (D).
9. This question asks for an inference, which, in a reading comprehension question, means something very likely to be true. In this case it asks for something that the author of the passage believes. The author's description of Marshall in the second paragraph as having a "distrust of the common people" leads to the reasonable conclusion that is expressed in choice (B), since Marshall was a governmental leader who, according to the point of

the passage as a whole, was near the mainstream in American politics. (B)

10. The question asks for a detail that is not mentioned in the passage regarding Marshall and property. Choices (A), (D), and (E) are explicitly mentioned in the first paragraph, and choice (B) is explicitly mentioned in the second paragraph. The one that is not mentioned is choice (C).

11. The question asks for the primary purpose of the passage, which is to explain the fundamental characteristics of Marshall's decisions as chief justice. It is accurately described in choice (A).

12. The question is about the detail of Marshall's attitude toward mass democratic politics. Review that attitude as discussed in the second paragraph. The word "distrust" is used in that discussion, and is repeated in choice (E).

13. The question asks for the key features of Marshall's jurisprudence "according to the author." Look at the third paragraph which begins with an assertion that the most important decisions of the Marshall court involved upholding the authority of the federal government against the states. This point is made in choice (E).

Questions 14–20

The passage contains five paragraphs. The first paragraph defines incrementalism as a budgeting strategy. Paragraph 2 states that incrementalism is especially useful for stable organizations. Paragraph 3 says that incrementalism puts the focus on new and expanded programs. Paragraph 4 explains that incrementalism deals with organization goals one at a time. Paragraph 5 explains how incrementalism facilitates problem solving. Taken together these paragraphs establish the main idea as this: Incrementalism is a budget-making strategy that is especially useful in stable organizations as they plan from year to year. It is a simple and straightforward passage.

14. The main idea is well stated in choice (B).

15. The question asks for something that the passage says about an organization that finds it necessary to consider alternatives beyond maintaining its existing services. This is mentioned at the end of the second paragraph, and applies to an organization "not meeting its constituency's needs," something repeated in choice (B).

16. The question asks about a specific phrase used in the first sentence of the fifth paragraph. The phrase "to look in one's own backyard" is used and explained as meaning to try something similar to what has been done previously, or to use a familiar method for problem solving. This is expressed in choice (D).

17. The question asks for something that is not mentioned in the passage. The answer is choice (A). Although the passage speaks of the goals of subunits of an organization, it does not characterize incrementalism as a method for preventing those various goals. The language in each of the other choices is explicitly included in the passage. Choice (B) is in paragraph 5; choice (C) is in paragraph 3; choice (D) is in the first paragraph; and choice (E) is in the second. (A)

18. The question asks for an inference from the passage and asks for an organization described in the answer choices that is best suited to the use of incrementalism as a strategy. Review the second and third paragraphs for discussion of organizations best suited for incrementalism, and note that they are especially stable with new alternatives that might come in the form of new programs or expansion of old ones. This is a good description of only the organization described in choice (E), but of none of the others. (E)

19. The primary purpose of the passage is to describe incrementalism and explain where it is useful. This is expressed best in choice (C).

20. The question asks for something with which the author would agree. This will be something compatible with the main idea and the author's attitude toward that main idea. The passage has simply described incrementalism and explained where it is useful. This point with which the author would agree and the main idea of his paragraph are well described in choice (D).

Questions 21–27

The passage has four paragraphs. The first paragraph introduces the Sophists as a group of philosophers in the fifth century B.C.E. who doubted the possibility of using reason to discover true knowledge. Paragraph 2 explains that these Sophists made the important contribution of focusing on human beings and their moral and political life. Paragraph 3 explains the position of the Sophists that the law is the product of custom or convention. Paragraph 4 compares the Sophists to many in the contemporary world, especially with regard to the claim that the laws protect only the powerful. Taken together the paragraphs express this main idea: The Sophists were a group of philosophers who focused on human beings and on their moral and political order and who were skeptics about rational knowledge of truth.

21. The main idea is best expressed in choice (E). Choice (B) might seem close, but it says that Sophists were "Greek political thinkers," whereas the passage, in the first paragraph, says they were from outside Greece. (E)

22. The question asks for the purpose of a detail, the mention of Thrasymachus in the third paragraph. Review of that part of the passage indicates that Thrasymachus is an example of the Sophists arguing that might makes right, an argument that was characteristic of Sophists. So the correct answer is in choice (C).

23. The question is a detail question, asking for something that is not mentioned in the passage. The correct answer is choice (C). Each of the other things is explicitly stated, but there is no statement that Sophists went so far as to claim it was foolish "ever" to obey the law. (C)

24. This question asks for the primary purpose, which is not advocacy or argument but explanation. The passage seeks to describe the Sophists, as is stated in choice (D).

25. This is an inference question about someone mentioned in the passage named Thrasymachus. Review the discussion of Thrasymachus in the third paragraph, noting that he argued that might makes right and that laws are there only to protect the interests of the powerful. The question asks for someone with whom Thrasymachus would agree, and that someone would have to be one of the Sophists. The only one in the list of five who is mentioned as a Sophist is Protagoras, who is named as "the best known of the Sophists" in the first paragraph. So the answer is in choice (B).

26. The question asks for something that the passage says the Sophists emphasized. This is mentioned in the second paragraph where it is said that the most important thing about the Sophists is that they turned philosophy to a study of human beings. So the answer is in choice (B).

27. This is an inference question, asking for something that would be "most consistent" with the Sophists' view. Recall that the Sophists doubted the possibility of using reason to come to true knowledge and claimed that law was a result of convention and served the interests of the powerful. This view, that there is no objective reason to obey a law, is consistent with the action in choice (D). Each of the others is driven by a belief in some moral principle. (D)

28. The question is a detail question, asking for something the author says about the views of a thinker the author mentions. Find the mention of Protagoras in the first paragraph and read the sentence about him. Choice (C) repeats—with almost the same wording—that Protagoras claimed that reality had whatever qualities that might be claimed for it. Again, detail questions are often answered correctly by focusing on the exact language of a part of the passage (C).

SECTION 4 – LOGICAL REASONING

1. **Question:** The question asks for something to weaken the conclusion in the passage.

   Analysis: The conclusion is contained in the final sentence: Unless people wish to continue education for its own sake they should choose to enter the workforce rather than go to graduate school. The reason is that, although there is still a differential between starting salaries of those with master's degrees and those without, the difference is not very large. There may be no obvious missing assumption to challenge here, so if it is unclear what is likely to weaken the conclusion, use this question: "Does this make it less likely that one should enter the workforce rather than go to graduate school?"

   Answer: Using the interrogation question with the answer choices reveals that choice (D) is the correct answer. It weakens the conclusion by offering another reason, other than salary, that could make a graduate degree advantageous. (D)

2. **Question:** This question deals with the same passage as the previous question but now seeks something to strengthen the conclusion.

   Analysis: The objective now is to support the conclusion that it makes more sense to enter the workforce rather than go to graduate school unless someone is interested in continuing education for its own sake. In this case, then, formulate the interrogation question for a strengthen problem: "Does this make it more likely that one should not go to graduate school, but should enter the workforce?"

   Answer: The correct answer to a strengthen question often adds new information to provide an additional reason for the conclusion. That happens in this case, as the interrogation question reveals that choice (A) is the correct answer. Not only is graduate school unlikely to make a substantial difference in income, but it could cause emotional distress as well. (A)

3. **Question:** This is a parallel flaw problem. There is a reasoning error in the passage, and the problem is to find the same reasoning error in one of the answer choices.

   Analysis: The passage presents an invalid syllogism. It says that if there were questions about astrophysics, then not everyone would pass. The next premise is that half the class did pass, which does not tell us whether everyone passed or not. No conclusion could follow, but this claims one in concluding that there must have been no questions about astrophysics. The error, then, is in a minor premise that does not address exactly one of the items in the major premise.

   Answer: The error is duplicated in choice (C), which has the same sort of minor premise that does not say whether the condition established in the major premise either happened or did not. (C)

4. **Question:** The question is about structure in asking about the technique that the passage relies upon to make its recommendation.

   Analysis: The passage concludes that a country should be told to stop giving cash subsidies to farmers. The reason for this, according to the passage, is that the only reliable indicator of what farmers should produce is market forces. So the passage uses this general rule that market forces should be used to decide what is produced, and applies it to this specific case. That is the strategy.

   Answer: The use of using a general principle to judge what to do in a particular case is exactly what is stated in choice (D).

5. **Question:** This is a structure question, asking what two people in a conversation disagree about.

   Analysis: The president is concerned as to whether relations with another country have been permanently damaged by the failure to appoint a special team of representatives, which appointment would develop an initial climate of trust. In response, Kesler does not claim that such a climate of trust can be created without the special team of representatives, but rather that the initial climate of trust itself is not needed for good relations with the other nation.

Answer: Analysis of the two statements shows that the correct answer is in choice (E).

6. **Question:** The question asks for an assumption on which the argument relies.

   Analysis: The conclusion in the passage is that more reliable methods for identifying melanoma are responsible for more reports of melanoma. The passage also notes that sun exposure is responsible for 45% of the cases of melanoma, but does not relate this information to the conclusion. Simply put, it must be true that there is no other cause for the increase in reported cases. Use the assumption test and ask, "Does this have to be true for it to be true that the increase in reported cases is due to the new methods of identifying melanoma?"

   Answer: Choice (C) has to be true, or if there is actually more melanoma, then the new method of reporting is not the sole reason for the increased reports. (C)

7. **Question:** The question asks for the main conclusion of the passage. Ordinarily in these cases the conclusion is included in the passage, but is not at the end and is not introduced by a typical conclusion indicator such as "therefore."

   Analysis: The passage is about Shakespeare's *Tempest.* It attempts to put the play in the context of English history and explains its contribution to political discourse of the time. It also puts the play in the context of political philosophy and the contribution it might make there. Adding the conclusion test "and so..." after the discussions of politics and philosophy leads back to the beginning of the passage, which is a statement that says that an assertion that *The Tempest* is a bad, boring play is not consistent with a careful and thoughtful reading. That point, contained in the second sentence, is what the passage is meant to prove.

   Answer: The conclusion is accurately expressed in choice (B).

8. **Question:** The question asks for something to support, or strengthen, the argument in the passage.

   Analysis: The conclusion is stated in the first sentence: that Leibniz's views on the weakness of will should be seen as central to his philosophical system. The rest of the passage establishes that weakness of will is interesting in and of itself and also that it is interesting in that it has to do with Leibniz's views on freedom. The passage moves from these considerations to its conclusion, but does not establish the importance of these considerations as being central to Leibniz's philosophical system. That importance is assumed, and the argument would be strengthened by confirming that assumption.

   Answer: The argument is strengthened by choice (D) which confirms the assumption that freedom is central to Leibniz's philosophical system, thereby making weakness of will also important because of its interaction with the concept of freedom. (D)

9. **Question:** The question asks for something that is most strongly supported by the statements in the passage. This will be something that is not explicit in the passage, but that the statements make true at least beyond a reasonable doubt.

   Analysis: The passage includes these statements: that the number of elderly is increasing; that the cost of caring for the elderly is increasing; that the number of wage earners is not increasing at the same rate; and that the funds for caring for the elderly will have to come from taxes paid by wage earners. Remember what kind of problem this is. It is not asking for assumptions or to be strengthened or weakened, but for something that is supported by the passage as stated. And that seems straightforward: that the taxes paid by the wage earners will have to increase.

   Answer: The statements in the passage strongly support choice (A).

10. **Question:** The question asks for something to support, or strengthen, the conclu-

sion. The phrasing of the question suggests especially that it will do what strengthen questions often do, and that it will add new information to offer another reason to reach the conclusion.

Analysis: The conclusion is stated in the final sentence, where it says that the need to recruit and provide staff development for new faculty is upon us. The argument is that examinations of future staffing needs show that in one state, for example, about 40% of full-time faculty will soon be eligible for retirement. The passage moves from that evidence about eligibility to a conclusion about the need for new faculty. It might be clear that there is an assumption here that, if granted, strengthens the conclusion. If not, use the strengthening test and interrogate each answer choice asking "Does this make it more likely that there is a need for new faculty?"

Answer: The conclusion about the need for new faculty is strengthened by choice (D). If those eligible for retirement in fact will retire, then that need is even more present. (D)

11. **Question:** The question asks for an assumption that is needed for a conclusion about *Paradise Lost* to be properly drawn.

Analysis: The conclusion is in the last sentence: *Paradise Lost* is a political work of great sophistication. The premises establish the subsidiary conclusion that the poem is a moral and religious one having to do with human liberty. So the premises are about the poem being moral and religious, but the conclusion is about it being political. The political nature appears for the first time in the conclusion. So for that conclusion to be legitimately drawn the connection between the moral and religious nature and the political nature needs to be made, and that is what the missing assumption must do. Remember, in a sound argument a major term cannot appear for the first time in a conclusion, but what is dealt with in the conclusion must appear in the premises as well.

Answer: The connection between the moral and the political that is required for the conclusion to be rightly drawn is contained in choice (C).

12. **Question:** The question seems unusual in that it asks for an action that "could not have moral worth," according to the argument. This suggests that the passage will describe certain criteria to be met for moral worth, and the task is to analyze the answer choices to determine whether they meet those criteria. So the question will behave like an inference question, asking, in effect, for what must be false, or what cannot have moral worth, given the criteria in the passage.

Analysis: The passage establishes that moral worth comes not from purpose, but on the principle of volition according to which the action has been done. That is to say, it is what is intended by the action and not its actual result that is responsible for moral worth.

Answer: According to the criteria established in the passage, the circumstance that could not have moral worth is in choice (C). Each of the others features or allows an action done with good intent, but choice (C) specifies that the intent is not good. (C)

13. **Question:** This is a structure question, presenting a conversation between two people and asking for what they disagree about.

Analysis: As always with problems of this nature asking for the subject of disagreement between two people, a good place to start is with the conclusion of the first speaker. Here, Martin's conclusion is that we must begin to develop the means to travel to and live on other planets in large numbers because eventually the resources of the earth will be exhausted. That George disagrees is clear from the first word: "nonsense." What is nonsense, according to George, is that there is a need to consider moving to other planets because, according to George, pollution controls can maintain acceptable living conditions on Earth for centuries. The other part of George's statement misinterprets Martin's statement by saying that current rocket resources would be inadequate to transport people to new planets. In fact, on that point the two agree. They disagree on whether exhaustion of the Earth's resources presents a problem for concern.

Answer: The disagreement between Martin and George is expressed in choice (B). It may seem that choice (D) is close, but note that Martin says that the Earth's resources will be exhausted "eventually," not immediately. (B)

14. Question: The question asks for an inference, or for something that must be true from the statements in the passage.

Analysis: The passage includes a chain of conditional statements. If the legislature does not increase appropriations, then the teachers will strike. If the legislature does increase appropriations, then it will cut back on highway repair. If it cuts back on highway repair, then that may anger motorists. So the legislature must either not increase appropriations or risk angering motorists. Note that the relationship between angering motorists and increasing appropriations can be put this way as well: If the legislature does not risk angering motorists, then it does not increase educational appropriations. So if it does not risk angering motorists, then the teachers will strike. As always with an inference question, it is not likely that one can know ahead of time what precisely the answer will be. With the content of the passage in mind, interrogate each choice and ask, "Can this be false?" Anything that can be false, which will be the case with four out of the five, is not the answer.

Answer: Using the interrogation question, realize that choice (A) could be false because the passage says only that the motorists "may" be angry. Choice (B) might also be false, for there might be other reasons for cutting back on highway repair. Choice (C) might also be false, again because cutting back on highway repair does not necessarily mean increasing appropriations for education. Choice (D) could be false because it deals only with "considering" increasing appropriations for education. Choice (E) must be true, for if the teachers do not strike, then the legislature will increase appropriations for education, which means that the legislature will cut back on highway repair. (E)

15. Question: This is an inference question, one that adds some information in the question itself. So begin by analyzing the passage, and then add the additional information.

Analysis: The passage cites three factors that professional painters say could be responsible for cracking latex paint, saying that some or all of them might be to blame. They are the following: (1) paint that was not thoroughly stirred; (2) a surface that was not clean; and (3) paint applied in one heavy coat rather than two or more light ones. Now the information from the question adds that the surface was clean, but the paint did crack and peel, and asks what must be true. Since the question also says that the professional painter's claims are correct, it must mean that either the paint was not thoroughly stirred or it was applied in one heavy coat.

Answer: The correct answer is in choice (C).

16. Question: The question is a structure question, asking for the function in the passage of a particular exchange involving the Prince of Wales.

Analysis: The passage is about architecture in England, and its point is that the kind of beautiful architecture found in other countries is not to be found in England. The reason presented is simply that the English do not tend to pattern themselves after others. This point is made through the exchange involving the Prince of Wales, who explains that he is not more like his father because he does not model himself after others. According to the passage, the situation of England as a whole is analogous. So the purpose of the Prince of Wales exchange is to clarify and indicate the reason why English architecture does not model architecture elsewhere.

Answer: Choice (A) offers an accurate characterization of the role of the exchange involving the Prince of Wales in the argument. The exchange does not confirm the absence of beautiful architecture, but rather attempts to explain the reason for that absence. (A)

17. **Question:** The question says that there is a choice in the passage that needs to be explained. This is likely to be either a principle question or a paradox question: Either there is a subtle choice that some belief or other will justify or there is an apparent contradiction which will need to be explained.

Analysis: The choice referred to in the question is this: Nellie chooses to turn down a promotion at one restaurant where she works and to accept a position at another restaurant. Now she works at restaurants to earn her way through college and is determined to earn her degree. What needs explaining, it seems, is why, if she needs money for college, she turned down the higher paying job. So it seems to be a paradox question: How could it be true that she works only to make money for her education on the one hand, and that she chooses the lower-paying job on the other?

Answer: With a paradox question, the right answer will usually offer additional information that makes it clear that both sides to the paradox can be true at the same time. In this case, additional information is needed that causes it to make sense that she works only to earn money for college and that she turns down the higher-paying job. Choice (C) causes it to make sense as it offers an explanation of how the choice serves Nellie's combination of goals. (C)

18. **Question:** This is a parallel structure problem. The question asks for the one of the answer choices that follows the same pattern of reasoning in the main passage.

Analysis: The passage involves first an argument to establish a conclusion that then becomes a minor premise in a more important argument. That first argument is "A loves B; therefore A is a lover." The overall argument is then: All the world loves a lover. A is a lover. So all the world, including B, loves A. The correct answer will involve the argument leading to the subsidiary conclusion that becomes a minor premise in the main argument as well as the items in the minor argument figuring in the conclusion in the main argument.

Answer: The answer choice that has the same number of players in the same logical roles is in choice (C).

19. **Question:** The question asks for an error in reasoning in the argument in the passage.

Analysis: The conclusion in the passage is that the crime rate must not be down, despite government statistics claiming it is. The evidence, however, is based not on rate or ratio but on numbers of crimes. So the argument makes the mistake of moving from absolute number to ratio, something which misuses percentages. A larger number of crimes could actually represent a smaller crime rate with an increased population.

Answer: The error is confusing ratio with number, and that is identified in choice (A).

20. **Question:** The question asks for a principle that would explain a decision by a Public Works director.

Analysis: In a principle problem there is normally a choice made in the passage, and the principle will be a belief that would lead the decision-maker to choose one alternative over the other. In this case the choice by the Public Works director is to allow a strip mining project to go forward. In favor of this alternative is the fact that there is a growing need for electrical power. In opposition to this alternative is the fact that the strip mining will cause environmental damage. The correct answer will be a belief that would lead someone to choose to accept the environmental damage in order to produce the power rather than to prevent the environmental damage even if it means less power produced.

Answer: The principle which could inform the Public Works director's choice is in choice (C). Each of the others has to do with power generation, but none of the other choices presents a principle that would be adequate for selecting between the alternatives presented by the passage. (C)

21. **Question:** The question asks for the main point of the argument made by an attorney in the passage.

Analysis: The passage begins with a statement that says that the case against the attorney's client was the result of the prosecutor's imagination as much as a result of any construction of the law. The rest of the passage provides evidence to back that up, likening the circumstance to the hysteria in the 17th century, and speaking of the dangers of trial by accusation and an overreaction to accusations of molesting children. The conclusion is that the case is not proven, or that the defendant is not guilty. The "and so..." test applied after any of the statements following the first sentence leads back to the claim that the client is not guilty.

Answer: The main idea is accurately stated in choice (A).

22. **Question:** The question asks for an assumption on which a forecast in the passage is based.

Analysis: The forecast is that the real estate market on the island in question in the decade of the 2020s will be less robust than it was in the first decade of that century. This forecast follows from evidence about the age of residents in the community and housing demand for people of particular ages. Housing demand is highest for residents in their 20s and declines for residents over 40. The evidence is that the housing demand was high in the first decade of the century and that it will decline in the third, and this reflects the fact that the group of people in their 20s at the beginning of the century was larger than it is expected to be in the third decade of the century. The evidence is about demand for housing, but the conclusion is about the market's being robust, or about actual sales of housing. For the data about demand to have results in actual sales it must be that those who demand housing can actually purchase it. As is often the case, there is a shift from the subject matter covered by the evidence to a new topic covered by the conclusion.

Answer: The missing link between demand and market is established in choice (E), which provides the assumption that people who seek housing can actually afford it. (E)

23. **Question:** The question says that the argument is vulnerable to criticism, meaning that there is a flaw in the reasoning.

Analysis: The conclusion of the argument is that the film version of *Crime and Punishment* is almost certain to be a flop. The reasoning is that important novels rarely become important or commercially successful films. Since *Crime and Punishment* is an important novel, therefore, the film of it is likely to be a flop. The error here is in assuming that what is true of a category as a whole is true of everything in that category. Because most important novels are unsuccessful as films does not compel the conclusion that this important novel will result in an unsuccessful film.

Answer: The error is correctly stated in choice (A).

24. **Question:** The question asks for explanation of a choice made in the passage. It is likely, then, that what will be lacking is a principle or belief to make selecting one alternative over another make sense, or that the passage will present a paradox, a choice that it does not seem ought to be made.

Analysis: Reading the passage indicates that the problem is a paradox problem. On the one hand, the chef knows that when boiling asparagus it is important to select stalks that are of uniform size and thin, yet on the other she chooses stalks that are thick. How could it be that the master chef would know that about asparagus, and yet make the shopping choices she makes?

Answer: The answer that resolves the apparent discrepancy is in choice (D), which denies neither part of the paradox, but makes the choice make sense by saying that the chef does not plan to boil the asparagus. (D)

SAMPLE ESSAY

The position of director of personnel and public relations at All Sports Sporting Goods is a difficult one to fill because it seeks a complex mix of skills and experience. And so the company is fortunate in having two quite promising applicants for the position. Of the two, Henry Able should be hired.

While it is understandable that the company needs to combine these roles in the same employee, it is also true that the skills of dealing with internal company personnel, on the one hand, and with external public relations, on the other, are different things. And the two candidates, in their experience and outlook, tend to represent different sides of that dichotomy. Mr. Able's expertise and experience in public relations is clear. In his previous position he was highly successful in advertising and public relations, and his firm thrived because of his efforts there. To be sure, he was less involved in employee relations, as that was not his principal job description. But he did have some involvement, however minor, and there is no record of any criticism of him for inadequacy in that role. Indeed, perhaps his sensitivity to public concerns can transfer itself to sensitivity about the needs and concerns of employees and management within the company.

Ms. Cole does have experience working with employee relations within the company and could be expected to perform that role well. Her innate wisdom and fairness would almost certainly, in time, become clear to those initially skeptical, and she could be expected to bring cordial and cooperative relationships within the company. Still, the perception of cordial employee relationships does not strengthen public perception of the value of products, and regarding the ability to do that, Ms. Cole's experience and qualifications are thin. Could she perform the role? It is something that is simply unknown. In the absence of another candidate whose ability to perform both roles is somewhat known, her strength of experience in labor relations might be enough to make her the intelligent choice. But since we know for certain of Mr. Able's strength in public relations and have some indication that he would develop strong personnel relationships as well, the more prudent move, the one that is more likely to offer success in both roles, is to hire Mr. Able.

LSAT

LAW SCHOOL ADMISSION TEST

ANSWER SHEETS

ANSWER SHEET

TEST 1

SECTION 1	SECTION 2	SECTION 3	SECTION 4
1. (A) (B) (C) (D) (E)	1. (A) (B) (C) (D) (E)	1. (A) (B) (C) (D) (E)	1. (A) (B) (C) (D) (E)
2. (A) (B) (C) (D) (E)	2. (A) (B) (C) (D) (E)	2. (A) (B) (C) (D) (E)	2. (A) (B) (C) (D) (E)
3. (A) (B) (C) (D) (E)	3. (A) (B) (C) (D) (E)	3. (A) (B) (C) (D) (E)	3. (A) (B) (C) (D) (E)
4. (A) (B) (C) (D) (E)	4. (A) (B) (C) (D) (E)	4. (A) (B) (C) (D) (E)	4. (A) (B) (C) (D) (E)
5. (A) (B) (C) (D) (E)	5. (A) (B) (C) (D) (E)	5. (A) (B) (C) (D) (E)	5. (A) (B) (C) (D) (E)
6. (A) (B) (C) (D) (E)	6. (A) (B) (C) (D) (E)	6. (A) (B) (C) (D) (E)	6. (A) (B) (C) (D) (E)
7. (A) (B) (C) (D) (E)	7. (A) (B) (C) (D) (E)	7. (A) (B) (C) (D) (E)	7. (A) (B) (C) (D) (E)
8. (A) (B) (C) (D) (E)	8. (A) (B) (C) (D) (E)	8. (A) (B) (C) (D) (E)	8. (A) (B) (C) (D) (E)
9. (A) (B) (C) (D) (E)	9. (A) (B) (C) (D) (E)	9. (A) (B) (C) (D) (E)	9. (A) (B) (C) (D) (E)
10. (A) (B) (C) (D) (E)	10. (A) (B) (C) (D) (E)	10. (A) (B) (C) (D) (E)	10. (A) (B) (C) (D) (E)
11. (A) (B) (C) (D) (E)	11. (A) (B) (C) (D) (E)	11. (A) (B) (C) (D) (E)	11. (A) (B) (C) (D) (E)
12. (A) (B) (C) (D) (E)	12. (A) (B) (C) (D) (E)	12. (A) (B) (C) (D) (E)	12. (A) (B) (C) (D) (E)
13. (A) (B) (C) (D) (E)	13. (A) (B) (C) (D) (E)	13. (A) (B) (C) (D) (E)	13. (A) (B) (C) (D) (E)
14. (A) (B) (C) (D) (E)	14. (A) (B) (C) (D) (E)	14. (A) (B) (C) (D) (E)	14. (A) (B) (C) (D) (E)
15. (A) (B) (C) (D) (E)	15. (A) (B) (C) (D) (E)	15. (A) (B) (C) (D) (E)	15. (A) (B) (C) (D) (E)
16. (A) (B) (C) (D) (E)	16. (A) (B) (C) (D) (E)	16. (A) (B) (C) (D) (E)	16. (A) (B) (C) (D) (E)
17. (A) (B) (C) (D) (E)	17. (A) (B) (C) (D) (E)	17. (A) (B) (C) (D) (E)	17. (A) (B) (C) (D) (E)
18. (A) (B) (C) (D) (E)	18. (A) (B) (C) (D) (E)	18. (A) (B) (C) (D) (E)	18. (A) (B) (C) (D) (E)
19. (A) (B) (C) (D) (E)	19. (A) (B) (C) (D) (E)	19. (A) (B) (C) (D) (E)	19. (A) (B) (C) (D) (E)
20. (A) (B) (C) (D) (E)	20. (A) (B) (C) (D) (E)	20. (A) (B) (C) (D) (E)	20. (A) (B) (C) (D) (E)
21. (A) (B) (C) (D) (E)	21. (A) (B) (C) (D) (E)	21. (A) (B) (C) (D) (E)	21. (A) (B) (C) (D) (E)
22. (A) (B) (C) (D) (E)	22. (A) (B) (C) (D) (E)	22. (A) (B) (C) (D) (E)	22. (A) (B) (C) (D) (E)
23. (A) (B) (C) (D) (E)	23. (A) (B) (C) (D) (E)	23. (A) (B) (C) (D) (E)	23. (A) (B) (C) (D) (E)
24. (A) (B) (C) (D) (E)	24. (A) (B) (C) (D) (E)	24. (A) (B) (C) (D) (E)	24. (A) (B) (C) (D) (E)
25. (A) (B) (C) (D) (E)	25. (A) (B) (C) (D) (E)		
	26. (A) (B) (C) (D) (E)		
	27. (A) (B) (C) (D) (E)		
	28. (A) (B) (C) (D) (E)		

WRITING SAMPLE RESPONSE SHEET

TEST 1

ANSWER SHEET

TEST 2

SECTION 1	SECTION 2	SECTION 3	SECTION 4
1. Ⓐ Ⓑ Ⓒ Ⓓ Ⓔ	1. Ⓐ Ⓑ Ⓒ Ⓓ Ⓔ	1. Ⓐ Ⓑ Ⓒ Ⓓ Ⓔ	1. Ⓐ Ⓑ Ⓒ Ⓓ Ⓔ
2. Ⓐ Ⓑ Ⓒ Ⓓ Ⓔ	2. Ⓐ Ⓑ Ⓒ Ⓓ Ⓔ	2. Ⓐ Ⓑ Ⓒ Ⓓ Ⓔ	2. Ⓐ Ⓑ Ⓒ Ⓓ Ⓔ
3. Ⓐ Ⓑ Ⓒ Ⓓ Ⓔ	3. Ⓐ Ⓑ Ⓒ Ⓓ Ⓔ	3. Ⓐ Ⓑ Ⓒ Ⓓ Ⓔ	3. Ⓐ Ⓑ Ⓒ Ⓓ Ⓔ
4. Ⓐ Ⓑ Ⓒ Ⓓ Ⓔ	4. Ⓐ Ⓑ Ⓒ Ⓓ Ⓔ	4. Ⓐ Ⓑ Ⓒ Ⓓ Ⓔ	4. Ⓐ Ⓑ Ⓒ Ⓓ Ⓔ
5. Ⓐ Ⓑ Ⓒ Ⓓ Ⓔ	5. Ⓐ Ⓑ Ⓒ Ⓓ Ⓔ	5. Ⓐ Ⓑ Ⓒ Ⓓ Ⓔ	5. Ⓐ Ⓑ Ⓒ Ⓓ Ⓔ
6. Ⓐ Ⓑ Ⓒ Ⓓ Ⓔ	6. Ⓐ Ⓑ Ⓒ Ⓓ Ⓔ	6. Ⓐ Ⓑ Ⓒ Ⓓ Ⓔ	6. Ⓐ Ⓑ Ⓒ Ⓓ Ⓔ
7. Ⓐ Ⓑ Ⓒ Ⓓ Ⓔ	7. Ⓐ Ⓑ Ⓒ Ⓓ Ⓔ	7. Ⓐ Ⓑ Ⓒ Ⓓ Ⓔ	7. Ⓐ Ⓑ Ⓒ Ⓓ Ⓔ
8. Ⓐ Ⓑ Ⓒ Ⓓ Ⓔ	8. Ⓐ Ⓑ Ⓒ Ⓓ Ⓔ	8. Ⓐ Ⓑ Ⓒ Ⓓ Ⓔ	8. Ⓐ Ⓑ Ⓒ Ⓓ Ⓔ
9. Ⓐ Ⓑ Ⓒ Ⓓ Ⓔ	9. Ⓐ Ⓑ Ⓒ Ⓓ Ⓔ	9. Ⓐ Ⓑ Ⓒ Ⓓ Ⓔ	9. Ⓐ Ⓑ Ⓒ Ⓓ Ⓔ
10. Ⓐ Ⓑ Ⓒ Ⓓ Ⓔ	10. Ⓐ Ⓑ Ⓒ Ⓓ Ⓔ	10. Ⓐ Ⓑ Ⓒ Ⓓ Ⓔ	10. Ⓐ Ⓑ Ⓒ Ⓓ Ⓔ
11. Ⓐ Ⓑ Ⓒ Ⓓ Ⓔ	11. Ⓐ Ⓑ Ⓒ Ⓓ Ⓔ	11. Ⓐ Ⓑ Ⓒ Ⓓ Ⓔ	11. Ⓐ Ⓑ Ⓒ Ⓓ Ⓔ
12. Ⓐ Ⓑ Ⓒ Ⓓ Ⓔ	12. Ⓐ Ⓑ Ⓒ Ⓓ Ⓔ	12. Ⓐ Ⓑ Ⓒ Ⓓ Ⓔ	12. Ⓐ Ⓑ Ⓒ Ⓓ Ⓔ
13. Ⓐ Ⓑ Ⓒ Ⓓ Ⓔ	13. Ⓐ Ⓑ Ⓒ Ⓓ Ⓔ	13. Ⓐ Ⓑ Ⓒ Ⓓ Ⓔ	13. Ⓐ Ⓑ Ⓒ Ⓓ Ⓔ
14. Ⓐ Ⓑ Ⓒ Ⓓ Ⓔ	14. Ⓐ Ⓑ Ⓒ Ⓓ Ⓔ	14. Ⓐ Ⓑ Ⓒ Ⓓ Ⓔ	14. Ⓐ Ⓑ Ⓒ Ⓓ Ⓔ
15. Ⓐ Ⓑ Ⓒ Ⓓ Ⓔ	15. Ⓐ Ⓑ Ⓒ Ⓓ Ⓔ	15. Ⓐ Ⓑ Ⓒ Ⓓ Ⓔ	15. Ⓐ Ⓑ Ⓒ Ⓓ Ⓔ
16. Ⓐ Ⓑ Ⓒ Ⓓ Ⓔ	16. Ⓐ Ⓑ Ⓒ Ⓓ Ⓔ	16. Ⓐ Ⓑ Ⓒ Ⓓ Ⓔ	16. Ⓐ Ⓑ Ⓒ Ⓓ Ⓔ
17. Ⓐ Ⓑ Ⓒ Ⓓ Ⓔ	17. Ⓐ Ⓑ Ⓒ Ⓓ Ⓔ	17. Ⓐ Ⓑ Ⓒ Ⓓ Ⓔ	17. Ⓐ Ⓑ Ⓒ Ⓓ Ⓔ
18. Ⓐ Ⓑ Ⓒ Ⓓ Ⓔ	18. Ⓐ Ⓑ Ⓒ Ⓓ Ⓔ	18. Ⓐ Ⓑ Ⓒ Ⓓ Ⓔ	18. Ⓐ Ⓑ Ⓒ Ⓓ Ⓔ
19. Ⓐ Ⓑ Ⓒ Ⓓ Ⓔ	19. Ⓐ Ⓑ Ⓒ Ⓓ Ⓔ	19. Ⓐ Ⓑ Ⓒ Ⓓ Ⓔ	19. Ⓐ Ⓑ Ⓒ Ⓓ Ⓔ
20. Ⓐ Ⓑ Ⓒ Ⓓ Ⓔ	20. Ⓐ Ⓑ Ⓒ Ⓓ Ⓔ	20. Ⓐ Ⓑ Ⓒ Ⓓ Ⓔ	20. Ⓐ Ⓑ Ⓒ Ⓓ Ⓔ
21. Ⓐ Ⓑ Ⓒ Ⓓ Ⓔ	21. Ⓐ Ⓑ Ⓒ Ⓓ Ⓔ	21. Ⓐ Ⓑ Ⓒ Ⓓ Ⓔ	21. Ⓐ Ⓑ Ⓒ Ⓓ Ⓔ
22. Ⓐ Ⓑ Ⓒ Ⓓ Ⓔ	22. Ⓐ Ⓑ Ⓒ Ⓓ Ⓔ	22. Ⓐ Ⓑ Ⓒ Ⓓ Ⓔ	22. Ⓐ Ⓑ Ⓒ Ⓓ Ⓔ
23. Ⓐ Ⓑ Ⓒ Ⓓ Ⓔ	23. Ⓐ Ⓑ Ⓒ Ⓓ Ⓔ	23. Ⓐ Ⓑ Ⓒ Ⓓ Ⓔ	23. Ⓐ Ⓑ Ⓒ Ⓓ Ⓔ
24. Ⓐ Ⓑ Ⓒ Ⓓ Ⓔ	24. Ⓐ Ⓑ Ⓒ Ⓓ Ⓔ	24. Ⓐ Ⓑ Ⓒ Ⓓ Ⓔ	24. Ⓐ Ⓑ Ⓒ Ⓓ Ⓔ
25. Ⓐ Ⓑ Ⓒ Ⓓ Ⓔ	25. Ⓐ Ⓑ Ⓒ Ⓓ Ⓔ		
26. Ⓐ Ⓑ Ⓒ Ⓓ Ⓔ			
27. Ⓐ Ⓑ Ⓒ Ⓓ Ⓔ			
28. Ⓐ Ⓑ Ⓒ Ⓓ Ⓔ			

WRITING SAMPLE RESPONSE SHEET

TEST 2

ANSWER SHEET

TEST 3

SECTION 1

1. Ⓐ Ⓑ Ⓒ Ⓓ Ⓔ
2. Ⓐ Ⓑ Ⓒ Ⓓ Ⓔ
3. Ⓐ Ⓑ Ⓒ Ⓓ Ⓔ
4. Ⓐ Ⓑ Ⓒ Ⓓ Ⓔ
5. Ⓐ Ⓑ Ⓒ Ⓓ Ⓔ
6. Ⓐ Ⓑ Ⓒ Ⓓ Ⓔ
7. Ⓐ Ⓑ Ⓒ Ⓓ Ⓔ
8. Ⓐ Ⓑ Ⓒ Ⓓ Ⓔ
9. Ⓐ Ⓑ Ⓒ Ⓓ Ⓔ
10. Ⓐ Ⓑ Ⓒ Ⓓ Ⓔ
11. Ⓐ Ⓑ Ⓒ Ⓓ Ⓔ
12. Ⓐ Ⓑ Ⓒ Ⓓ Ⓔ
13. Ⓐ Ⓑ Ⓒ Ⓓ Ⓔ
14. Ⓐ Ⓑ Ⓒ Ⓓ Ⓔ
15. Ⓐ Ⓑ Ⓒ Ⓓ Ⓔ
16. Ⓐ Ⓑ Ⓒ Ⓓ Ⓔ
17. Ⓐ Ⓑ Ⓒ Ⓓ Ⓔ
18. Ⓐ Ⓑ Ⓒ Ⓓ Ⓔ
19. Ⓐ Ⓑ Ⓒ Ⓓ Ⓔ
20. Ⓐ Ⓑ Ⓒ Ⓓ Ⓔ
21. Ⓐ Ⓑ Ⓒ Ⓓ Ⓔ
22. Ⓐ Ⓑ Ⓒ Ⓓ Ⓔ
23. Ⓐ Ⓑ Ⓒ Ⓓ Ⓔ
24. Ⓐ Ⓑ Ⓒ Ⓓ Ⓔ

SECTION 2

1. Ⓐ Ⓑ Ⓒ Ⓓ Ⓔ
2. Ⓐ Ⓑ Ⓒ Ⓓ Ⓔ
3. Ⓐ Ⓑ Ⓒ Ⓓ Ⓔ
4. Ⓐ Ⓑ Ⓒ Ⓓ Ⓔ
5. Ⓐ Ⓑ Ⓒ Ⓓ Ⓔ
6. Ⓐ Ⓑ Ⓒ Ⓓ Ⓔ
7. Ⓐ Ⓑ Ⓒ Ⓓ Ⓔ
8. Ⓐ Ⓑ Ⓒ Ⓓ Ⓔ
9. Ⓐ Ⓑ Ⓒ Ⓓ Ⓔ
10. Ⓐ Ⓑ Ⓒ Ⓓ Ⓔ
11. Ⓐ Ⓑ Ⓒ Ⓓ Ⓔ
12. Ⓐ Ⓑ Ⓒ Ⓓ Ⓔ
13. Ⓐ Ⓑ Ⓒ Ⓓ Ⓔ
14. Ⓐ Ⓑ Ⓒ Ⓓ Ⓔ
15. Ⓐ Ⓑ Ⓒ Ⓓ Ⓔ
16. Ⓐ Ⓑ Ⓒ Ⓓ Ⓔ
17. Ⓐ Ⓑ Ⓒ Ⓓ Ⓔ
18. Ⓐ Ⓑ Ⓒ Ⓓ Ⓔ
19. Ⓐ Ⓑ Ⓒ Ⓓ Ⓔ
20. Ⓐ Ⓑ Ⓒ Ⓓ Ⓔ
21. Ⓐ Ⓑ Ⓒ Ⓓ Ⓔ
22. Ⓐ Ⓑ Ⓒ Ⓓ Ⓔ
23. Ⓐ Ⓑ Ⓒ Ⓓ Ⓔ
24. Ⓐ Ⓑ Ⓒ Ⓓ Ⓔ
25. Ⓐ Ⓑ Ⓒ Ⓓ Ⓔ

SECTION 3

1. Ⓐ Ⓑ Ⓒ Ⓓ Ⓔ
2. Ⓐ Ⓑ Ⓒ Ⓓ Ⓔ
3. Ⓐ Ⓑ Ⓒ Ⓓ Ⓔ
4. Ⓐ Ⓑ Ⓒ Ⓓ Ⓔ
5. Ⓐ Ⓑ Ⓒ Ⓓ Ⓔ
6. Ⓐ Ⓑ Ⓒ Ⓓ Ⓔ
7. Ⓐ Ⓑ Ⓒ Ⓓ Ⓔ
8. Ⓐ Ⓑ Ⓒ Ⓓ Ⓔ
9. Ⓐ Ⓑ Ⓒ Ⓓ Ⓔ
10. Ⓐ Ⓑ Ⓒ Ⓓ Ⓔ
11. Ⓐ Ⓑ Ⓒ Ⓓ Ⓔ
12. Ⓐ Ⓑ Ⓒ Ⓓ Ⓔ
13. Ⓐ Ⓑ Ⓒ Ⓓ Ⓔ
14. Ⓐ Ⓑ Ⓒ Ⓓ Ⓔ
15. Ⓐ Ⓑ Ⓒ Ⓓ Ⓔ
16. Ⓐ Ⓑ Ⓒ Ⓓ Ⓔ
17. Ⓐ Ⓑ Ⓒ Ⓓ Ⓔ
18. Ⓐ Ⓑ Ⓒ Ⓓ Ⓔ
19. Ⓐ Ⓑ Ⓒ Ⓓ Ⓔ
20. Ⓐ Ⓑ Ⓒ Ⓓ Ⓔ
21. Ⓐ Ⓑ Ⓒ Ⓓ Ⓔ
22. Ⓐ Ⓑ Ⓒ Ⓓ Ⓔ
23. Ⓐ Ⓑ Ⓒ Ⓓ Ⓔ
24. Ⓐ Ⓑ Ⓒ Ⓓ Ⓔ
25. Ⓐ Ⓑ Ⓒ Ⓓ Ⓔ
26. Ⓐ Ⓑ Ⓒ Ⓓ Ⓔ
27. Ⓐ Ⓑ Ⓒ Ⓓ Ⓔ
28. Ⓐ Ⓑ Ⓒ Ⓓ Ⓔ

SECTION 4

1. Ⓐ Ⓑ Ⓒ Ⓓ Ⓔ
2. Ⓐ Ⓑ Ⓒ Ⓓ Ⓔ
3. Ⓐ Ⓑ Ⓒ Ⓓ Ⓔ
4. Ⓐ Ⓑ Ⓒ Ⓓ Ⓔ
5. Ⓐ Ⓑ Ⓒ Ⓓ Ⓔ
6. Ⓐ Ⓑ Ⓒ Ⓓ Ⓔ
7. Ⓐ Ⓑ Ⓒ Ⓓ Ⓔ
8. Ⓐ Ⓑ Ⓒ Ⓓ Ⓔ
9. Ⓐ Ⓑ Ⓒ Ⓓ Ⓔ
10. Ⓐ Ⓑ Ⓒ Ⓓ Ⓔ
11. Ⓐ Ⓑ Ⓒ Ⓓ Ⓔ
12. Ⓐ Ⓑ Ⓒ Ⓓ Ⓔ
13. Ⓐ Ⓑ Ⓒ Ⓓ Ⓔ
14. Ⓐ Ⓑ Ⓒ Ⓓ Ⓔ
15. Ⓐ Ⓑ Ⓒ Ⓓ Ⓔ
16. Ⓐ Ⓑ Ⓒ Ⓓ Ⓔ
17. Ⓐ Ⓑ Ⓒ Ⓓ Ⓔ
18. Ⓐ Ⓑ Ⓒ Ⓓ Ⓔ
19. Ⓐ Ⓑ Ⓒ Ⓓ Ⓔ
20. Ⓐ Ⓑ Ⓒ Ⓓ Ⓔ
21. Ⓐ Ⓑ Ⓒ Ⓓ Ⓔ
22. Ⓐ Ⓑ Ⓒ Ⓓ Ⓔ
23. Ⓐ Ⓑ Ⓒ Ⓓ Ⓔ
24. Ⓐ Ⓑ Ⓒ Ⓓ Ⓔ

WRITING SAMPLE RESPONSE SHEET

TEST 3

NOTES

NOTES

Installing REA's TESTware®

System Requirements

Pentium 75 MHz (300 MHz recommended) or a higher or compatible processor; Microsoft Windows 98 or later; 64 MB available RAM; Internet Explorer 5.5 or higher.

Installation

1. Insert the Annotated LSAT CD-ROM into the CD-ROM drive.
2. If the installation doesn't begin automatically, from the Start Menu choose the run command. When the run dialog box appears, type **d:\setup** (where d is the letter of your CD-ROM drive) at the prompt and click ok.
3. The installation process will begin. A dialog box proposing the directory **"C:\Program Files\REA\LSAT"** will appear. If the name and location are suitable, click ok. If you wish to specify a different name or location, type it in and click ok.
4. Start the Annotated LSAT TEST*ware*® application by double-clicking on the icon.

REA's Annotated LSAT TEST*ware*® is easy to learn and use. To achieve maximum benefits, we recommend that you take a few minutes to go through the on-screen tutorial on your computer.

Testing Accomodations

If you qualify for additional test time, please contact us at info@rea.com so we can customize your database.

Technical Support

REA's TEST*ware*® is backed by customer and technical support. For questions about installation or operation of your software, contact us at:

Research & Education Association
Phone: (732) 819-8880 (9 a.m. to 5 p.m. ET, Monday–Friday)
Fax: (732) 819-8808
Website: *www.rea.com*
E-mail: info@rea.com

Note to Windows XP Users: In order for the TEST*ware*® to function properly, please install and run the application under the same computer administrator-level user account. Installing the TEST*ware*® as one user and running it as another could cause file-access path conflicts.